THE KINGFISHER

Children's
FACTFINDER

First published in 1985 by Kingfisher Books Limited
Elsley Court, 20–22 Great Titchfield Street
London W1P 7AD, a Grisewood & Dempsey Company.

BRITISH LIBRARY CATALOGUING IN PUBLICATION DATA
Children's Factfinder
   1. Children's encyclopedias and dictionaries
   I. Beal, George
   082   AG5
   ISBN 0-86272-158-X

Printed in Yugoslavia
Phototypeset by Southern Positives and Negatives (SPAN)
Lingfield, Surrey
Cover design by The Pinpoint Design Company

THE KINGFISHER

Children's FACTFINDER

Compiled by John Grisewood
Edited by George Beal

KINGFISHER BOOKS

Contents

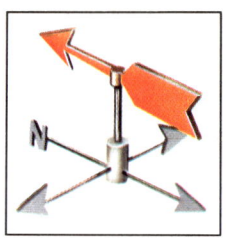

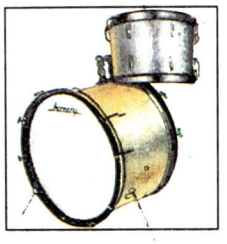

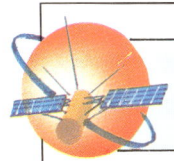 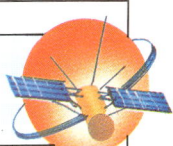

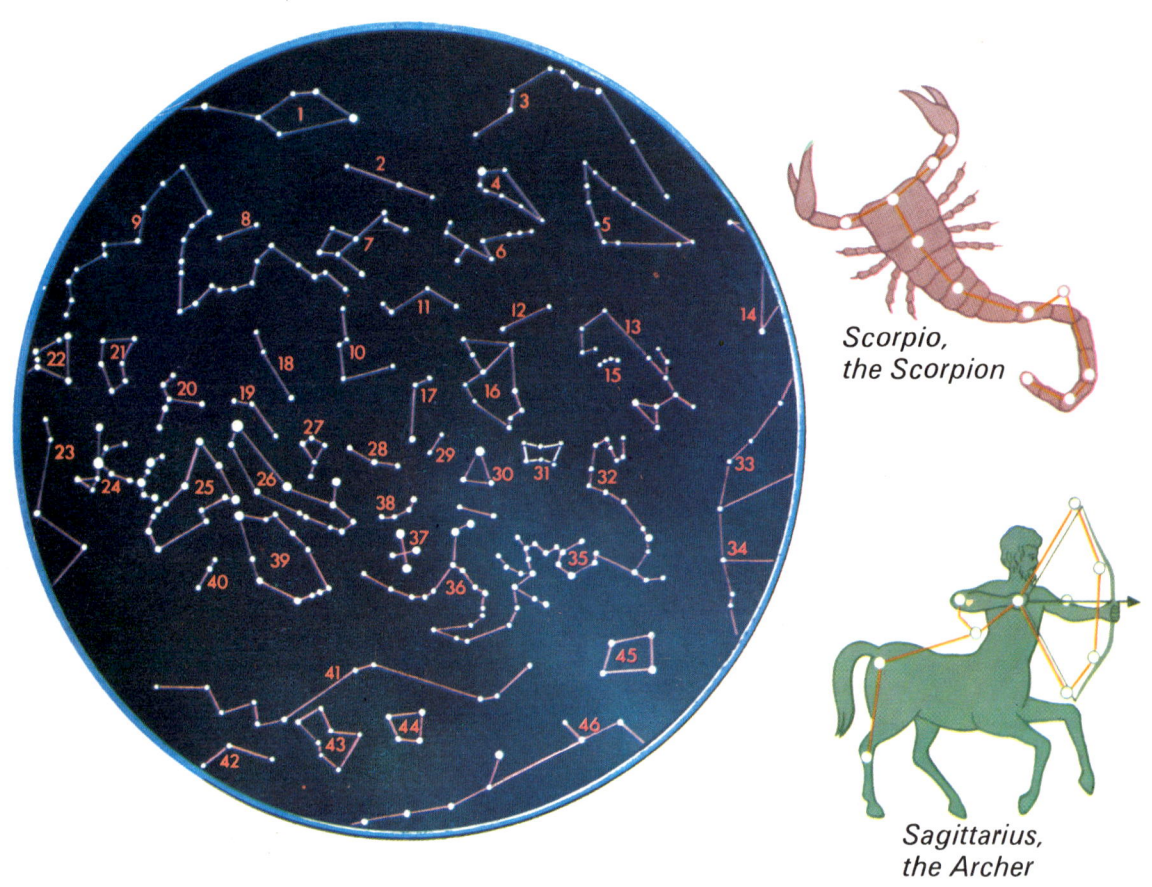

Scorpio,
the Scorpion

Sagittarius,
the Archer

CONSTELLATIONS OF THE SOUTHERN HEMISPHERE

1 Cetus, Sea Monster
2 Sculptor, Sculptor
3 Aquarius, Water-Bearer
4 Piscis Austrinus,
   Southern Fish
5 Capricornus, Sea Goat
6 Grus, Crane
7 Phoenix, Phoenix
8 Fornax, Furnace
9 Eridanus, River Eridanus
10 Hydrus, Little Snake
11 Tucana, Toucan
12 Indus, Indian
13 Sagittarius, Archer
14 Aquila, Eagle
15 Corona Australis,
   Southern Crown

16 Pavo, Peacock
17 Octans, Octant
18 Dorado, Swordfish
19 Pictor, Painter's Easel
20 Columba, Dove
21 Lepus, Hare
22 Orion, Hunter
23 Monoceros, Unicorn
24 Canis Major, Great Dog
25 Puppis, Poop
26 Carina, Keel
27 Volans, Flying Fish
28 Chamaeleon,
   Chamaeleon
29 Apus, Bird of Paradise
30 Triangulum Australe,
   Southern Triangle

31 Ara, Altar
32 Scorpio, Scorpion
33 Serpens, Serpent
34 Ophiuchus, Serpent-
   Bearer
35 Lupus, Wolf
36 Centaurus, Centaur
37 Crux, Southern Cross
38 Musca, Fly
39 Vela, Sails
40 Pyxis, Compass Box
41 Hydra, Sea Serpent
42 Sextans, Sextant
43 Crater, Cup
44 Corvus, Crow
45 Libra, Scales
46 Virgo, Virgin

CONSTELLATIONS OF THE NORTHERN HEMISPHERE

1 Equuleus, Colt
2 Delphinus, Dolphin
3 Pegasus, Flying Horse
4 Pisces, Fishes
5 Cetus, Sea Monster
6 Aries, Ram
7 Triangulum, Triangle
8 Andromeda, Chained Maiden
9 Lacerta, Lizard
10 Cygnus, Swan
11 Sagitta, Arrow
12 Aquila, Eagle
13 Lyra, Lyre
14 Cepheus, King

15 Cassiopeia, Lady in Chair
16 Perseus, Champion
17 Camelopardus, Giraffe
18 Auriga, Charioteer
19 Taurus, Bull
20 Orion, Hunter
21 Lynx, Lynx
22 Polaris, Pole Star
23 Ursa Minor, Little Bear
24 Draco, Dragon
25 Hercules, Kneeling Giant
26 Ophiuchus, Serpent-Bearer
27 Serpens, Serpent

28 Corona Borealis, Northern Crown
29 Boötes, Herdsman
30 Ursa Major, Great Bear
31 Gemini, Twins
32 Cancer, Crab
33 Canis Minor, Little Dog
34 Hydra, Sea Serpent
35 Leo, Lion
36 Leo Minor, Little Lion
37 Canes Venatici, Hunting Dogs
38 Coma Berenices, Berenice's Hair
39 Virgo, Virgin

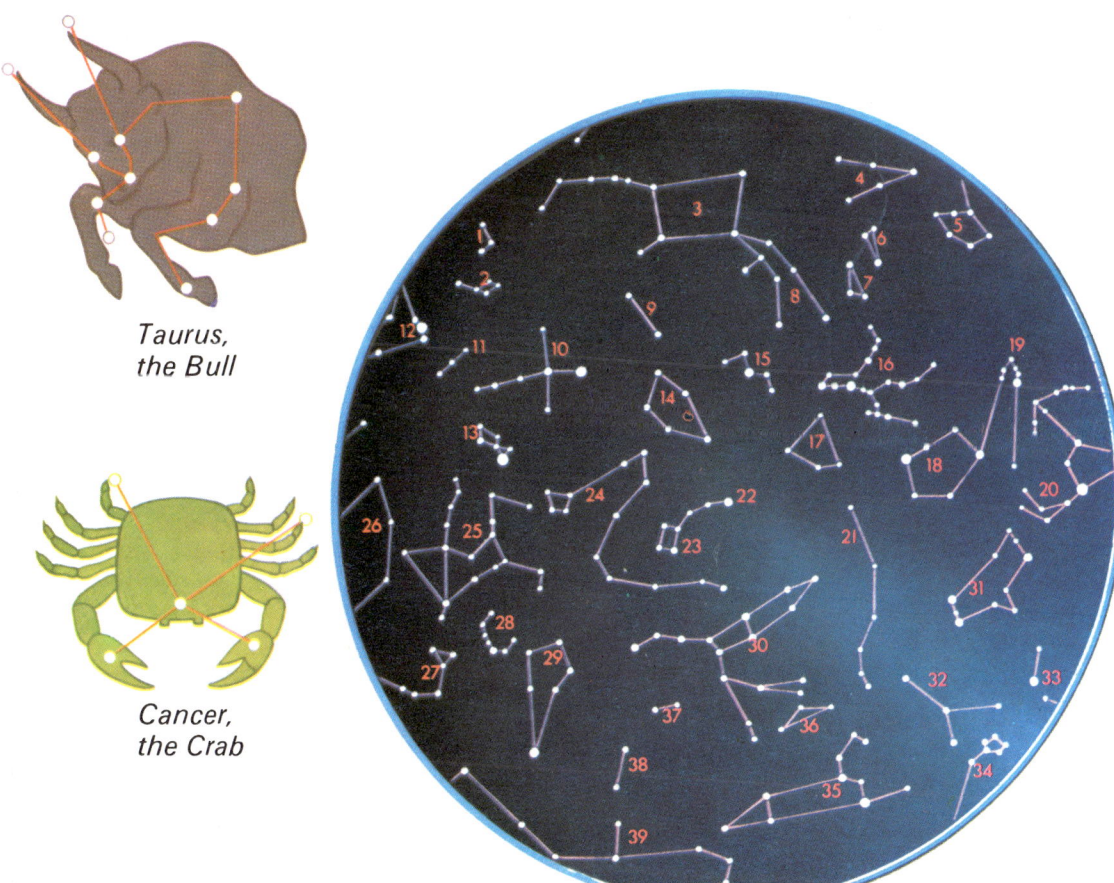

Taurus, the Bull

Cancer, the Crab

The Milky Way

On a clear moonless night, you can see a fuzzy band across part of the sky. When looked at through a telescope, this band is seen to be made up of hundreds upon hundreds of stars. We call it the *Milky Way*. We also give this name to the *galaxy*, or star system, to which our Sun belongs.

The Milky Way galaxy is a huge disc of stars with a bulge in the middle. When you look at the fuzzy band in the night sky, you are actually looking at a cross-section of the disc. Most of the stars in the galaxy are found on arms which spiral out from the bulge. In all, there are about 100,000 million stars in the whole galaxy. The galaxy also includes great clusters of stars, called *globular clusters*; and clouds of gas and dust, called *nebulae* (singular, *nebula*). Some nebulae are bright; others are dark and prevent us seeing through them.

The galaxy is so big that light takes 100,000 years to travel from one side to the other. Like everything else in the universe, the whole galaxy is spinning round. The part of the galaxy where the Sun is turns around once in 225 million years.

Someone at the Equator looking up into the night sky will see the stars move across the sky in straight *parallel lines. Above: Someone looking up into the sky from farther north or south will see the stars move across the sky in* curved *parallel lines. In both cases, the star movement is really caused by the Earth spinning on its axis. The difference in star movement is explained by how near, or far, the observer is from the Poles around which the Earth spins. In the northern hemisphere, the Pole Star (yellow) will not move at all.*

Below: The Great Galaxy in the constellation Andromeda

Famous Astronomers

Aristarchus (200s BC), a Greek, suggested that the Earth travels round the Sun.

Brahe, Tycho (1546–1601), a Dane, was a brilliant observer of the heavens.

Copernicus, Nicolaus (1473–1543), a Polish priest, revived the idea that the Earth circles the Sun.

Einstein, Albert (1879–1955), a German physicist and mathematician, revolutionized many astronomical concepts with his theories of relativity.

Galileo (1564–1642), an Italian scientist, constructed a telescope in 1609 and became the first great observer with such an instrument.

Halley, Edmund (1656–1742), the second British Astronomer Royal, is best known for his work on comets. He showed that the comet now named after him had appeared many times before at regular intervals.

Hipparchus (100s BC), a Greek, was the best astronomer of ancient times.

Hubble, Edwin (1899–1953), an American, founded the study of the universe beyond our own galaxy.

Kepler, Johannes (1571–1630), a German who became Tycho Brahe's assistant, developed the laws of planetary motion. The first of these states that planets travel round the Sun in elliptical orbits.

Lowell, Percival (1885–1916), an American, correctly predicted that a ninth planet exists (Pluto).

Newton, Isaac (1642–1727), a brilliant English scientist and mathematician, developed the law of gravitation, explained why the heavenly bodies move as they do, and calculated their orbits.

Ptolemy of Alexandria (AD 100s), a Greek, surveyed in his famous astronomical book the *Almagest* ('The Greatest') the work of Hipparchus.

All About Astronomy

astronomy The scientific study of the heavens.

celestial sphere An imaginary sphere surrounding the Earth in space.

cosmology The study of the form and nature of the universe.

eclipse What happens when one heavenly body passes in front of another and blots out its light.

ecliptic The apparent path of the Sun across the celestial sphere during the year.

light-year A unit of distance astronomers use. It is the distance light, moving at 300,000 km a second, travels in a year.

observatory The place where professional astronomers work.

radio astronomy The study of radio waves from the heavens.

radio telescope Apparatus built to concentrate and magnify radio signals from space.

spectrum A band of colour produced when light is passed through a spectroscope. Light from the Sun and the stars – that is, white light – is made up of light of different colours, or wavelengths.

stellar Relating to the stars.

telescope An instrument used to collect and concentrate light from the heavenly bodies and produce a magnified image. Refracting telescopes use lenses to do this. Reflecting telescopes use mirrors.

transit An event when a smaller heavenly body (e.g. Venus) passes over the disc of another (e.g. the Sun).

universe Everything that exists – the Earth, the Sun, the planets, the stars, the galaxies, and space.

zodiac The constellations through which the Sun appears to pass during the year. They are Aries, Taurus, Gemini, Cancer, Leo, Virgo, Libra, Scorpio, Sagittarius, Capricornus, Aquarius, and Pisces.

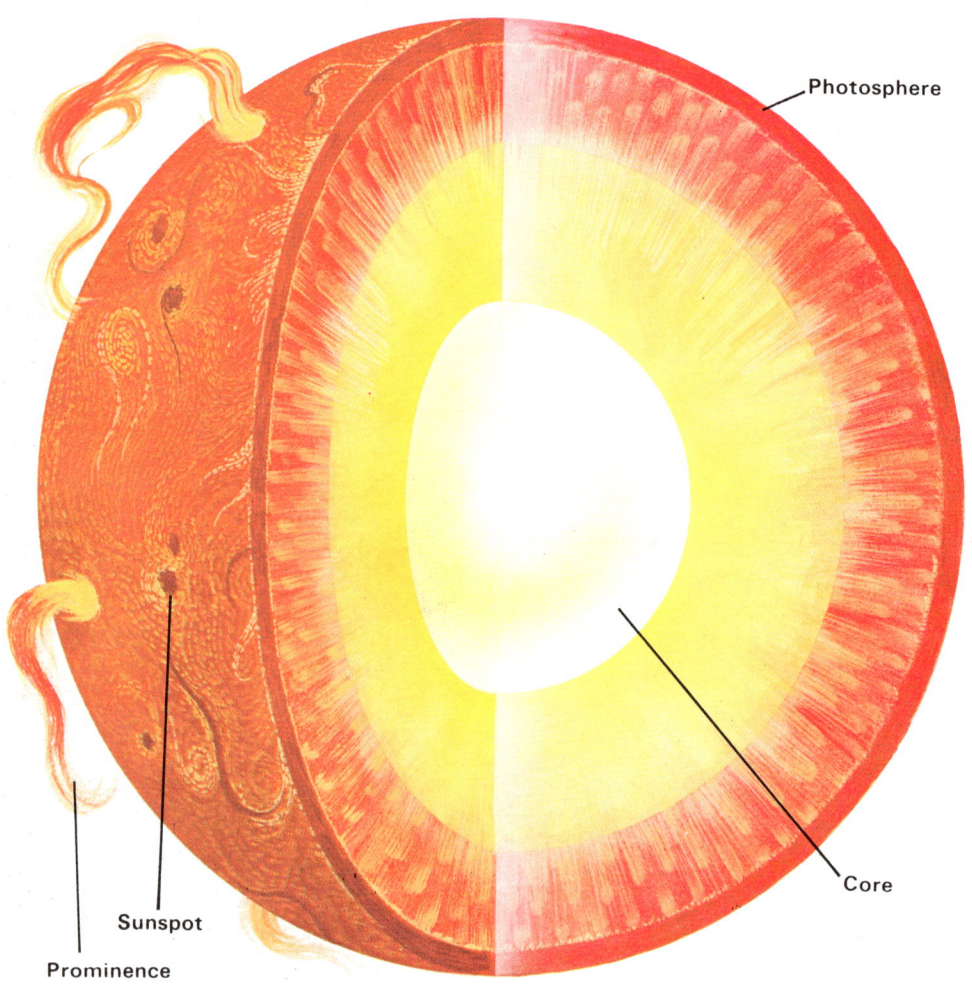

Photosphere

Core

Sunspot

Prominence

SUN STATISTICS	
Diameter	1,392,000 km
	(865,000 miles)
Volume	1,304,000 Earths
Relative density	1·4
Mass	333,000 Earth's
Gravitational pull	28 × Earth's
Temperature	
at surface	6000°C
at the centre	15,000,000°C
Spins on axis in	25⅓ days
Speed of travel through space	250 km/sec 155 miles per second

Our Star, the Sun

The Sun is especially important to us, but it is a very ordinary star, really. It is a kind astronomers call a 'yellow dwarf'. It has been shining like it does today for at least 5000 million years, and it will continue to shine as it does today for at least another 5000 million years. Then it may swell up into a giant reddish star called a 'red giant'.

The energy that makes the Sun shine comes from deep inside, where the temperature is millions of degrees celsius. At this temperature atoms of hydrogen join together to form atoms of helium. In this so-called 'fusion process', vast amounts of energy are given out as light, heat, and other forms.

Spheres of light and colour

The bright surface of the Sun which gives out light is called the *photosphere* ('light sphere'). It is so bright that it makes the light of the Sun's atmosphere. The inner part of the atmosphere is known as the *chromosphere* ('colour-sphere'), because it has a reddish colour.

The outer part is called the *corona* ('crown'). It reaches out millions of kilometres into space. The only time when we can see the chromosphere and corona is during a total eclipse of the Sun. Then the bright disc of the Sun is covered by the dark disc of the Moon.

The Sun's surface is seething as hot gases boil up from beneath. Patterns of bright specks continually come and go. Some features remain for days or indeed months at a time. They are *sunspots*, which show up as dark patches on the Sun's disc. Some measure up to about 200,000 km across (125,000 miles).

A total solar eclipse reveals the Sun's corona.

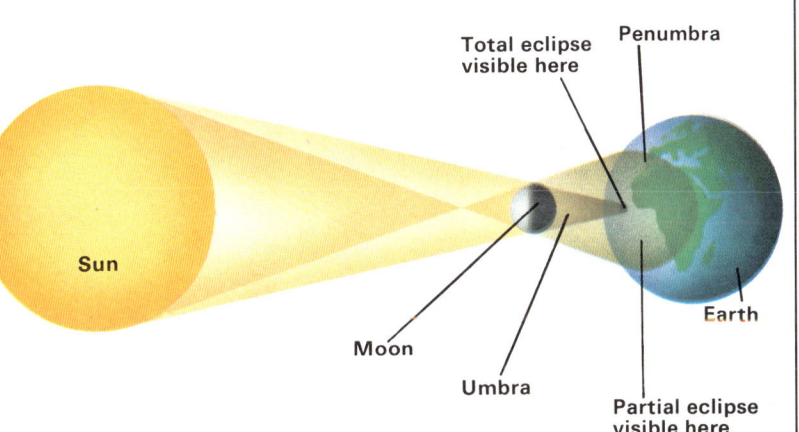

This diagram shows a solar eclipse caused as the Moon's shadow falls on the Earth, and a lunar eclipse as the Earth's shadow falls on the Moon. Only the umbra – the dark middle part of each shadow – is shown.

Total eclipse visible here

Penumbra

Sun

Moon

Umbra

Earth

Partial eclipse visible here

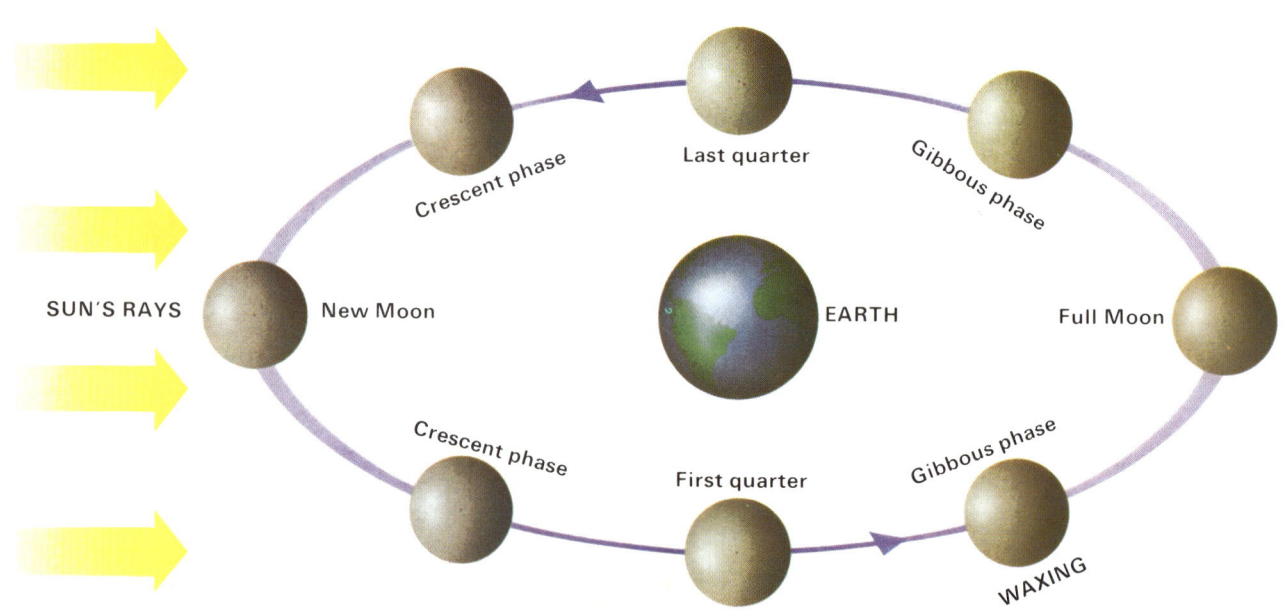

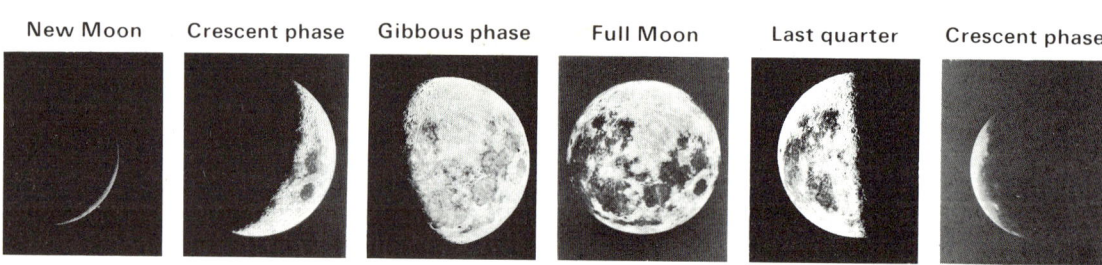

| New Moon | Crescent phase | Gibbous phase | Full Moon | Last quarter | Crescent phase |

As the Moon travels round the Earth every month, more or less of its surface is lit by the Sun. It depends on where the Moon is in its orbit. We call the varying appearance of the Moon, its phases. When the Moon is directly between us and the Sun, we cannot see it. And we call this the new moon. After a while, as the Moon moves on, a thin crescent of light appears. This gradually gets bigger until half the surface is lit. We call this the Moon's first quarter. Later, we see all the surface – the full moon. Up to this point we say the Moon has been 'waxing'. Now it starts to 'wane'. The sunlit portion gets smaller and smaller, until it disappears completely at the next new Moon. It takes the Moon $29\frac{1}{2}$ days to go through its phases.

MOON DATA

Diameter at Equator	3476 km (2160 miles)
Volume	$\frac{1}{49}$ Earth's
Density (water=1)	3·34
Mass	$\frac{1}{81}$ Earth's
Gravitational attraction at surface	$\frac{1}{6}$ Earth's
Average distance from Earth	384,400 km (238,860 miles)
Spins on its axis once in:	$27\frac{1}{3}$ days
Circles the Earth once in:	$27\frac{1}{3}$ days

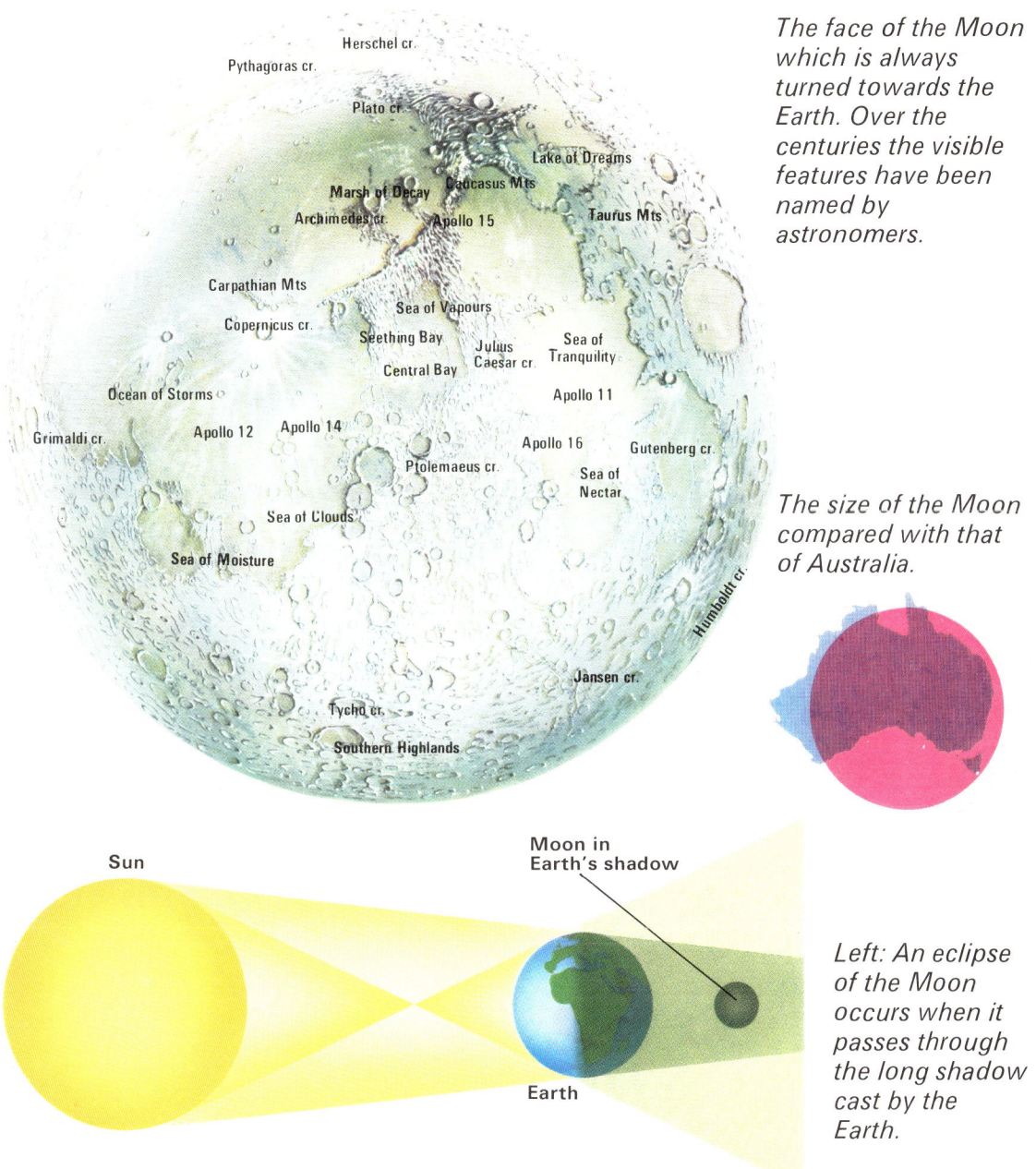

The face of the Moon which is always turned towards the Earth. Over the centuries the visible features have been named by astronomers.

Herschel cr.
Pythagoras cr.
Plato cr.
Lake of Dreams
Caucasus Mts
Marsh of Decay
Archimedes cr.
Apollo 15
Taurus Mts
Carpathian Mts
Sea of Vapours
Copernicus cr.
Seething Bay
Julius Caesar cr.
Central Bay
Sea of Tranquility
Ocean of Storms
Apollo 11
Grimaldi cr.
Apollo 12
Apollo 14
Apollo 16
Gutenberg cr.
Ptolemaeus cr.
Sea of Nectar
Sea of Clouds
Sea of Moisture
Humboldt cr.
Jansen cr.
Tycho cr.
Southern Highlands

The size of the Moon compared with that of Australia.

Sun

Moon in Earth's shadow

Earth

Left: An eclipse of the Moon occurs when it passes through the long shadow cast by the Earth.

Eclipses

The diameter of the Moon is 400 times as small as that of the Sun, but the Moon is 400 times closer to the Earth. As a result, the Moon appears more or less the same size as the Sun to our eyes. At certain times of the year, the Moon comes between us and the Sun and blots out the Sun from our sight. We say that an *eclipse of the Sun* has occurred. Only a narrow band of the Earth's surface ever has a *total eclipse*. This is the region in complete shadow *(umbra)*. A total eclipse never lasts longer than about 7 minutes.

One question that astronomers have not, so far, been able to answer is whether there is life elsewhere in the universe. But when we think about the vast distances to other worlds, this is not surprising. If the Sun were the size of a football, the nearest star – Alpha Centauri – would be about 13,000 km (8000 miles) away. This shows how alone in space we are. But it now seems almost certain that there must be intelligent life somewhere other than on Earth.

FACTS ABOUT THE SOLAR SYSTEM

Name	Average distance from Sun (millions) km)	Diameter at equator km	(miles)	Circles Sun in:	Turns on axis in:
Sun	—	1,392,000	(865,000)	—	$25\frac{1}{3}$ days
Moon	—	3476	(2160)	—	$27\frac{1}{3}$ days
Mercury	58	4850	(3015)	88 days	59 days
Venus	108	12,140	(7545)	224 days	244 days
Earth	150	12,756	(7926)	$365\frac{1}{4}$ days	23:56 hours
Mars	228	6790	(4220)	687 days	24:37 hours
Jupiter	778	142,600	(88,600)	11·9 years	9:50 hours
Saturn	1427	120,200	(74,700)	29·5 years	10:14 hours
Uranus	2870	49,000	(30,500)	84 years	15:48 hours
Neptune	4497	50,000	(31,200)	164·8 years	15:48 hours
Pluto	5900	3000	(1800)	247·7 years	153 hours

In our galaxy alone – the Milky Way – there may be 1000 million planets on which people something like ourselves could develop. And our galaxy is only one among millions of other galaxies in the universe. Scientists believe that somewhere among this inconceivably large number of planets there must be living creatures not too different from us. But getting in touch with them over the vast distances and time involved will not be easy.

The Planets

Mercury is the smallest planet and also the one closest to the Sun. It is difficult to see in the night sky because it is always low on the horizon just before sunrise and just after sunset.

Being close to the Sun, Mercury's surface is very hot, rising to 400°C (750°F) or more. It has a barren, rocky surface covered in craters, much like the Moon's. Like the Moon, it has no atmosphere.

Venus is similar in size to the Earth. It has a thick atmosphere of carbon dioxide gas, containing thick white clouds. These hide the surface from us. The temperature on the surface is more than 400°C (750°F). And the pressure of the atmosphere is nearly 100 times the air pressure on Earth.

We can see Venus very clearly because it is the brightest body in the night sky after the Moon. We can see it as a 'morning star' at sunrise and an 'evening star' at sunset.

Mars can also be clearly seen for much of the year. It has an orange-red colour and is known as the 'Red Planet'. It has a bare surface that is often lashed by sandstorms. Temperatures on Mars are generally very low, and seldom rise above freezing point (0°C or 32°F). In the Martian winter, the north and south poles are capped with 'ice'. The ice is not water ice like the polar ice caps on Earth. It is probably frozen carbon dioxide gas.

The surface is covered with craters, although there are one or two smooth regions. One of the main Martian features is a great canyon 5000 km (3000 mile) long and 70 km (44 miles) wide.

The Minor Planets, or Asteroids, circle in a broad belt between the orbits of Mars and Jupiter. They are chunks of rock covered in frozen gases. Most are too small to be detected from Earth, but a few are quite large. Largest is Ceres, which is about 760 km (470 miles) in diameter.

Jupiter is the giant of the planets. It could swallow more than 1300 Earths. But it is only about 300 times more massive than Earth, because it is made mainly of hydrogen, the lightest element. It has a thick hydrogen atmosphere beneath which are layers of liquid hydrogen. It may have a rocky centre.

Jupiter can easily be seen from Earth. The four largest of its 14 moons can be seen through binoculars. The largest moon, Ganymede, is 5200 km (3230 miles) in diameter. Through a telescope, cloud belts can be seen floating in the atmosphere. A giant red spot can often be seen too. It is thought to be a great storm, which has been raging for hundreds of years.

Saturn is called the ringed planet. It has a flat ring round its middle, made up of three separate bands. The second biggest planet, it consists mainly of hydrogen gas. It also contains methane. The largest of Saturn's 10 moons is Titan, with a diameter of 4880 km (3032 miles).

Uranus and Neptune are nearly identical twins. They are nearly the same size and are thought to be similar in make-up. They are very cold worlds (about −200°C or, −328°F) made probably of hydrogen and methane. Uranus can scarcely ever be seen with the naked eye. Neptune can be seen only through a telescope.

Pluto is so far away that we know little about it. We are not even sure of its size. But we do know that it must be very cold indeed.

The giant planet Jupiter seen through a telescope. Clouds hide its surface. The planet spins so fast that it pulls the clouds into dark bright stripes.

Comet West, 1976 was one of the brightest comets of the century. It is photographed here over Kitt Peak National Observatory.

Comets

The appearance of a bright comet is one of the finest sights in the heavens. A comet is a mass of dust and frozen gas which travels around the Sun. For most of the time we cannot see it. But when it nears the Sun, it begins to reflect the Sun's light and we can see it.

The comet sometimes grows a tail, which can stretch more than half-way across the sky. The tail does not stream out behind the comet, but always points away from the Sun. This is because the stream of particles coming from the Sun (the *solar wind*) pushes matter away from the comet's head, or *coma*.

Some comets do not travel very far. They take only a few years to orbit the Sun. Encke's comet takes only $3\frac{1}{3}$ years. Other comets take much longer. Halley's comet takes about 76 years. This is the most famous comet of all, which has been seen for centuries. It appeared at the Battle of Hastings in 1066.

Shooting Stars

Sometimes in the night sky you can see a sudden streak of light. It looks as if a star is falling from the sky, and we call it a *falling*, or *shooting* star. But its proper name is a *meteor*. Fiery meteor trails are made by chunks of rock as they hurtle through the Earth's upper air. The rubbing action, or friction, of the air against the rock, heats it and usually makes it burn up to dust.

If the lump of rock is very big, parts of it may reach the Earth. We call these lumps *meteorites*. Some of them are stony. Others are made up mainly of iron and nickel. The biggest meteorite yet found is the Hoba meteorite from Namibia. It weighs 60 tonnes.

How the Universe Began

No one really knows how and when the universe began, but astronomers have made some guesses. Many think that the universe began about 15,000 million years ago, literally 'with a bang'. They call it the *big-bang theory*. In the beginning, these astronomers say, all the matter in the universe was lumped together in a massive ball. Then, 15,000 million years ago, the ball exploded, scattering matter in all directions. From this matter, the stars eventually formed.

Astronomers have found some possible evidence of a 'big bang'. They have found that the galaxies are racing away from each other. This shows that the universe is still expanding.

Several astronomers are against the big-bang theory. They think instead that the universe has always been like it is now. This is the *steady-state theory*.

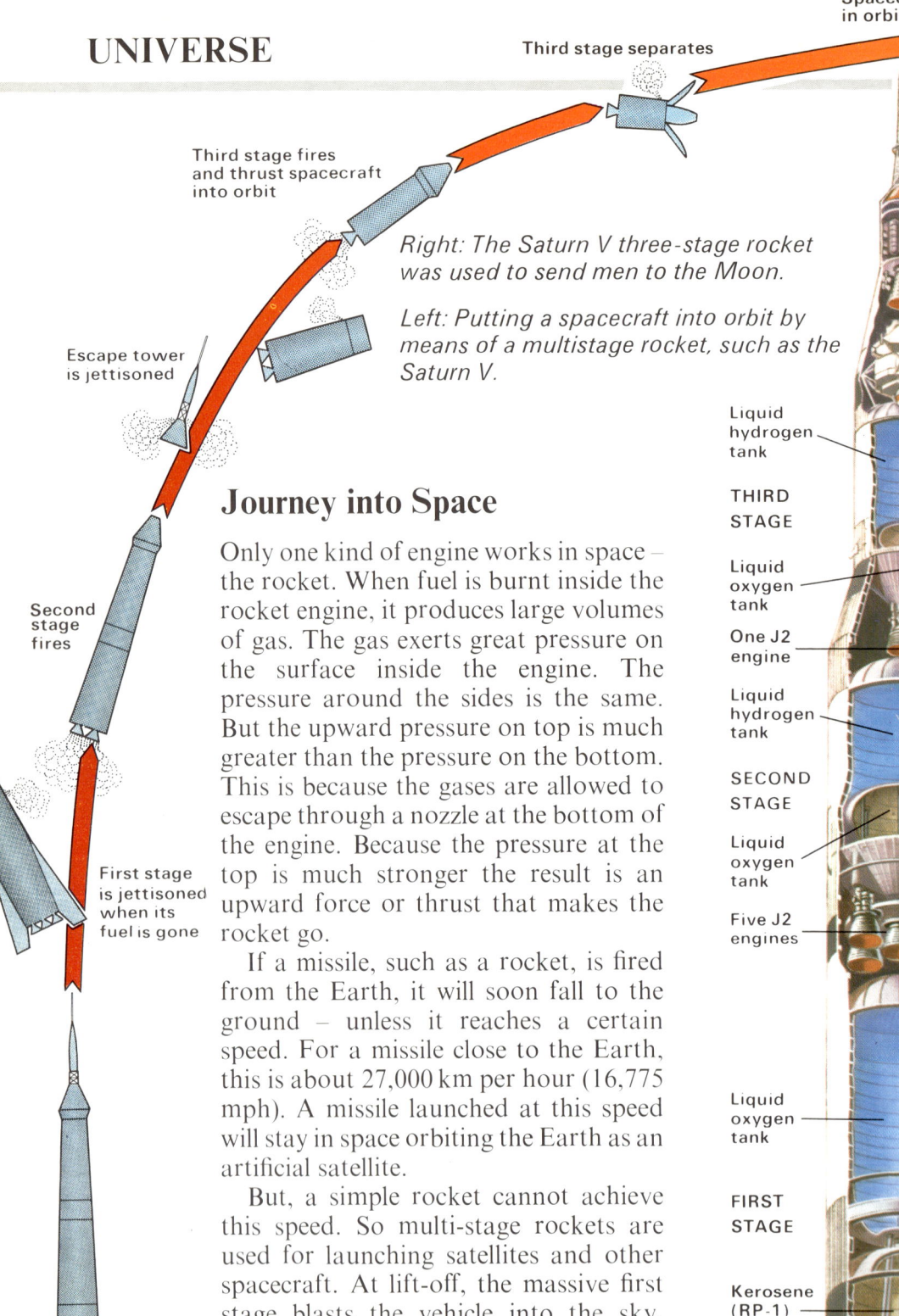

Third stage separates

Spacecraft continues in orbit

Third stage fires and thrust spacecraft into orbit

Escape tower

Escape tower is jettisoned

Right: The Saturn V three-stage rocket was used to send men to the Moon.

Left: Putting a spacecraft into orbit by means of a multistage rocket, such as the Saturn V.

Second stage fires

First stage is jettisoned when its fuel is gone

first stage fires

Liquid hydrogen tank

THIRD STAGE

Liquid oxygen tank

One J2 engine

Liquid hydrogen tank

SECOND STAGE

Liquid oxygen tank

Five J2 engines

Liquid oxygen tank

FIRST STAGE

Kerosene (RP-1) tank

Stabilizer fins

Fairing

Five F1 engines

Journey into Space

Only one kind of engine works in space – the rocket. When fuel is burnt inside the rocket engine, it produces large volumes of gas. The gas exerts great pressure on the surface inside the engine. The pressure around the sides is the same. But the upward pressure on top is much greater than the pressure on the bottom. This is because the gases are allowed to escape through a nozzle at the bottom of the engine. Because the pressure at the top is much stronger the result is an upward force or thrust that makes the rocket go.

If a missile, such as a rocket, is fired from the Earth, it will soon fall to the ground – unless it reaches a certain speed. For a missile close to the Earth, this is about 27,000 km per hour (16,775 mph). A missile launched at this speed will stay in space orbiting the Earth as an artificial satellite.

But, a simple rocket cannot achieve this speed. So multi-stage rockets are used for launching satellites and other spacecraft. At lift-off, the massive first stage blasts the vehicle into the sky. When the first stage has burnt out, it is dumped and a second-stage rocket takes over. Then this is dumped and, a third-stage rocket provides the final burst of acceleration.

Steps into Space

1942 German scientists successfully tested the VI rocket, later used to bombard London.

1957 USSR launched the first artificial satellite, Sputnik 1, on 4 October, and the second, Sputnik 2, on 3 November. Sputnik 2 contained the first space traveller, a dog called Laika.

1959 Russian probe Luna 2 crash-landed on the Moon. Luna 3 sent back pictures of the Moon's hidden side.

1960 Russia launched two dogs into orbit and recovered them.

1961 Soviet cosmonaut Yuri Gagarin became the first man to orbit the Earth, on 12 April.

1962 USSR and the USA launched probes to Mars and Venus.

1964 US Moon probe Ranger 7 sent back close-up pictures of the Moon, before crash-landing.

1965 Russian cosmonaut Alexei Leonov made the first 'walk' in space. US Mariner 4 probe sent back pictures of Mars from a distance of 220 million km (137 million miles). A Russian Venera probe crash-landed on Venus.

1966 Moon probes Luna 9 and Surveyor 1 soft-landed on the Moon's surface and sent back pictures.

1968 Apollo 8 astronauts travelled round the Moon and back, approaching to within 120 km of the surface.

1969 Apollo 11 astronaut Neil Armstrong became the first 'man on the Moon' on 20 July. He and Edwin Aldrin explored the Moon on foot for nearly 3 hours. In November a Russian robot spacecraft landed on the Moon, scooped up some soil, and then returned with it to Earth. Another landed a 'moon-walker', Lunokhod.

1971 Russia launched Salyut 1 space station. US probe Mariner 9 went into orbit round Mars. A Russian probe soft-landed on Mars.

1972 Last Apollo flight to the Moon (Apollo 17).

1973 US launched space station Skylab, which was visited by two three-man crews. US Pioneer 10 probe sent back pictures of Jupiter.

1974 Third Skylab crew remained in space for 84 days. Mariner 10 became the first probe to use the gravitational pull of one planet, Venus, to reach another, Mercury. It sent back the first close-up pictures of Mercury.

1975 Russian cosmonauts and American astronauts linked up in space in Soyuz and Apollo spacecraft. Russian Venus probes Venera 9 and 10 sent back the first close-up pictures of Venus.

1976 US Viking probes enter Martian orbit and dropped landers on to the surface, which transmitted the first close-up pictures of the planet.

1977 Russian craft docked with a space laboratory, and the US launched two spacecraft to fly to Venus.

1979 Russian cosmonauts spent a record 175 days in space.

1980 An American Pioneer/Venus orbiter mapped almost all of Venus.

1981 The American space shuttle Columbia made its first flight.

1982 Two Russian cosmonauts spent 211 days in space.

1983 The American space shuttle took off with six astronauts aboard.

1984 A Russian woman cosmonaut became the first woman to walk in space.

First Woman in Orbit. *Valentina Tereshkova was launched into space on 16 June 1963 in the spacecraft Vostok 6. She joined fellow cosmonaut Valery Bykovsky in orbit in Vostok 5. Her trip lasted three days, during which time she made 49 orbits of the Earth.*

First Man on the Moon. *Astronaut Neil Armstrong was assured of a place in history when he stepped on to the Moon on 20 July 1969. 'That's one small step for a man, one giant leap for mankind', he said.*

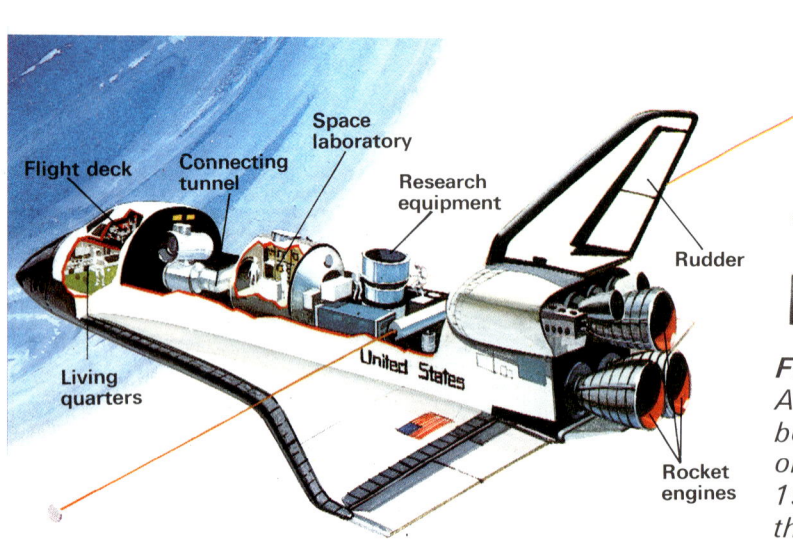

Flight deck
Connecting tunnel
Space laboratory
Research equipment
Rudder
Living quarters
United States
Rocket engines

The Space Shuttle Columbia is launched by rockets, orbits like a spacecraft and can land back on Earth like an airliner.

First Man in Orbit. *Yuri Alekseyevich Gagarin became the first person to orbit the Earth, on 12 April 1961. He made one orbit in the spacecraft Vostok 1 (Vostok means 'east'). He reached a height of more than 300 km in his 108-minute flight.*

Our Planet

Great Ice Age

Ice ages are periods in the Earth's history when large parts of its surface have been covered with thick sheets of ice. Scientists believe that these periods of excessive cold occur every few million years. The last ice age, called the Great Ice Age, began nearly 2 million years ago. There were a series of *glaciations*, during which the ice sheets spread out from the North Pole and covered much of the northern part of the world.

In northern Europe and North America, the ice was up to 3000 m thick (9840 ft). The Scandinavian Peninsula was the centre of the great European ice cap. Ice flowed almost to Moscow and covered northern England, western Denmark, and Germany. It covered an area of over 6 million sq km. In North America it flowed west and south to spread out over an area of more than 12 million sq km.

As the great ice sheets advanced, they scraped the land clear of soil and loose rocks. They levelled the surface of the land and smoothed out the mountain peaks. The ice, in the form of *glaciers*, swept down the river beds to the sea, scooping out deep valleys and fiords on its way.

Scientists who study the Ice Age have given names to the four periods of glaciation and to the periods in between, called *interglacials*. The longest period of glaciation in the Great Ice Age lasted over 150,000 years, and the longest interglacial period, when the climate warmed up again, lasted 90,000 years. The last great retreat of ice began about 10,000 to 25,000 years ago. This may mean that the Earth has entered a fourth interglacial period, and that some time in the future, perhaps in about 50,000 to 100,000 years' time, another intense period of cold may develop and the ice sheets will advance again.

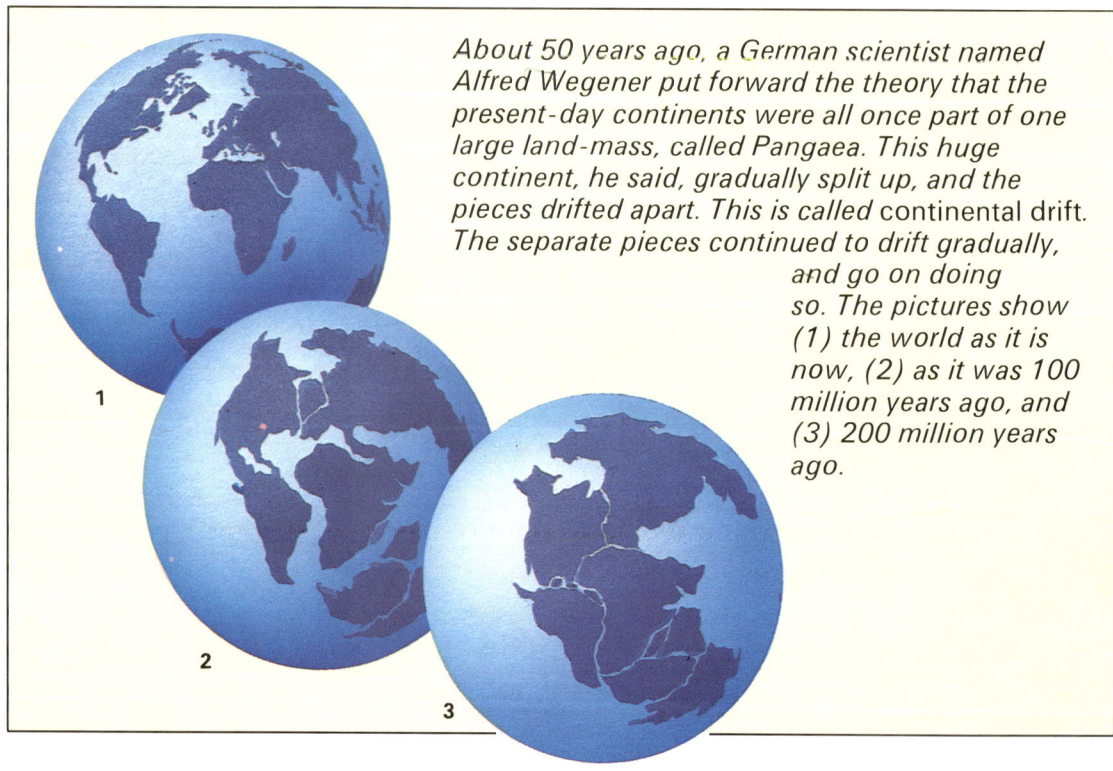

About 50 years ago, a German scientist named Alfred Wegener put forward the theory that the present-day continents were all once part of one large land-mass, called Pangaea. This huge continent, he said, gradually split up, and the pieces drifted apart. This is called continental drift. The separate pieces continued to drift gradually, and go on doing so. The pictures show (1) the world as it is now, (2) as it was 100 million years ago, and (3) 200 million years ago.

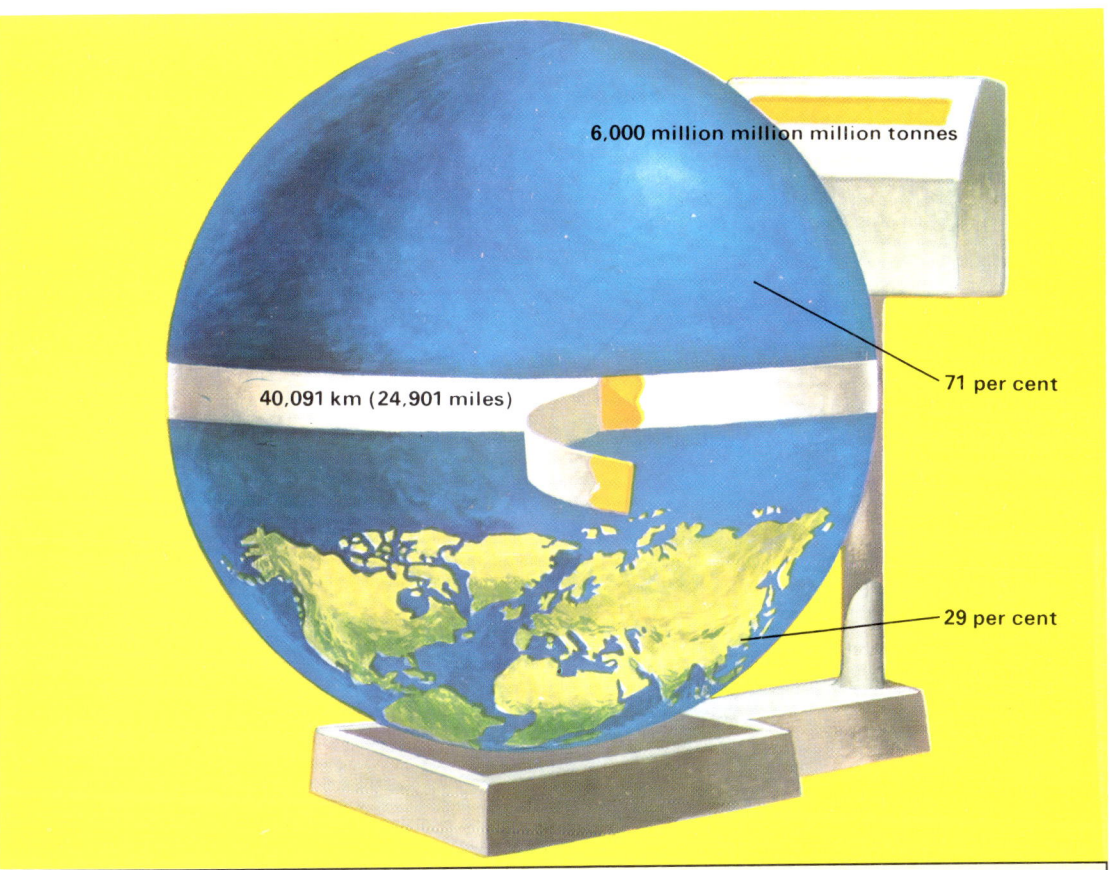

6,000 million million million tonnes

40,091 km (24,901 miles)

71 per cent

29 per cent

Earth's Vital Statistics

Age: about 4600 million years

Weight: about 6000 million million million tonnes

Diameter: from Pole to Pole through the Earth's centre 12,719 km (7900 miles)
across the Equator through the Earth's centre 12,757 km (7927 miles)

Circumference: round the Poles 40,020 km (24,857 miles)
round the Equator 40,091 km (24,901 miles)

Area: 149,142,560 sq. km 57,584,000 sq miles – 29%
Water 360,932,040 sq. km 139,356,000 sq miles – 71%
Total 510,074,600 sq. km 196,940,000 sq miles – 100%

Volume: 1,084,000 million cubic km (260,000 million cubic miles)

Volume of the oceans: 1321 million cubic km (317 million cubic miles)

Average height of land: 840 m (2757 ft) above sea level

Average depth of ocean: 3795 m (12,450 ft) below sea level

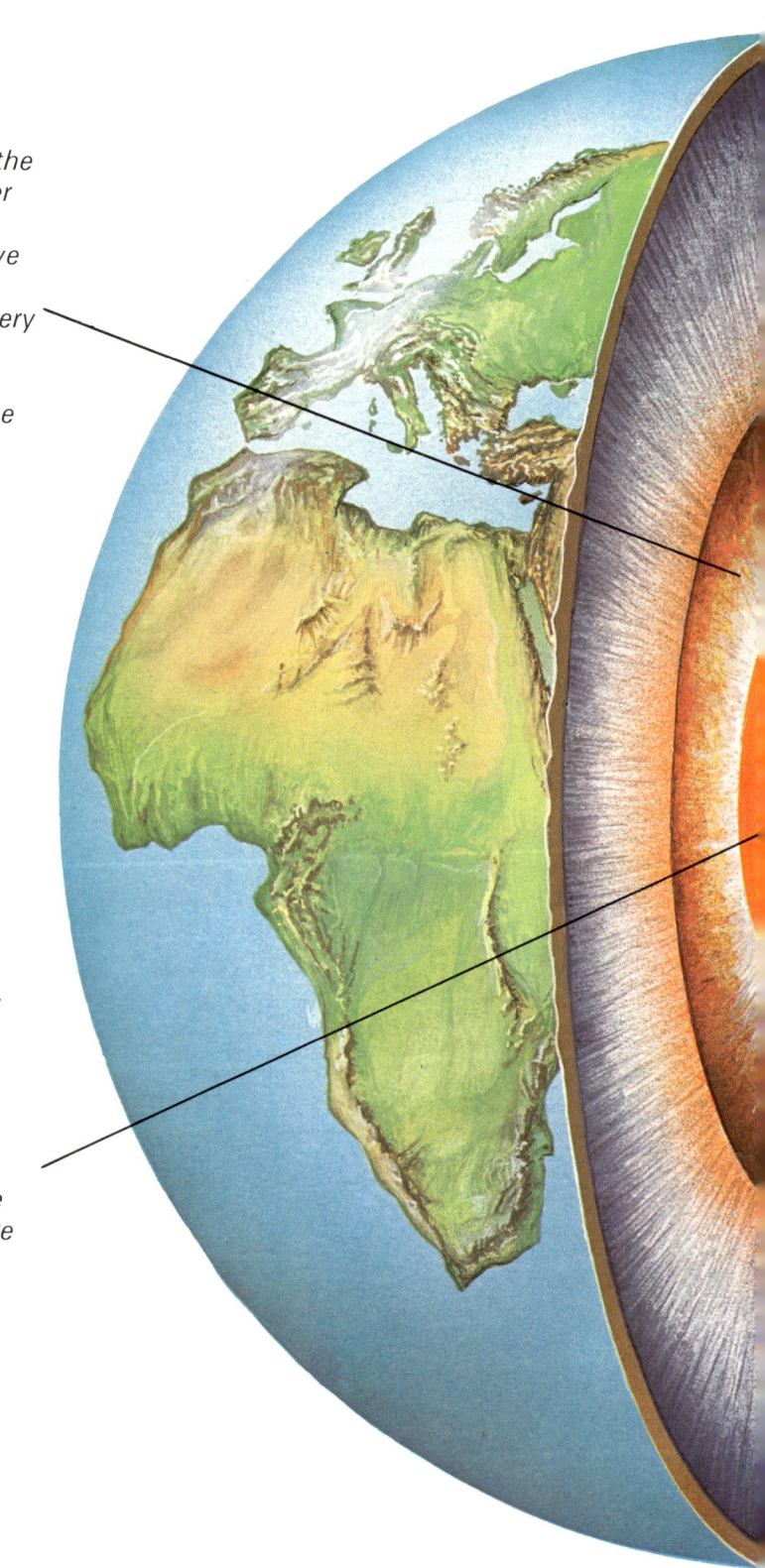

The outer core lies below the mantle and above the inner core. It is 2240 km (1400 miles) thick. Experts believe that it is mainly made of molten metals which are very hot and under enormous pressure. Four-fifths of it may be iron and nickel. The rest probably consists of silicon.

Earth's inner core is a solid ball 2440 km (1540 miles) across. It is 13 times as dense as water. Like the outer core, it may be made mainly of iron and nickel. The core has a temperature of 3700°C, and the pressure there is 3800 tonnes per square centimetre (24,000 tons per square inch).

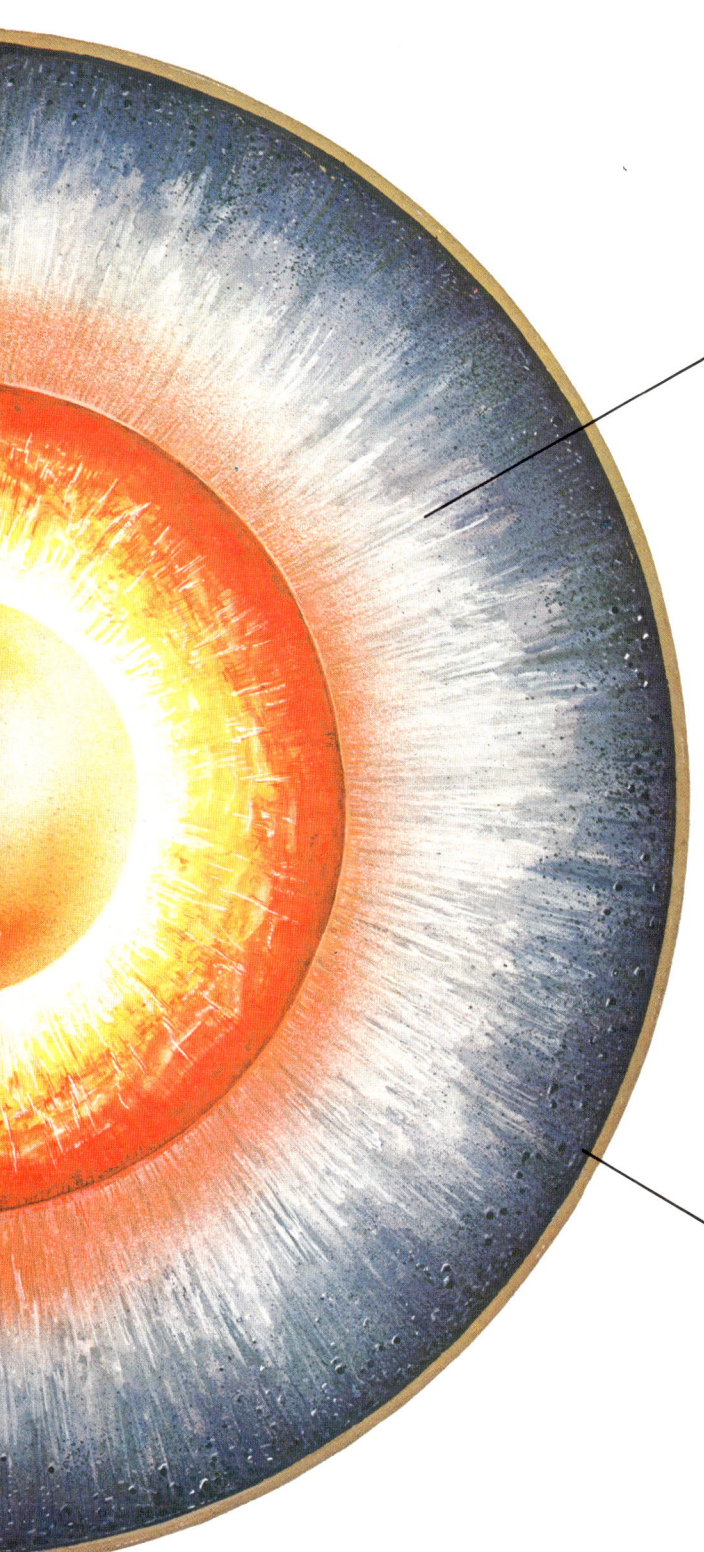

The mantle lies beneath the crust and above the outer core. It is nearly 2900 km (1800 miles) thick. It consists of dense hot rocks. The temperature and pressure here are lower than those of the core. But much of the mantle rock is semi-molten and flows in sluggish currents.

The crust is the Earth's solid outer layer. It is up to 30 km (19 miles) thick beneath mountains, but only 6 km (4 miles) thick under the oceans. Its rocks 'float' on the denser rocks that make up the mantle.

Weather Terms

air mass Large body of air having certain characteristics of temperature or moisture. Winds are movements of air masses.

altitude Height of a place above sea level. Temperature decreases by about 1°C for each 200 m (655 ft).

altocumulus Greyish-white cloud formation, made up of small rounded heaps.

altostratus Greyish 'veil' of cloud, often signalling a depression.

anemometer Instrument for measuring wind speed.

anticyclone A region of high pressure, usually associated with good weather.

barometer Instrument for measuring air pressure: indicates changes in weather.

Beaufort Scale Scale of numbers representing wind force in open ground; devised in 1805 by Admiral Sir Francis Beaufort.

blizzard Violent snowstorm with icy winds.

cirrocumulus Thin patch of cloud in

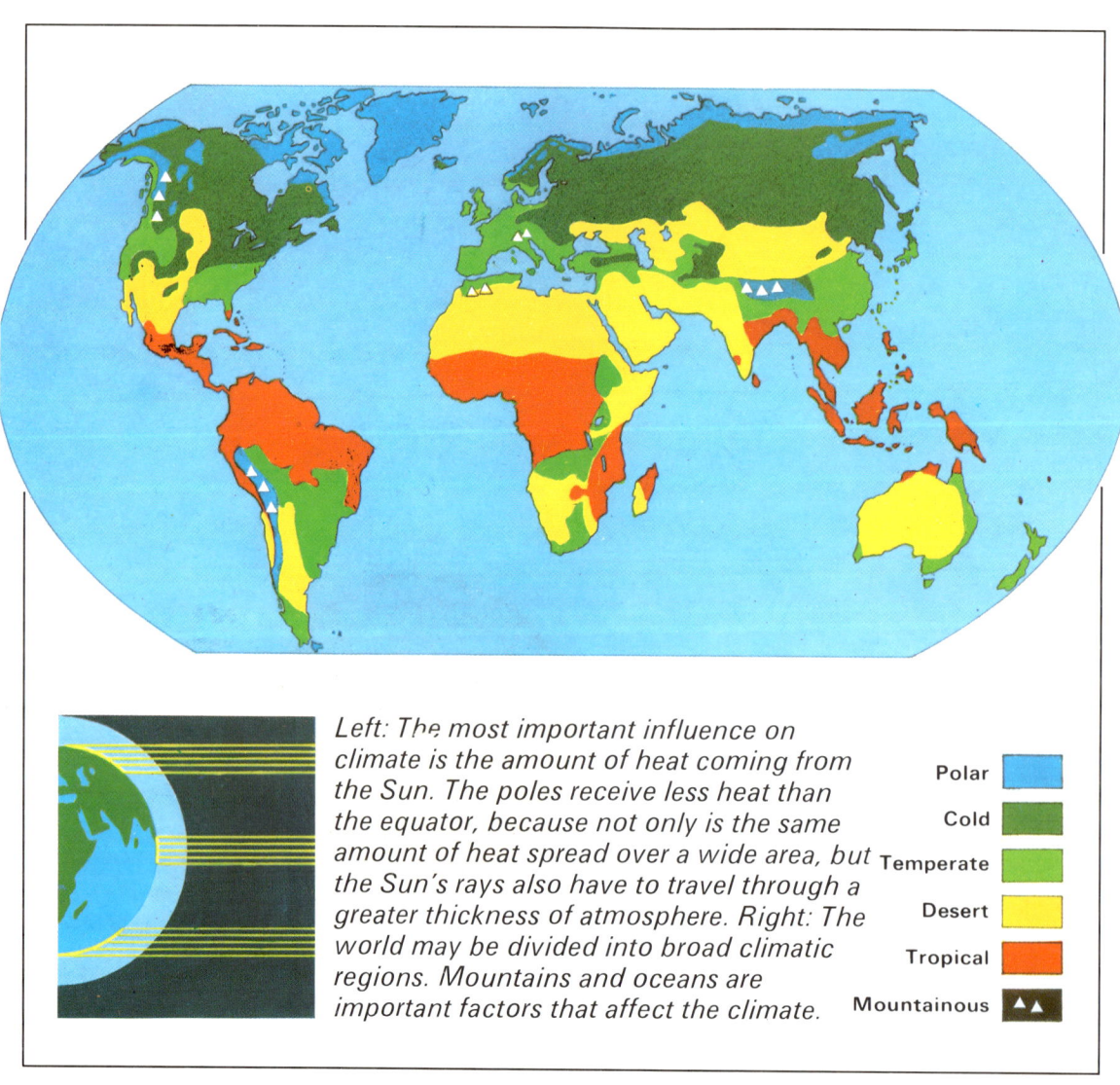

Left: The most important influence on climate is the amount of heat coming from the Sun. The poles receive less heat than the equator, because not only is the same amount of heat spread over a wide area, but the Sun's rays also have to travel through a greater thickness of atmosphere. Right: The world may be divided into broad climatic regions. Mountains and oceans are important factors that affect the climate.

Polar
Cold
Temperate
Desert
Tropical
Mountainous

ripple form, sometimes producing characteristic 'mackerel sky'.

cirrostratus Thin, milky, fibrelike cloud formation, often seen before depression. Causes 'halo' round Sun or Moon.

cirrus Highest cloud formation in sky, having a delicate white fibrelike appearance.

cloud Mass of water droplets or ice crystals suspended in the air.

condensation Formation of water droplets or round small particles when the air has more water vapour than it can hold.

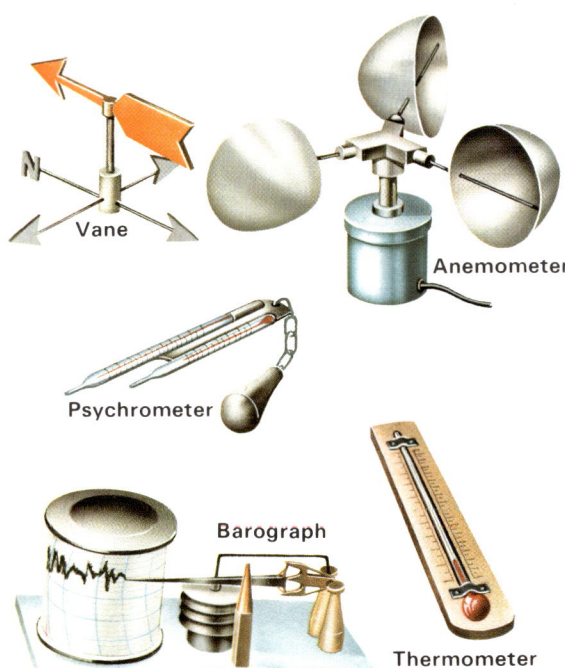

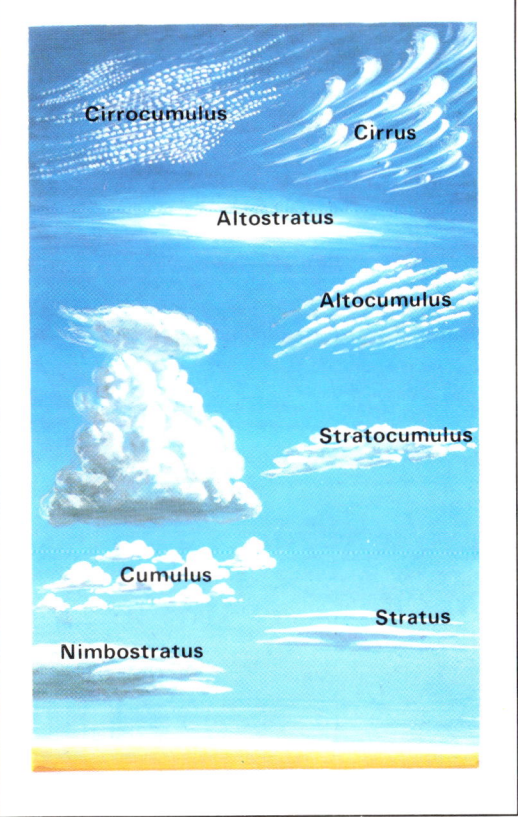

Different kinds of clouds. In cloud names, the term 'alto' means 'high', 'nimbo' or 'nimbus' means 'rain', 'cumulo' means 'pile' or 'heap', 'strato' means 'layerlike' or 'sheetlike', and 'cirro' means 'curl'.

Various instruments used to measure the conditions of the air. Anemometers measure wind speeds and vanes show wind direction.

convection Transfer of heat by flow of air from hotter to colder parts of the atmosphere.

cumulonimbus Thundercloud, often having typically anvil-shaped top and dark base.

cumulus Cloud formation made up of detached white heaps ('cauliflower heads').

cyclone Region of low pressure with winds spiralling inwards, usually signalling a spell of bad weather; called a *low* or *depression* in temperate regions.

depression Region of low pressure causing unsettled weather, with rain and winds.

dew Condensation on objects close to the ground.

equatorial climate High temperatures and heavy rainfall the whole year round.

fog Low cloud, close to the ground.

front Boundary between air masses with different temperatures and humidities.

frost Ice crystals or frozen particles of moisture that form when the temperature drops below freezing point 0°C (−32°F).

hail Pellets of ice that fall during storms.

high An *anticyclone*.

humidity The amount of moisture in the air.

hurricane A violent storm or cyclone, with winds spiralling inwards towards a centre of low pressure (the 'eye').

hygrometer Instrument for measuring humidity (moisture in the air)

isobar A line drawn on a weather map to connect points of equal pressure.

isotherm A line drawn on a weather map to connect points of equal temperature.

lightning Large discharge of electricity between clouds or cloud and Earth or within a cloud.

low A *cyclone*.

meteorology The study of weather.

mist Thin fog.

monsoon A seasonal wind that blows in certain parts of the world, usually bringing a long period of heavy rain; particularly severe between Asia and Australia.

nimbostratus Dark-grey rain cloud, thick enough to blot out sun.

occluded front Combination of warm and cold front.

precipitation Any form of moisture (rain, snow, etc.) that falls from a cloud.

pressure Force exerted by the weight of air over a place on the Earth. It is measured in bars.

rain Droplets of water that fall to Earth from a cloud.

rainbow Arc seen in the sky as the result of sunlight passing through raindrops and being split into its constituent colours (red, orange, yellow, green, blue indigo, violet).

sea breeze A current of cool air that comes in from the sea to replace the rising warm air on land that has been rapidly heated during the day.

seasons Periods of the year marked by regular overall changes in the weather and in the lengths of the days and nights. The seasons (spring, summer, autumn, winter) are caused by the varying amounts of warmth received on different regions of the Earth as it travels round the Sun.

sleet A mixture of snow and rain, or snow partly melting as it falls.

snow Crystals of ice that fall from clouds and are still frozen when reaching Earth.

storm A violent disturbance in the atmosphere, usually accompanied by heavy rain and strong winds.

stratocumulus Cloud formation, extensive layer of irregular light and dark patches.

stratus Lowest and most uniform cloud formation, like fog.

temperate climates Climates not exhibiting extremes of heat or cold.

thunder The noise caused by lightning flash when it heats air so that it expands explosively.

tornado Small but intense storms, with violent whirling winds.

tropical climates There are two kinds: *tropical marine* (on eastern coasts of Americas and Africa), with high temperatures, much rain, and hurricanes and typhoons; *tropical continental* (inland from the coasts), warm, moderate to considerable rainfall, dry winters.

troposphere Lowest layer of the atmosphere; it carries the weather.

wind Movement of air masses over surface of Earth; denoted by direction *from* which it blows.

The Earth's Atmosphere

The band of gases surrounding the Earth forms the atmosphere, and this has been divided by scientists into several layers.

The outermost layer of all is called the exosphere; next is the ionosphere, and below that is the mesosphere. Beneath these is the stratosphere, and lowest of all, the troposphere.

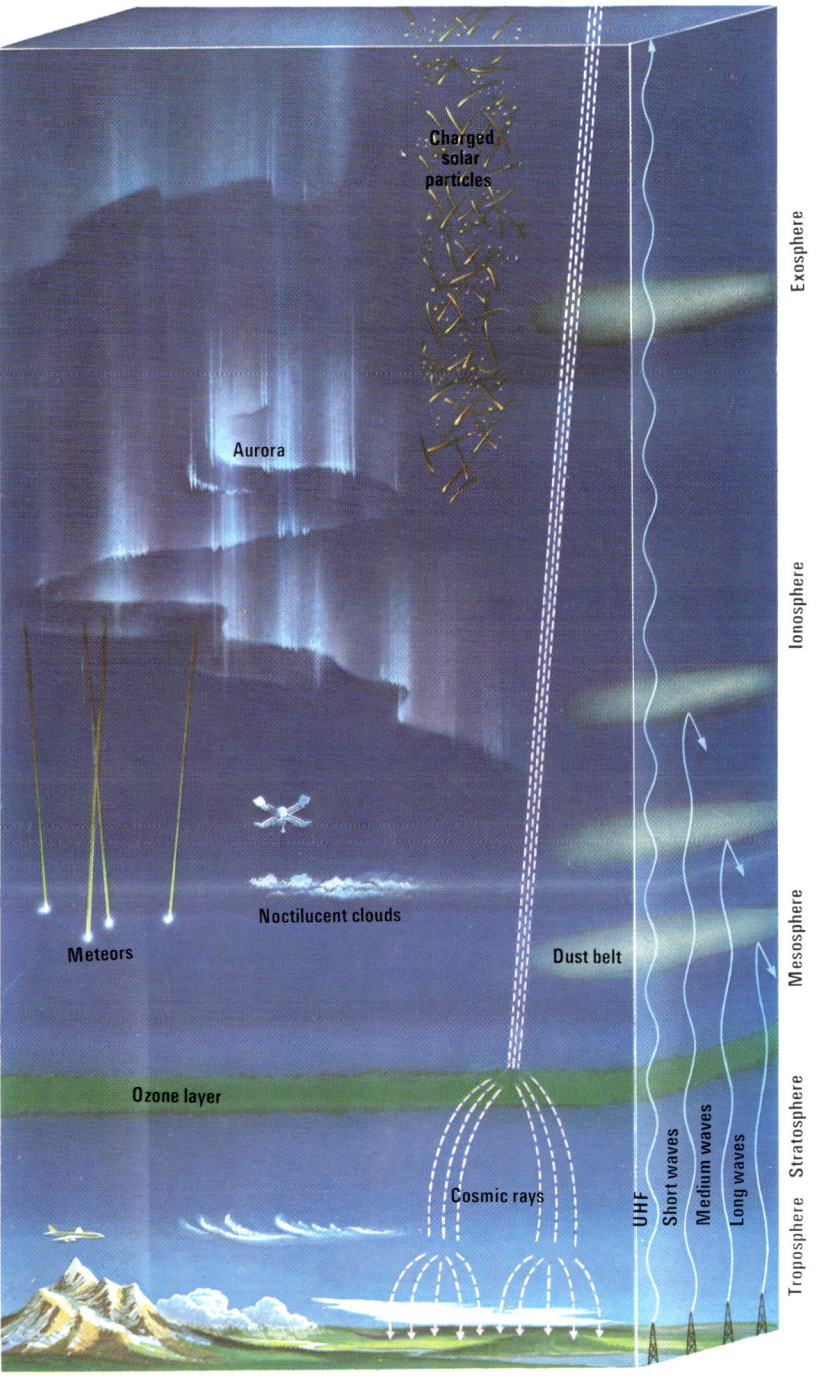

Charged solar particles

Aurora

Meteors

Noctilucent clouds

Dust belt

Ozone layer

Cosmic rays

UHF

Short waves

Medium waves

Long waves

Exosphere

Ionosphere

Mesosphere

Stratosphere

Troposphere

The exosphere starts at about 500 km (300 miles) from the surface of the Earth.

The ionosphere begins about 80 km (50 miles) above the Earth.

The mesosphere is between 50 and 80 km (30 and 50 miles) above the Earth.

The stratosphere is from 8 km (5 miles) to 50 km (30 miles) above Earth.

The troposphere is the bottom layer, up to 8–15 km (5–10 miles) above the Earth.

World Facts and Figures

HIGHEST MOUNTAINS

Asia	metres	feet
Everest (Himalaya-Nepal/Tibet)	8848	29,028
Godwin Austen (Pakistan/India)	8611	28,250
Kanchenjunga (Himalaya-Nepal/Sikkim)	8597	28,146
Makalu (Himalaya-Nepal/Tibet)	8470	27,790
Dhaulagiri (Himalaya-Nepal)	8172	26,795
Nanga Parbat (Himalaya-India)	8126	26,660
Annapurna (Himalaya-Nepal)	8075	26,492

South America		
Aconcagua (Andes-Argentina)	6960	22,834

North America		
McKinley (Alaska-USA)	6194	20,320

Africa		
Kilimanjaro (Tanzania)	5895	19,340

Europe		
Elbruz (Caucasus-USSR)	5633	18,481
Mont Blanc (Alps-France)	4810	15,781

Antarctica		
Vinson Massif	5139	16,860

Australasia		
Wilhelm (Bismarck Range New Guinea)	4694	15,400

LONGEST RIVERS

	km	miles
Nile (Africa)	6670	4145
Amazon (S. America)	6437	4000
Mississippi-Missouri-Red Rock (N. America)	6231	3872
Yangtze (China)	5470	3400
Ob-Irtysh (USSR)	5150	3200
Zaire* (Africa)	4828	3000
Lena (USSR)	4828	3000
Amur (Asia)	4506	2800
Yenisey (USSR)	4506	2800
Hwang Ho (China)	4345	2700
Mekong (SE Asia)	4184	2600
Niger (Africa)	4000	2486

*Formerly Congo River

WATER DEPTHS

Greatest ocean depth: 11,022 m (36,161 ft), Marianas trench, Pacific Ocean.

Deepest gorge: 24,000 m (7315 ft), Hells Canyon, Idaho, USA.

Longest gorge: 349 km (217 miles), Grand Canyon, Arizona, USA.

Highest navigated lake: Titicaca, Peru/Bolivia, 3810 m (4175 ft) above sea level.

Deepest lake: Baikal Siberia, USSR, 1940 m (2121 ft).

Highest mountain: the peak of Everest.

Largest desert: sand dunes in the Sahara, in Morocco.

Highest waterfall: part of the Angel Falls, Venezuela.

GREAT CITIES
(over 4 million population)

City	Population	Year
Tokyo (Japan)	11,695,000	1977
Shanghai (China)	11,320,000	1980
Buenos Aires (Argentina)	9,677,000	1980
Mexico City (Mexico)	9,618,000	1977
Peking (China)	8,706,000	1980
Paris (France)	8,550,000	1975
São Paulo (Brazil)	8,408,000	1979 est
Seoul (S Korea)	8,367,000	1980
Moscow (USSR)	8,099,000	1980
Tientsin (China)	7,390,000	1980
Calcutta (India)	7,031,000	1971
New York City (USA)	7,016,000	1980
London (UK)	6,696,000	1981
Jakarta (Indonesia)	6,506,000	recent est
Chungking (China)	6,200,000	1980
Bombay (India)	5,971,000	1971
Cairo (Egypt)	5,715,000	1974 est
Rio de Janeiro (Brazil)	5,395,000	1979 est
Canton (China)	5,000,000	1973 est
Leningrad (USSR)	4,683,000	1980
Tehran (Iran)	4,496,000	1976
Shenyang (China)	4,400,000	1975
Lüta (China)	4,200,000	1973 est
Milan (Italy)	4,000,000	1980 est

OCEANS

	sq km	sq miles
Pacific	181,000,000	70,000,000
Atlantic	106,000,000	41,000,000
Indian	73,490,000	28,400,000
Arctic	14,350,000	5,400,000

LARGEST ISLANDS

	sq km	sq miles
Greenland (N. Atlantic)	2,175,600	840,000
New Guinea (SW Pacific)	794,090	317,000
Borneo (SW Pacific)	751,078	287,400
Madagascar (Indian Ocean)	587,041	227,800
Baffin I. (Canadian Arctic)	476,066	183,810
Sumatra (Indian Ocean)	431,982	182,860
Honshu (NW Pacific)	230,822	88,031
Great Britain (N. Atlantic)	229,522	84,186
Ellesmere (Canadian Arctic)	198,393	82,119
Victoria I. (Canadian Arctic)		

DESERTS

	sq km	sq miles
Sahara	8,400,000	3,250,000
Australian Desert	1,550,000	600,000
Arabian Desert	1,300,000	500,000
Gobi	1,040,000	400,000
Kalahari	520,000	200,000

LARGEST LAKES

	sq km	sq miles
Caspian Sea (USSR/Iran)	438,695	170,000
Superior (USA/Canada)	82,409	31,820
Victoria Nyanza (Africa)	69,484	26,828
Aral (USSR)	67,770	26,000
Huron (USA/Canada)	59,570	23,010
Michigan (USA)	58,016	22,400
Baikal (USSR)	34,180	13,197
Tanganyika (Africa)	31,999	12,355
Great Bear (Canada)	31,598	12,275
Malawi* (Africa)	28,490	11,430

*Also called Lake Nyasa

WEATHER EXTREMES

Hottest shade temperature recorded: 57·7°C (136°F) at Al'Aziziyah, Libya, on 13.9.22.

Coldest temperature recorded: −88·3°C (−94°F) at Vostock, Antartica, on 24.8.60.

Highest annual rainfall: 11,680 mm (460 inches) at Mt Waialeale, Hawaii.

Driest place on earth: Arica, Chile, averages 0·76 mm (0·030 inches) of rain per year.

Greatest tides: 16·3 (534 ft) Bay of Fundy, Nova Scotia, Canada.

Strongest surface wind recorded: 372 km/h (231 mph) at Mt Washington, N.H., USA, in 1934.

MAJOR WATERFALLS

Highest	metres	feet
Angel Falls (Venezuela)	979	3212
Tugela Falls (South Africa)	948	3110
Yosemite Falls (California)	739	2425

Greatest Volume	m³/sec	ft³/sec
Niagara (N. America)	6000	212,200

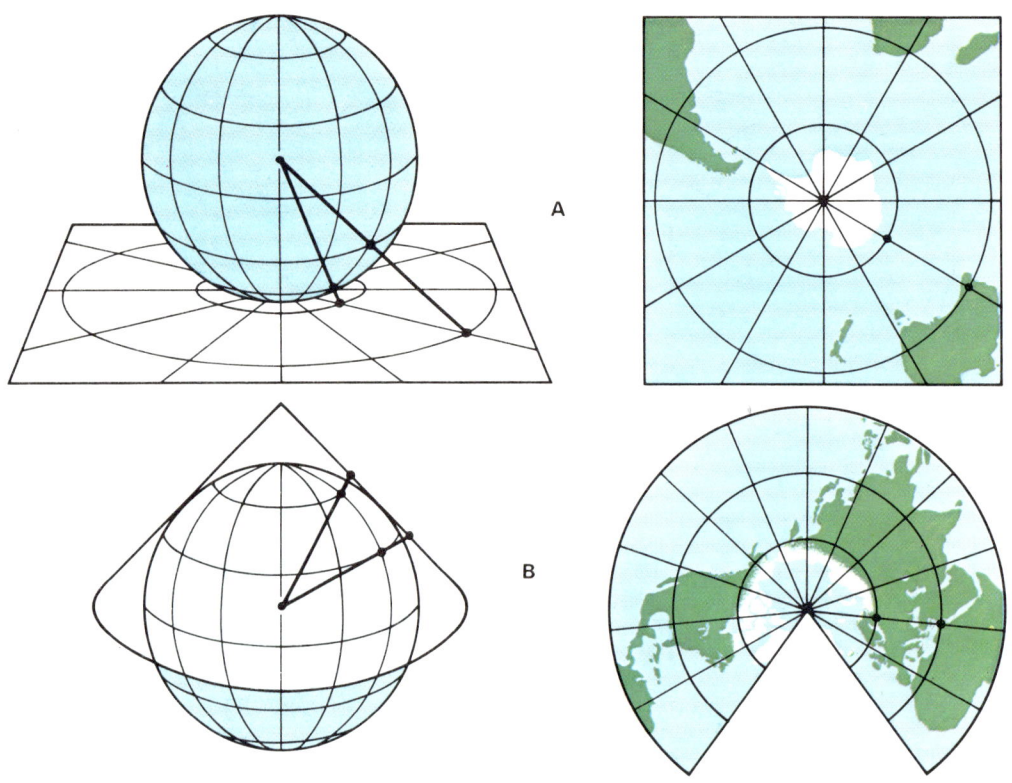

A

B

Two Famous Map-Makers

Ptolemy of Alexandria (AD 100s) was a famous astronomer, but his contributions to map-making were also very important. In his book, *Geography*, he put forward a very good idea about map projection, listed places with their latitude and longitude, drew 26 regional maps of Europe in colour, and produced a map of the world as it was known at that time. But he made a serious mistake in estimating the size of the world, exaggerating the amount of land from Spain to China. But it was because of this mistake that Columbus was encouraged to make his famous voyage of discovery to America over 1300 years later.

Mercator, Gerhardus (1512–94), a Flemish geographer, invented the Mercator map projection. He was first to use the term 'atlas' for a collection of maps, published an accurate map of Europe, and used his projection to produce a map of the Earth drawn in a way most familiar to us today.

Map Projections

The world is a globe, or sphere, so maps, which are flat, will not be able to show details in quite the same way as a globe. Maps are 'projections' from a globe, like the cone-shaped and cylinder-shaped ones shown in the diagrams. Imagine a globe touching a flat surface at one point. If a light could be placed in the centre of the globe, it would reflect a shadow of the lines of latitude and longitude on to the paper. This projection (A) becomes more and more distorted away from the point of contact.

Imagine a cone of paper placed on a globe, as in diagram B. A light in the

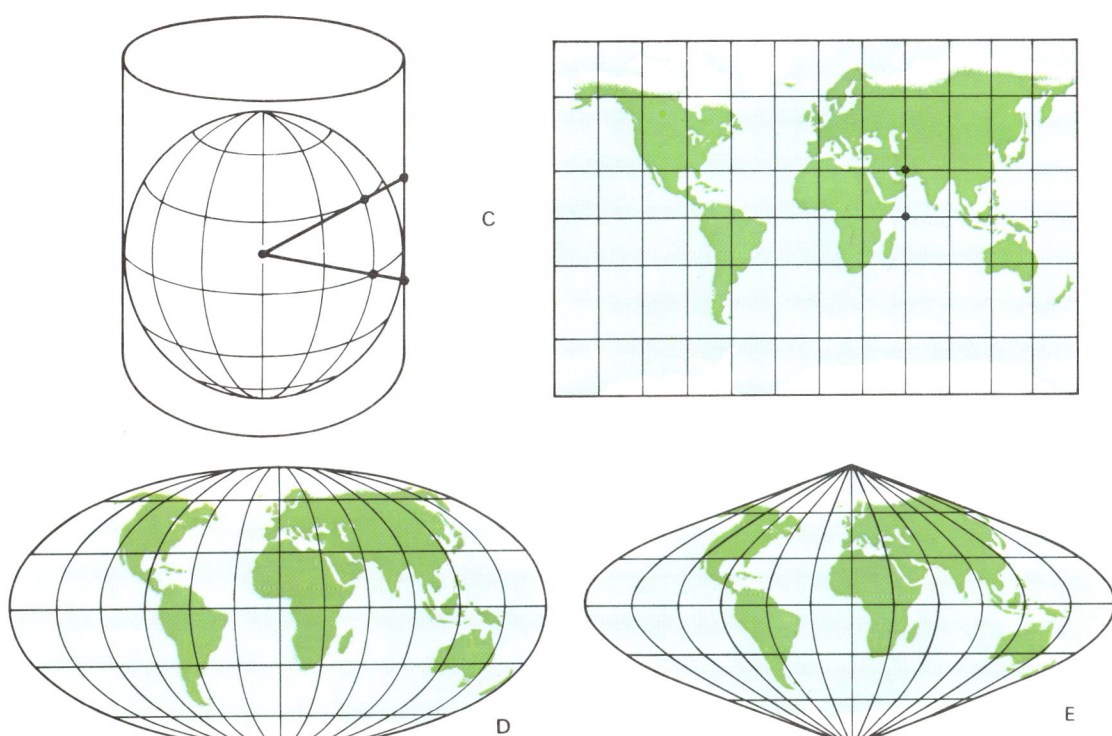

centre of the globe would project a shadow of the lines of latitude and longitude on to the paper. If the paper cone is unrolled, the position of the shadow would appear as a conical projection.

Diagram C shows the third perspective projection, which is cylinder-shaped. Imagine a paper cylinder wrapped around a globe, touching it along the line of the equator. A light inside the globe would project the lines of latitude and longitude on to the paper. Projections made in this way are distorted away from the equator. Lines of latitude appear wrongly as lines of equal length.

The projection shown at diagram D was invented by the German professor Mollweide. It shows the entire Earth's surface on one map. Diagram E shows another projection which is distorted away from the centre.

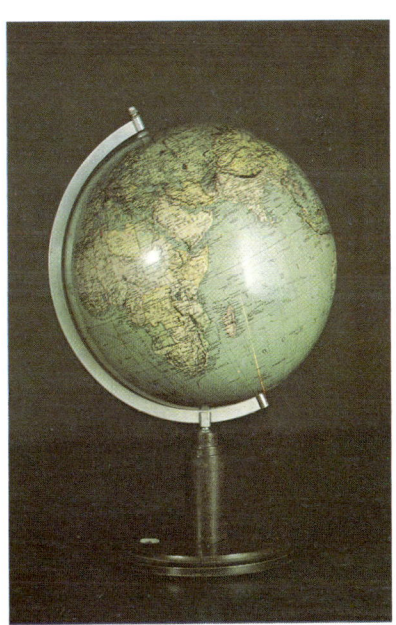

A modern globe on a stand. Only a globe can show the Earth's surface as it really is.

Geography Terms

agriculture Cultivating the land to grow crops. Sometimes the word is used for pastoral farming (keeping animals) as well as arable farming (growing crops).

atmosphere The layer of moving air which surrounds the Earth. It consists of nitrogen, oxygen, water vapour and other gases. The atmosphere is concentrated near the Earth's surface, and gets thinner away from the Earth.

axis An imaginary straight line around which a spinning object rotates. The Earth's axis goes from the North Pole, through the centre of the Earth, to the South Pole. The Earth travels round the Sun, and its axis is tilted in relation to the path of the Earth's orbit.

barchan Crescent-shaped dunes which move in the direction of the prevailing wind.

canyon A deep, steep-sided valley, usually cut by a river in a *desert* area where the sides do not get very worn away by rain-water and streams. The most

Rivers are a major factor in shaping the land. Fed by mountain glaciers and rain and snow, they carve out valleys and carry debris to the sea.

famous is the Grand Canyon, on the Colorado River, USA.

cash crops Crops grown mainly for sale and not for the farmer's own food supply. They may include food crops, for example, wheat from the Canadian prairies. Many have to be processed in factories, for example, sugar cane, cocoa, rubber.

climate The average weather conditions of a place. Climate figures are averages of figures collected over a number of years (usually at least 30 years), so extremes of heat and cold, drought and flood are hidden.

colony Usually a country that has been settled by people who have moved far away from their native land, and is now governed by the settlers' home country. The Falkland Islands are a British colony with a Governor sent from the UK.

coral Coral is made by tiny creatures called polyps which live in warm sunny seas. They build skeletons outside their bodies. When they die new polyps build on the old skeletons to form coral reefs.

core The inner part of the Earth.

crust The outer layer of the Earth.

delta The Greek letter Δ (delta), used to describe an area of sediments deposited at the mouth of some rivers. Deltas occur when a river brings more alluvia (sand and mud) than sea or lake currents can carry away. Rivers with large deltas include the Nile and the Ganges.

deserts A dry area where little grows. Sometimes defined as an area with less than 250 mm (10 inches) of rain a year on average. Bahrain is an example of a place with a desert climate; the Sahara is the largest desert; the Atacama is the driest.

dunes Mounds or ridges of sand. They are found on some sandy coasts and in sandy *deserts*. Sand dunes move when strong winds blow sand up the side of the dune facing the wind, and the grains roll down the sheltered side. Sometimes dunes can be 'fixed' by planting special grasses or trees.

A delta is found at the mouth of some large rivers. It is a kind of flat plain caused by mud carried down the river and deposited at the mouth.

Barchans are crescent-shaped dunes which move in the direction of the prevailing wind.

The Giant's Causeway in County Antrim, Northern Ireland. This natural wonder consists of about 40,000 columns of basalt (solidified lava).

dyke This word can mean four different things: 1. A bank or wall to hold back flood water or the sea (such as dykes built round polders in the Netherlands). 2. A ditch for draining land. 3. A man-made ditch built to defend an area (for example Offa's Dyke along the boundary of England and Wales). 4. A wall of solidified volcanic lava formed when the edge of a layer of lava sticks out of the ground.

earthquake A sudden movement within the Earth's *crust* which causes shock waves which make the Earth's surface shake. Earthquake tremors are recorded on a seismograph.

estuary The mouth of a river where it enters the sea. Usually it is much wider than the rest of the river. An estuary has tides so river water and sea water mix.

fiord (fjord) A long, steep-sided inlet of the sea in a mountainous coastal area. Originally it was a valley eroded by a glacier. After the glacier melted, the valley was drowned as the sea level rose. Spectacular fiords are found in Norway, New Zealand and southern Chile.

fodder crops Crops grown as food for animals.

fold mountains Mountains formed by folding layers of rocks. When parts of the Earth's crust move together from each side, the rocks in between are folded. The Andes are an example of a fold mountain range.

geyser (geysir) A hot spring which throws out a jet of hot water regularly or occasionally. Geysers occur in volcanic areas where water underground is heated so much that it turns to steam. The best-known geysers are in the USA, Iceland and New Zealand.

glacier A mass of ice which moves slowly downhill. It follows the easiest route – usually along a river valley which it deepens and straightens.

hurricane A severe tropical storm with spiralling winds of up to 340 km per hour (210 mph) and very low air pressure. The wind does a great deal of damage, the accompanying rain and high tides cause floods. The term is mainly used for Atlantic storms, which cause much damage in the USA, Central America and the West Indies. In the Pacific the same kind of storm is called a typhoon; in the Indian Ocean it is called a cyclone.

ice ages Periods in the Earth's history when ice sheets have spread over large areas of the world which now have a much warmer climate. Between 700,000 and 10,000 years ago there were at least four Ice Ages in Europe.

irrigation Watering the land to help grow crops. In many irrigation schemes, channels lead from a lake or river to the edge of fields. Gaps can be opened in these channels to let water flow on to each field when it is needed.

latitude and **longitude** These are lines drawn on a globe. Lines which run through the poles north to south are called lines of longitude. The Equator and lines parallel to it are lines of latitude.

Mediterranean climate Summers are hot and dry; winters are warm and wet. Such a climate is found around the Mediterranean Sea and also in central California, central Chile, near Cape Town (South Africa) and Perth (Australia).

monsoon The word means season and usually refers to winds that bring an exceptionally wet season for part of the year. The most spectacular monsoon climates are in Asia. In summer, the continent heats up and becomes an area of low pressure. Winds are drawn in from the sea, bringing rain. In winter, the continent is cold with high pressure, and winds blow out from the land towards the ocean.

moraine Loose rocks, gravel and clay carried by glaciers and ice sheets. Moraine is found on, in and under glaciers and ice sheets, and when they melt this material is dumped on the ground. Areas of moraine often have poor soil and poor drainage, giving marshy areas, such as in northern Poland.

oasis An area in a desert with water at or near the surface. Crops can be grown, and people can live there, obtaining water from springs or wells.

peninsula An area of land almost surrounded by water, but not completely cut off from the mainland. A good example is the Malay Peninsula.

plain A lowland area with a fairly level surface, though there may be hills. The North European Plain and the Great Plains of North America are examples of very large plains.

plantation A large farm or estate on which only one cash crop is usually grown. Sometimes the first stages of processing take place there, such as drying the beans on a coffee plantation, or drying and crushing the leaves on a tea plantation.

plateau An upland area with a fairly level surface, though a plateau may have some hills and may be divided by deep valleys. Much of Eastern and Southern Africa is a plateau.

polder An area of land reclaimed from a lake or the sea.

porous rocks Rocks which allow water to sink through, for example chalk and sandstone. Water can often be collected from such rocks by wells or pumps.

precipitation When used of the weather, refers to rain and snow.

rain forest Tropical forest in hot rainy or monsoon areas.

relief A term used to mean the shape of the land. Relief maps use colour or contour lines to indicate the shape of the land.

savanna Tropical grassland where it is hot all through the year. There are two seasons, a wet and a dry. The tall savanna grass is lush and green in the wet season but brown and dry in the dry season. The scattered trees are the kind that can survive a long hot drought, such as the baobab and acacia.

sedimentary rocks Rocks formed from sediments which once accumulated on land or sea. Most built up layer by layer under water and were gradually squeezed and cemented into layers of rocks. Clay, sandstone and limestone are examples of sedimentary rocks.

soil erosion The removal of valuable top soil. It is usually caused by bad farming methods. If large areas of soil are left bare, they may be washed away by heavy rain, and light soils may be blown away by strong winds. Some solutions are to terrace hillsides; to plant belts of trees to shelter fields; to plough along a slope instead of up and down it; to move animals before they eat all the grass and other plants.

temperate lands Those parts of the world between the tropics and the Polar areas which have a cold season and a hot season. Places such as the Mediterranean which have warm winters may be called warm temperate. Places with cold winters may be called cold temperate because they still have warm summers

tropics Lines of latitude marking where the sun is directly overhead on midsummer's day. On 21 June, the sun is overhead at the Tropic of Cancer. On 21 December, it is overhead at the Tropic of Capricorn.

tundra A treeless zone around the Arctic Circle where lichens and small plants grow in the short summers.

wadi A dry watercourse in a desert. After a storm it may suddenly be filled with water.

Quartz is a common mineral.
Some kinds are used in jewellery.

Birthstones are also supposed to have a special meaning:

Month	Stone	Meaning
January	Garnet	Constancy
February	Amethyst	Sincerity
March	Bloodstone	Courage
April	Diamond	Innocence
May	Emerald	Success in love
June	Agate	Health and long life
July	Carnelian	Content
August	Sardonyx	Married bliss
September	Chrysolite	Antidote to madness
October	Opal	Hope
November	Topaz	Fidelity
December	Turquoise	Prosperity

Above: Calcite is a mineral composed of calcium carbonate.

Fluorite or flat spar.
One variety is Blue John, which is used to make ornaments.

Yellow crystals of sulphur often occur in volcanic areas.

Halite is rock salt.

PRECIOUS STONES AND THEIR MEANING

Some people believe that dreams have meaning. To dream of precious stones also is supposed to have a significance, according to the following list

Stone	Meaning
Agate	A journey
Amber	A voyage
Amethyst	Protection from harm
Aquamarine	New friends
Beryl	Happiness to come
Bloodstone	Unhappy news
Carbuncle	Acquirement of wisdom
Carnelian	Troubles ahead
Chalcedony	Friends reunited
Chrysoberyl	A time of need
Chrysolite	Caution needed
Coral	Recovery from illness
Crystal	Freedom from enemies
Diamond	Victory over enemies
Emerald	Much to look forward to
Garnets	Solution of a mystery
Heliotrope	Long life
Jade	Good fortune
Jasper	Love returned
Jet	Sorrow
Lapis-lazuli	Enduring love
Moonstone	Impending danger
Moss-agate	An unsuccessful journey
Onyx	A happy marriage
Opal	Important possessions
Pearl	Faithful friends
Porphyry	Misfortune
Rock Crystal	Pure faith
Ruby	Unexpected guests
Sapphire	Escape from danger
Sardonyx	Love of friends
Topaz	No harm shall occur
Tourmaline	An accident
Turquoise	Prosperity

Cassiterite is a major source of tin.

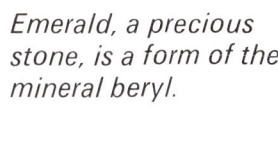

Emerald, a precious stone, is a form of the mineral beryl.

Pyrite, or fool's gold, contains iron and sulphur.

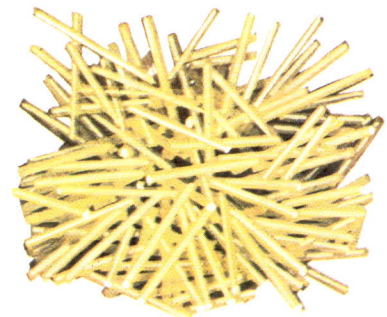

Gypsum is a soft mineral. A very dense form of it is known as alabaster.

Diamond, a precious stone and a form of carbon, is the hardest natural substance.

OUR PLANET

Earthquakes

The intensity of an earthquake is measured on the Modified Mercalli Scale. The numbers on this scale refer to the effects produced.

1. Very slight. Felt only by instruments.
2. Felt by people resting.
3. Feels like passing traffic.
4. Furniture and windows rattle.
5. Can be felt outdoors. Clocks stop. Doors swing.
6. Furniture moves about. Cracks appear in walls.
7. People knocked over. Masonry cracks and falls
8. Chimneys and monuments fall. Buildings move on foundations.
9. Heavy damage to buildings. Large cracks open in ground.
10. Most buildings destroyed. Landslides occur. Water thrown out of canals and lakes.
11. Railway lines badly bent.
12. No buildings left standing.

The strength of the earthquake itself is measured on another scale, which is based on the amount of energy released by the earthquake. This is called the Gutenberg-Richter scale, numbered from 1 to 10. Below are three of the greatest quakes recorded in modern times and their magnitude on the scale:

Year Location
1906 Columbia-Ecuador frontier area (8·9).
1933 At sea, about 161 km (100 miles) east of northern Japan (8·9).
1964 Prince William Sound, Alaska (8·3).

Each of these earthquakes released about the same amount of energy as would be released by 7000 atomic bombs of the size that devastated Hiroshima and Nagasaki in 1945. None of these earthquakes did as much damage as the greatest known killer quake, which occurred in Shensi, China, in 1556. It killed over 800,000 people.

Volcanoes occur where the Earth's crust is being squeezed or stretched as new mountains are formed. The enormous pressures melt the solid rock to liquid magma. When the pressures become too great, gases and hot liquid rock, *lava*, may burst through the centre of a volcano and out of a crater at the top.

Volcanoes are usually cone-shaped with a crater at the top. Active volcanoes erupt for short periods and then remain dormant for long periods. If the lava remains bubbling in a lava lake, eruptions are just overflows. If the lava solidifies, the next eruption will explode.

Inside a volcano, lava, which is hot liquid rock, together with gases and rocky lumps, spouts up from the central vent. The mountain is made from layers of cold ash and lava. Deep down in the depths, a substance called magma is formed, a boiling mass of gas and rock in liquid form.

Tsunamis

In connection with earthquakes is a destructive water force called *tsunami*, a deadly wave caused by seismic jolts or the shifting of the ocean floor. When Lisbon suffered a severe earthquake in 1755, tsunamis up to 12 m (40 ft) high destroyed the lower parts of the city. In 1946 tsunamis created by an underwater disturbance near the Aleutian Islands raced southwards at speeds of up to 483 km/h (300 mph), straight towards the Hawaiian islands. Without warning, the tsunamis smashed into the island, one after another, tearing up piers and houses and flinging boats into the treetops. Over 170 people lost their lives. Since then, seismographic stations have been set up around the Pacific to give early warning of earthshocks.

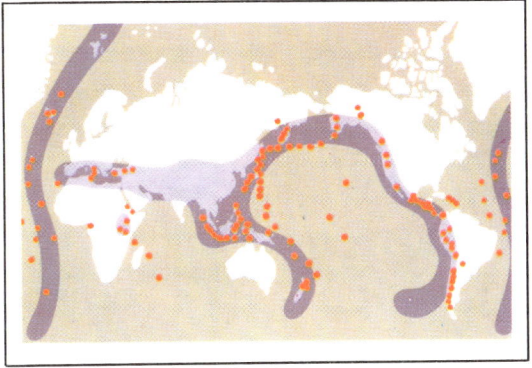

This map shows the earthquake areas of the world, with the red dots indicating volcanoes. Most of the world's active volcanoes are found in a band reaching across the Pacific Ocean, and continuing north of Australia through New Guinea and Indonesia. It is here where the greatest number of active volcanoes are grouped.

Far right: Low volcanoes (1) are made of liquid lava. This spreads out a long way before it hardens. Cone volcanoes (2) are made from thick lava. Sometimes it turns into a solid plug. Pressure builds up inside the volcano and the plug blows out (3).

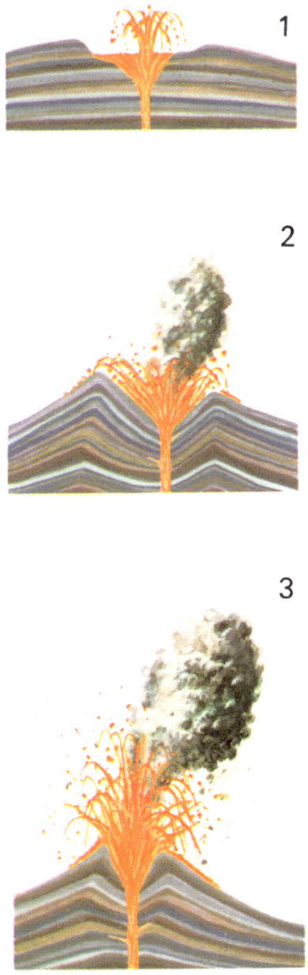

Above: (1) The coral continues to build up as the sea mount wears away, (2), when it eventually leaves a coral ring around a lagoon.

Waves

Most waves are caused by wind, but although it seems as if the wind is pushing the water along, this is not so. Each tiny droplet of water is going round and round in a circular movement, ending up exactly where it began. It is possible to see this if you watch a beach ball floating on the water on a windless day. The ball stays in more or less the same place, although it travels in a circle with the passing of the wave.

Waves break when the water at the top, or crest, is moving faster than the wave itself. Then, the top water falls forward, making a foamy cap, which we call 'white horses'.

Atolls

Atolls are reefs made of coral, which is formed into rings or broken rings surrounding a central lagoon. Islands form part of these rings, on which grow coconut palms and other scanty plants. Originally, the reefs grew around mountain or volcano peaks, which gradually sank, leaving the coral ring above water.

Below: Diagrams showing the movement of a ball on waves.

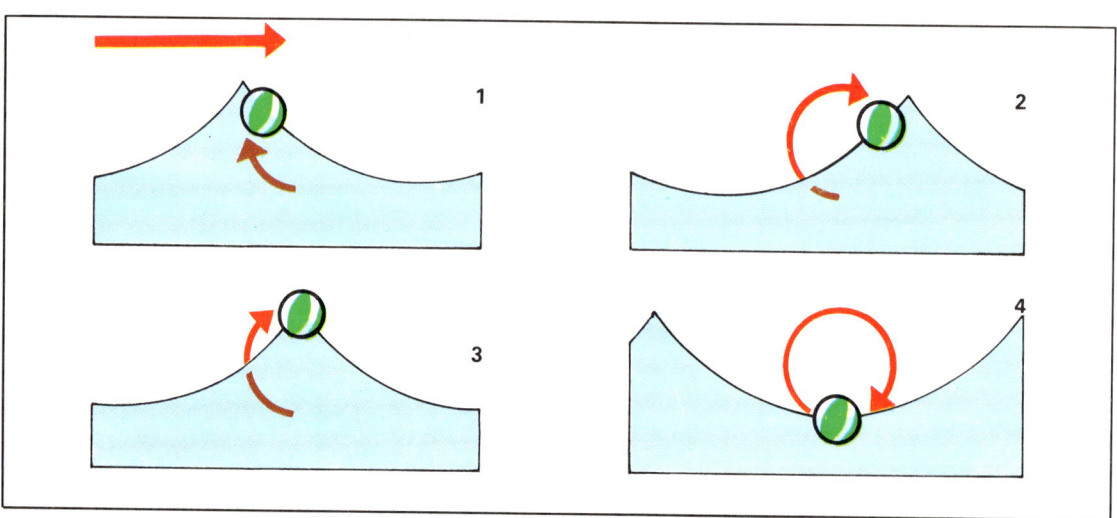

Ocean Terms

abyssal plain Sea bed below about 4000 m (13,125 ft). It is used as a general term to describe the bed of the ocean that lies deeper than the continental shelves but shallower than the deep-sea trenches.

continental shelf Relatively shallow part of the sea floor adjoining the continents. It is rarely more than 200 m (655 ft) deep, and represents the submerged part of the continental plate.

continental slope Slope of the sea bed that links the shallows of the *continental shelf* with the deeps of the *abyssal plain*.

current Flow of water in a particular direction through an ocean. Currents may be of warm water or of cold, and they may run on the surface or at great depths.

guyot *Seamount* with a flat top. The flat tops look as if they have been planed down by wave action, but they are so deep that they are well below the level of the waves.

neap tide Tide formed when the Moon is in the first or last quarter, when the gravitational pulls of the Moon and Sun are acting at right-angles to one another. This gives low high tides and high low tides.

ocean The expanse of salt water that covers most of the Earth, or any one of its subdivisions.

salinity The saltiness of the sea water. It varies from place to place. In warm areas, where water evaporates fairly quickly, salinity is high (there is a greater proportion of salt in the water). At the mouths of big rivers, where the fresh water is constantly being added to the sea, the salinity is low.

seamount Hill that rises from the bed of the sea but does not reach the surface.

spring tide Tide formed when the Moon is new or full, when the gravitational pulls of the Moon and Sun are acting in the same direction. This gives high high tides and low low tides.

submarine canyon Deep canyon cut into the *continental shelf* and *continental slope*, usually offshore from the mouth of a big river.

tide The raising and lowering of the sea water at any point on the surface of the ocean twice a day, caused by the gravitational pulls of the Moon and Sun. See *neap tide* and *spring tide*.

trench Long, deep depression in the *abyssal plain*. These are formed where the oceanic crust is sliding under the continental crust.

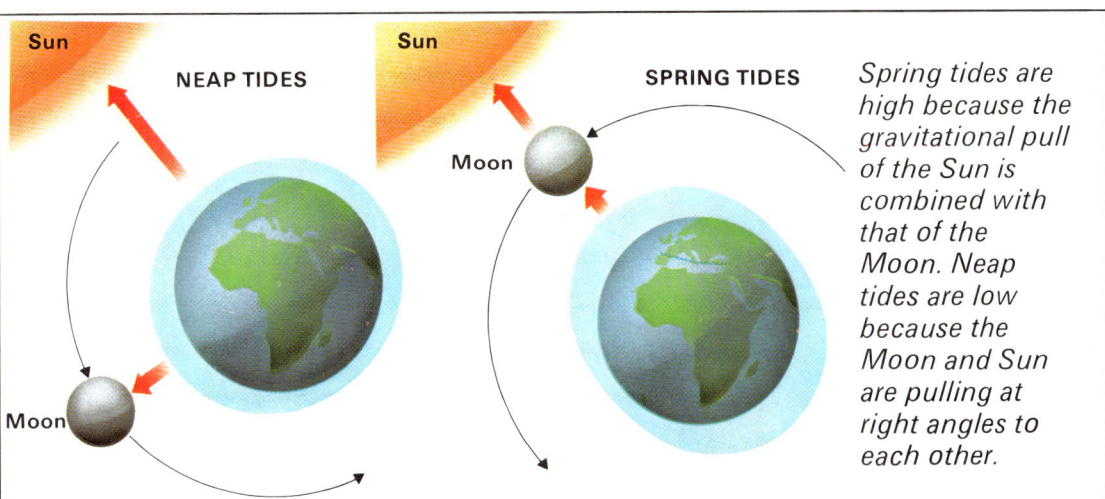

NEAP TIDES — Sun, Moon

SPRING TIDES — Sun, Moon

Spring tides are high because the gravitational pull of the Sun is combined with that of the Moon. Neap tides are low because the Moon and Sun are pulling at right angles to each other.

The World's Oceans

Arctic Ocean
The most northerly of the oceans, the Arctic is covered with sea ice which varies in thickness from 1·5 to 9 m (5 to 30 ft). During the winter months, the ice, is of course, at its thickest and is solid all over. When the summer arrives, the mass breaks up into ice floes, which start to move, and can be a danger to ships. The North Pole is at the centre of the ocean, where the water depth is 2743 m (900 ft).

Atlantic Ocean
Unlike the Pacific, the Atlantic is not scattered with groups of islands, except in the West Indies. Otherwise, the islands are widely placed, the most well-known being the British Isles in the North. Others are the Azores, the Canary Islands, with such smaller ones as St Helena, Tristan da Cunha and the Falkland Islands.

Along either side of the equator, a warm current flows westward, and this divides as it reaches the coast of South America, sweeping to the North and South. This makes the temperature of the sea higher in the Caribbean and the Gulf of Mexico.

Another warm current, the Gulf Stream, flows up the coast of North America to Newfoundland, and then across the Atlantic to Europe.

Indian Ocean
This large sea area is bounded on the north by India and Iran, on the south by Antarctica, on the east by Australia and the East Indies and on the west by the

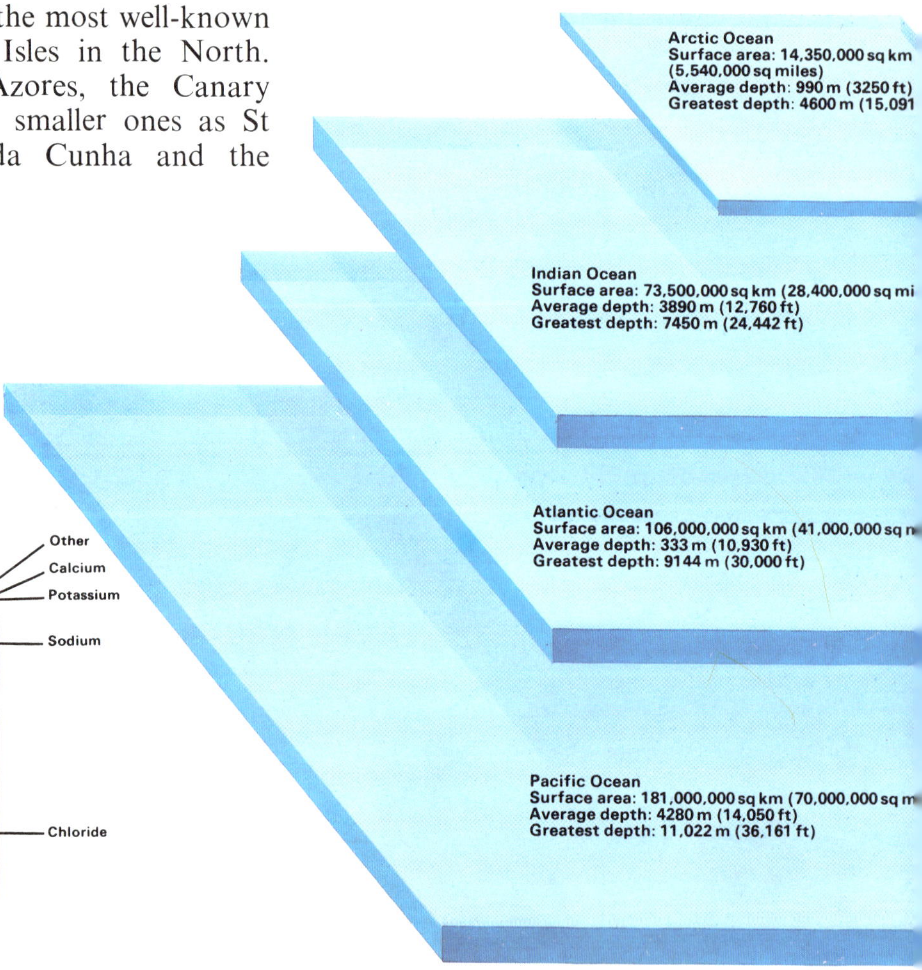

Arctic Ocean
Surface area: 14,350,000 sq km (5,540,000 sq miles)
Average depth: 990 m (3250 ft)
Greatest depth: 4600 m (15,091

Indian Ocean
Surface area: 73,500,000 sq km (28,400,000 sq mi
Average depth: 3890 m (12,760 ft)
Greatest depth: 7450 m (24,442 ft)

Atlantic Ocean
Surface area: 106,000,000 sq km (41,000,000 sq m
Average depth: 333 m (10,930 ft)
Greatest depth: 9144 m (30,000 ft)

Pacific Ocean
Surface area: 181,000,000 sq km (70,000,000 sq m
Average depth: 4280 m (14,050 ft)
Greatest depth: 11,022 m (36,161 ft)

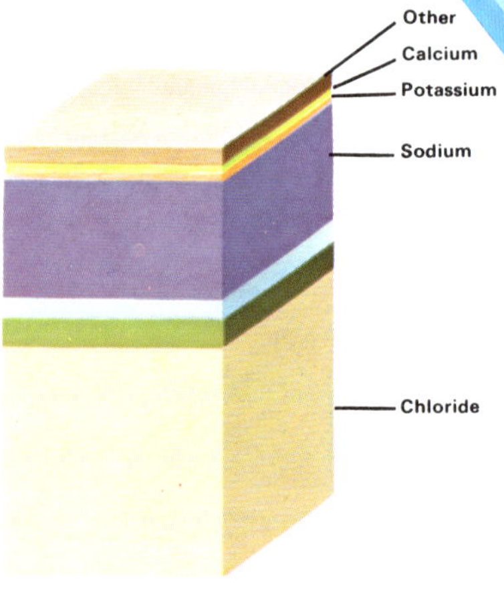

Other
Calcium
Potassium
Sodium
Chloride

continent of Africa. It contains several large islands, the biggest being Madagascar, the others being Socotra and Sri Lanka.

The small islands include such places as Mauritius, Réunion, the Seychelles, the Maldives, Chagos and Cocos groups.

The equator runs through the centre, and much of the area is tropical.

Ocean currents move in two branches, one on each side of the equator. The southerly currents flow from Australia to Madagascar, where they turn southwards, and are driven by winds back towards Australia. North of the equator, the currents flow in the Bay of Bengal and the Arabian sea.

Pacific Ocean

This is the largest of all the oceans, and also contains the deepest place in any ocean. That is in the Marianas Trench, where the bottom is 11,022 m (36,161 ft) down. This is over 11 km (6·78 miles), and a heavy object dropped into the water would take over an hour to reach the bottom.

There are thousands of small islands covering the ocean area, mainly in the southern half, including a large number of coral groups.

SEAWATER

Seawater is salt because it contains many salty chemicals, although most of this dissolved matter is common salt. But it also contains the salts of many metals, including gold, silver, copper, nickel, iron, cobalt and zinc. The actual saltiness (or salinity) varies from about 33 to 37 parts of salt to a thousand parts of water.

Most of the Earth's surface is covered by water, being 71% of the total, the remaining 29% being the land.

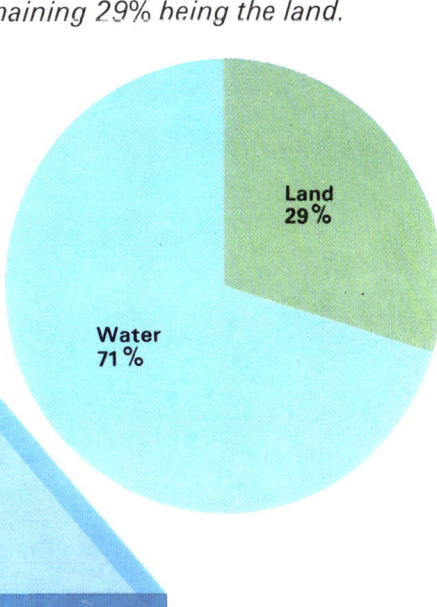

The Rain and the Snow

Water on the Earth is turned into water vapour by the Sun. In other words, it evaporates. This water vapour rises into the air, and condenses into tiny droplets, forming a cloud. The droplets are too small to fall as they are, for they seem almost to float on the air. Cool air will cause the droplets to become larger, when they fall as rain. It takes many thousands of droplets to form together before this happens.

A cloud passing over a mountain will encounter cold air, and sometimes this air is so cold that the droplets form into ice crystals. These fall to Earth, but melt as they reach the warmer air below.

Some of the moisture reaches Earth as dew or frost, while other forms are snow, sleet and hail. Snow is formed in much the same way as are raindrops, except that the temperature is lower.

The word *precipitation* is used to describe all the various ways in which water falls upon the Earth.

Sometimes the ice crystals formed in a cloud become compacted into a solid mass of ice, which falls as a hailstone. A hailstone is not just frozen rain, but a pellet made up of many layers of ice. When the temperature of the cloud is below freezing point, ice crystals form together into snowflakes, and then we have snow falling to the ground.

Dew is formed because the Earth loses heat as the day grows to an end, and the water vapour in the air condenses on the cool surfaces. If it is below freezing point, the tiny drops of water vapour turn into ice, and this is called frost.

There is a continual exchange of water between the Earth and the atmosphere, this forming what is called the water cycle. In this cycle water evaporates from the seas, rivers and lakes, and from growing plants. The vapour condenses into clouds in cool air, and returns to the ground as rain, snow or some other form of precipitation.

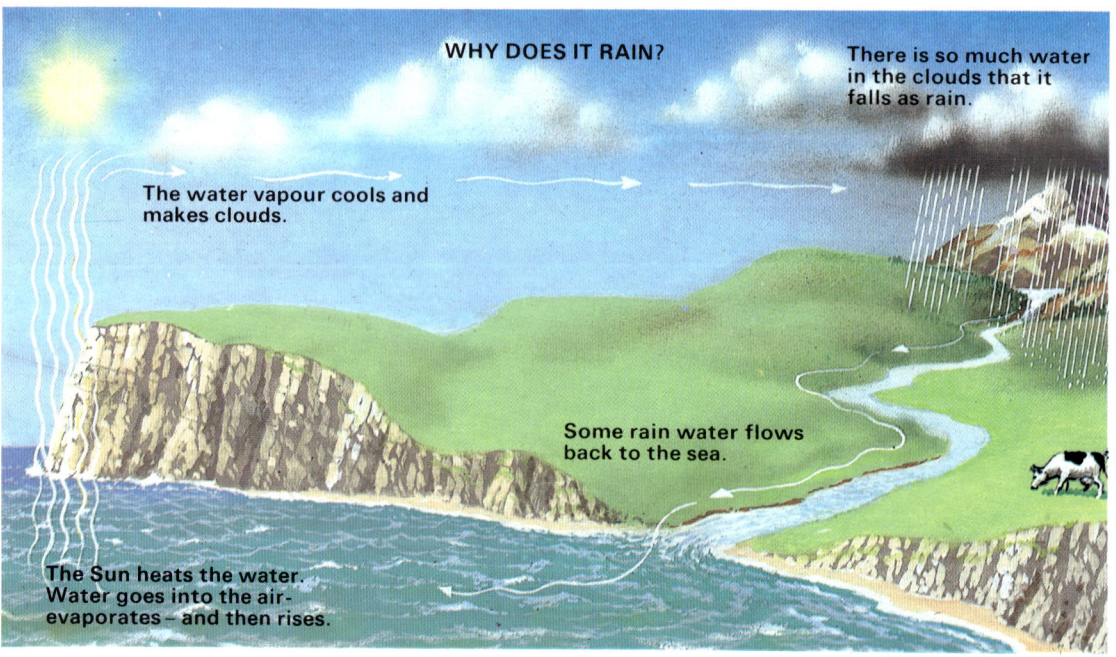

WHY DOES IT RAIN?

There is so much water in the clouds that it falls as rain.

The water vapour cools and makes clouds.

Some rain water flows back to the sea.

The Sun heats the water. Water goes into the air – evaporates – and then rises.

 # Countries of the World

Area: 30,319,000 sq. km (11,707,000 sq. m). **Population:** 484,000,000. **Independent countries** (1982): 53 (including island nations); **Highest peak:** Mt Kilimanjaro, 5895 m (19,341 ft); **Lowest point:** Lake Assal (Djibouti), 155 m (509 ft) below sea level; **Largest lake:** Victoria, 69,484 sq. km (26,828 sq. m) in Kenya, Tanzania and Uganda; **Longest rivers:** Nile, Zaire, Niger, Zambezi.

ALGERIA Republic of North Africa. **Area:** 2,382,000 sq. km (919,600 sq. m). **Population:** 20,000,000. **Capital:** Algiers.

ANGOLA Republic of west-central Africa. **Area:** 1,247,000 sq. km (481,000 sq. m). **Population:** 7,414,000. **Capital:** São Paulo de Luanda.

ASCENSION Island in the South Atlantic, a dependency of St Helena. **Area:** 88 sq. km (34 sq. m). **Population:** 1000. **Capital:** Georgetown.

BENIN Republic on the Gulf of Guinea, West Africa. **Area:** 112,600 sq. km (43,480 sq. m). **Population:** 3,734,000. **Capital:** Porto Novo.

BURKINA FASO Republic of West Africa. **Area:** 274,200 sq. km (105,900 sq. m). **Population:** 6,000,000. **Capital:** Ouagadougou.

BOTSWANA Republic of Southern Africa, a member of the Commonwealth. Formerly Bechuanaland Protectorate. **Area:** 600,400 sq. km (232,000 sq. m). **Population:** 820,000. **Capital:** Gaborone.

BURUNDI Republic of Central Africa. Formerly the Belgian territory Ruanda-Urundi. **Area:** 27,800 sq. km (10,750 sq. m). **Population:** 4,293,000. **Capital:** Bujumbura.

CAMEROON Republic of West Africa.

Area: 475,450 sq. km (183,580 sq. m). **Population:** 8,804,000. **Capital:** Yaoundé.

CAPE VERDE Republic, a number of islands in the North Atlantic, about 300 miles off West Africa. **Area:** 4030 sq. km (1560 sq. m). **Population:** 324,000. **Capital:** Praia.

CENTRAL AFRICAN REPUBLIC Republic of Equatorial Africa within the French Community. **Area:** 622,984 sq. km (240,550 sq. m). **Population:** 2,086,000. **Capital:** Bangui.

CHAD Republic of Equatorial Africa within the French Community. **Area:** 1,284,000 sq. km (496,000 sq. m). **Population:** 4,714,000. **Capital:** N'djamena.

COMOROS Island republic off Mozambique, in Africa. **Area:** 2170 sq. km (838 sq. m). **Population:** 343,000. **Capital:** Moroni.

CONGO A republic of Equatorial Africa within the French Community. **Area:** 342,000 sq. km (132,000 sq. m). **Population:** 1,613,000. **Capital:** Brazzaville.

DJIBOUTI Republic of north-east Africa within the French Community, on the Red Sea. **Area:** 22,000 sq. km (8500 sq. m). **Population:** 371,000. **Capital:** Djibouti.

EGYPT Arab republic of north-east Africa. **Area:** 1,000,000 sq. km (387,000 sq. m). **Population:** 43,600,000. **Capital:** Cairo.

EQUATORIAL GUINEA Republic of West Africa. Area 28,000 sq. km (10,800 sq. m). **Population:** 378,000. **Capital:** Malabo.

ETHIOPIA Republic of north-east Africa. **Area:** 1,222,000 sq. km (472,000 sq. m). **Population:** 34,244,000. **Capital:** Addis Ababa.

ATLANTIC
OCEAN

Mediterranean Sea

Tangier
Rabat
Casablanca
Marrakech
Fès
MOROCCO
ATLAS MOUNTAINS
Oran
Algiers
Constantine
TUNISIA
Tunis
Sfax
Tripoli
Benghazi
Alexandria
Cairo
Suez

Canary Is
Las Palmas
El Aaiun
WESTERN SAHARA

ALGERIA

LIBYA

EGYPT

Nile

Aswan

SAHARA DESERT

MAURITANIA
Nouakchott

MALI

NIGER

CHAD

Dongola

Red Sea

Timbuktu

Niamey

Agadez

L. Chad

Khartoum

DJIBOUTI
Djibouti

Senegal
SENEGAL
GAMBIA
Bamako
GUINEA-BISSAU
GUINEA
nakry
eetown
SIERRA
LEONE
LIBERIA
Monrovia

UPPER VOLTA
Ouagadougou

Kano

N'Djamena

SUDAN

Addis Ababa

ETHIOPIAN
HIGHLANDS
ETHIOPIA

NIGERIA

IVORY
COAST
GHANA
Abidjan
Accra
Lomé
Porto-Novo
BENIN
TOGO
Niger
Ibadan
Lagos
Malabo
EQUATORIAL
GUINEA
SAO TOME
& PRINCIPE
ator
Libreville
GABON
CAMEROON
Yaoundé
CENTRAL AFRICAN
REPUBLIC
Bangui

CONGO
Congo Basin
Brazzaville
Kinshasa
Cabinda
Zaire

UGANDA
Kampala
Kigali
RWANDA
Bujumbura
BURUNDI
L. Victoria
Mt Kenya
Nairobi
Mt Kilimanjaro
Mombasa
KENYA
SOMALI

Luanda

ZAIRE

L. Tanganyika

Tabora
Dodoma
Zanzibar
Dar es Salaam
TANZANIA

Benguela
Huambo

ANGOLA

L. Malawi
MALAWI
Lilongwe

MOZAMBIQUE

ZAMBIA
Lusaka

Zambezi

NAMIBIA

BOTSWANA

Harare
ZIMBABWE
Beira

Walvis Bay
Namib Desert
Windhoek
Kalahari
Gaborone
Pretoria
Johannesburg
Maputo
Mbabane
SWAZILAND
Limpopo

Orange
Maseru
LESOTHO
Durban
East London
Port Elizabeth
SOUTH
AFRICA
DRAKENSBERG
Cape Town

0   500   1000 miles
0   500   1000   1500 kilometres
■ Capital Cities

51

GABON Republic of Equatorial Africa within the French Community. **Area:** 268,000 sq. km (103,000 sq. m). **Population:** 667,000. **Capital:** Libreville.

GAMBIA A republic within the Commonwealth in West Africa. **Area:** 11,300 sq. km (4300 sq. m). **Population:** 642,000. **Capital:** Banjul.

GHANA Republic of West Africa, a member of the Commonwealth. **Area:** 239,000 sq. km (92,000 sq. m). **Population:** 12,413,000. **Capital:** Accra.

GUINEA Republic of West Africa. **Area:** 246,000 sq. km (95,000 sq. m). **Population:** 5,741,000. **Capital:** Conakry.

GUINEA-BISSAU Republic of West Africa. **Area:** 36,000 sq. km (14,000 sq. m). **Population:** 817,000. **Capital:** Bissau.

IVORY COAST Republic of West Africa. **Area:** 322,500 sq. km (124,000 sq. m). **Population:** 9,564,000. **Capital:** Abidjan.

KENYA Republic of East Africa, a member of the Commonwealth. **Area:** 582,700 sq. km (225,000 sq. m). **Population:** 16,922,000. **Capital:** Nairobi.

LESOTHO Kingdom of Southern Africa. **Area:** 30,360 sq. km (11,700 sq. m). **Population:** 1,406,000. **Capital:** Maseru.

LIBERIA Republic of West Africa. **Area:** 111,370 sq. km (43,000 sq. m). **Population:** 1,992,000. **Capital:** Monrovia.

LIBYA Republic of North Africa. **Area:** 1,760,000 sq. km (680,000 sq. m). **Population:** 3,224,000. **Capital:** Tripoli.

MADAGASCAR An island republic 250 miles east of Africa. **Area:** 587,000 sq. km (226,700 sq. m). **Population:** 9,167,000. **Capital:** Antananarivo.

MALAWI Republic of Southern Africa. **Area:** 118,500 sq. km (45,800 sq. m). **Population:** 6,376,000. **Capital:** Lilongwe.

MALI Republic of north-west Africa. **Area:** 1,240,000 sq. km (479,000 sq. m). **Population:** 6,966,000. **Capital:** Bamako.

MAURITANIA A republic of north-west Africa. **Area:** 1,030,700 sq. km (400,000 sq. m). **Population:** 1,721,000. **Capital:** Nouakchott.

MAURITIUS An independent state in the Indian Ocean, made up of two main islands. A member of the Commonwealth. **Area:** 2050 sq. km (790 sq. m). **Population:** 973,000. **Capital:** Port Louis.

MAYOTTE A French territory, an island in the Comoro Archipelago. **Area:** 374 sq. km (145 sq. m). **Population:** 32,000. **Capital:** Dzaoudzi.

MOROCCO A monarchy of north-west Africa. **Area:** 446,500 sq. km (172,400 sq. m). **Population:** 21,280,000. **Capital:** Rabat.

MOZAMBIQUE Republic of south-east Africa. **Area:** 783,000 sq. km (302,000 sq. m). **Population:** 10,987,000. **Capital:** Maputo.

NAMIBIA A disputed territory of south-west Africa known to the Republic of South Africa as South West Africa. A mandate was granted to South Africa in 1920 by the League of Nations, but the United Nations and South Africa have been unable to reach agreement on its present status. **Area:** 824,000 sq. km (318,000 sq. m). **Population:** 1,066,000. **Capital:** Windhoek.

NIGER Republic of West Africa. **Area:** 1,267,000 sq. km (489,000 sq. m). **Population:** 5,600,000. **Capital:** Niamey.

NIGERIA Republic of West Africa. **Area:** 923,000 sq. km (356,700 sq. m). **Population:** 88,847,000. **Capital:** Lagos (Abuja).

RÉUNION A French overseas department in the Indian Ocean. **Area:** 2500 sq. km (969 sq. m). **Population:** 546,000. **Capital:** St Denis.

RWANDA Republic of Central Africa. **Area:** 26,400 sq. km (10,000 sq. m). **Population:** 5,067,000. **Capital:** Kigali.

ST HELENA British colony, including the island of Ascension and the four islands of Tristan da Cunha, in the South Atlantic. St Helena **area:** 122 sq. km (47 sq. m). **Population:** 5,200. **Capital:** Jamestown.

TRISTAN DA CUNHA Island in the South Atlantic, a dependency of St Helena. **Area:** 98 sq. km (38 sq. m). **Population:** 320. **Capital:** Edinburgh.

SÃO TOMÉ AND PRINCIPE Island republic in the Gulf of Guinea, Africa. **Area:** 964 sq. km (372 sq. m). **Population:** 110,000. **Capital:** Saõ Tomé.

SENEGAL Republic of West Africa. **Area:** 196,000 sq. km (76,000 sq. m). **Population:** 6,000,000. **Capital:** Dakar.

SEYCHELLES Island republic of the Indian Ocean, a member of the Commonwealth. **Area:** 108 sq. km (280 sq. m). **Population:** 70,000. **Capital:** Victoria.

SIERRA LEONE Republic of West Africa, an independent member of the Commonwealth. **Area:** 71,700 sq. km (27,700 sq. m). **Population:** 3,643,000. **Capital:** Freetown.

SOMALI REPUBLIC Republic of Africa, facing Aden. **Area:** 637,700 sq. km (246,000 sq. m). **Population:** 4,125,000. **Capital:** Mogadishu.

SOUTH AFRICA Republic of Southern Africa. **Area:** 1,221,000 sq. km (471,500 sq. m). **Population:** 30,844,000. **Capital:** Cape Town (seat of Legislature); Pretoria (seat of Government).

SUDAN Republic of north-east Africa. **Area:** 2,506,000 sq. km (967,500 sq. m). **Population:** 19,373,000. **Capital:** Khartoum.

SWAZILAND Kingdom of southern Africa, a member of the Commonwealth. **Area:** 17,400 sq. km (6,700 sq. m). **Population:** 580,000. **Capital:** Mbabane.

TANZANIA Republic of East Africa, a member of the Commonwealth. **Area:** 945,000 sq. km (365,000 sq. m). **Population:** 19,388,000. **Capital:** Dodoma.

TOGO Republic of West Africa. **Area:** 56,000 sq. km (21,600 sq. m). **Population:** 2,700,000. **Capital:** Lomé.

TUNISIA Republic of North Africa. **Area:** 163,000 sq. km (63,000 sq. m). **Population:** 6,625,000. **Capital:** Tunis.

UGANDA Republic of Equatorial Africa. A member of the Commonwealth. **Area:** 236,000 sq. km (91,000 sq. m). **Population:** 14,000,000. **Capital:** Kampala.

UPPER VOLTA *see* **BURKINA FASO**

WESTERN SAHARA A North African territory facing the Atlantic. **Area:** 266,000 sq. km (102,700 sq. m). **Population:** 76,000. **Capital:** El Aiun.

ZAIRE Republic of west-central Africa. **Area:** 2,345,400 sq. km (905,600 sq. m). **Population:** 29,826,000. **Capital:** Kinshasa.

ZAMBIA A land-locked republic in south-central Africa. A member of the Commonwealth. **Area:** 752,600 sq. km (290,600 sq. m). **Population:** 5,992,000. **Capital:** Lusaka.

ZIMBABWE Republic of Southern Africa (the former Rhodesia). A member of the Commonwealth. **Area:** 390,600 sq. km (150,800 sq. m). **Population:** 7,878,000. **Capital:** Harare.

A to Z of Africa

Afrikaans Modified form of Dutch spoken in South Africa (official language, with English).

Afrikaners South African of European descent (Dutch rather than British); sometimes spelt *Afrikanders*.

apartheid Policy of racial segregation, or 'separate development', in South Africa.

Arabs The people who make up the greater part of the population of northern Africa (Morocco, Algeria, Tunisia, Libya, Sudan, Egypt). They are mainly Muslims.

Aswan High Dam Dam nearly 5 km (3 miles) long and 107 m (351 ft) high, built on the Nile in the 1960s in southern Egypt. It controls the floodwaters of the Nile.

Atlas Mountains Range extending 2500 km across north-western Africa, from Atlantic to Mediterranean, crossing Morocco, Algeria, and Tunisia. Rise over 4000 m.

Bantu Large group of Negroid races living in equatorial and southern Africa; also languages spoken by them.

Bedouins Arab tribes that roam the deserts.

Benin Kingdom that became powerful in 1400s in what is now Nigeria. Sculptures are among finest examples of African art. Declined in 1600s; conquered by Britain in 1897.

Berbers People living on western Mediterranean coast and in Sahara. Similar to Arabs; mainly fair skinned, but some types are dark. They are Muslims and speak Berber or Arabic.

Boers Old name for descendants of Dutch settlers in Africa. *Boer* is Dutch for 'farmer'.

Bushmen An African people who live in small bands in the Kalahari desert. They have dark, yellowish skin and tightly curled hair, and stand about 150 cm (59 inches) high. Among the oldest peoples of Africa, they live by hunting animals and digging up wild roots.

Cape Coloureds South Africans of mixed black and white descent.

Drakensberg Mountains South Africa's largest range, extending from Cape Province to northern Transvaal, and rising to heights of 3350 m (10,990 ft).

Fulani Nomadic people of mixed Negroid and Mediterranean stock, scattered through northern Africa from Senegal to Sudan; also, their language.

Ghana, Ancient kingdom in western Africa that became rich from trade in gold and salt sometime before AD 800. It was about 800 km (500 miles) north-west of present-day Ghana.

Hausa Negroid people of Sudan and northern Nigeria; also their Hamitic language, used widely in west Africa, especially in trade.

Hottentots Short, stocky people of southern Africa, related to *Bushmen*.

Ibos A Negroid people of the lower Niger region.

Kalahari Desert in southern Africa, covering 500,000 sq. km (195,000 square miles), mainly in Botswana.

Kanem Ancient kingdom that reached the height of its power in the 1200s. It grew up north-east of Lake Chad in about AD 800, and declined in the 1600s.

Kush Ancient kingdom on the Nile. Formerly a province of Egypt, it was a great trading power for about 300 years until AD 50.

Mali Now the name of a country in western Africa, Mali was an ancient empire that flourished in that area for 500 years, until it was overthrown in AD 1500 by the Songhai empire. Ruled by the Muslims, it was prosperous and its laws were just.

Masai Nomadic, cattle-owning group of people who live around the Kenya–Tanzania border. A proud, warlike people, they have largely maintained their old ways of life.

Moors Arabic-speaking Muslims of north-western Africa, or any Muslims of European (Spanish, Turkish) descent living in northern Africa.

Negroes Most of the people who live south of the Sahara are Negroes. There are 'true' Negroes, Nilotes, pygmies, and Bushmen and Hottentots. The largest group are the 'true' Negroes, who have skin ranging from light brown to brown-black in colour, kinky hair, broad noses, and thick lips.

Niger River Flows 4200 km (2610 miles) from Guinea, in western Africa, north-east and then sharply south-east to drain into the Atlantic. It has a broad marshy delta along the Nigerian coast.

Nile The world's longest river, flowing more than 6600 km (4100 miles) through north-eastern Africa. Its farthest source rises in Rwanda and flows through Uganda to join the *White Nile* in the Sudan. The *Blue Nile* rises in Ethiopia and joins the White Nile at Khartoum in the Sudan. The Nile runs through a series of cataracts (rapids) in the Sudan and Egypt before emptying into the Mediterranean. Its delta is one of the finest farming regions in the world.

nomads People with no settled home, who wander from place to place. Arabs and Berbers in the Sahara lead nomadic lives, living in tents and moving around with their camels, goats, and sheep in search of grass and water. Other African nomads include the pygmies.

pygmies There are between 100,000 and 200,000 African pygmies. They are characterized by yellow-brown skin, round heads, and tightly curled red-brown hair. They are known as Negrillos or Twides, and are only about 1·4 metres tall. They live mainly in the tropical rain forests of the Zaïre basin.

Red Sea Arm of the Indian Ocean separating Africa from Arabia, connected to the Mediterranean by the Suez Canal.

religions There are about 100 million Christians in Africa and nearly 100 million Muslims. Most of the rest follow tribal religions.

Sahara World's largest desert (about 8,400,000 sq. km (3,250,000 square miles), extending across northern Africa from Atlantic to Red Sea.

Songhai Empire that dominated much of western Africa in the 1500s, stretching from what is now Niger to Senegal. Crushed by Moroccans in 1591.

Tanganyika, Lake World's longest (675 km / 420 miles) lake, and second deepest (1433 m / 4600 feet). Bordered for most of length by Zaïre on west and Tanzania on east.

Tuaregs Nomadic Arab tribes of the desert, similar to the Bedouins.

Tugela Falls Second-highest waterfall (948 m) in the world, in Natal, South Africa.

veld (Afrikaans for 'grassland') Vast grassy plateaus covering much of South Africa.

Victoria, Lake Largest lake (69,484 sq km / 26,825 square miles) in Africa, second-largest freshwater lake in world; lies in Kenya, Uganda, and Tanzania.

Victoria Falls Largest waterfall (in volume of water) in Africa; on the Zambezi, between Zimbabwe and Zambia.

wadi (Arabic for 'ravine') Dry river bed through which water flows in rainy season. Often formed in sand, especially in northern Africa.

Zaïre, River (formerly Congo) flows 4500 km (2800 miles) through west-central Africa to the Atlantic.

Zulus Brave and powerful African tribe of the 1800s, eventually subdued by the British. More than half a million now live in Zululand in Natal, South Africa.

COUNTRIES

Area: 44,387,000 sq. km (17,139,000 sq. m), including 75 per cent of the USSR (east of the Urals and Caspian Sea) and 97 per cent of Turkey: **Population:** 2,693,000,000; **Independent countries** (1982): 40; **Highest peak:** Mt Everest, 8848 m (29,028 ft); **Lowest point:** Shore of Dead Sea, 393 m (1289 ft) below sea level; **Largest lake:** Caspian Sea, 438,695 sq. km (170,000 sq. m); **Longest rivers:** Yangtze, Lena, Yenisey, Hwang Ho, Ob, Mekong, Amur.

AFGHANISTAN Republic of Asia. **Area:** 650,000 sq. km (250,000 sq. m). **Population:** 16,024,000. **Capital:** Kabul.

BAHRAIN Group of islands forming a State in the Persian Gulf. **Area:** 622 sq. km (240 sq. m). **Population:** 467,000. **Capital:** Manama.

BANGLADESH Republic in south-east Asia. A member of the Commonwealth. **Area:** 144,000 sq. km (55,600 sq. m). **Population:** 94,472,000. **Capital:** Dacca.

BHUTAN Kingdom of the Himalayas. **Area:** 47,000 sq. km (18,000 sq. m). **Population:** 1,352,000. **Capital:** Thimphu.

BRUNEI Sultanate of Borneo. A member of the Commonwealth. **Area:** 5,760 sq. km (2,230 sq. m). **Population:** 248,000. **Capital:** Seria.

BURMA Republic of south-east Asia. **Area:** 676,500 sq. km (261,230 sq. m). **Population:** 35,211,000. **Capital:** Rangoon.

CHINA (People's Republic) Republic of south-east Asia. **Area:** 9,597,000 sq. km (3,706,000 sq. m). **Population:** 1,012,358,000. **Capital:** Beijing (Peking).

ASIA

ARCTIC OCEAN

URAL MOUNTAINS

Yenisey

Ob

Lena

USSR

Omsk

Novosibirsk

Irkutsk

Amur

L. Baikal

Darya

L. Balkhash

Ulan Bator

MONGOLIA

Sapporo

Harbin

Vladivostok

JAPAN

TIEN SHAN

Hwang Ho

Gobi Desert

Peking

Tientsin

NORTH KOREA

Pyongyang

Lü-ta

Seoul

SOUTH KOREA

Pusan

Taiyuan

Yokohama

Kyoto

Kobe

Nagoya

Osaka

Kitakyushu

Nagasaki

Tokyo

STAN

Kabul

Islamabad

Lahore

Kashmir

Lanchow

Sian

Nanking

Shanghai

CHINA

Wuhan

Tibet

HIMALAYAS

Lhasa

Chengtu

Yangtze-Kiang

Chungking

Taipei

TAIWAN

AN

Delhi

New Delhi

Mt Everest

NEPAL

Katmandu

Thimphu

BHUTAN

Brahmaputra

Kunming

Si-Kiang

Canton

HONG KONG

MACAO

yderabad

Kanpur

Lucknow

Varanasi

Ganges

BURMA

Dacca

Ahmadabad

INDIA

Calcutta

Mandalay

Hanoi

LAOS

Nagpur

BANGLADESH

Irrawaddy

Salween

Vientiane

VIETNAM

Mekong

Manila

Quezon City

nbay

Godavari

Rangoon

THAILAND

PHILIPPINES

Hyderabad

Bangkok

CAMBODIA

Bangalore

Madras

Phnom Penh

Saigon
(Ho Chi Minh City)

Bandar Seri
Begawan

SRI LANKA

BRUNEI

Colombo

Sarawak

MALDIVE IS

Malé

Penang

MALAYSIA

Kuala Lumpur

SINGAPORE

West Irian

OCEAN

Sumatra

Borneo

Sulawesi

INDONESIA

Djakarta

Java

Timor

CHRISTMAS ISLAND Australian territory in the Indian Ocean. **Area:** 135 sq. km (52 sq. m). **Population:** 3,200. **Capital:** Flying Fish Cove.

COCOS (KEELING) ISLANDS Australian territory in the Indian Ocean. **Area:** 14 sq. km (5½ sq. m). **Population:** 500. **Capital:** Bantam Village.

HONG KONG British colony on the south-east coast of China. **Area:** 1045 sq. km (403 sq. m). **Population:** 4,957,000. **Capital:** Victoria.

INDIA Republic of south-east Asia, a member of the Commonwealth. **Area:** 3,287,600 sq. km (1,270,000 sq. m). **Population:** 700,000,000. **Capital:** Delhi.

INDONESIA Island republic of south-east Asia. **Area:** 2,027,000 sq. km (782,700 sq. m). **Population:** 146,527,000. **Capital:** Jakarta.

IRAN Republic of south-west Asia. **Area:** 1,648,000 sq. km (636,000 sq. m). **Population:** 40,288,000. **Capital:** Tehran.

IRAQ Republic of south-west Asia. **Area:** 435,000 sq. km (168,000 sq. m). **Population:** 14,000,000. **Capital:** Baghdad.

ISRAEL Republic of the Middle East. **Area:** 20,700 sq. km (8000 sq. m). **Population:** 4,100,000. **Capital:** Jerusalem.

JAPAN Constitutional monarchy of the Far East. **Area:** 372,300 sq. km (143,800 sq. m). **Population:** 120,055,000. **Capital:** Tokyo.

JORDAN Kingdom of the Middle East. **Area:** 97,740 sq. km (37,700 sq. m). **Population:** 3,403,000. **Capital:** Amman.

KAMPUCHEA Republic of south-east Asia. **Area:** 181,000 sq. km (70,000 sq. m). **Population:** 8,600,000. **Capital:** Phnom Penh.

KOREA, NORTH Republic of the Far East. **Area:** 120,500 sq. km (46,500 sq. m). **Population:** 18,900,000. **Capital:** Pyongyang.

KOREA, SOUTH Republic of the Far East. **Area:** 98,000 sq. km (38,000 sq. m). **Population:** 39,546,000. **Capital:** Seoul.

KUWAIT An Emirate on the Persian Gulf. **Area:** 17,800 sq. km (6900 sq. m). **Population:** 1,516,000. **Capital:** Kuwait.

LAOS A republic of south-east Asia. **Area:** 236,800 sq. km (91,400 sq. m). **Population:** 3,611,000. **Capital:** Vientiane.

LEBANON Republic of the Middle East. **Area:** 10,400 sq. km (4000 sq. m). **Population:** 3,325,000. **Capital:** Beirut.

MACÃO An overseas territory of Portugal on the south-east coast of China. **Area:** 16 sq. km (6 sq. m). **Population:** 330,000. **Capital:** Macão.

MALAYSIA A state of south-east Asia. A member of the Commonwealth. **Area:** 330,000 sq. km (127,300 sq. m). **Population:** 14,777,000. **Capital:** Kuala Lumpur.

MALDIVES An island republic of the Indian Ocean, with about 2000 islands. A member of the Commonwealth. **Area:** 300 sq. km (115 sq. m). **Population:** 167,000. **Capital:** Malé.

MONGOLIA Republic of central Asia. **Area:** 1,565,000 sq. km (604,300 sq. m). **Population:** 1,772,000. **Capital:** Ulan Bator.

NEPAL A monarchy of the Himalayas between China and India. **Area:** 140,800 sq. km (54,000 sq. m). **Population:** 14,932,000. **Capital:** Katmandu.

OMAN A sultanate at the eastern end of the Arabian peninsula. **Area:** 212,400 sq. km (82,000 sq. m). **Population:** 950,000. **Capital:** Muscat.

PAKISTAN Republic of Southern Asia. **Area:** 804,000 sq. km (310,400 sq. m). **Population:** 85,558,000. **Capital:** Islamabad.

PHILIPPINES Republic of south-east Asia. **Area:** 330,000 sq. km (116,000 sq. m). **Population:** 50,697,000. **Capital:** Manila.

QATAR An Emirate, a peninsula in the Persian Gulf. **Area:** 11,000 sq. km (4000 sq. m). **Population:** 294,000. **Capital:** Doha.

SAUDI ARABIA Kingdom of the Arabian peninsula. **Area:** 2,150,000 sq. km (830,000 sq. m). **Population:** 9,418,000. **Capital:** Riyadh.

SINGAPORE Island republic off the Malay peninsula, a member of the Commonwealth. **Area:** 580 sq. km (224 sq. m). **Population:** 2,476,000. **Capital:** Singapore.

SRI LANKA Republic of South Asia, a member of the Commonwealth. **Area:** 65,600 sq. km (25,000 sq. m). **Population:** 15,400,000. **Capital:** Colombo.

SYRIA Republic of the Middle East. **Area:** 185,000 sq. km (71,500 sq. m). **Population:** 9,227,000. **Capital:** Damascus.

TAIWAN (Republic of China). Nationalist republic. **Area:** 36,000 sq. km (14,000 sq. m). **Population:** 17,000,000. **Capital:** Taipei.

THAILAND Kingdom of south-east Asia.

Area: 514,000 sq. km (198,000 sq. m). **Population:** 49,414,000. **Capital:** Bangkok.

TURKEY Republic, in Europe/Asia. **Area:** 780,600 sq. km (301,400 sq. m). **Population:** 47,663,000. **Capital:** Ankara.

UNITED ARAB EMIRATES A federation of seven emirates, formerly the British-protected Trucial States, in the Persian Gulf. They are: Abu Dhabi, Ajman, Dubai, Fujairah, Ras al Khaimah, Sharjah and Umm al Qaiwain. **Area:** 83,600 sq. km (32,300 sq. m). **Population:** 1,040,000. **Capital:** Abu Dhabi.

VIETNAM Republic of south-east Asia. **Area:** 330,000 sq. km (127,250 sq. m). **Population:** 51,742,000. **Capital:** Hanoi.

YEMEN ARAB REPUBLIC (in the Arabian peninsula). **Area:** 195,000 sq. km (75,300 sq. m). **Population:** 6,142,000. **Capital:** San'a.

YEMEN PEOPLE'S DEMOCRATIC REPUBLIC (in the Arabian peninsula). **Area:** 333,000 sq. km (128,600 sq. m). **Population:** 1,905,000. **Capital:** Aden.

A to Z of Asia

Angkor Capital of the Khmer Empire (802–1413), rediscovered in 1860s. Ruins, together with those of temple of Angkor Wat, have been restored.

Arabia Vast desert peninsula in south-western Asia, between Red Sea and Persian Gulf. Most of it belongs to Saudi Arabia.

Asia Minor Peninsula in western Asia, between Black Sea and Mediterranean, mostly occupied by Turkey. Home of some of world's earliest civilizations.

Assyria Ancient empire in the Tigris valley, in what is now northern Iraq. Flourished from about 1800 to 612 BC, with periods of great power and culture.

COUNTRIES

Babylonia Ancient empire south of *Assyria*. One of the earliest civilizations. Flourished from about 1850 to 539 BC, closely connected with Assyria in culture and development. The two countries were for periods in control of each other.

Black Sea Lies between western Asia (Turkey, USSR) and Europe.

Brahmaputra River in southern Asia, flowing 2700 km (1675 miles) from Tibet to join the Ganges in India.

Caspian Sea Largest inland body of water in the world, the Caspian Sea (438,695 sq. km / 170,000 sq. miles) is a salt lake that lies between Europe and western Asia. It is bordered by the USSR on three sides and by Iran, and lies 28 m below sea level.

Caucasus Mountain range in the USSR extending about 1200 km (745 miles) between the Black and Caspian seas, forming boundary between Asia and Europe.

Dead Sea Inland sea between Israel and Jordan, saltiest body of water in world. It is also the lowest place on the Earth's surface, lying 392 m below the average sea level.

Euphrates River that flows about 2700 km (1680 miles) from Turkey, through Syria and Iraq, to the Persian Gulf. Its lower valley, in southern Iraq, was the centre of one of the world's oldest civilizations. See also *Tigris*.

Everest Highest mountain (8848 m / 29,028 ft) in the world; in the Himalaya, on the border between Tibet and Nepal.

Ganges Indian river that flows from Himalaya to Bay of Bengal. Considered sacred by Hindus.

Gobi Sandy, treeless desert in east-central Asia, mainly in China and Mongolia.

Himalaya Highest mountain system in world, extending some 2400 km (1490 miles) between the Indus and Brahmaputra rivers, separating northern India from Tibet. Consists of several ranges, including the Karakoram, the most northerly chain. Many peaks over 700 m (22,965 ft), including Everest, Godwin Austen and Kanchenjunga.

Hwang Ho (Yellow River). Flows about 4500 km (2800 miles) in northern China, emptying into the Yellow Sea. Nicknamed 'China's sorrow' because of many disastrous floods.

Mesopotamia Name, literally 'between the rivers', given by ancient Greeks to land between Tigris and Euphrates rivers in what is now mostly Iraq. Settled at least 6000 years ago, and was home of Sumerian civilization by 3000 BC.

Ob River that flows more than 4000 km (2500 miles) from Altai Mountains in western Siberia to the Arctic Ocean. Navigable for most of length, it is one of Asian Russia's chief trade routes.

Palestine The Holy Land of the Bible, and regarded as such by Christians, Jews, and Muslims. On eastern shore of Mediterranean, it includes Israel and parts of adjacent countries.

Red Sea Long (2250 km / 1367 miles), narrow, sea between Arabia and Africa, opening into Indian Ocean and connected by the Suez Canal to the Mediterranean.

Sumer Region in lower *Mesopotamia* whose people developed one of the first great civilizations, based on agriculture and with a fine culture. Flourished from before 3000 BC to about 2000 BC.

Tamils A dark-skinned people who live in Madras (southern India). Burma, Malaysia, and Sri Lanka.

Tartars Early Mongol peoples of central Asia who founded the Mongol Empire in the AD 800s. Today the term refers chiefly to peoples of Turkish origin living in western Asia.

Tigris River that flows 1850 km (1200 miles) from eastern Turkey, through Iraq, where it joins the Euphrates and empties into the Persian Gulf.

Urals Mountain system extending for 2500 km (1560 miles) north to south across the USSR, from the Arctic.

Yangtze Kiang World's fourth longest river, winding 5470 km (3400 miles) from Tibet to the East China Sea near Shanghai. Much of China's trade centres on this river.

Area: 24,249,000 sq. km (9,363,000 sq. m), including Mexico, Central America, the West Indies and Greenland, a self-governing country of Denmark; **Population:** 382,000,000; **Independent countries** (1982): 22; **Highest peak:** Mt McKinley (Alaska), 6194 m (20,322 ft); **Lowest point:** Death Valley (California), 86 m (282 ft) below sea level; **Largest lake:** Lake Superior, 82,409 sq. km (31,820 sq. m); **Longest rivers:** Mississippi-Missouri-Red Rock.

ANGUILLA British colony of the Leeward Islands, West Indies. **Area:** 90 sq. km (35 sq. m). **Population:** 6,500. **Capital:** The Valley.

ANTIGUA and BARBUDA British Associated State of the West Indies. **Area:** 440 sq. km (170 sq. m). **Population:** 77,000. **Capital:** St. John's.

BAHAMAS An independent member of the Commonwealth in the West Atlantic. **Area:** 14,000 sq. km (5380 sq. m). **Population:** 237,000. **Capital:** Nassau.

BARBADOS An independent member of the Commonwealth in the West Indies. **Area:** 430 sq. km (166 sq. m). **Population:** 257,000. **Capital:** Bridgetown.

BELIZE State on the east coast of Central America, a member of the Commonwealth. **Area:** 22,960 sq. km (8860 sq. m). **Population:** 135,400. **Capital:** Belmopan.

BERMUDA British dependent territory in the West Atlantic. **Area:** 53 sq. km (20 sq. m). **Population:** 62,000. **Capital:** Hamilton.

CANADA Independent member of the Commonwealth in the north of North America. **Area:** 9,976,000 sq. km (3,852,000 sq. m). **Population:** 24,670,000. **Capital:** Ottawa.

CAYMAN ISLANDS British colony, a number of islands in the West Indies. **Area:** 260 sq. km (100 sq. m). **Population:** 11,000. **Capital:** George Town.

COSTA RICA Republic of Central America. **Area:** 50,700 sq. km (19,600 sq. m). **Population:** 2,330,000. **Capital:** San José.

CUBA Republic of the West Indies. **Area:** 114,550 sq. km (44,220 sq. m). **Population:** 10,346,000. **Capital:** Havana.

DOMINICA Republic within the Commonwealth in the Windward Islands, West Indies. **Area:** 751 sq. km (290 sq. m). **Population:** 82,000. **Capital:** Roseau.

DOMINICAN REPUBLIC Republic of the West Indies, occupying the eastern two-thirds of the island of Hispaniola. **Area:** 49,000 sq. km (18,800 sq. m). **Population:** 5,776,000. **Capital:** Santo Domingo.

EL SALVADOR Republic of Central America. **Area:** 21,000 sq. km (8000 sq. m). **Population:** 4,820,000. **Capital:** San Salvador.

GREENLAND A self-governing county of Denmark in the North Atlantic. **Area:** 2,176,000 sq. km (840,000 sq. m). **Population:** 50,000. **Capital:** Godthaab.

Canada	
Capital	**Province**
Edmonton	1. Alberta
Victoria	2. British Columbia
Winnipeg	3. Manitoba
Fredericton	4. New Brunswick
St John's	5. Newfoundland
Yellowknife	6. Northwest Terr.
Halifax	7. Nova Scotia
Toronto	8. Ontario
Charlottetown	9. Prince Edward Is.
Quebec	10. Quebec
Regina	11. Saskatchewan
Whitehorse	12. Yukon Territory

GRENADA An independent country within the Commonwealth, located in the West Indies, one of the Windward Islands. **Area:** 344 sq. km (133 sq. m). **Population:** 113,000. **Capital:** St. George's.

GUADELOUPE A French overseas department in the West Indies. **Area:** 1780 sq. km (688 sq. m). **Population:** 332,000. **Capital:** Basse-Terre.

GUATEMALA Republic of Central America. **Area:** 108,900 sq. km (42,000 sq. m). **Population:** 7,436,000. **Capital:** Guatemala City.

HAITI Republic of the West Indies, occupying the western third of the island of Hispaniola. **Area:** 28,000 sq. km (10,700 sq. m). **Population:** 5,220,000. **Capital:** Port-au-Prince.

HONDURAS Republic of Central America. **Area:** 112,000 sq. km (43,000 sq. m). **Population:** 4,000,000. **Capital:** Tegucigalpa.

JAMAICA An independent member of the Commonwealth in the West Indies. **Area:** 11,000 sq. km (4,200 sq. m). **Population:** 2,300,000. **Capital:** Kingston.

MARTINIQUE A French overseas department in the West Indies. **Area:** 1,100 sq. km (426 sq. m). **Population:** 326,000. **Capital:** Fort-de-France.

MEXICO Republic of North America. **Area:** 1,970,000 sq. km (761,000 sq. m). **Population:** 74,600,000. **Capital:** Mexico City.

MONTSERRAT British colony in the Leeward Islands, West Indies. **Area:** 98 sq. km (38 sq. m). **Population:** 12,000. **Capital:** Plymouth.

NETHERLANDS ANTILLES Two groups of Dutch islands in the Caribbean, with full internal autonomy. **Area:** 960 sq. km (370 sq. m). **Population:** 273,000. **Capital:** Willemstad.

NICARAGUA Republic of Central America. **Area:** 130,000 sq. km (50,000 sq. m). **Population:** 2,851,000. **Capital:** Managua.

PANAMA Republic of Central America. **Area:** 75,700 sq. km (29,000 sq. m). **Population:** 2,012,000. **Capital:** Panama.

PUERTO RICO A United States self-governing Commonwealth in the West Indies. **Area:** 8900 sq. km (3435 sq. m). **Population:** 3,666,000. **Capital:** San Juan.

ST KITTS-NEVIS A State in the Leeward Islands of the West Indies, associated with the Commonwealth. **Area:** 260 sq. km (100 sq m). **Population:** 51,000. **Capital:** Basseterre.

ST LUCIA An independent state within the Commonwealth; one of the Windward Islands in the West Indies. **Area:** 616 sq. km (238 sq.m). **Population:** 130,000. **Capital:** Castries.

ST PIERRE AND MIQUELON A French overseas department, eight islands off Newfoundland, Canada. **Area:** 242 sq. km (93 sq. m). **Population:** 6,000. **Capital:** St Pierre.

ST VINCENT AND THE GRENADINES An independent member of the Commonwealth in the Windward Islands, West Indies. **Area:** 388 sq. km (150 sq. m). **Population:** 113,000. **Capital:** Kingstown.

TRINIDAD AND TOBAGO Island Republic of the West Indies within the Commonwealth. **Area:** 5000 sq. km (2000 sq. m). **Population:** 1,193,000. **Capital:** Port-of-Spain.

NORTH AMERICA

Greenland

Yukon **Alaska**

Fairbanks •

•Anchorage

Mackenzie

Baffin Is

Great Bear L.

•Whitehorse

Juneau •

Great Slave L.

CANADA

Churchill •

Hudson Bay

Edmonton •

Vancouver •

•Calgary

L. Winnipeg

Seattle •

•Regina

Portland •

•Winnipeg

Quebec •

Missouri

Montreal

L. Superior

Ottawa

Halifax

St Lawrence

Minneapolis • •St Paul

L. Huron

Toronto

Boston

Francisco •

Salt Lake City •

USA

Milwaukee •

L. Michigan

Detroit •

Cleveland

L. Erie *L. Ontario*

New York

Philadelphia

Chicago

Pittsburgh

•Denver

Columbus

Baltimore

Washington DC

ROCKY MOUNTAINS

Colorado

Kansas City •

St Louis •

Indianapolis •

Bermuda

Las Vegas •

Los Angeles •

Santa Fe •

Albuquerque •

Memphis •

San Diego •

Phoenix •

•Tucson

Red

•Atlanta

ATLANTIC OCEAN

El Paso •

Dallas •

Mississippi

Jacksonville •

PACIFIC OCEAN

SIERRA MADRE

G. of California

Rio Grande

San Antonio •

Houston •

•New Orleans

•Monterrey

Gulf of Mexico

Miami •

•Nassau

BAHAMAS

MEXICO

Havana ■

CUBA

DOMINICAN REPUBLIC

San Juan ■

•Guadalajara

HAITI

PUERTO RICO

Port-au-Prince ■

Santo Domingo

■ Mexico City

JAMAICA

■Kingston

BARBADOS

NORTH AMERICA

Belmopan

BELIZE

Caribbean Sea

Port-of-Spain •

0	500	1000 miles
0	500 1000	1500 kilometres

GUATEMALA

Guatemala City ■

HONDURAS

Tegucigalpa ■

TRINIDAD & TOBAGO

San Salvador ■

NICARAGUA

EL SALVADOR

Managua ■

■ Capital Cities

COSTA RICA

Panama Canal Zone

San José •

Panama ■

PANAMA

COUNTRIES

TURKS AND CAICOS ISLANDS
British colony in the Caribbean. **Area:** 430 sq. km (166 sq. m). **Population:** 7,200. **Capital:** Cockburn Town.

UNITED STATES OF AMERICA
Federal republic of North America. **Area:** 9,363,123 sq. km (3,615,319 sq. m). **Population:** 226,505,000. **Capital:** Washington, District of Columbia.

VIRGIN ISLANDS
(British) Group of 36 islands in the West Indies. **Area:** 153 sq. km (59 sq. m). **Population:** 11,500. **Capital:** Road Town.

VIRGIN ISLANDS
(US) A territory near Puerto Rico in the West Indies. **Area:** 344 sq. km (133 sq. m). **Population:** 119,000. **Capital:** Charlotte Amalie.

A to Z of North America

Appalachians Range of mountains running parallel to the Atlantic coast, extending about 2400 km (1500 miles) from Gulf of St Lawrence to northern Alabama.
Canadian Shield Vast rocky region that curves around Hudson Bay, covering half of Canada.
Colorado River Flows 2300 km (1400 miles) from the Rockies in Colorado to the Gulf of California.

THE UNITED STATES OF AMERICA

Name and Abbreviation	Area sq. km	Area sq. m	Population	Capital	Date of Admission to the Union
Alabama (Ala.)	133,667	51,612	3,890,000	Montgomery	1819
Alaska (Alas.)	1,518,800	586,444	400,500	Juneau	1959
Arizona (Ariz.)	295,023	113,915	2,718,000	Phoenix	1912
Arkansas (Ark.)	137,539	53,107	2,285,000	Little Rock	1836
California (Calif.)	411,013	158,702	23,668,500	Sacramento	1850
Colorado (Colo.)	269,998	104,253	2,889,000	Denver	1876
Connecticut (Conn.)	12,973	5,009	3,107,500	Hartford	1788*
Delaware (Del.)	5,328	2,057	595,000	Dover	1787*
District of Columbia (D.C.)	–	–	–	Washington	1791
Florida (Fla.)	151,670	58,563	9,740,000	Tallahassee	1845
Georgia (Ga.)	152,488	58,879	5,465,000	Atlanta	1788*
Hawaii (Hi.)	16,705	6,450	965,000	Honolulu	1959
Idaho (Id.)	216,412	83,562	944,000	Boise	1890
Illinois (Ill.)	146,075	56,403	11,418,500	Springfield	1818
Indiana (Ind.)	93,993	36,293	5,490,000	Indianapolis	1816
Iowa (Ia.)	145,790	56,293	2,913,000	Des Moines	1846
Kansas (Kans.)	213,063	82,269	2,363,000	Topeka	1861
Kentucky (Ky.)	104,623	40,397	3,662,000	Frankfort	1792
Louisiana (La.)	125,674	48,526	4,204,000	Baton Rouge	1812
Maine (Me.)	86,026	33,127	1,125,000	Augusta	1820
Maryland (Md.)	27,394	10,577	4,217,000	Annapolis	1788*
Massachusetts (Mass.)	21,386	8,258	5,737,000	Boston	1788*
Michigan (Mich.)	150,779	58,219	9,258,000	Lansing	1837
Minnesota (Minn.)	217,735	84,073	4,077,000	St. Paul	1858
Mississippi (Miss.)	123,584	47,719	2,521,000	Jackson	1817
Missouri (Mo.)	180,486	69,690	4,917,500	Jefferson City	1821

Death Valley Deep trough in eastern California, 200 km (125 miles) long and 10-20 km wide. Contains Badwater, the lowest land in the Western Hemisphere, 86 metres (282 ft) below sea level.

Eskimos About 35,000 Eskimos live in Alaska and northern Canada.

Grand Canyon Massive, spectacular gorge formed in Arizona by the Colorado River. More than a mile (1600 km) deep.

Great Lakes Five lakes that make up N. America's chief inland waterway: Erie, Superior, Huron, Michigan, Ontario.

Indians The original peoples of North America, also known as *Amerinds* or *Amerindians*. They are believed to have come from Asia, across a land bridge, some 20,000 years ago. The Aztec and Maya of Central America built large cities. In Canada and the USA, the Indians lived mainly by hunting and farming. In Canada today, about 200,000 Indians live on some 2000 *reserves*. In the USA there are about 275 reservations, where more than half the country's 650,000 Indians live.

Mississippi River Second-longest N. American river. Only its chief tributary, the Missouri, is longer. Rises in Lake Itasca, in Minnesota.

Missouri River Chief tributary of Mississippi and longest river in N. America.

Negroes The Negroes of N. America are descendants of slaves brought over from

THE UNITED STATES OF AMERICA

Name and Abbreviation	Area sq. km	sq. m	Population	Capital	Date of Admission to the Union
Montana (Mont.)	381,086	147,146	786,700	Helena	1889
Nebraska (Nebr.)	200,017	77,231	1,570,000	Lincoln	1867
Nevada (Nev.)	286,297	110,546	800,000	Carson City	1864
New Hampshire (N.H.)	24,097	9,304	920,600	Concord	1788*
New Jersey (N.J.)	20,295	7,836	7,364,000	Trenton	1787*
New Mexico (N. Mex.)	315,113	121,672	1,300,000	Santa Fé	1912
New York (N.Y.)	128,401	49,579	17,557,000	Albany	1788*
North Carolina (N.C.)	136,197	52,589	5,874,500	Raleigh	1789*
North Dakota (N. Dak.)	183,022	70,669	653,000	Bismarck	1889
Ohio (Oh.)	106,765	41,224	10,798,000	Columbus	1803
Oklahoma (Okla.)	181,089	69,923	3,025,000	Oklahoma City	1907
Oregon (Ore.)	251,180	96,986	2,632,000	Salem	1859
Pennsylvania (Pa.)	117,412	45,336	11,867,000	Harrisburg	1787*
Rhode Island (R.I.)	3,144	1,214	947,000	Providence	1790*
South Carolina (S.C.)	80,432	31,057	3,120,000	Columbia	1788*
South Dakota (S. Dak.)	199,551	77,051	690,000	Pierre	1889
Tennessee (Tenn.)	109,411	42,246	4,591,000	Nashville	1796
Texas (Tex.)	692,402	267,353	14,228,000	Austin	1845
Utah (Ut.)	219,931	84,920	1,461,000	Salt Lake City	1896
Vermont (Vt.)	24,887	9,609	511,456	Montpelier	1791
Virginia (Va.)	105,716	40,819	5,346,000	Richmond	1788*
Washington (Wash.)	176,617	68,196	4,130,000	Olympia	1889
West Virginia (W. Va.)	62,629	24,183	1,945,000	Charlestown	1863
Wisconsin (Wis.)	145,438	56,157	4,705,000	Madison	1848
Wyoming (Wyo.)	253,596	97,919	471,000	Cheyenne	1890

One of the Thirteen Original States

COUNTRIES

Africa. About one in every 10 people in the USA is a Negro or has mixed Negro and White ancestry.

Niagara Falls Spectacular waterfalls on Canada—US border. Horseshoe Falls (Canada) 640 m (2100 ft wide, 57 m (187 ft) high; American Falls 335 m (1099 ft) wide, 59 m (193½ ft) high.

Rio Grande River that flows from Colorado through south-western USA and forms nearly two-thirds of boundary with Mexico.

Rocky Mountains System of jagged peaks extending about 5000 km (1650 miles) along western North America, from Alaska, through Canada, to New Mexico.

St Lawrence River Canada's longest river, flowing 3130 km (10,270 miles) from Lake Ontario to Gulf of St Lawrence.

South America

Area: 17,832,000 sq. km (6,885,000 sq. m); **Population:** 262,000,000; **Independent countries** (1982): 12; **Highest peak:** Mt Aconcagua, 6960 m (22,835 ft); **Largest lake:** Maracaibo (Venezuela), 16,300 sq. km (6300 sq. m); **Longest river:** Amazon; **Highest waterfall:** Angel Falls in Venezuela.

ARGENTINA Republic of South America. **Area:** 2,766,890 sq. km (1,068,360 sq. m).
Population: 27,796,000. **Capital:** Buenos Aires.

BOLIVIA Republic of South America. **Area:** 1,093,500 sq. km (424,000 sq. m). **Population:** 5,897,000. **Capital:** La Paz.

BRAZIL Republic, largest country of South America. **Area:** 8,512,000 sq. km (3,286,670 sq. m). **Population:** 133,880,000. **Capital:** Brasilia.

CHILE Republic of South America. **Area:** 757,000 sq. km (292,274 sq. m). **Population:** 11,478,000. **Capital:** Santiago.

COLOMBIA Republic of South America. **Area:** 1,139,000 sq. km (440,000 sq. m). **Population:** 28,000,000. **Capital:** Bogotá.

ECUADOR Republic of South America. **Area:** 283,600 sq. km (109,500 sq. m). **Population:** 8,893,000. **Capital:** Quito.

FALKLAND ISLANDS British colony in the South Atlantic. **Area:** 12,200 sq. km (4700 sq. m). **Population:** 2000. **Capital:** Stanley.

FRENCH GUIANA A French overseas department in north-east South America. **Area:** 91,000 sq. km (35,000 sq. m). **Population:** 76,000. **Capital:** Cayenne.

GUYANA Republic of north-east South America, a member of the Commonwealth. **Area:** 215,000 sq. km (83,000 sq. m). **Population:** 887,000. **Capital:** Georgetown.

PARAGUAY Republic of South America. **Area:** 406,700 sq. km (157,000 sq. m). **Population:** 3,254,000. **Capital:** Asunción.

PERU Republic of western South America. **Area:** 1,285,000 sq. km (496,000 sq. m). **Population:** 18,786,000. **Capital:** Lima.

SURINAM Republic of north-east South America. **Area:** 163,300 sq. km (63,000 sq. m). **Population:** 404,000. **Capital:** Paramaribo.

URUGUAY Republic of South America. **Area:** 176,200 sq. km (68,000 sq. m). **Population:** 2,934,000. **Capital:** Montevideo.

VENEZUELA Republic of South America. **Area:** 912,000 sq. km (352,000 sq. m). **Population:** 15,920,000. **Capital:** Caracas.

SOUTH AMERICA

Barranquilla • Maracaibo • Caracas

Orinoco

VENEZUELA

• Medellin

Llanos

Georgetown •

Paramaribo •

GUYANA

SURINAM

Cayenne •

FRENCH GUIANA

■ Bogotá

• Cali

COLOMBIA

Equator

■ Quito

ECUADOR

Guayaquil•

Amazon

• Belém

• Manáus

Selvas

Fortaleza•

Chiclayo•

PERU

BRAZIL

Recife •

Trujillo•

São Francisco

Callão ■ Lima

• Cuzco

• Salvador

A N D E S   M O U N T A I N S

BOLIVIA

■ Brasília

• La Paz

• Cochabamba

Oruro •

■ Sucre

Brazilian Highlands

PACIFIC OCEAN

Atacama Desert

Paraná

PARAGUAY

• Rio de Janeiro

São Paulo •

Gran Chaco

■ Asunción

CHILE

Córdoba•

Rosario

• Pôrto Alegre

Valparaíso•

▲Mt Aconcagua

■ Santiago

ARGENTINA

Buenos Aires

URUGUAY

■ Montevideo

La Plata •

Pampas

ATLANTIC OCEAN

• Bahía Blanca

Colorado

Chubut

Pàtagonia

0   500   1000 miles

0   500   1000   1500 kilometres

■ Capital Cities

Falkland Is

Cape Horn   **Tierra del Fuego**

A to Z of South America

Aconcagua Highest mountain in the Americas; rises 6960 metres (22,835 ft) in the Andes, in western Argentina, near the border with Chile. It is an extinct volcano, and its peak is always covered with snow.

Amazon Second-longest river in the world (to the Nile), rising in the lowlands of north-eastern Peru and flowing eastwards, through the jungles of Brazil, for 6437 km (4000 miles) before emptying into the Atlantic. It is fed by over 200 branches. Slow-moving, it contains more water than any other river.

Andes Longest chain of mountains in the World, stretching 7250 km (4,500 miles) along the whole west coast of South America, from Cape Horn, in the south, to Panama. They contain more than 50 peaks over 6000 metres (19,600 ft) high. Only the Himalaya mountains in Asia are higher.

Angel Falls The highest waterfall in the world, with an unbroken drop of 807 metres (2647 ft) and a total fall of 979 metres (3215 ft). Located on Mt Auyantepui, a high plateau in south-eastern Venezuela.

Atacama Desert One of the driest areas in the world, a region rich in minerals, situated between southern Ecuador and central Chile.

Gran Chaco A vast low-lying plain covering western Paraguay, northern Argentina, and southern Bolivia. It has swamps, jungles, and grassy plains.

Guaira Falls Massive waterfalls on the Paraná River in south-western Brazil, spanning nearly 5 km (3 miles). It has a greater volume of flow than any other waterfall in the world, about 13,000 cubic metres (45,900 cubic ft) per second.

Iguaçu Falls Spectacular waterfalls on the Brazil-Argentina border.

Lake Maracaibo Largest lake in S. America, 16,300 sq km (6300 sq miles) in area. It lies in north-western Venezuela, and is connected by a short channel with the Gulf of Venezuela, an area of the Caribbean Sea.

Lake Titicaca Highest lake in the world, 3812 metres (12,506 ft) above sea level. Situated on the Bolivia-Peru border, it lies in a basin in the Andes.

llanos Literally, 'level lands.' Term used in S. America for the vast treeless plain of the Orinoco basin, in Colombia and Venezuela. After the wet season, rich grass provides grazing land for livestock.

Machu Picchu Ancient Inca city in Peru, discovered in 1911 on a mountain, 2000 metres (6,500 ft) up in the Andes. Ruins include a temple and terraced gardens.

pampas Spanish for 'plains' used of several great plains of South America, but in particular for the vast, grass-covered plain of central Argentina, between the Rio Salado and Rio Negro. A rich, fertile area, the Argentinian pampa is excellent pasture land for cattle and sheep.

Paraná Second-longest river in S. America, rising in southern Brazil and flowing 3950 km (2455 miles) before emptying into the Rio de la Plata estuary, in Argentina.

Patagonia Dry tableland occupying the southern part of the continent and shared by Argentina and Chile. Largely desert, it has frequent dust storms and water is scarce. But it is one of the world's largest sheep-grazing regions.

Tierra del Fuego Archipelago (group of islands) at southern tip of S. America separated from mainland by Strait of Magellan.

The areas of the Antarctic controlled by different nations.

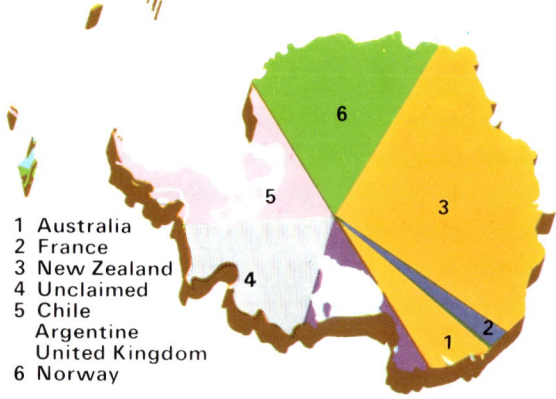

1 Australia
2 France
3 New Zealand
4 Unclaimed
5 Chile
  Argentine
  United Kingdom
6 Norway

A to Z of the Polar Regions

ANTARCTICA

Area: 13,209,000 sq. km (5,100,000 sq. mi); **Population:** there is no permanent population; **Highest point:** 5139 m (16,860 ft) in the Vinson Massif; **Ice sheet:** Antarctica contains the world's largest ice sheet; the average thickness of the ice is 2000–3800 m (6560–12,470 ft).

Americanoids Term for several tribes of north-eastern Siberia who resemble the American Indians of the north-west coast. They either fish and hunt seals, or herd reindeer. The main tribes include the Chukchi, Koryaks, and Kamchadals.

Antarctic Treaty Agreement signed in 1959 by 12 nations to reserve the area for peaceful purposes and provide for international co-operation in scientific investigation and research.

Arctic Circle Imaginary line drawn round the North Pole at a distance of about 2623 km (1630 miles), at a northern latitude of $66\frac{1}{2}°$. It marks the edge of an area where, for at least one day of the year, the sun never sets.

Erebus The only active volcano in Antarctica, 3794 metres (12,445 ft) high.

Eskimos A hardy people who live in the Arctic regions of North America and Asia, from Greenland across Canada and Alaska to Siberia.

ice-cap Thick layer of ice and snow that covers large areas in polar regions, such as Greenland and Antarctica. The antarctic ice-cap covers 13 million sq km (5 million square miles).

permafrost Permanently frozen soil, which in parts of the Arctic (Siberia) reaches depths of 500-600 metres (1600-1950 ft).

Polar Ice-Pack The floating masses of broken, piled-up ice that cover most of the Arctic Ocean.

subarctic Region south of the true Arctic that is almost as cold in the winter, but has warmer summers.

taiga Subarctic forests that thrive south of the *tree line,* consisting mainly of firs.

Transantarctic Mountains Chain of mountains crossing the entire continent of Antarctica, some of the ranges being completely buried by the ice-cap.

tundra Low, swampy, treeless plains lying mainly along the Arctic Circle in northern Europe, Siberia, and North America, covered mostly by mosses, lichens, and low shrubs. The ground is mainly *permafrost*, but a thin layer at the surface thaws in summer, when flowers such as poppies and bluebells bloom even in northern Greenland.

Tungus Members of a Mongoloid people who live mainly in Siberia, along the eastern branches of the Yenisey River. They depend chiefly on reindeer.

Yakuts A Mongoloid people of north-central Siberia. They number about 300,000 and breed reindeer and dogs.

Europe

Area: 10,531,000 sq. km (4,066,000 sq. m), including 25 per cent of the USSR (west of the Urals and Caspian Sea) and 3 per cent of Turkey; **Population:** 695,000,000, Europe is the most densely populated continent; **Independent countries:** 32, not including the USSR and Turkey; **Highest point:** Mt Elbruz, 5633 m (18,481 ft); **Largest lake:** Caspian Sea on Europe-Asia border, 438,695 sq. km (170,000 sq. m); **Longest rivers:** Volga, Danube.

ALBANIA Republic of Europe in the Balkans. **Area:** 28,5000 sq. km (11,000 sq. m). **Population:** 2,873,000. **Capital:** Tirana.

ANDORRA Tiny country of the Pyrenees: sovereignty divided between France and the Spanish Bishop of Urgel. **Area:** 453 sq. km (175 sq. m). **Population:** 32,700. **Capital:** Andorra la Vella.

COUNTRIES

AUSTRIA Republic of Central Europe.
Area: 83,850 sq. km (32,376 sq. m).
Population: 7,526,000.
Capital: Vienna.

BELGIUM Kingdom of Northern Europe.
Area: 30,500 km (11,800 sq. m).
Population: 9,940,000.
Capital: Brussels.

BULGARIA Republic of Europe in the
Balkans. **Area:** 111,000 sq. km (42,855
sq. m). **Population:** 8,990,000. **Capital:**
Sofia.

CYPRUS Island republic in the Mediterranean, at the moment divided after
Turkish forces occupied the North in
1974. A member of the Commonwealth.
Area: 9,250 sq. km (3600 sq. m).
Population: 665,000. **Capital:** Nicosia.
The Turkish occupied area, proclaimed as
the 'Turkish Cypriot Federated State' is
40% of the total.

CZECHOSLOVAKIA Republic of
Central Europe. **Area:** 128,000 sq. km
(50,000 sq. m). **Population:** 15,556,000.
Capital: Prague.

DENMARK Kingdom of Northern
Europe. **Area:** 45,000 sq. km (17,400 sq.
m). **Population:** 5,175,000. **Capital:**
Copenhagen.

FINLAND Republic of north-east Europe.
Area: 337,000 sq. km (130,000 sq. m).
Population: 4,829,000.
Capital: Helsinki.

FRANCE Republic of Western Europe.
Area: 547,000 sq. km (213,000 sq. m).
Population: 54,414,000. **Capital:** Paris.

GERMAN DEMOCRATIC REPUBLIC
Republic of Eastern Europe. **Area:**
108,000 sq. km (41,800 sq. m). **Population:** 16,748,000. **Capital:** East Berlin.

GERMANY, FEDERAL REPUBLIC OF
Republic of Western Europe. **Area:**
248,000 sq. km (96,000 sq. m). **Population:** 61,392,000. **Capital:** Bonn.

GIBRALTAR British colony at the entrance to the Mediterranean. **Area:** 6.5 sq.
km ($2\frac{1}{2}$ sq. m). **Population:** 31,000.
Capital: Gibraltar.

GREECE Republic of south-east Europe.
Area: 132,000 sq. km (51,000 sq. m).
Population: 9,665,000.
Capital: Athens.

HUNGARY Republic of Central Europe.
Area: 93,000 sq. km (36,000 sq. m).
Population: 10,850,000.
Capital: Budapest.

ICELAND Island republic of the Northern
Atlantic. **Area:** 103,000 sq. km (40,000
sq. m). **Population:** 234,000. **Capital:**
Reykjavik.

IRELAND, REPUBLIC OF Republic of
Northern Europe. **Area:** 70,200 sq. km
(27,000 sq. m). **Population:** 3,366,000.
Capital: Dublin.

ITALY Republic of Southern Europe.
Area: 301,000 sq. km (116,000 sq. m).
Population: 56,189,000. **Capital:**
Rome.

LIECHTENSTEIN A principality of
Western Europe. **Area:** 157 sq. km (62 sq.
m). **Population:** 26,000. **Capital:**
Vaduz.

LUXEMBOURG A Grand Duchy of
Western Europe. **Area:** 2600 sq. km
(1000 sq. m). **Population:** 360,000.
Capital: Luxembourg.

MALTA An island republic of the
Mediterranean, a member of the Commonwealth. **Area:** 316 sq. km (122 sq.

EUROPE

ARCTIC OCEAN

Reykjavik   ICELAND

NORWEGIAN SEA

Faroe Is

Shetland Is

Orkney Is

ATLANTIC OCEAN

Murmansk

Narvik

KJOLEN MOUNTAINS

FINLAND

L. Onega

Arkhangelsk

Trondheim

NORWAY

SWEDEN

Sundsvall

Tampere

L. Ladoga

Vyborg

Leningrad

Yaroslavl

Bergen

Oslo

Stavanger

Vänern

Vättern

Gothenburg

Stockholm

Moscow

BALTIC SEA

Riga

Dvina

Smolensk

Aberdeen

Glasgow

Edinburgh

Belfast

NORTH SEA

DENMARK

Copenhagen

Malmö

Kaliningrad

Minsk

IRELAND

UNITED KINGDOM

Dublin

Manchester

Liverpool

Sheffield

Cork

NETHERLANDS

Bremen

Hamburg

Elbe

Berlin

POLAND

Poznań

Warsaw

Łódź

UNION OF SOVIET SOCIALIST REPUBLIC

Kharkov

Cardiff

Birmingham

Amsterdam

Hannover

EAST GERMANY

Wrocław

Kiev

Dnepr

Thames

London

Plymouth

Southampton

Rotterdam

Antwerp

Cologne

Bonn

Brussels

BELGIUM

Frankfurt

Prague

Kraków

Dnepropetrovsk

Brest

Le Havre

LUXEMBOURG

Rhine

WEST GERMANY

CZECHOSLOVAKIA

Dnestr

Paris

Seine

Stuttgart

Strasbourg

Munich

Linz

Vienna

CARPATHIANS

Prut

Odessa

Nantes

Loire

Basel

Bern

Zürich

LIECH.

AUSTRIA

Budapest

FRANCE

SWITZERLAND

Geneva

ALPS

Lyon

HUNGARY

ROMANIA

BLACK SEA

Bordeaux

Rhône

Milan

Po

Turin

Trieste

Venice

Zagreb

Belgrade

Bucharest

Danube

a Coruña

Santander

Bilbao

Ebro

Toulouse

Marseille

Genoa

SAN MARINO

YUGOSLAVIA

Sofia

Oporto

Douro

Valladolid

PYRENEES

ANDORRA

Zaragoza

Barcelona

Nice

MONACO

Toulon

Corsica

Florence

ITALY

APENNINES

Dubrovnik

ALBANIA

BULGARIA

isbon

Tagus

Madrid

Ajaccio

Rome

Naples

Bari

Tirana

Thessaloniki

TURKEY

Istanbul

PORTUGAL

Guadiana

SPAIN

Valencia

Sardinia

Balearic Is

Taranto

Sevilla

Cádiz

Málaga

Cartagena

Cagliari

GREECE

Athens

GIBRALTAR

MEDITERRANEAN SEA

Palermo

Messina

Sicily

MALTA

Crete

EUROPE

0   100   200   300   400 miles

0   200   400   600 kilometres

■ Capital Cities

m). **Population:** 340,000. **Capital:** Valetta.

MONACO A principality on the Mediterranean coast, in south-east France. **Area:** 1.9 sq. km (467 acres). **Population:** 25,000. **Capital:** Monaco.

NETHERLANDS Kingdom of Western Europe. **Area:** 40,800 sq. km (15,800 sq. m). **Population:** 14,324,000. **Capital:** Amsterdam.

NORWAY Kingdom of Northern Europe. **Area:** 324,000 sq. km (125,000 sq. m). **Population:** 4,138,000. **Capital:** Oslo.

POLAND Republic of Eastern Europe. **Area:** 312,700 sq. km (120,700 sq. m). **Population:** 36,300,000. **Capital:** Warsaw.

PORTUGAL Republic of Western Europe. **Area:** 92,000 sq. km (35,500 sq, m). **Population:** 10,390,000. **Capital:** Lisbon.

ROMANIA Republic of Eastern Europe. **Area:** 237,500 sq. km (91,700 sq. m). **Population:** 22,653,000. **Capital:** Bucharest.

SAN MARINO Republic in the Apennines, Italy. **Area:** 61 sq. km (24 sq. m). **Population:** 21,000. **Capital:** San Marino.

SPAIN Kingdom of Western Europe. **Area:** 504,700 sq. km (195,000 sq. m). **Population:** 38,670,000. **Capital:** Madrid.

SWEDEN Kingdom of Northern Europe. **Area:** 450,000 sq. km (173,700 sq. m). **Population:** 8,340,000. **Capital:** Stockholm.

SWITZERLAND Republic of Western Europe. **Area:** 41,000 sq. km (16,000 sq. m). **Population:** 6,350,000. **Capital:** Berne.

UNITED KINGDOM Kingdom of north-west Europe. **Area:** 244,046 sq. km (94,232 sq. m). **Population:** 55,670,000. **Capital:** London. The United Kingdom consists of the following:

England Kingdom; **Area:** 130,363 sq. km (50,336 sq. m). **Population:** 46,221,000. **Capital:** London.

Scotland Kingdom; **Area:** 78,772 sq. km (30,416 sq. m). **Population:** 5,116,000. **Capital:** Edinburgh.

Wales Principality; **Area:** 20,763 sq. km (8017 sq. m). **Population:** 2,790,000. **Capital:** Cardiff.

Northern Ireland Area: 14,148 sq. km (5463 sq. m). **Population:** 1,543,000. **Capital:** Belfast.

Isle of Man Area: 588 sq. km (227 sq. m). **Population:** 62,000. **Capital:** Douglas.

Channel Islands Group of islands off north-west coast of France. **Area:** 195 sq. km (75 sq. m). **Population:** 131,000. The islands are: **Jersey. Area:** 116 sq. km (45 sq. m). **Population:** 73,000. **Capital:** St. Helier. **Guernsey. Area:** 63 sq. km ($24\frac{1}{2}$ sq. m). Dependencies: Alderney 8 sq. km (3 sq. m), Sark 5 sq. km (2 sq. m), Herm 130 hectares (320 acres), Brechou 30 hectares (74 acres), Jethou 18 hectares (44 acres), Lithou 15 hectares (38 acres). **Total population:** 131,000. **Capital:** St. Peter Port.

UNION OF SOVIET SOCIALIST REPUBLICS Usually abbreviated to USSR, this is the world's largest nation, and occupies territory stretching from Europe to Asia. **Total area:** 22,402,200 sq. km (8,650,000 sq. m). **Population:** 270,376,000. **Capital:** Moscow. **Republics of the USSR:** Armenia; Azerbaijan; Belorussia; Estonia; Georgia;

Kazakhstan; Kirgizia; Latvia; Lithuania; Moldavia; Russian SFSR; Tadzhikistan; Turkmenistan; Ukraine; and Uzbekistan.

VATICAN CITY State in north-west Rome, Italy, in which is located the government of the Roman Catholic Church, headed by the Pope. **Area:** 44 hectares (108.7 acres). **Population:** 1000.

YUGOSLAVIA A federal republic on the Adriatic. **Area:** 255,800 sq. km (98,800 sq. m). **Population:** 22,745,000. **Capital:** Belgrade.

A to Z of Europe

Alps Largest mountain system in Europe, extending about 1100 km (685 miles) from south-eastern France, through Switzerland, northern Italy, southern Germany, Austria, and Yugoslavia, as far east as Romania. See also *Mont Blanc.*

Apennines Low mountain range that covers two-thirds of Italy's area, extending from Gulf of Genoa in north to 'toe' of Italy.

Balkans Group of countries in south-eastern Europe occupying a peninsula projecting into the Mediterranean. Countries: Yugoslavia, Albania, Bulgaria, Greece, and Eastern Turkey.

Baltic Sea Separates Scandinavia from rest of northern Europe.

Basques A people living on the slopes of the Pyrenees, on the France-Spain border. They have retained their own language and customs.

Benelux Economic union formed in 1948 by Belgium, the Netherlands, and Luxembourg.

Berlin Wall Barricade built by East Germans in 1961 to seal off the east-west border and prevent people from Eastern Germany fleeing to West Berlin, which is part of Western Germany.

Black Sea Inland sea bounded by USSR, Romania, Bulgaria, and Turkey' area 450,000 sq km (180,000 sq miles). Con-

nected to Mediterranean by Bosporus, Sea of Marmara and Dardanelles.

Bosporus Strait, through Turkey, that connects Black Sea with Sea of Marmara; 30 km long. Istanbul lies on western side.

British Isles Island group off west coast of mainland Europe, consisting chiefly of Great Britain and Ireland.

Carpathians Mountain range extending 1450 km (800 miles) in semicircle between Romania and Czechoslovakia in central Europe.

Celts People of southern Germany in about 500 BC who spread out over western Europe, particularly the British Isles. Forerunners of Irish, Highland Scots, Welsh, and Cornish peoples.

Common Market See *European Economic Community.*

Crimea Russian peninsula extending into Black Sea area 25,000 sq km.

Danube River of central Europe, flowing 2775 km (1725 miles) from Germany to the Black Sea, at the Russian-Romanian border. An important trade route for ships and barges, it flows through three capital cities – Vienna, Budapest, and Belgrade.

Dardanelles Strait 60 km (37 miles), through Turkey, joining Mediterranean with Sea of Marmara and thence the Black Sea.

Don River in southern Russia, flowing 1960 km from a lake about 150 km (93 miles) south of Moscow to the Sea of Azov.

Eastern Europe Term used for Communist Europe, i.e. USSR and its satellites (Albania, Bulgaria, Czechoslovakia, East Germany, Hungary, Poland, Romania, and Yugoslavia).

Elbe Important waterway that flows over 1100 km (683 miles) from Czechoslovakia, through Germany, to the North Sea. The largest ships can travel 88 km ($54\frac{1}{2}$ miles), as far as Hamburg.

Elbruz Highest mountain in Europe, rising 5633 metres in Caucasus, USSR.

English Channel Channel between the North Sea and the Atlantic separating England and France. About 560 km (348

COUNTRIES

miles) long and 32 km (20 miles) wide at narrowest point.

Etna Active volcano rising 3390 metres (10,570 ft) on east coast of Sicily.

European Economic Community EEC Set up in 1957 to establish a common market without trade barriers and a closer union between European peoples. Members: Belgium, Denmark, France, Great Britain, Greece, Ireland (Republic), Italy, Luxembourg, the Netherlands, West Germany, Spain and Portugal.

fiord Long deep narrow inlet of the sea, found particularly along the coast of Norway.

Iberian Peninsula The peninsula occupied by Spain and Portugal.

languages About 60 languages are spoken in Europe, from three major groups *Germanic* in northern Europe, such as English, German, Danish, Dutch, and Swedish, *Romance,* in south and west, such as Spanish Italian, French, and Portuguese, *Baltic-Slavic,* in the east, such as Russian, Polish, and Bulgarian.

Lapland Region of northernmost Europe, mostly within Arctic Circle, extending across Norway, Sweden, Finland, and USSR. Inhabited by *Lapps,* a short, hardy people, many of whom live a nomadic life herding reindeer.

Low Countries Term for Belgium, Luxembourg, and the Netherlands.

Macedonia Mountainous region in central Balkans covering parts of Greece, Yugoslavia, and Bulgaria.

Mediterranean Sea Sea that borders the countries of south-western Europe, as well as Africa and Asia; area 3,000,000 sq km (969,100 sq miles).

North Sea Area of the North Atlantic between Britain and mainland Europe. Rich deposits of oil and natural gas began to be exploited in the 1970s.

Olympia Valley in southern Greece, which in ancient times was a religious and athletics centre. Ancient Olympic Games held there every four years. Many ancient ruins excavated since 1800s.

Pyrenees Mountain chain that forms border between France and Spain, about 435 km (270 miles) long. Tiny republic of Andorra lies on southern slopes.

Rhine River flowing over 1100 km (680 miles) from Switzerland, through Austria, Germany, and the Netherlands, to the North Sea. Europe's most important inland waterway, particularly in West Germany, it is connected by canal to the chief rivers near its course, including the Rhone, Danube, and Elbe. Major cities on its banks include Basel, Strasbourg, Cologne, Dusseldorf, and Rotterdam.

Rhone River that flows more than 800 km (500 miles) from Switzerland, through Lake Geneva and France, to the Mediterranean, important commercially.

Scandinavia Name for the peninsula in northern Europe consisting of Norway and Sweden. Historically and culturally, Denmark is regarded as a Scandinavian country, as also in some respects is Finland.

Seine Principal river of France, winding 765 km (475 miles) from the east, flowing through Paris, north-west to the English Channel.

Simplon Tunnel Important route through Swiss Alps, once longest tunnel 20 km (12.4 miles) in world.

Slavs People from Eastern Europe and Siberia who speak one of the Slavonic languages such as Russian, Polish, Czech, Slovak, Serbian, and Bulgarian.

Strait of Gibraltar Narrow channel between Gibraltar, on the southern tip of Spain, and Africa, joining the Mediterranean with the Atlantic; about 51 km ($31\frac{1}{2}$ miles) long and 13 km (8 miles) wide at narrowest.

Vesuvius Only active volcano on the European mainland, located near Naples, in Italy; frequent eruptions.

Vikings Bands of Scandinavian seafarers who raided and plundered many parts of Europe between the 700s and 1100s, including Germany, France, England, Ireland, Spain, and Italy. They also settled in Iceland and Greenland, and probably sailed down coast of North America.

Volga Europe's longest river, and Russia's most important waterway. Rises in Valdai Hills, 485 km (300 miles) south-east of Leningrad, and winds first east and then south, down to Caspian Sea.

Warsaw Pact Military alliance between Communist countries of Europe, first signed in 1955.

Oceania

Area: 8,510,000 sq. km (3,286,000 sq. m), of which Australia and New Zealand make up 93,5 per cent; **Population:** 24,500,000. **Independent countries:** 11; **Highest peak:** Mt Wilhelm (Papua New Guinea), 4694 m (15,400 ft); **Lowest point:** Lake Eyre (Australia), 12 m (39 ft) below sea level; **Longest rivers** (Australia): Murray, 2575 km (1600 m) and its tributary, the Darling, 2740 km (1702 m).

AUSTRALIA An independent member of the Commonwealth occupying the whole of the continent of Australia and outlying islands. **Area:** 7,686,800 sq. km (2,968,000 sq. m). **Population:** 15,066,000. **Capital:** Canberra. *States and territories:* Australian Capital Territory; New South Wales; Northern Territory; Queensland; South Australia; Tasmania; Victoria; and Western Australia.

COOK ISLANDS Self-governing territory of New Zealand in the South Pacific. **Area:** 234 sq. km (90 sq. m). **Population:** 18,000. **Capital:** Avarua.

FIJI An independent member of the Commonwealth in south-west Pacific. **Area:** 18,300 sq. km (7050 sq. m). **Population:** 656,000. **Capital:** Suva.

FRENCH POLYNESIA A French overseas department in the Eastern Pacific. **Area:** 4000 sq. km (1550 sq. m). **Population:** 166,000. **Capital:** Papeete.

GUAM A territory of the United States in the Marianas archipelago in the North Pacific. **Area:** 549 sq. km (212 sq. m). **Population:** 99,000. **Capital:** Agana.

KIRIBATI Island republic of the Central Pacific, a member of the Commonwealth. **Area:** 930 sq. km (360 sq. m). **Population:** 60,000. **Capital:** Tarawa.

NAURU An island republic in the Western Pacific, with special relations with the Commonwealth. **Area:** 21 sq. km (8 sq. m). **Population:** 7000. **Capital:** Nauru.

NEW ZEALAND An independent member of the Commonwealth in the south-west Pacific. **Area:** 268,000 sq. km (103,700 sq. m). **Population:** 3,400,000. **Capital:** Wellington.

NIUE A self-governing territory of New Zealand in the Cook Islands, South Pacific. **Area:** 260 sq. km (100 sq. m). **Population:** 4000. **Capital:** Alofi.

NORFOLK ISLAND An Australian territory in the south-west Pacific. **Area:** 36 sq. km (14 sq. m). **Population:** 2000. **Capital:** Kingstown.

PACIFIC ISLANDS TRUST TERRITORY Group of islands, including the Marianas, Caroline and Marshall Island, governed by the United States. **Area:** 1780 sq. km (687 sq. m). **Population:** 149,000. **Capital:** Saipan.

PAPUA NEW GUINEA An independent state within the Commonwealth in the south-west Pacific. **Area:** 461,700 sq. km (178,200 sq. m). **Population:** 3,221,000. **Capital:** Port Moresby.

PITCAIRN ISLAND British colony in the South Pacific. **Area:** 5 sq. km (2 sq. m). **Population:** 63. **Capital:** Adamstown.

SAMOA, AMERICAN Group of eight islands in the South Pacific, governed by the United States. **Area:** 197 sq. km (76 sq. m). **Population:** 35,000. **Capital:** Pago Pago.

Equator

Kiribati

NAURU

Arafura Sea

PAPUA NEW GUINEA ▲Mt Wilhelm

Bismarck Archipelago

Solomon Is

Tuvalu Is

Port Moresby ■

INDIAN OCEAN

Darwin ●

Coral Sea

New Hebrides (UK & Fr)

FIJI

Suva

Roebourne ●

Northern Territory

●Townsville

New Caledonia (Fr)

●Noumea

Gt Sandy Desert

A U S T R A L I A

●Cloncurry

Alice Springs ●

Queensland

G R E A T   D I V I D I N G   R A N G E

Gibson Desert

Toowoomba ● ●Brisbane

Western Australia

Kalgoorlie ●

Gt Victoria Desert

South Australia

L. Eyre

Tasman Sea

Perth ●

Nullarbor Plain

Darling

New South Wales

●Newcastle
●Sydney
●Wollongong

● Albany

Great Australian Bight

Adelaide ●

Murray

■Canberra

NEW ZEALAND

Nor

Auckland ●
Hamilton ●
Rotorua ●
Na

OCEANIA

Victoria

Ballarat ●
Geelong ●   ●Melbourne

Mt Kosciusko

Nelson ● ■Welling

0	400	800	1200 miles
0	400	800	1200 1600 kilometers

South Is
Mt Cook ▲

Christchurch ●

■ Capital Cities

●Launceston

Tasmania

●Hobart

Invercargill ● ●Dunedin

Stewart Is

SAMOA, WESTERN An independent state, a member of the Commonwealth, in the Pacific. **Area:** 2900 sq. km (1090 sq. m). **Population:** 164,000. **Capital:** Apia.

SOLOMON ISLANDS An independent state, a member of the Commonwealth, in the south-west Pacific. **Area:** 28,500 sq. km (11,000 sq. m). **Population:** 242,000. **Capital:** Honiara.

TONGA Island kingdom in the South Pacific within the Commonwealth. **Area:** 700 sq. km (270 sq. m). **Population:** 100,000. **Capital:** Nuku'alofa.

TUVALU An independent member of the Commonwealth, a group of islands in the South Pacific. **Area:** 8 sq. km (3 sq. m). **Population:** 7,400. **Capital:** Fongafale or Funafuti.

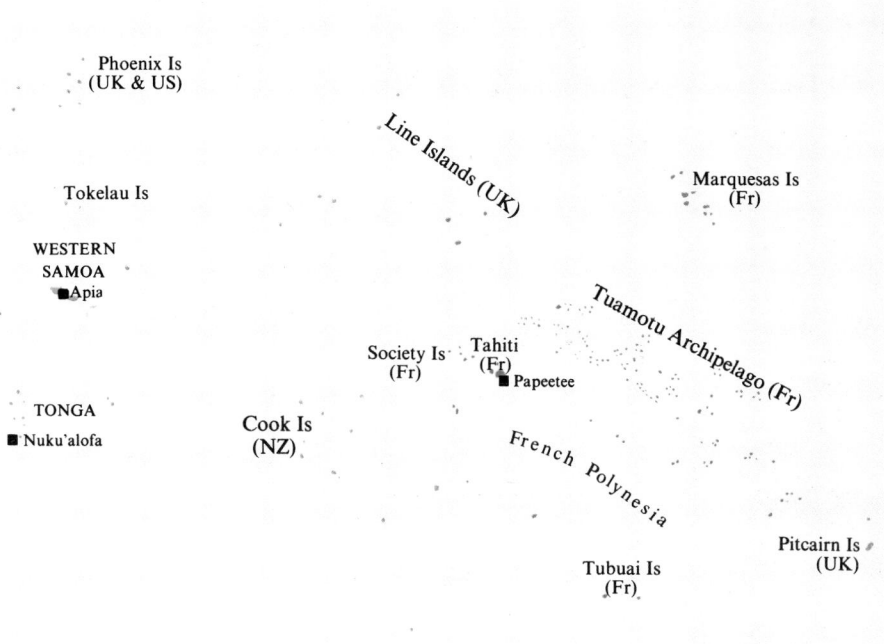

Phoenix Is
(UK & US)

Line Islands (UK)

Marquesas Is
(Fr)

Tokelau Is

WESTERN
SAMOA
■Apia

Tuamotu Archipelago (Fr)

Society Is   Tahiti
(Fr)   (Fr)
■ Papeetee

TONGA
■ Nuku'alofa

Cook Is
(NZ)

French Polynesia

Pitcairn Is
(UK)

Tubuai Is
(Fr)

Kermadec Is
(NZ)

PACIFIC OCEAN

Chatham Is
(NZ)

VANUATU Island republic in the southwest Pacific, a member of the Commonwealth. **Area:** 14,800 sq. km (5700 sq. m). **Population:** 113,000. **Capital:** Port Vila.

WALLIS AND FUTUNA ISLANDS A French overseas territory in the southwest Pacific. **Area:** 200 sq. km (77 sq. m). **Population:** 9000. **Capital:** Mata-Uta.

A to Z of Oceania

Aborigines The original peoples of Australia.

atoll Ring of coral, common in the Pacific, enclosing shallow pool or lagoon. See *coral reef*.

Bismarck Archipelago Group of volcanic islands east of New Guinea, including New Britain (largest), New Ireland, Admiralty Islands. Part of Papua New Guinea.

coral reef Limestone ridge under water formed from the skeletons of millions of tiny sea animals. Some build up above the water to form coral islands. Many Pacific islands were formed in this way.

Darling Australia's longest river (2740 km/1700 miles), draining a vast area in Queensland and New South Wales, before joining the Murray.

Easter Island Solitary island in South Pacific, 3850 km (2390 miles) from South America; famous for stone statues erected hundreds of years ago.

French Polynesia French territory in the central South Pacific, including Society Islands (Tahiti, etc.) and the Marquesas.

Friendly Islands Another name for the Tonga group.

Great Artesian Basin Large area chiefly in southern Queensland, where water for farming comes from over 2000 artesian wells (holes bored through layers of rock to reach water trapped in porous layers of stone, the water then rising to the surface under its own pressure).

Great Barrier Reef Largest *coral reef* in the world; stretches along Queensland's eastern coast and north into Torres Strait; 2000 km (1250 miles) long, 70 km (44 miles) at widest point.

Great Dividing Range Low system of mountains stretching along the eastern coast of Australia and through most of Victoria in the south; also called the Eastern Highlands.

Hawaiian Islands Group of Polynesian islands (a state of the United States – Hawaii) in the North Pacific, about 3800 km (2375 miles) west of North America.

highest elevation Djaya Peak (5030 metres/16,495 ft), in New Guinea (Indonesia).

lowest point Lake Ayre, in South Australia, 12 metres (39 ft) below sea level.

Maoris Early inhabitants of New Zealand, a Polynesian people.

Melanesia South-west area of the Pacific that is regarded as one of the three main divisions of Oceania; includes New

The kiwi looks for food after dark

Young koalas ride on their mother's back after leaving the pouch.

Guinea, Fiji, Bismarck Archipelago, and the Solomon Islands. The Melanesians are tall and stocky, with frizzy hair and dark skins. Melanesia means 'black islands'.

Micronesia Area of the Pacific north of Melanesia and regarded as one of the three main divisions of Oceania. Contains about 2500 islands, mostly low coral atolls. Micronesians resemble the Polynesians, but have darker skins. Micronesia means 'little islands'.

Murray Australia's second-longest river, rising in the Snowy Mountains and flowing 2580 km (1600 miles) to its estuary near Adelaide; forms the boundary between New South Wales and Victoria.

New Guinea Apart from Australia and Greenland, the largest island in the world (794,000 sq km/317,000 sq. miles). Western part, West Irian, belongs to Indonesia; eastern part independent as Papua New Guinea.

A kangaroo with its young, called a joey, in its pouch.

Nullabor Plain Dry, featureless plateau that runs across the southern coast of Western Australia and part of South Australia.

peoples Most of the people of Australia and New Zealand are of European descent. Native peoples of Australasia and Oceania include the Aborigines of Australia, the Maoris of New Zealand, and the Melanesians, Micronesians, and Polynesians of the Pacific islands.

Polynesia Vast area of the central Pacific, taking in most of the far-flung islands, and including New Zealand and the Hawaiian Islands. Regarded as one of the three main divisions of Oceania. Polynesians are tall, powerful people, the lightest skinned of the Pacific islanders.

Sutherlands Falls Fifth highest in the world, dropping 580 metres (1902 ft) in three leaps, in the Southern Alps of New Zealand.

The United Nations

The United Nations (UN) is an international organization that works for world peace and security and for the betterment of mankind. More than 140 independent nations belong to the UN. Member countries send representatives to the UN headquarters in New York City. There are six major organs of the UN, which carry on the work of the organization at the headquarters. There are also a number of specialized agencies, such as the Food and Agricultural Organization, the World Health Organization, and the International Monetary Fund. These are self-governing international organizations that have a special relationship with the UN, and have headquarters in various parts of the world.

Principal Organs of the UN

General Assembly consists of all members, each having one vote. Most of work done in committees: (1) Political Security, (2) Economic and Financial, (3) Social, Humanitarian, and Cultural, (4) Trust and Non-Self-Governing Territories, (5) Administrative and Budgetary, (6) Legal.

Security Council consists of 15 members each with 1 vote. There are 5 permanent members – China, France, UK, USA, and USSR – the others being elected for two-year terms. Main object: maintenance of peace and security.

Economic and Social Council is responsible under General Assembly for carrying out functions of the UN with regard to international economic, social, cultural, educational, health, and related matters.

Trusteeship Council administers Trust Territories.

International Court of Justice composed of 15 judges (all different nationalities)

COUNTRIES

elected by UN. Meets at The Hague.

The Secretariat is composed of the Secretary-General, who is chief administrative officer of the UN and is appointed by the General Assembly, and an international staff appointed by him.

The symbol of the United Nations, a map of the world inside olive branches, for peace.

'ARCHIES AND 'OCRACIES	
Term	**Rule by . . .**
anarchy	harmony, without law
aristocracy	a privileged order
autocracy	one person
bureaucracy	officials
democracy	the people
ergatocracy	the workers
gynocracy	women
matriarchy	female head
monarchy	hereditary head of state
ochlocracy	the mob
oligarchy	small exclusive class
patriarchy	male head of family
plutocracy	the wealthy

United Nations: Member Countries

Country	Joined*	Country	Joined*	Country	Joined*
Afghanistan	1946	Canada	1945	France	1945
Albania	1955	Cape Verde	1975	Gabon	1960
Algeria	1962	Central African		Gambia	1965
Angola	1976	Republic	1960	Germany, East	1973
Antigua and Barbuda	1981	Chad	1960	Germany, West	1973
Argentina	1945	Chile	1945	Ghana	1957
Australia	1945	China†	1945	Greece	1945
Austria	1955	Colombia	1945	Grenada	1974
Bahamas	1973	Comoros	1975	Guatemala	1945
Bahrain	1971	Congo	1960	Guinea	1958
Bangladesh	1974	Costa Rica	1945	Guinea-Bissau	1974
Barbados	1966	Cuba	1945	Guyana	1966
Belgium	1945	Cyprus	1960	Haiti	1945
Belize	1981	Czechoslovakia	1945	Honduras	1945
Benin	1969	Denmark	1945	Hungary	1955
Bhutan	1971	Djibouti	1977	Iceland	1946
Bolivia	1945	Dominica	1978	India	1945
Botswana	1966	Dominican Republic	1945	Indonesia	1950
Brazil	1945	Ecuador	1945	Iran	1945
Bulgaria	1955	Egypt	1945	Iraq	1945
Burkina Faso	1960	El Salvador	1945	Ireland, Rep. of	1955
Burma	1948	Equatorial Guinea	1968	Israel	1949
Burundi	1962	Ethiopia	1945	Italy	1955
Byelorussian SSR	1945	Fiji	1970	Ivory Coast	1960
Cameroon	1960	Finland	1955	Jamaica	1962

The Commonwealth of Nations

This is a voluntary association of independent states. The Head of the Commonwealth is HM Queen Elizabeth II. Present members of the Commonwealth (with date of independence in brackets) are: Antigua & Barbuda (1981), Australia (1901), Bahamas (1973), Bangladesh: (from Pakistan, 1971), Barbados (1966), Belize (1981), Botswana (1966), Brunei (1984), Canada (1931), Cyprus (1960), Dominica (1978), Fiji (1970), The Gambia (1965), Ghana (1957), Great Britain, Grenada (1974), Guyana (1966), India (1947), Jamaica (1962), Kenya (1963), Kiribati (1979), Lesotho (1966), Malawi (1964), Malaysia (1957), Maldives (1965), Malta (1964), Mauritius (1968), Nauru (1968), New Zealand (1907), Nigeria (1960), Papua New Guinea (1975), St Kitts-Nevis (1983), St Lucia (1979), St Vincent (1979), Seychelles (1976), Sierra Leone (1961), Singapore (1965), Solomon Islands (1978), Sri Lanka (1948), Swaziland (1968), Tanzania (1961), Tonga (1970), Trinidad & Tobago (1962), Tuvalu (1978), Uganda (1962), Vanuatu (1980), Western Samoa (1962), Zambia (1964), Zimbabwe (1980).

Country	Joined*	Country	Joined*	Country	Joined*
Japan	1956	Nigeria	1960	Sri Lanka	1955
Jordan	1955	Norway	1945	Sudan	1956
Kampuchea	1955	Oman	1971	Surinam	1975
Kenya	1963	Pakistan	1947	Swaziland	1968
Kuwait	1963	Panama	1945	Sweden	1946
Laos	1955	Papua New Guinea	1975	Syria	1945
Lebanon	1945	Paraguay	1945	Tanzania	1961
Lesotho	1966	Peru	1945	Thailand	1946
Liberia	1945	Philippines	1945	Togo	1960
Libya	1955	Poland	1945	Trinidad & Tobago	1962
Luxembourg	1945	Portugal	1955	Tunisia	1956
Madagascar	1960	Qatar	1971	Turkey	1945
Malawi	1964	Romania	1955	Uganda	1962
Malaysia	1957	Rwanda	1962	Ukrainian SSR	1945
Maldives, Rep. of	1965	St Lucia	1979	USSR	1945
Mali	1960	St Vincent &		United Arab Emirates	1971
Malta	1964	the Grenadines	1980	United Kingdom	1945
Mauritania	1961	Samoa	1976	United States	1945
Mauritius	1968	São Tomé & Principe	1975	Uruguay	1945
Mexico	1945	Saudi Arabia	1945	Vanuatu	1981
Mongolian PR	1961	Senegal	1960	Venezuela	1945
Morocco	1956	Seychelles	1976	Vietnam	1976
Mozambique	1975	Sierra Leone	1961	Yemen Arab Republic	1947
Nepal	1955	Singapore	1965	Yemen PDR	1967
Netherlands	1945	Solomon Islands	1978	Yugoslavia	1945
New Zealand	1945	Somali Republic	1960	Zaire	1960
Nicaragua	1945	South Africa	1945	Zambia	1964
Niger	1960	Spain	1955	Zimbabwe	1980

COUNTRIES

Afghanistan

Albanie

Algérie

Argentine

Australie

Autriche

Belgique

Bolivie

Brésil

Bulgarie

Birmanie

Canada

Sri Lanka

Chili

Chine

Colombie

Cuba

Chypre

Tchécoslovaquie

Danemark

Équateur

Éthiopie

Finlande

France

R.D.A.

R.F.A.

Ghana

Grèce

Hongrie

Islande

Inde

Indonésie

Iran

Irak

Irlande

Israël

Italie

Jamaïque

Japon

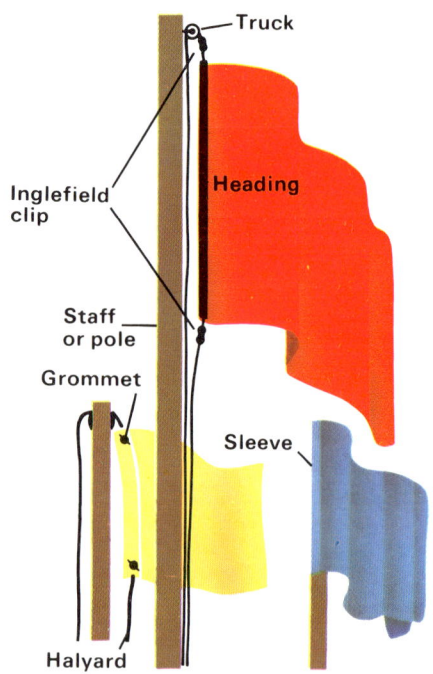

The names of the different parts of a flag.

Flag Terms

badge Any emblem added to a flag and which can generally be used separately.
banner Any kind of flag, especially one with a complex design or coat-of-arms, or a flag hanging from a crossbar.
bunting A strong cloth used for flags; also a string of small decorative flags in that material.
burgee The flag of a yacht club, generally triangular or swallow-tailed.
canton A rectangular area in the top corner of a flag near the staff.
charge A symbol or other object on a flag, not normally used separately.
colour or colours The flag of a military unit, such as a regiment.
courtesy flag The merchant flag of the host country flown by a visiting foreign ship.
dexter The right-hand side of a flag from the bearer's viewpoint, or the left side as seen by the viewer.

dipping Briefly lowering a flag as an expression of courtesy.

dress ship To decorate a ship with flags on a special occasion.

emblem A heraldic device or other distinguishing symbol representing a person, country or organization.

ensign A flag indicating nationality flown by ships at the stern or by government services on land, such as the air force.

field The background colour of a flag or heraldic shield.

fly Part of a flag farthest away from the staff and usually occupying that half of its area.

hoist To raise a flag; also part of a flag nearest the staff, usually occupying that half of its area.

house flag The flag of a commercial organization.

jack A small flag of nationality flown at the prow of a ship.

Jolly Roger A black flag with white emblems associated with pirates.

merchant flag The flag of nationality flown by merchant ships; also known as the civil ensign.

national flag In this book, the flag used by private citizens of a country.

naval ensign The flag of nationality flown from the stern of a warship.

obverse The side of a flag seen when the staff is on the viewer's left.

pennant Generally a small tapering flag used as a rank flag on ships or as a wall souvenir or decoration.

reverse The side of a flag seen when the staff is on the viewer's right.

sinister The left-hand side of a flag from the bearer's viewpoint, or the right side as seen by the viewer.

state ensign The government flag flown on non-military vessels, such as those used by fisheries or customs.

state flag The government flag flown on land on state property.

streamer A very long narrow flag, or a ribbon.

tricolour A flag with three colours, generally arranged in stripes.

Jordanie

Corée du Nord

Corée du Sud

Liban

Libéria

Malaysia

Malte

Mexique

Maroc

Pays-Bas

Nouvelle-Zélande

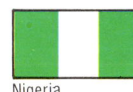
Nigeria

Norvège

Pakistan

Paraguay

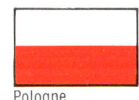
Pérou

Philippines

Pologne

Portugal

Roumanie

Arabie Saoudite

Sierra Léone

Singapour

Afrique du Sud

Espagne

Suède

Suisse

Thaïlande

Trinidad et Tobago

Tunisie

Turquie

Royaume-Uni

États-Unis

Uruguay

U.R.S.S.

Cité du Vatican

Vénézuela

Yougoslavie

Zaïre

Zero Fever

In the early 1920's a catastrophic inflation swept through Germany. The rise in prices began immediately after the First World War. By 1921, prices stood some 14 times as high as they were in 1913, the year before the war. Then, inflation suddenly took off at a gallop. A year later, prices rose to 1500 times their 1913 level and continued upwards without any sign of slowing down. Eleven months later they had soared to a staggering 1,422,900,000 times their pre-war level. Outbreaks of a strange new disease called 'zero fever' began to be reported in the newspapers. People were being driven to despair trying to calculate prices which had risen to billions and trillions of marks. They collapsed with nervous exhaustion under the strain of handling so many zeros.

This rate of inflation upset all the conventions of commercial life. Banks refused to make loans that would only be paid back a few weeks later in money worth a tiny fraction of its original value. People who had lent money frantically tried to dodge those owing them money lest they be forced to accept near worthless pieces of paper.

A customer in one restaurant indicated that he wished to buy a dollar's worth of supper rather than pay with German marks. A substantial meal was brought to him, but before he could leave a second supper began to arrive with the explanation that the value of the mark had declined yet again while he was eating the first.

Above: This one billion mark note was issued in Cologne in 1928. It would have bought less than a single German mark does today.

The Great Crash

On 29 October, 1929, still known as 'Black Tuesday', prices on the New York Stock Exchange plummeted through the floor. A record 16 million shares were traded during a single hectic day as thousands of shareholders desperately tried to cash in their holdings. Stock markets the world over were dragged down in the wake of New York. The world slipped into the Great Depression of the 1930s. Over the next few years banks failed, production ground down and the jobless figures were staggering. Not until the Second World War, which broke out in 1939, did the economy begin to boom again.

Coins with animals in their design make an interesting subject for a collection. Many coins, such as those below, carry a picture of the animal which is regarded as a national emblem, such as the kiwi of New Zealand. Ireland, an agricultural nation, has had a hen and chick a pig and a bull on its coins. Horses, antelope, and mythical and heraldic beasts are all found on coins.

● The heaviest coin of all time was the 10 daler piece. This coin was minted in Sweden in the mid-seventeenth century, and each 20 kilogram (44 lb) slab could purchase two cows.

● The Nepalese jawa of 1740 is the smallest known coin ever to have been minted. This sliver of silver weighed a mere 0.014 gram.

The World's Currencies

Country	Currency	Country	Currency
Afghanistan	afghani (100 puls)	Guinea	syli
Albania	lek (100 qindarka)	Guyana	dollar (100 cents)
Algeria	dinar (100 centimes)	Haiti	gourde (100 centimes)
Andorra	franc (Fr) & peseta (SP)	Honduras	lempira (100 centavos)
Angola	kwanza (100 lweis)	Hungary	forint (100 fillér)
Antigua	dollar (100 cents)	Iceland	krona (100 aurar)
Argentina	peso (100 centavos)	India	rupee (100 paise)
Australia	dollar (100 cents)	Indonesia	rupiah (100 sen)
Austria	schilling (100 groschen)	Iran	rial (100 dinars)
Bahamas	dollar (100 cents)	Iraq	dinar (1000 fils)
Bahrain	dinar (1000 fils)	Ireland Rep. of	pound (100 pence)
Bangladesh	taka (100 paise)	Israel	shekel (100 agorot)
Barbados	dollar (100 cents)	Italy	lira
Belgium	franc (100 centimes)	Ivory Coast	franc
Belize	dollar (100 cents)	Jamaica	dollar (100 cents)
Benin	franc	Japan	yen
Bermuda	dollar (100 cents)	Jordan	dinar (1000 fils)
Bhutan	ngultrum	Kampuchea	riel (100 sen)
Bolivia	peso (100 centavos)	Kenya	shilling (100 cents)
Botswana	pula (100 thebe)	Korea, North	won (100 jun)
Brazil	cruzeiro (100 centavos)	Korea, South	won (100 jun)
Brunei	dollar (100 sen)	Kuwait	dinar (1000 fils)
Bulgaria	lev (100 stotinki)		
Burkina Faso	franc		
Burma	kyat (100 pyas)		
Burundi	franc		
Cameroon	franc		
Canada	dollar (100 cents)		
Central African Republic	franc		
Chad	franc		
Chile	new peso (100 old escudos)		
China: People's Republic	yuan (10 chiao; 100 fen)		
Colombia	peso (100 centavos)		
Congo	franc		
Costa Rica	colón (100 centimos)		
Cuba	peso (100 centavos)		
Cyprus	pound (1000 mils)		
Czechoslovakia	koruna (100 haleru)		
Denmark	krone (100 öre)		
Dominica	dollar (100 cents)		
Dominican Republic	peso (100 centavos)		
Ecuador	sucre (100 centavos)		
Egypt	pound (100 piastres) 1000 millièmes)		
Equatorial Guinea	ekuele		
Ethiopia	dollar (100 cents)		
Fiji	dollar (100 cents)		
Finland	markka (100 penniä)		
France	franc (100 centimes)		
Gabon	franc		
Gambia	dalasi (100 bututs)		
Germany, East	mark (100 pfennigs)		
Germany, West	mark (100 pfennigs)		
Ghana	cedi (100 pesewas)		
Gibraltar	pound (100 pence)		
Greece	drachma (100 lepta)		
Grenada	dollar (100 cents)		
Guatemala	quetzal (100 centavos)		

Country	Currency	Country	Currency
Laos	kip (100 ats)	**New Zealand**	dollar (100 cents)
Lebanon	pound (100 piastres)	**Nicaragua**	córdoba (100 centavos)
Lesotho	loti	**Niger**	franc
Liberia	dollar (100 cents)	**Nigeria**	naira (100 kobo)
Libya	dinar (1000 dirhams)	**Norway**	krone (100 öre)
Liechtenstein	franc (Swiss)	**Oman**	rial (1000 baiza)
Luxembourg	franc (100 centimes)	**Pakistan**	rupee (100 paisas)
Macau (Port.)	pataca (100 avos)	**Panama**	balboa (100 cents)
Madagascar	franc	**Paraguay**	guarani (100 céntimos)
Malawi	kwacha (100 tambala)	**Peru**	ita (100 centavos)
Malaysia	dollar (100 cents)	**Philippines**	peso (100 centavos)
Maldives, Rep of	rupee (100 laris)	**Poland**	zloty (100 groszy)
Mali	franc	**Portugal**	escudo (100 centavos)
Malta	pound (100 cents; 1000 mils)	**Qatar**	riyal (100 dirhams)
		Romania	leu (100 bani)
Mauritania	ouguiya (5 khoums)	**Rwanda**	franc
Mauritius	rupee (100 cents)	**St Kitts-Nevis**	dollar (100 cents)
Mexico	peso (100 centavos)	**St Lucia**	dollar (100 cents)
Monaco	franc (French)	**St Vincent**	dollar (100 cents)
Mongolian People's		**El Salvador**	colön (100 centavos)
Republic	tugrik (100 möngö)	**San Marino**	lira (Italian)
Morocco	dirham (100 centimes)	**Saudi Arabia**	riyal (20 qursh)
Nauru	dollar (100 cents)	**Senegal**	franc
Nepal	rupee (100 pice)	**Sierra Leone**	leone (100 cents)
Netherlands	guilder (100 cents)	**Singapore**	dollar (100 cents)
		Somali Republic	shilling (100 cents)
		South Africa	rand (100 cents)
		South-West Africa	rand (100 cents) (SA)
		Spain	peseta (100 céntimos)
		Sri Lanka	rupee (100 cents)
		Sudan	pound (100 piastres; 1000 milliemes)
		Surinam	guilder (100 cents)
		Swaziland	lilangeni (pl. emalangeni) (100 cents)
		Sweden	krona (100 ore)
		Switzerland	franc (100 centimes)
		Syria	pound (100 piastres)
		Taiwan	dollar (100 cents)
		Tanzania	shilling (100 cents)
		Thailand	baht (100 satangs)
		Togo	franc
		Tonga	pa'anga (100 senite)
		Trinidad & Tobago	dollar (100 cents)
		Tunisia	dinar (1000 millimes)
		Turkey	lira (100 kurus)
		Uganda	shilling (100 cents)
		United Arab Emirates	dirham (100 fils)
		United Kingdom	pound (100 pence)
		United States	dollar (100 cents)
		Uruguay	peso (100 centésimos)
		USSR	rouble (100 copecks)
		Vatican City State	lira
		Venezuela	bolivar (100 céntimos)
		Vietnam	dong (100 xu)
		Western Samoa	tala (100 sene)
		Yemen Arab Republic	riyal (40 bogaches)
		Yemen PDR	dinar (1000 fils)
		Yugoslavia	dinar (100 paras)
		Zaire	zaire (100 makuta [sing. likuta]; 1000 sengi)
		Zimbabwe	dollar (100 cents)

TALKING OF COINS

The 'obverse' or head side of a coin.

The edge of some coins is 'grained'. This was originally done to prevent clipping of coins.

The legend is the words or, figure on the coin.

The 'reverse' or tails side of the coin.

Left: Nowadays coins and notes like these are the small change of the world of money. Nearly 90 percent of the money supply is actually in bank deposits. Most currencies have a main unit which is often divided into 100 smaller units. The smaller units are often called 'cents' (or centavos, centimos, centimes, or centesimos) from 'centum' the Latin for one hundred.

British Knighthood

The main British orders of knighthood are: The Order of the Garter (founded 1394); the Order of the Thistle (1687); the Order of the Bath (1725); the Order of St. Patrick (1788); the Order of St. Michael and St. George (1818); the Order of the Star of India (1861); and the Royal Victorian Order (1896). In 1917, the Order of the British Empire was started. This Order has Knights Grand Cross, Knights Commander, Commanders, Officers and Members.

Women who are given a rank similar to knighthood are called Dames.

International Organizations

COMECON Council for Mutual Economic Assistance. Established 1949. Members are Bulgaria, Czechoslovakia, East Germany, Hungary, Poland, Romania, USSR, Yugoslavia (associate member). Cuba, Mongolia and Vietnam are non-European members.

EEC European Economic Community or Common Market. Established 1957. Members are Belgium, Denmark, France, Greece, Ireland, Italy, Luxembourg, Netherlands, United Kingdom, West Germany, Spain and Portugal.

EFTA European Free Trade Area. Established 1961. Members are Austria, Iceland, Norway, Portugal, Sweden, Switzerland, Finland (associate).

NATO North Atlantic Treaty Organization. Belgium, Canada, Denmark, France, West Germany, Greece, Iceland, Italy, Luxembourg, Netherlands, Norway, Portugal, Turkey, United Kingdom, United States.

Warsaw Pact Albania, Bulgaria, Czechoslovakia, East Germany, Hungary, Poland, Romania, USSR.

Monarchs of the World

Almost all countries of the world today have a parliamentary system – that is, a council of people elected to rule.

By far the majority of nations have at their head a President, in most cases elected every few years. Those which still have hereditary monarchs are:

Country	Ruler	Came to Throne
Belgium	King Baudouin I	1951
Bhutan	King Jigme Singye Wangchuk	1972
Denmark	Queen Margrethe II	1972
Great Britain	Queen Elizabeth II	1952
Japan	Emperor Hirohito	1926
Jordan	King Hussein	1952
Liechtenstein	Prince Franz Joseph II	1938
Luxembourg	Grand Duke Jean	1964
Monaco	Prince Ranier III	1949
Morocco	King Hassan II	1961
Nepal	King Mahendra Bir Bikram Shah Deva	1955
Netherlands	Queen Beatrix	1980
Norway	King Olav V	1957
Saudi Arabia	King Faisal bin Abdul Aziz	1964
Spain	King Juan Carlos I	1975
Sweden	King Carl XVI Gustav	1973
Thailand	King Bhumibol Adulaydej	1946

Parliaments by Other Names

Name	Country
Althing	Iceland
Bundesrat	Austria & Germany
Bundestag	West Germany
Congress	USA
Cortes	Spain
Dail	Ireland
Folketing	Denmark
Knesset	Israel
Nationalrat	Austria & Switzerland
Riksdag	Sweden
Sobranie	Bulgaria
Soviet	USSR
Ständerat	Switzerland
States-General	Netherlands
Storting	Norway

**Medal of Honor
(USA)**

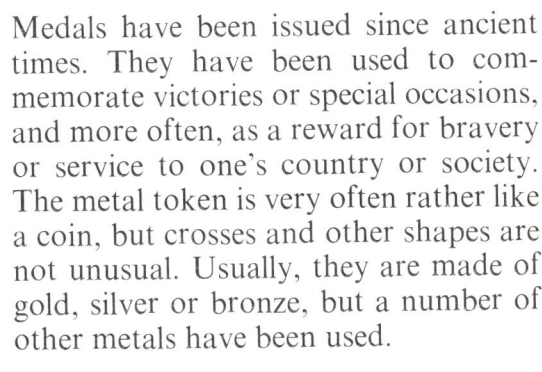

**Victoria Cross
(Great Britain)**

**Decoration Militaire
(Belgium)**

Medals and Decorations

Medals have been issued since ancient times. They have been used to commemorate victories or special occasions, and more often, as a reward for bravery or service to one's country or society. The metal token is very often rather like a coin, but crosses and other shapes are not unusual. Usually, they are made of gold, silver or bronze, but a number of other metals have been used.

**Iron Cross
(Germany)**

**Croix de Guerre
(France)**

**Service Medal
with 'Korea' clasp
(United Nations)**

**Order of Victory
(USSR)**

**Purple heart
(USA)**

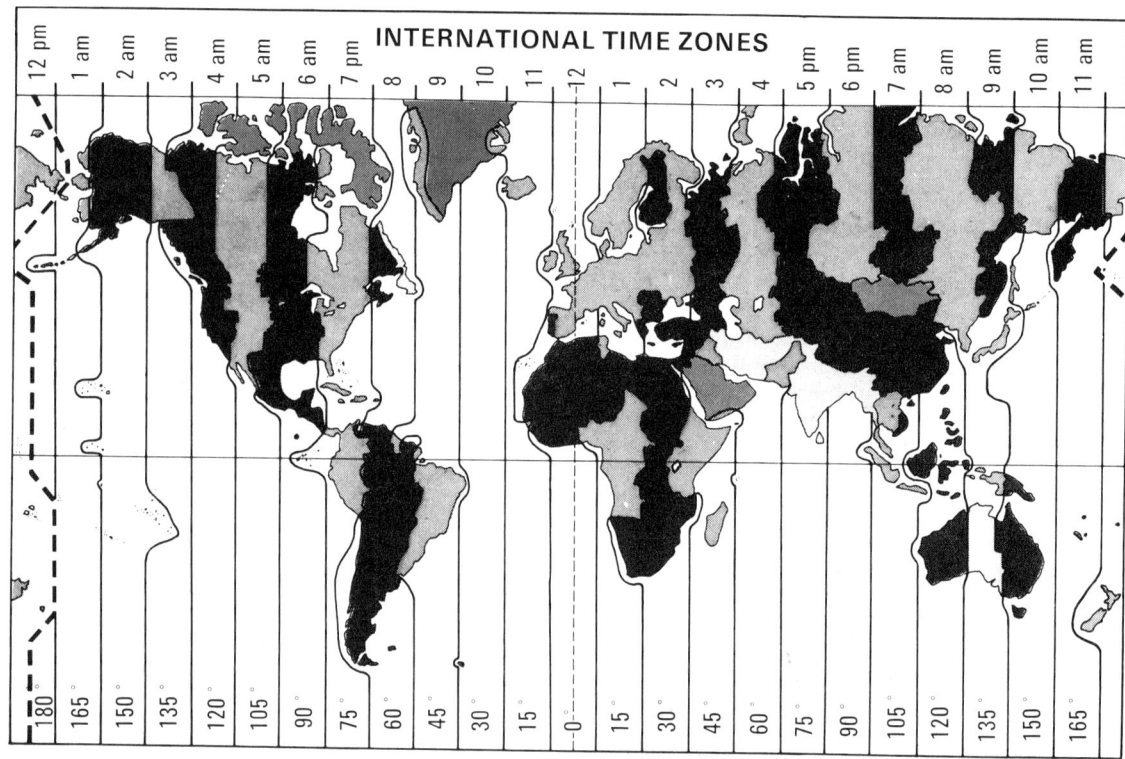

INTERNATIONAL TIME ZONES

Calendars

Gregorian In 1582, Pope Gregory XIII corrected the Julian calendar. Augustus had previously taken a day from February and added it to August; and now Pope Gregory ordered 10 days to be dropped from October 1582. To maintain the correction for the future, he decreed that in century years that could not be divided by 400, February would not have an extra day.

Hebrew Calendar based on the Moon, usually with 12 months. The months are alternately 30 and 29 days long. But there are seven occasions during every 19-year period when an extra 29-day month is added to the year, and one 29-day month is given an extra day.

Islamic Calendar based on a 354-day year. This means that the Islamic New Year moves backwards through the seasons. The year is based on the Moon, with 12 months of 30 and 29 days

The time-zone chart above shows what time is in force at different zones of the world, based on 12 noon at Greenwich.

alternately. There are 30-year cycles during which 19 years have 354 days each, and the remaining 11 have an extra day each.

Roman A calendar based on a year of 10 months (304 days). Every other year a short month (22/23 days) was added. The 10 months were Martius, Aprilis, Maius, Junius, Quintilis, Sextilis, September, October, November, and December.

Julian In 46 BC, Julius Caesar decreed that the new Roman calendar would have a year made up of 12 months of 31 and 30 days. February would have 29 days but every fourth year (leap year) it would have an extra day (making 30). This calendar was based on a year of $365\frac{1}{4}$ days, but was just over 11 minutes longer than a solar year.

HISTORY

EUROPE		AMERICAS		ASIA	
BC				**BC**	
c 40,000	Last Ice Age			c 8000	Agriculture develops in the Middle East
c 20,000	Cave paintings in France and Spain			c 6000	Rice cultivated in Thailand
c 6500	First Farming in Greece			c 4000	Bronze casting begins in Near East
		BC		c 3000	Development of major cities in Sumer
		c 3000	First pottery in Mexico		
		c 2000	First metal working in Peru		
c 2600	Beginnings of Minoan civilization in Crete			c 2750	Growth of civilizations in Indus Valley
c 1600	Beginnings of Mycenaean civilization in Greece			c 2200	Hsia dynasty in China
c 1450	Destruction of Minoan Crete			c 1750	Collapse of Indus Valley civilization
c 1200	Collapse of Mycenaean empire			c 1500	Rise of Shang dynasty in China
c 1100	Phoenician supremacy in Mediterranean Sea			c 1200	Beginning of Jewish religion
900–750	Rise of city-states in Greece			c 1050	Shang dynasty overthrown by Chou in China
766	First Olympic Games			c 770	Chou dynasty is weakening
753	Foundation of Rome (traditional date)				
				c 720	Height of Assyrian power
				c 650	First iron used in China
				586	Babylonian captivity of Jews
				483–221	'Warring States' period in China
510	Foundation of Roman Republic				
477–405	Athenian supremacy in Aegean				
431–404	War between Athens and Sparta				
290	Roman conquest of central Italy			202	Han dynasty re-unites China
146	Greece comes under Roman domination			**AD**	
31	Battle of Actium. Octavian defeats Mark Antony			c 0	Buddhism introduced to China from India
				25	Han dynasty restored in China
AD				45	Beginning of St Paul's missionary journeys
43	Roman invasion of Britain			132	Jewish rebellion against Rome
116	Emperor Trajan extends Roman Empire to Euphrates			220	End of Han dynasty; China splits into three states
238	Beginnings of raids by Goths into Roman Empire			330	Capital of Roman Empire transferred to Constantinople
293	Division of Roman Empire by Diocletian	c 300	Rise of Mayan civilization in Central America	350	Huns invade Persia and India
370	Huns from Asia invade Europe	c 400	Incas established on parts of South American Pacific coast	407–553	First Mongol Empire
410	Visigoths sack Rome				
449	Angles, Saxons and Jutes invade Britain				
486	Frankish kingdom founded by Clovis				
497	Franks converted to Christianity				

AFRICA		PEOPLE		INVENTIONS & DISCOVERIES	
BC				**BC**	
c 5000	Agricultural settlements in Egypt			**c 6000**	First known pottery and textiles
				c 5000	First known use of irrigation
c 3100	King Menes unites Egypt			**c 4000**	Invention of plough and sail
				c 3100	First known use of writing on clay tablets
		BC			
c 2685	Beginning of 'Old Kingdom' in Egypt	**c 2650**	Death of King Zoser of Egypt, for whom first pyramid was built	**c 2590**	Cheops builds Great Pyramid at Giza in Egypt
c 1570	Beginning of 'New Kingdom' in Egypt	**1792–50**	Rule of Hammurabi in Babylon		
		1361–52	Rule of Tutankhamun in Egypt		
		1304–1237	Rule of Ramasses II in Egypt		
		1198–66	Reign of Ramasses III, last great Pharaoh	**c 1100**	Phoenicians develop alphabet
814	Carthage founded by Phoenicians				
		c 605–520	Lao-tzu, founder of Taoism		
		563–479	Siddhartha Gautama (the Buddha)		
		551–479	Confucius, Chinese thinker		
		427–347	Plato, Greek thinker		
		384–322	Aristotle, Greek thinker		
		356–323	Alexander the Great		
				c 214	Building of Great Wall of China
		100–44	Julius Caesar		
		AD			
AD		**63 BC–**	Augustus (Octavian), first		
30	Egypt becomes Roman province	**14 AD**	Roman Emperor		
		c 4 BC–	Jesus Christ, founder of		
		c AD 29	Christianity		
		54–68	Reign of Emperor Nero		
		97–117	Reign of Emperor Trajan	**AD**	
				142	First stone bridge built over River Tiber
				c 105	First use of paper in China
				c 271	Magnetic compass in use in China
				c 300	Foot stirrup for riding invented
		306–337	Reign of Emperor Constantine		
		340–420	St Jerome, Bible translator		
		354–430	St Augustine of Hippo		
		379–395	Theodosius I, Roman Emperor in the East		
429–535	Vandal kingdom in northern Africa	**480–543**	St Benedict, founder of first monastery		

HISTORY

EUROPE		AMERICAS		ASIA	
597	St Augustine's mission to England			552	Buddhism introduced to Japan
		c 600	Height of Mayan civilization		
				624	China re-united under T'ang dynasty
				635	Muslims begin conquest of Syria and Persia
				674	Muslim conquest reaches River Indus
711	Muslim conquest of Spain				
793	Viking raids begin				
800	Charlemagne crowned Emperor in Rome				
				821	Conquest of Tibet by Chinese
843	Partition of Carolingian Empire at Treaty of Verdun				
874	First Viking settlers in Iceland				
886	King Alfred defeats Danish King Guthrum. Danelaw established in England			907	Last T'ang Emperor deposed in China
911	Vikings granted duchy of Normandy by Frankish king			939	Civil wars in Japan
				979	Sung dynasty re-unites China
		c 990	Expansion of Inca Empire		
1016	King Cnut rules England, Denmark and Norway			1054	Break between Greek and Latin Christian churches begins
1066	William of Normandy defeats Anglo-Saxons at Hastings				
1071	Normans conquer Byzantine Italy			1071	Seljuk Turks conquer most of Asia Minor
1095	Pope summons First Crusade				
		1100s	Inca family under Manco Capac settle in Cuzco	c 1100	Polynesian Islands colonized
1147–9	Second Crusade	1151	End of Toltec Empire in Mexico		
		1168	Aztecs leave Chimoztoc Valley	1156–89	Civil wars in Japan
1170	Murder of Thomas à Becket at Canterbury			1174	Saladin conquers Syria
1189–92	Third Crusade			1187	Saladin captures Jerusalem
1198	Innocent III elected Pope			1190	Temujin begins to create Empire in Eastern Asia
1202–1204	Fourth Crusade leads to capture of Constantinople			1206	Temujin proclaimed Genghis Khan
1215	King John of England signs Magna Carta			1210	Mongols invade China
1217–1222	Fifth Crusade			1234	Mongols destroy Chinese Empire
1228–9	Sixth Crusade			1261	Greek Empire restored at Constantinople
1236	Mongols invade Russia				
1241	Mongols invade Poland, Hungary, Bohemia, then withdraw			1279	Mongols conquer Southern China
1248–70	Seventh Crusade			1281	Mongols fail in attempt to conquer Japan
1250	Collapse of imperial power in Germany and Italy on death of Frederick II			1299	Ottoman Turks begin expansion

AFRICA		PEOPLE		INVENTIONS & DISCOVERIES	
				c 520	Rise of mathematics in India. Invention of decimal system
533–552	Justinian restores Roman power in North Africa	527–565	Reign of Emperor Justinian		
		570–632	Muhammad, founder of Islam		
		590–604	Reign of Pope Gregory I		
641	Conquest of Egypt by Muslims	673–735	Venerable Bede, historian		
c 700	Rise of Empire of Ghana				
		711–814	Reign of Charlemagne		
				c 730	First printing in China
				c 750	Paper-making spreads to Muslim world
				760	Muslims adopt numerals
				788	Great Mosque built at Cordoba in Spain
850	Acropolis of Zimbabwe built			850	First printed book in China
				860	Discovery of Iceland by Vikings
				982	Erik the Red discovers Greenland
920–1050	Height of Ghana Empire				
969	Fatimids conquer Egypt and found Cairo	987–996	Reign of Hugh Capet, first King of France		
c 1000	First Iron Age settlement at Zimbabwe	980–1037	Avicenna, great Arab physician	c 1000	Vikings discover America
				c 1000	Great age of Chinese painting
		1066–1087	Reign of William I, King of England	c 1045	Moveable type printing invented in China
		1138–93	Saladin, Sultan of Egypt and Syria	c 1100	Foundation of first universities in Europe
c 1150	Beginning of Yoruba city-states (Nigeria)				
		1155–90	Reign of Emperor Frederick I		
1174	Saladin conquers Egypt	1154–89	Reign of Henry II of England		
		1162–1227	Genghis Khan	1161	Explosives used in China
c 1200	Rise of Empire of Mali in West Africa	1170–1221	St Dominic, founder of Dominicans	1167	Foundation of Oxford University
c 1200	Emergence of Hausa city-states (Nigeria)	1182–1226	St Francis of Assisi, founder of Franciscans	1209	Foundation of Cambridge University
1240	Collapse of Empire of Ghana	1214–1294	Roger Bacon, philosopher		
		1216–1294	Kublai Khan		
		1225–74	Thomas Aquinas, philosopher		
		1265–1321	Dante, Italian poet	1271–95	Journey to China by Marco Polo, father and uncle
		1254–1324	Marco Polo, traveller		
c 1300	Emergence of Ife Kingdom (West Africa)	1267–1337	Giotto, Italian painter	1290	Spectacles invented in Italy

HISTORY

EUROPE		AMERICAS		ASIA	
1305	Papacy moves from Rome to Avignon	c 1300	Inca Roca takes title of Sapa Inca		
		1325	Rise of Aztecs. Founding of Tenochtitlan		
1337	Hundred Years' War begins between France and England				
1346	English defeat French at Battle of Crecy			c 1341	Black Death begins
1348	Black Death reaches Europe				
1356	English defeat French at Battle of Poitiers			1363	Tamerlane begins conquest of Asia
		1370	Expansion of Chimu kingdom	1368	Ming dynasty founded in China
		c 1375	Beginning of Aztec expansion		
1378–1417	Great Schism: (break between Rome and Avignon) rival popes elected			1398	Tamerlane ravages kingdom of Delhi
1381	Peasants' Revolt in England			1401	Tamerlane conquers Damascus and Baghdad
1385	Independence of Portugal			1402	Tamerlane overruns Ottoman Empire
1415	Henry V defeats French at Battle of Agincourt			1421	Peking becomes capital of China
		1438	Inca Empire established in Peru		
		1440–69	Montezuma rules Aztecs		
		1450	Incas conquer Chimu kingdom		
1453	England loses all French possessions except Calais			1453	Ottoman Turks capture Constantinople
1455–85	Wars of the Roses in England				
1492	Last Muslims in Spain conquered by Christians	1486–1502	Aztec Empire reaches sea		
		1493	Spanish make first settlement in New World (Hispaniola)		
1517	Martin Luther nails 95 Theses to church door at Wittenberg	1502–20	Aztec conquests under Montezuma II		
1519	Zwingli leads Reformation in Switzerland	c 1510	First African slaves taken to America	1516	Ottomans overrun Syria, Egypt and Arabia
1529	Reformation Parliament begins in England	1521	Cortes conquers Aztec capital, Tenochtitlan	1526	Foundation of Mughal Empire
1532	Calvin starts Protestant movement in France	1533	Pizarro conquers Peru	1533	Ivan the Terrible succeeds to Russian throne
1536	Suppression of monasteries begins in England	1535	Spaniards explore Chile		
1545	Council of Trent marks start of Counter-Reformation				
1558	England loses Calais to French			1556	Ivan the Terrible conquers Volga basin
1562–98	Wars of Religion in France				
1571	Battle of Lepanto: end of Turkish sea power			1565	Mughal power extended
1572	Dutch revolt against Spain				
1588	Spanish Armada defeated by English				

	AFRICA	PEOPLE	INVENTIONS & DISCOVERIES
		1320–84 John Wycliffe, religious reformer	
		1336–1405 Tamerlane, Mongol Emperor	
		1340–1400 Geoffrey Chaucer, English poet	
		1369–1415 John Huss, German religious reformer	
		1377–1446 Brunelleschi, Italian architect	
		1386–1466 Donatello, Italian sculptor	
		1394–1460 Henry the Navigator	
		1412–31 Joan of Arc of France	**1405** Chinese voyages in the Indian Ocean
1415	Beginning of Portugal's African Empire	**1422–91** William Caxton, English printer	
		1443–96 Francis Drake, English sailor	
		1451–1506 Christopher Columbus	
1450	Height of Songhai Empire in West Africa	**1452–1519** Leonardo da Vinci	**1445** Gutenburg prints first book from moveable type (in Europe)
		1469–1524 Vasco da Gama, explorer	
		1466–1536 Erasmus, Renaissance writer	**1488** Bartolomeo Dias sails round Cape of Good Hope
		1475–1564 Michelangelo, artist	
1482	Portuguese settle Gold Coast (now Ghana)	**1480–1521** Fernando Magellan, explorer	**1492** Columbus reaches West Indies
1492	Spain begins conquest of North African coast	**1483–1520** Raphael, Renaissance painter	**1497** John Cabot reaches Newfoundland
1505	Portuguese establish trading posts in East Africa	**1483–1546** Martin Luther, German religious reformer	**1498** Vasco da Gama reaches India round Cape of Good Hope
		1491–1556 Ignatius Loyola, Spanish founder of Jesuits	**1501** Vespucci explores Brazilian coast
		1497–1543 Hans Holbein, German painter	**1522** Magellan completes first circumnavigation of world
		1500–33 Atahualpa, last Inca ruler	
		1505–72 John Knox, Scottish Protestant reformer	**1525** Potato introduced to Europe
		1509–64 John Calvin, French religious reformer	**1535** Cartier navigates St Lawrence River
		1512–94 Mercator, Flemish cartographer	**1543** Copernicus declares that Earth revolves around Sun
1546	Destruction of Mali Empire by Songhai	**1547–1616** Cervantes, Spanish writer	
		1548–1614 El Greco, Spanish painter	**1559** Tobacco introduced to Europe
		1564–1616 William Shakespeare	
1570	Bornu Empire in the Sudan flourishes	**1564–1642** Galileo, Italian astronomer	
1571	Portuguese establish colony in Angola (Southern Africa)	**1577–1640** Rubens, Flemish painter	**1577–80** Drake sails round world
		1588–1679 Thomas Hobbes, English philosopher	**1582** Introduction of Gregorian calendar
1591	Moroccans destroy Songhai Empire	**1596–1650** Descartes, French thinker	

HISTORY

EUROPE		AMERICAS		ASIA	
1600	English East India Company founded				
1605	Gunpowder Plot				
1609	Dutch win freedom from Spain	1607	First English settlement in America		
1618–48	Thirty Years' War	1608	French colonists found Quebec		
		1620	Puritans land in New England		
1642–6	English Civil War	1626	Dutch settle New Amsterdam		
1649	Execution of Charles I in London				
		1644	New Amsterdam seized by British and re-named New York	1644	Ch'ing dynasty founded in China by Manchus
1688	England's 'Glorious Revolution'	1654	Portuguese take Brazil from Dutch	1690	Foundation of Calcutta by British
1701	Act of Settlement in Britain	1693	Gold discovered in Brazil		
1701–13	War of Spanish Succession				
1704	Battle of Blenheim				
1704	Union of England and Scotland			1707	Break up of Mughal Empire
1713	Treaty of Utrecht			1724	Hyderabad in India gains freedom from Mughals
1740–48	War of Austrian Succession				
1746	Jacobites defeated at Culloden in Scotland				
1756	Start of Seven Year's War			1757	Battle of Plassey establishes British rule in India
		1759	British capture Quebec from French		
		1765	Stamp Act in American colonies		
		1773	Boston Tea Party		
		1775–8	American War of Independence	1775	Peasant uprising in Russia
		1776	Declaration of American Independence	1783	India Act gives Britain control of India
1789	French Revolution	1789	Washington becomes first US President		
1804	Napoleon proclaimed Emperor	1791	Slave revolt in Haiti	1799	Napoleon invades Syria
1805	Battle of Trafalgar	1803	Louisiana Purchase doubles size of USA	1804–15	Serbs revolt against Turkey
1812	Napoleon's Russian campaign	1808–28	Independence movements in South America		
1815	Napoleon defeated at Waterloo	1819	Spain cedes Florida to US		
1821–29	Greek War of Independence			1819	British found Singapore
1830	Revolutions in France, Germany, Poland and Italy	1836	Texas independent of Mexico	1830–54	Russia conquers Kazakhstan
				1842	Hong Kong ceded to Britain
1846	Irish potato famine	1840	Union of Upper and Lower Canada	1845–8	Anglo-Sikh wars in India
1846	Britain repeals Corn Laws			1850/56	Australia and New Zealand granted responsible governments
1848	Year of Revolutions	1848	California Gold Rush begins		
1851	Great Exhibition in London			1854	Trade treaty between Japan and US
1854–6	Crimean War			1857	Indian Mutiny
1860	Unification of Italy	1861–5	American Civil War		
		1865	Abraham Lincoln assassinated		

AFRICA	PEOPLE	INVENTIONS & DISCOVERIES
	1602–61 Mazarin, French statesman	
	1606–69 Rembrandt, Dutch painter	
	1608–74 John Milton, English poet	
		1609 Invention of telescope
		1618 Imbert (French) reaches Timbuktu
	1622–73 Molière, French dramatist	
	1642–1727 Isaac Newton, scientist	
1652 Foundations of Cape Colony by Dutch	**1643–1715** Reign of Louis XIV	**1643** Invention of barometer
	1650–1722 Duke of Marlborough	
	1689–1725 Reign of Peter the Great	
1686 French annex Madagascar	**1685–1750** J. S. Bach, composer	
	1685–1759 Handel, composer	
	1694–1778 Voltaire, French writer	**1698** Thomas Savery invents steam pump
	1703–91 John Wesley, English preacher	
	1706–90 Benjamin Franklin, American inventor	**1709** Darby pioneers iron smelting
1705 Turks overthrown in Tunis	**1712–78** J. J. Rousseau, French philosopher	**1712** Thomas Newcomen's steam engine
	1725–74 Robert Clive, ruler in India	**1728** Bering discovers Bering Strait
	1728–79 James Cook, explorer	**1733** John Kay's flying shuttle
	1743–1826 Thomas Jefferson, American statesman	**1752** Franklin's lightning conductor
	1756–91 W. A. Mozart, German composer	**1764** Hargreave's spinning jenny
	1769–1821 Napoleon Bonaparte	**1765** James Watt's steam engine
	1769–1850 Duke of Wellington	**1768** Cook begins Pacific exploration
	1770–1827 Beethoven, German composer	
	1776–1837 John Constable, English painter	**1782** Watt's double acting steam engine
	1783–1830 Simon Bolivar, 'Liberator'	**1785** Cartwright's power loom
	1788–1850 Robert Peel, English statesman	**1793** Eli Whitney's cotton gin
1787 British acquire Sierra Leone	**1806–59** I. K. Brunel, British engineer	**1805** Mungo Park explores Niger River
1798 Napoleon attacks Egypt	**1810–61** Cavour, Italian unifier	
1802–11 Portuguese cross Africa	**1813–83** Richard Wagner, German composer	
1807 British abolish slave trade		
1811 Mohammad Ali takes control in Egypt	**1815–98** Otto von Bismarck, German statesman	**1815** Davy's miners' safety lamp
		1825 First passenger steam railway
1818 Zulu Empire founded in southern Africa	**1821–90** Richard Burton, explorer	**1825** Neilson's blast furnace
1822 Liberia founded for free slaves	**1828–1910** Leo Tolstoy, Russian writer	**1831** Faraday's dynamo
1830 French begin conquest of Algeria	**1837–1901** Reign of Queen Victoria	**1844** Invention of safety match
	1840–1926 Claude Monet, French painter	
1835–37 Great Trek of Boers in South Africa	**1840–1917** Rodin, French sculptor	
	1853–1902 Cecil Rhodes, colonizer	
	1856–1939 Sigmund Freud, psychoanalyst	
	1858–1928 Emmeline Pankhurst, women's leader	**1853–6** Livingstone crosses Africa
		1855 Bessemer's converter
1860 French expansion in West Africa	**1860–1904** Anton Chekhov, Russian playwright	**1859** Lake Tanganyika discovered
		1862 Gatling's rapid fire gun

HISTORY

EUROPE		AMERICAS		ASIA	
1867	North German Confederation	1867	Dominion of Canada formed		
1871	Proclamation of German Empire				
1872–1914	Triple Alliance between Germany, Austria and Italy			1877	Victoria becomes Empress of India
				1885	Indian National Congress formed
		1876	Battle of Little Big Horn	1886	British annex Burma
		1898	Spanish-American war	1894–5	Sino-Japanese war
1904	Anglo-French Entente	1903	Panama Canal Zone to US	1901	Unification of Australia
1905	First revolution in Russia			1906	Revolution in Persia
				1910	Japan annexes Korea
		1911	Revolution in Mexico	1911	Chinese revolution under Sun Yat-sen
1912–13	Balkan Wars				
1914–18	First World War				
		1914	Panama Canal opens		
1917	Russian Revolution	1917	US declares war on Central Powers	1917	Balfour Declaration promises Jewish homeland
1919	Treaty of Versailles				
1920	League of Nations established	1920	US refuses to join League of Nations	1922	Republic proclaimed in Turkey
1922	Irish Free State created			1926	Chiang Kai-shek unites China
1926	General Strike in Britain				
		1929	Wall Street Crash	1931	Japanese occupy Manchuria
1933	Hitler becomes German Chancellor	1933	Roosevelt introduces New Deal in America		
				1934	Mao Tse-tung's Long March in China
1936–9	Spanish Civil War			1937	Japanese capture Peking
1939–45	Second World War			1940	Japan allies with Germany
		1941	US enters World War II		
1945	United Nations established			1945	First A-bombs dropped on Japan
1949	Formation of NATO			1946–9	Civil war in China
1955	Warsaw Pact signed			1947	India and Pakistan independent
1957	European Common Market set up			1956	Arab-Israeli war
		1959	Cuban revolution	1957	Malaysia independent
1961	Berlin Wall built				
		1962	Cuba missile crisis	1962	Sino-Indian war
1963	Nuclear Test Ban Treaty	1963	President Kennedy assassinated		
1968	Russian troops in Czechoslovakia			1965	United States sends troops to Vietnam
1973	Britain, Eire and Denmark join European Economic Community			1971	East Pakistan becomes Bangladesh
				1973	Arab-Israeli war
		1974	Resignation of President Nixon	1974	Portuguese African colonies independent
1975	Monarchy restored in Spain				
1978	John Paul II elected as first non-Italian Pope for 450 years	1978	US agrees to diplomatic relations with China and ends those with Taiwan		
				1979	Shah of Iran deposed. An Islamic republic is declared
1980	President Tito of Yugoslavia dies. Polish Solidarity trade union, led by Lech Walesa, confronts Communist government			1980	Iran-Iraq war
1981	Greece becomes 10th member of the Common Market	1981	US hostages held in Iran released after 444 days First flight of US space shuttle	1982	Israel invades Lebanon to drive Palestine Liberation Organization from the country.
1985	Mikhail Gorbachev elected new Soviet leader	1982	Argentines invade Falkland Islands		

AFRICA		PEOPLE		INVENTIONS & DISCOVERIES	
1869	Opening of Suez Canal	1863–1947	Henry Ford, US car maker	1866	Nobel invents dynamite
1875	Disraeli buys Suez Canal shares	1866–1925	Sun Yat-sen, Chinese statesman		
1879	Zulu War	1872–1928	Roald Amundsen, explorer		
1882	British occupy Egypt	1874–1965	Winston Churchill, British statesman		
1884	Germany acquires African colonies				
1885	Belgium acquires Congo	1879–1955	Albert Einstein, German physicist	1871	Stanley finds Livingstone
1886	Germany and Britain divide East Africa			1876	Bell invents telephone
		1881–1973	Pablo Picasso, Spanish painter	1884	Waterman's fountain pen
1899–1902	Anglo-Boer War			1886–7	Benz and Daimler invent internal combustion engine
1909	Union of South Africa formed	1883–1945	Mussolini, Italian dictator		
1911	Italians conquer Libya	1889–1945	Adolf Hitler, German Nazi leader	1895	Marconi's wireless
1914	British Protectorate in Egypt	1889–1964	Nehru, Indian leader	1903	First successful flight by Wright brothers
1919	Nationalist revolt in Egypt	1890–1970	General de Gaulle, French statesman	1909	Peary reaches North Pole
		1892–1975	Franco, Spanish dictator	1911	Amundsen reaches South Pole
1922	Egypt becomes independent	1893–1976	Mao Tse-tung, Chinese revolutionary	1913	Geiger counter invented
		1913–	Willi Brandt, German statesman	1918	Automatic rifle invented
				1919	Rutherford splits atom
		1914–	Thor Heyerdahl, explorer	1919	First crossing of Atlantic by air
		1921–	John Glenn, first American in space	1925	Baird invents television
1936	Italy annexes Ethiopia	1924–	Kenneth Kaunda, Zambian leader	1926	First liquid fuel rocket
		1926–	Fidel Castro, Cuban leader	1930	Whittle's jet engine
				1935	Invention of nylon
		1930–	Neil Armstrong, first on moon	1939	Development of penicillin
1949	Apartheid established in South Africa	1934–68	Yuri Gagarin, first in space	1947	First supersonic flight
1956	Suez crisis			1948	Transistor developed
1957	Ghana becomes independent, followed by other African States			1953	The conquest of Everest
				1957	First satellite launched
				1961	First man in space
1967–70	Nigerian civil war			1969	First man lands on Moon
				1976	Microcomputers on a single chip
1979	General Amin flees from Uganda				
1980	Last British colony in Africa achieves independence as Zimbabwe				
				1982	First successful, permanent artificial heart operation

Great Pyramid

Pharos Lighthouse

Tomb of Mausolus

Hanging Gardens of Babylon

Statue of Zeus

Temple of Diana

Colossus of Rhodes

Wonders of the East

Shwe Dagon Pagoda A Buddhist shrine near Rangoon, Burma. The present structure was constructed between the 15th and 18th centuries. It is a large tower, called a *stupa*, rising to 112 m (358 ft), and this is surrounded by a large number of much smaller towers. The tower is built of brick, and is gilded over from base to summit.

Angkor Wat This temple in Kampuchea is dedicated to the Hindu god Vishnu, and building was started in AD 1112, and completed in 1180 during the times of the Khmer kings. It is one of the world's largest temples, built as an enormous oblong with conical towers at each corner. It is 243 m (796 ft) long and 180 m (588 ft) wide, with a central pagoda 76 m (250 ft) high.

Persepolis Although in ruins today, 2400 years ago this was a great city of ancient Persia. A great central hall had a hundred columns supporting the roof, although today only 13 of these huge columns remain. The city was destroyed by Alexander the Great in 331 BC.

The Taj Mahal This is a mausoleum at Agra, in India, in which lie the bodies of Shah Jehan, Mughal emperor of India 1627–58, and his favourite wife, Mumtaz Mahal. It was built by the Shah when his wife died in 1629. The Taj Mahal is built of white marble, carved, and inlaid with semi-precious stones.

Seven Wonders of the World*

*Originally compiled by Antipater of Sidon, a Greek poet, in the 100s BC.

Pyramids of Egypt Oldest and only surviving 'wonder'. Built in the 2000s BC as royal tombs, about 80 are still standing. The largest, the Great Pyramid of Cheops, at el-Gizeh, was 147 m (481 ft) high.

Hanging Gardens of Babylon Terraced gardens adjoining Nebuchadnezzar's palace said to rise from 23–91 m (75 to 300 ft). Supposedly built by the king about 600BC to please his wife, a princess from the mountains, but they are also associated with Assyrian Queen Semiramis.

Statue of Zeus at Olympia Carved by Phidias, the 12 m (40 ft) statue marked the site of the original Olympic Games in the 400s BC. It was constructed of ivory and gold, and showed Zeus (Jupiter) on his throne.

Temple of Artemis (Diana) at Ephesus Constructed of Parian marble and more than 122 m (400 ft) long with over 100 columns 18 m (60 ft) high, it was begun about 350 BC and took some 120 years to build. Destroyed by the Goths in AD 262.

Colossus of Rhodes Gigantic bronze statue of sungod Helios (or Apollo); stood about 36 m (117 ft) high, dominating the harbour entrance at Rhodes. The sculptor Chares supposedly laboured for 12 years before he completed it in 280 BC. It was destroyed by an earthquake in 244 BC.

Pharos of Alexandria Marble lighthouse and watchtower built about 270 BC on the island of Pharos in Alexandria's harbour. Possibly standing 122 m (400 ft) high, it was destroyed by an earthquake in 1375.

Mausoleum at Halicarnassus Erected by Queen Artemisia in memory of her husband King Mausolus of Caria (in Asia Minor), who died in 353 BC. It stood 43 m (140 ft) high. All that remains are a few pieces in the British Museum and the word 'mausoleum' in the English language.

Wonders of the West

The Eiffel Tower The great iron structure dominates the city of Paris in France, from where it stands on the south bank of the River Seine. It was designed by Gustave Eiffel for the Paris Exhibition of 1889. There are three platforms, the topmost being 300 m (985 ft) high.

The Alhambra This Moorish palace is at Granada, in Spain, and was built by the caliph Al Ahmar from 1238–1358, combining a royal palace, fortress and residence. Within are the Court of the Lions, with fountain, pavilions and arches; the Court of the Myrtles, containing delicate columns of jasper and alabaster; and the Magnificent Hall of the Ambassadors with its cedarwood ceiling.

The Hoover Dam Originally called the Boulder Dam, this great construction is on the Colorado River, USA, and forms the border between Nevada and Arizona. Built in 1936, the dam is 221 m (726 ft) high, and although no longer the world's highest (the Grand Coulee Dam is higher), it was the first engineering feat of its size and capacity ever completed.

Chichen Itza This is a ruined city of the Maya empire, situated at Yucatan, Mexico, and built about 1500 years ago. The central pyramid is 21 m (70 ft) high, and is 168 m (550 ft) square. Here, the Maya people worshipped the god Quetzalcoatl.

Explorers and Travellers

Amundsen, Roald (1872–1928), Norwegian explorer, reached the South Pole (1911) and flew across the North Pole in an airship (1926); perished in a rescue flight to the North Pole.

Cabot, John (c.1450–c.1499), Venetian explorer who visited England, and in 1497 discovered the mainland of North America on behalf of Henry VII of England.

Columbus, Christopher (1451–1506), Genoese navigator, traditional discoverer of America. In 1492, on an

hugged the west coast of Africa. Strong winds then drove him off the land and southwards to unknown latitudes. He then sailed east and, when no land appeared, turned north and realized he had rounded the African continent.

Livingstone, David (1813–73), Scottish missionary and doctor, explored much of central Africa. He discovered Lake Ngami, the upper reaches of the Zambezi, and Victoria Falls. He became the first man to cross the African continent. In 1870, with no word from Livingstone for nearly five years, journalist Henry Morton Stanley was sent from the USA

On his first expedition to the South Seas in 1768, James Cook sailed to Tahiti and then on to New Zealand. In 1770 he reached Botany Bay in Australia and claimed it for Britain.

expedition financed by Spain, he reached the Bahamas, and also discovered Cuba and Haiti. Made three further voyages to West Indies (1493, 1498, 1502).

Cook, James (1728–79), English navigator, explored much of the South Pacific, including the east coast of Australia, which he claimed for Britain.

Da Gama, Vasco (1469?–1524), Portuguese navigator, rounded the Cape of Good Hope (1497), crossed the Indian Ocean, and reached Calicut, India, after a voyage of 11 months.

Dias, Bartolomeu (1450?–1500), Portuguese navigator, was the first man to round the Cape of Good Hope. He left Lisbon with three ships (1487) and

to look for him. He and Livingstone eventually had a historic meeting by Lake Tanganyika in 1871.

Magellan, Ferdinand (1480?–1521), Portuguese navigator, led the first expedition to sail round the world (1519–22). Financed by King Charles V of Spain, Magellan sailed with 5 ships and 300 men, first to South America, round Cape Horn, through the straits that are named after him, across the Pacific, round the tip of Africa, and back to Spain.

Peary, Robert Edwin (1856–1920), American admiral and Arctic explorer, survived a dangerous sled trip across the ice to reach the North Pole (1909).

KEY DATES IN EXPLORATION

BC

3000	Hennu the Egyptian sails to the Land of Punt (Somalia)
3000	Minoans explore the Mediterranean.
600	Phoenicians reach Britain.
530	Hanno the Carthaginian explores west African coast.
330	Pythias reaches the Arctic.

AD

870	Norwegian Vikings discover and settle Iceland.
900	Icelanders discover Greenland.
1000	Leif Ericsson reaches Newfoundland.
1270	Marco Polo travels to China.
1418	Henry the Navigator instigates discovery and exploration of West Africa, Madeira, Azores, and Cape Verde Islands.
1487	Bartolomeu Dias rounds Cape of Good Hope.
1492	Columbus reaches the West Indies.
1497	Vasco da Gama sails round Africa to India
1497	Cabot seeks North-west Passage.
1499	Amerigo Vespucci discovers Brazil.
1519–22	Magellan sails round world.
1519	Cortés explores Mexico.
1530	Pizarro explores Peru.
1577–80	Drake sails round world.
1594	Barents seeks North-east Passage.
1607	Hudson seeks North-east Passage.
1642	Tasman explores South Seas.
1768	Cook explores South Pacific.
1789	Mackenzie explores west Canada.
1795	Mungo Park traces the Niger.
1819	Bellingshausen sails round Antarctica.
1840	Livingstone goes to Africa.
1895	Nansen nears North Pole.
1909	Peary reaches North Pole.
1911	Amundsen reaches South Pole.
1912	Scott reaches South Pole.
1957	Fuchs leads International Geophysical Year expedition's crossing of Antarctica.

Polo, Marco (1254–1324), Venetian traveller and diplomat, accompanied his father and uncle on an overland journey to China. He stayed 17 years in Peking and became the first European to explore eastern Asia.

Scott, Robert Falcon (1868–1912), British Antarctic explorer, was beaten in the race to the South Pole by Amundsen, by a mere five weeks. Scott and his companions perished on the return journey.

Tasman, Abel (1603–59), Dutch seafarer, explored the South Seas (1642); discovered Tasmania, New Zealand, and some of the Friendly Islands.

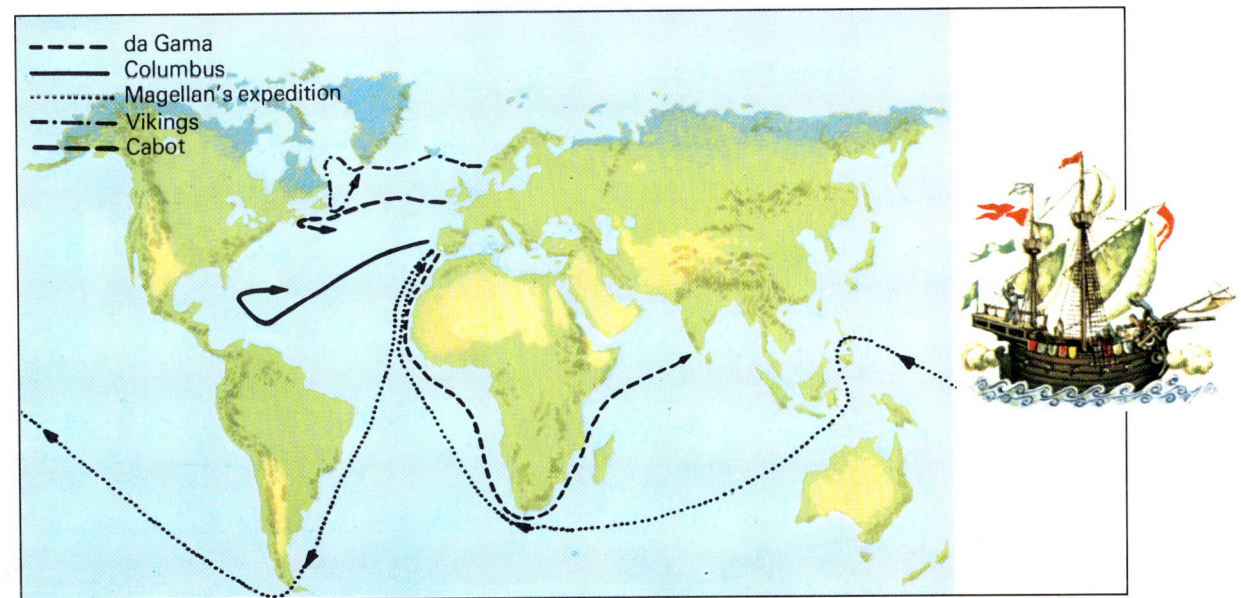

- – – – da Gama
- ——— Columbus
- ·········· Magellan's expedition
- – · – · – Vikings
- – – – Cabot

Who's Who in History

Alexander the Great (356–323) Became king of Macedon at 20 and then set out to conquer the world. By 323, his empire stretched from Greece to the River Indus in NW India and south to include Egypt. He was – perhaps the world's greatest military commander.

Amundsen, Roald see page 104

Atatürk, Kemal (1881–1938) Turkish general and statesman – founder of modern Turkey. Atatürk was a general in the First World War, he overthrew the Sultan and turned Turkey into a republic becoming its president in 1923. Made Turkey secular, forbade the wearing of the fez (hat) and discouraged women using the veil.

Baber (1483–1530) Mongol descendant of Genghis Khan, he became ruler at Kabul when aged 21. From there set out upon the conquest of northern India to establish the Mughal empire which lasted until the coming of the British to India in the 18th century.

Becket, Thomas à (1118–1170) Friend and Chancellor of Henry II. The king made him Archbishop of Canterbury, but he then quarrelled with the king over the balance of church and state power. He was murdered in Canterbury Cathedral by followers of the king.

Bismarck, Prince Otto von (1815–1898) Prussian statesman, prime minister of Prussia and then Germany from 1862 to 1890. He is the creator of modern – united Germany. He was known as the 'Iron Chancellor'.

Boadicea (died AD 62) Queen of Iceni tribe of Britain, she revolted against the Roman occupation. Only defeated after a major campaign that endangered Roman control of Britain.

Caesar, Julius (100–44 BC) Roman statesman and general, Conquered Gaul and wrote his account – De Bello Gallico. Defied orders of the Senate and crossed the River Rubicon with his army to invade Italy and become dictator. Assassinated by his political rivals and in the power struggle that followed Augustus emerged victorious to become the first Roman emperor.

Canute (994–1035) Son of Sweyn Forkbeard of Denmark. King of England from 1016 to his death. Strong king who restored order to the country after a period of weakness. The famous story of Canute telling the sea to stop has often been misunderstood. He wished to demonstrate the limit of kingly power to foolish courtiers, who said he could do anything.

Catherine II, the Great (1729–1796) Deposed her mad husband Tsar Peter III of Russia and became empress (1762). Strengthened power of nobility; captured Crimea, Black Sea coast and much of Poland.

Charles V (1500–1558) Holy Roman emperor from 1519. King of Spain as Charles I from 1516. Ruled over more of Europe than any other Habsburg. Abdicated 1556.

Chiang Kai-shek (1888–1975) Chinese Nationalist leader who succeeded Sun Yat-sen in 1925 as leader of the Kuomintang (Nationalist Party). He and his followers were forced from China by the victorious communists under Mao Tse-tung in 1949. He established a Nationalist government on Formosa (Taiwan).

Churchill, Winston S. (1874–1965) British soldier, statesman and author. First Lord of Admiralty 1911–1915 and 1939–1940, Chancellor of Exchequer 1924–1929. Britain's war time prime minister from 1940–1945 and again from 1951–1955. Also a writer – he won the Nobel prize for literature in 1953.

Cleopatra VII (69–30 BC) Macedonian queen of Egypt from 51 to 30 BC. Caesar supported her against a rival claimant to the throne. She became his lover and bore him a son. After his death she became the lover and later wife of Marcus Antonius. Attempted but failed to captivate Augustus and in 30 BC committed suicide. Her great beauty is almost certainly a later exaggeration but she used her attractions to keep her throne.

Clive, Robert (1725–1774) British soldier who did much to bring India under British control in

Alexander the Great, from a mosaic found in the ruins at Pompeii in Southern Italy.

the 18th century. Governor of Bengal (1764–1767). On his return to England he was censured for misgovernment and corruption and said that in retrospect he was astonished at his own moderation. Committed suicide.

Columbus, Christopher See page 104.

Cook, James See page 104.

Cortes, Hernando (1485–1547) Greatest Spanish *Conquistador* who conquered Mexico (the Aztecs) in 1519–1521 with a mere 550 men. He ruled as governor until 1530.

Cromwell, Oliver (1599–1658) Leader of the Roundhead (Parliamentary) faction in the civil war in England. Brilliant soldier and great statesman. Had Charles I executed and ruled as Lord Protector of England (1653–1658).

Cyrus (600–529 BC) King of Persia and founder of the Persian empire. He overthrew Croesus and conquered Babylon, freeing the Jews from captivity there.

Da Gama see page 104.

De Gaulle, Charles (1890–1970) French general and statesman. Only French soldier who successfully withstood the German panzer tank tactics of 1940. After the fall of France in 1940 he organized the Free French movement from London. President of France from 1945–1946 and during the important period from 1956–1969, with a new constitution (the Fifth Republic). Granted full independence to France's African colonies in 1960 and ended the war in Algeria in 1962. Retired from politics.

Dias, Bartolomeu see page 104.

Sir Francis Drake, the Elizabethan seaman, was known to the Spaniards as 'el Draque', the Dragon.

Drake, Sir Francis (1543–1596) English adventurer, plundered Spanish settlements in America. Sailed round the world in 1577–1580. Burned a Spanish fleet at Cadiz in 1587 and helped to defeat Spanish Armada in 1588.

Edward, the Black Prince (1330–1376) Son of Edward III, he won his spurs' at the Battle of Crecy. Regarded as the greatest knight of his age. He died a year before his father and his son became king of England as Richard II.

Fox, Charles James (1749–1806) British politician, arch opponent of George III, rival to Pitt. One of the few British parliamentarians to support the French Revolution.

Franklin, Benjamin (1706–1790) American statesman and scientist and one of the founding fathers of the USA. He invented bifocal glasses and the lightning conductor.

Frederick II, the Great (1712–1786) King of Prussia from 1740, brilliant general. Fought Empress Maria Theresa in War of Austrian Succession. Skilled flautist.

Gandhi, Mohandas Karamchand (1869–1948) Indian lawyer, ascetic, and Hindu spiritual leader; worked for independence from Britain. largely by non-violent civil disobedience; jailed several times; assassinated by Hindu fanatic because he preached peace with Muslims.

Garibaldi, Giuseppe (1807–1882) Italian patriot who played a major part in the struggle to bring about the unification of Italy (1861). His most famous feat was the conquest of the kingdom of the Two Sicilies in 1860 with 1000 men (Redshirts). Twice he tried to conquer Rome (1862, 1867). Fought for France (1870–1871). Member of Italian parliament (1874).

Gladstone, William Ewart (1809–1898) British Liberal statesman who was four times prime minister of Britain. Failed in several attempts to persuade Parliament to agree to Home Rule for Ireland.

Hammurabi the Great (1792–50 BC) Sixth king of the first Babylonian dynasty, he conquered all Mesopotamia. He was a great builder and his code of laws was not surpassed until Roman times.

Hannibal (247–183 BC) Greatest of Carthaginian soldiers and statesmen. Crossed the Alps (with elephants) to invade Italy, where he defeated the Romans in many battles. He was, himself, defeated at Zama in 202 by the Romans and was later exiled. He committed suicide so as not to fall into Roman hands.

Homer (c.850 BC) Traditionally a Greek poet,

HISTORY

author of the *Iliad* and the *Odyssey*, though nothing certain is known of him.

Ivan IV, the Terrible (1530–1584) First tsar of all Russia. Became ruler 1533, assumed personal power 1546. Vicious and cruel, had many people murdered and tortured. Developed religious mania, murdered eldest son, repented and became a monk on his death bed.

Joan of Arc (Jeanne d'Arc) (1412–1431) The peasant girl who 'heard voices' and led the French armies against the English in the Hundred Years' War. She was burnt as a witch.

Justinian I (483–565) Last great Roman emperor, he became emperor of the eastern empire in 526 at Constantinople, and reconquered much of the old western empire (Italy) which was then in the hands of the barbarians.

Kenyatta, Jomo (c.1883–1978) Kenyan nationalist leader who spent much of his life campaigning for Kenyan independence from British rule. His book *Facing Mount Kenya* was a landmark in African nationalism. He became the first prime minister and then president of an independent Kenya (1963).

Kitchener, Horatio Herbert (1850–1916) Governor-general Sudan, recapturing Khartoum from Muslim fanatics. British soldier who won the battle of Omdurman in 1898. Became c-in-c in South Africa during the Boer War (1900) and was secretary of state for war in 1914. His features became famous on the First World War poster 'Your Country Needs You'. Drowned when ship hit mine.

Lenin, Vladimir (1870–1924) Russian revolutionary who was exiled from Russia from 1895–1917. He founded the Bolshevik (later the Communist) party. Allowed across Germany in a sealed train after the February Revolution, he then led the October Revolution. Fell ill and lost control of government in 1922. Succeeded by Stalin in 1924.

Livingstone, David See page 104.

Magellan, Ferdinand see page 104.

Mao Tse-tung (1893–1976) Chinese Communist leader who defeated the Nationalists, under Chiang Kai-shek, in 1949 to rule all China. His revolutionary method was constantly to upset the Chinese establishment and after his death the Maoist notion of continuous cultural revolution was rejected.

Maria Theresa (1717–1780) Austrian empress of Holy Roman empire from 1740. Defended her right to the throne in the War of Austrian Succession, 1740–1748. Her husband, Francis of Lorraine, was recognized as emperor in 1748.

The Emperor Napoleon, from a chalk drawing.

Marx, Karl (1818–1883) German Jewish philosopher who in his writings laid the foundations of Communism. In 1848 (with Engels) he published the Communist Manifesto. His doctrine in *Das Kapital* (1867) revolutionized political thinking.

Napoleon (1769–1821) Corsican soldier, made himself emperor of France in 1804. Conquered Italy, Spain, Egypt, Netherlands and most of central Europe. Invasion of Russia failed (1812). Defeated Leipzig (1813), abdicated 1814. Returned to power 1815, defeated at Waterloo, exiled to St. Helena.

Nasser, Gamal Abdel (1918–1970) Egyptian revolutionary and army officer. Helped depose King Farouk (1952). While president from 1956 tried to modernize country.

Nehru, Jawahalal (1889–1964) Indian statesman who played a leading part in the nationalist struggle to gain independence from Britain. Prime minister of India from 1947–1964. He was one of the founders of the political movement known as Non-Alignment.

Nelson, Horatio (1758–1805) British naval hero, lost eye and arm in battle. Destroyed French fleet at Battle of Nile (1798), won Battle of Copenhagen (1801), destroyed another French fleet at Trafalgar (1805), dying in moment of victory. Created viscount, 1801. Liaison with Emma, Lady Hamilton, a public scandal.

Nero (37–68) Roman emperor from 54 to 68. Rebuilt city after the great fire and was wrongly depicted by later Christian writers as playing the lyre while Rome burnt. He led a dissolute private

Tamerlane, the Tatar ruler was descended from Genghis Khan.

life and committed suicide in 68 when the army revolted.

Nightingale, Florence (1820–1910) English reformer, became nurse. Against great opposition she organized nursing reforms during the Crimean War when she became known as the 'Lady with the Lamp'. Her system of sanitary barrack hospitals was to be adopted worldwide.

Nkrumah, Kwame (1909–1972) Gold Coast nationalist, he founded the Convention People's Party and became the country's first prime minister at independence and then its first president when Ghana became a republic in 1960. He was ousted in a coup in 1966 and died in exile in Guinea. He was the author of several books including *I Speak of Freedom.*

Peary, Robert see page 104.

Pericles (495–429 BC) Greatest Athenian of its 'golden age', he led Athens from 460 to 430 and was responsible for making Athens the 'most beautiful city in the world'. He died in 429 of the plague. Known as the 'father of democracy'.

Pizarro, Francisco (1474–1541) One of the greatest of the Spanish *Conquistadores*, he conquered the Inca empire of Peru in 1528 with only 180 men. Assassinated.

Polo, Marco See page 105.

Ptolemy I Sotor (?–283 BC) Half-brother to Alexander the Great and one of his most trusted generals. Ptolemy took Egypt as his 'share' of Alexander's empire when Alexander died and founded the Ptolemaic line of pharaohs which lasted until the time of Julius Caesar.

Raleigh, Sir Walter (1552–1618) English soldier and courtier who established the first colony of Virginia and introduced the habit of smoking to England. Explored Guiana region of South America and was executed by James I (VI) after failing to find gold.

Richelieu, Cardinal Armand Jean du Plessis (1585–1642) French statesman who became the first minister of Louis XIII from 1624–1642 and virtually ruled France. He curbed the old nobility, broke the independent power of the Huguenots and extended France's boundaries and power in Europe.

Robespierre, Maximilien (1758–1794) Leader of the Jacobins in the French Revolution, became the most important figure in the 'Reign of Terror'. Almost a dictator for a time, he himself was denounced and guillotined.

Roosevelt, Franklin Delano (1884–1945) Four times president of the USA, he was responsible for the New Deal in the 1930s to help end the great Depression. He led his country through the Second World War until his death in 1945.

Scott, Robert Falcon see page 105.

Smuts, Jan Christian (1870–1950) Boer general in the Boer War of 1899–1902, he was twice prime minister of South Africa and a supporter of the connection with Britain.

Stuart, Charles Edward (1720–1788) Known as the 'Young Pretender' to the British crown. Son of James Edward Stuart and grandson of King James II. Led the unsuccessful 1745 invasion of Scotland in an attempt to bring about a Jacobite rebellion against the Hanoverian dynasty. Defeated at Culloden (1746), lived rest of his life in exile.

Sun Yat-sen (1866–1925) Chinese revolutionary who overthrew the Manchu dynasty and turned China into a republic. He was president of China from 1921 to his death.

Tamerlane (1336–1405) Name means Timur the Lame. He created a huge Mongol empire from Turkey to India and north to Moscow. A brilliant soldier, feared for his ruthlessness.

Tasman, Abel see page 105.

Trotsky, Leon (Lev Davidovich Bronstein; 1879–1940) Russian revolutionary. Minister under Lenin (1917). Organized Red Army in civil war of 1918–1921. Opposed Stalin – exiled 1929. Assassinated by a Stalin agent in Mexico.

Walpole, Sir Robert (1676–1745) Britain's first and one of her longest serving prime ministers (1721–1742). His general motto was 'let sleeping dogs lie'.

Rulers of England

Saxons

Egbert	827–839
Ethelwulf	839–858
Ethelbald	858–860
Ethelbert	860–866
Ethelred I	866–871
Alfred the Great	871–899
Edward the Elder	899–924
Athelstan	924–939
Edmund	939–946
Edred	946–955
Edwy	955–959
Edgar	959–975
Edward the Martyr	975–978
Ethelred I the Unready	978–1016
Edmund Ironside	1016

Danes

Canute	1016–1035
Harold I Harefoot	1035–1040
Hardicanute	1040–1042

Saxons

Edward the Confessor	1042–1066
Harold II	1066

House of Normandy

William I the Conqueror	1066–1087
William II	1087–1100
Henry I	1100–1135
Stephen	1135–1154

House of Plantagenet

Henry II	1154–1189
Richard I	1189–1199
John	1199–1216
Henry III	1216–1272
Edward I	1272–1307
Edward II	1307–1327
Edward III	1327–1377
Richard II	1377–1399

House of Lancaster

Henry IV	1399–1413
Henry V	1413–1422
Henry VI	1422–1461

House of York

Edward IV	1461–1483
Edward V	1483
Richard III	1483–1485

House of Tudor

Henry VII	1485–1509
Henry VIII	1509–1547
Edward VI	1547–1553
Mary I	1553–1558
Elizabeth I	1558–1603

Rulers of Scotland

Malcolm II	1005–1034
Duncan I	1034–1040
Macbeth (usurper)	1040–1057
Malcolm III Canmore	1057–1093
Donald Bane	1093–1094
Duncan II	1094
Donald Bane (restored)	1094–1097
Edgar	1097–1107
Alexander I	1107–1124
David I	1124–1153
Malcolm IV	1153–1165
William the Lion	1165–1214
Alexander II	1214–1249
Alexander III	1249–1286
Margaret of Norway	1286–1290
(*Interregnum* 1290–1292)	
John Balliol	1292–1296
(*Interregnum* 1296–1306)	
Robert I (Bruce)	1306–1329
David II	1329–1371

House of Stuart

Robert II	1371–1390
Robert III	1390–1406
James I	1406–1437
James II	1437–1460
James III	1460–1488
James IV	1488–1513
James V	1513–1542
Mary	1542–1567
James VI (I of Great Britain)	1567–1625

Rulers of Great Britain

House of Stuart

James I	1603–1625
Charles I	1625–1649
(*Commonwealth* 1649–1659)	
Charles II	1660–1685
James II	1685–1688
William III ⎫ jointly	1689–1702
Mary II ⎭	1689–1694
Anne	1702–1714

House of Hanover		*House of Saxe-Coburg*	
George I	1714–1727	Edward VII	1901–1910
George II	1727–1760	*House of Windsor*	
George III	1760–1820	George V	1910–1936
George IV	1820–1830	Edward VIII	1936
William IV	1830–1837	George VI	1936–1952
Victoria	1837–1901	Elizabeth II	1952–

British Prime Ministers

Sir Robert Walpole (W)	1721–42	Benjamin Disraeli (C)	1874–80
Earl of Wilmington (W)	1742–43	William Gladstone (L)	1880–85
Henry Pelham (W)	1743–54	Marquess of Salisbury (C)	1885–86
Duke of Newcastle (W)	1754–56	William Gladstone (L)	1886
Duke of Devonshire (W)	1756–57	Marquess of Salisbury (C)	1886–92
Duke of Newcastle (W)	1757–62	William Gladstone (L)	1892–94
Earl of Bute (T)	1762–63	Earl of Rosebery (L)	1894–95
George Grenville (W)	1763–65	Marquess of Salisbury (C)	1895–1902
Marquess of Rockingham (W)	1765–66	Arthur Balfour (C)	1902–05
Earl of Chatham (W)	1766–67	Sir Henry Campbell-	
Duke of Grafton (W)	1767–70	Bannerman (L)	1905–08
Lord North (T)	1770–82	Herbert Asquith (L)	1908–15
Marquess of Rockingham (W)	1782	Herbert Asquith (Cln)	1915–16
Earl of Shelbourne (W)	1782–83	David Lloyd-George (Cln)	1916–22
Duke of Portland (Cln)	1783	Andrew Bonar Law (C)	1922–23
William Pitt (T)	1783–1801	Stanley Baldwin (C)	1923–24
Henry Addington (T)	1801–04	James Ramsay	
William Pitt (T)	1804–06	MacDonald (Lab)	1924
Lord Grenville (W)	1806–07	Stanley Baldwin (C)	1924–29
Duke of Portland (T)	1807–09	James Ramsay	
Spencer Perceval (T)	1809–12	MacDonald (Lab)	1929–31
Earl of Liverpool (T)	1812–27	James Ramsay	
George Canning (T)	1827	MacDonald (Cln)	1931–35
Viscount Goderich (T)	1827–28	Stanley Baldwin (Cln)	1935–37
Duke of Wellington (T)	1828–30	Neville Chamberlain (Cln)	1937–40
Earl Grey (W)	1830–34	Winston Churchill (Cln)	1940–45
Viscount Melbourne (W)	1834	Winston Churchill (C)	1945
Sir Robert Peel (T)	1834–35	Clement Atlee (Lab)	1945–51
Viscount Melbourne (W)	1835–41	Sir Winston Churchill (C)	1951–55
Sir Robert Peel (T)	1841–46	Sir Anthony Eden (C)	1955–57
Lord John Russell (W)	1846–52	Harold Macmillan (C)	1957–63
Earl of Derby (T)	1852	Sir Alec Douglas-Home (C)	1963–64
Earl of Aberdeen (P)	1852–55	Harold Wilson (Lab)	1964–70
Viscount Palmerston (L)	1855–58	Edward Heath (C)	1970–74
Earl of Derby (C)	1858–59	Harold Wilson (Lab)	1974–76
Viscount Palmerston (L)	1859–65	James Callaghan (Lab)	1976–79
Earl Russell (L)	1865–66	Margaret Thatcher (C)	1979–
Earl of Derby (C)	1866–68		
Benjamin Disraeli (C)	1868	W=Whig. T=Tory. Cln=Coalition. P=Peelite.	
William Gladstone (L)	1868–74	L=Liberal. C=Conservative. Lab=Labour.	

American Presidents

	president (party)	term
1	George Washington (F)	1789–97
2	John Adams (F)	1797–1801
3	Thomas Jeffferson (DR)	1801–09
4	James Madison (DR)	1809–17
5	James Monroe (DR)	1817–25
6	John Quincy Adams (DR)	1825–29
7	Andrew Jackson (D)	1829–37
8	Martin Van Buren (D)	1837–41
9	William H. Harrison* (W)	1841
10	John Tyler (W)	1841–45
11	James K. Polk (D)	1845–49
12	Zachary Taylor* (W)	1849–50
13	Millard Fillmore (W)	1850–53
14	Franklin Pierce (D)	1853–57
15	James Buchanan (D)	1857–61
16	Abraham Lincoln† (R)	1861–65
17	Andrew Johnson (U)	1865–69
18	Ulysses S. Grant (R)	1869–77
19	Rutherford B. Hayes (R)	1877–81
20	James A. Garfield† (R)	1881
21	Chester A. Arthur (R)	1881–85
22	Grover Cleveland (D)	1885–89
23	Benjamin Harrison (R)	1889–93
24	Grover Cleveland (D)	1893–97
25	William McKinley† (R)	1897–1901
26	Theodore Roosevelt (R)	1901–09
27	William H. Taft (R)	1909–13
28	Woodrow Wilson (D)	1913–21
29	Warren G. Harding* (R)	1921–23
30	Calvin Coolidge (R)	1923–29
31	Herbert C. Hoover (R)	1929–33
32	Franklin D. Roosevelt* (D)	1933–45
33	Harry S. Truman (D)	1945–53
34	Dwight D. Eisenhower (R)	1953–61
35	John F. Kennedy† (D)	1961–63
36	Lyndon B. Johnson (D)	1963–69
37	Richard M. Nixon (R)	1969–74
38	Gerald R. Ford (R)	1974–77
39	James E. Carter (D)	1977–80
40	Ronald Reagan (R)	1980–

*Died in office   †Assassinated in office
F=Federalist DR=Democratic–Republican
D=Democratic. W=Whig. R=Republican. U=Union

Tsars of Russia

The last tsar of Russia, Nicholas II (1894–1917) with his family.

Ivan III the Great	1462–1505
Basil III	1505–1533
Ivan IV the Terrible	1533–1584
Fëdor I	1584–1598
Boris Godunov	1598–1605
Fëdor II	1605
Demetrius	1605–1606
Basil (IV) Shuiski	1606–1610
[Interregnum, 1610–1613]	
Michael Romanov	1613–1645
Alexis	1645–1676
Fëdor III	1676–1682
Ivan V and Peter the Great	1682–1689
Peter the Great (alone)	1689–1725
Catherine I	1725–1727
Peter II	1727–1730
Anna	1730–1740
Ivan VI	1740–1741
Elizabeth	1741–1762
Peter III	1762
Catherine II the Great	1762–1796
Paul I	1796–1801
Alexander I	1801–1825
Nicholas I	1825–1855
Alexander II	1855–1881
Alexander III	1881–1894
Nicholas II	1894–1917

Rulers of France

Capetian

Hugh Capet	987–996
Robert	996–1031
Henry I	1031–1060
Philip I	1060–1108
Louis VI	1108–1137
Louis VII	1137–1180
Philip II, Augustus	1180–1223
Louis VIII	1223–1226
Louis IX, the Saint	1226–1270
Philip III	1270–1285
Philip IV	1285–1314
Louis X	1314–1316
Philip V	1316–1322
Charles IV	1322–1328

House of Valois

Philip VI	1328–1350
John	1350–1364
Charles V	1364–1380
Charles VI	1380–1422
Charles VII	1422–1461
Louis XI	1461–1483
Charles VIII	1483–1498
Louis XII	1498–1515
Francis I	1515–1547
Henry II	1547–1559
Francis II	1559–1560
Charles IX	1560–1574
Henry III	1574–1589

House of Bourbon

Henry IV	1589–1610
Louis XIII	1610–1643
Louis XIV	1643–1715
Louis XV	1715–1774
Louis XVI	1774–1793

FIRST REPUBLIC 1792–1804

FIRST EMPIRE
House of Buonaparte
Napoleon I *(abdicated)* 1804–1814

MONARCHY
House of Bourbon (restored)

Louis XVIII	1814–1822
Charles X *(abdicated)*	1822–1830

House of Bourbon-Orléans
Louis Philippe *(abdicated)* 1830–1848

SECOND REPUBLIC
President
Louis Napoleon Buonaparte 1849–1851

SECOND EMPIRE
House of Buonaparte (restored)
Napoleon III *(abdicated)* 1851–1870

THIRD REPUBLIC
Presidents

Adolphe Thiers	1871–1873
Marshal MacMahon	1873–1879
Julés Grévy	1879–1887
Sadi Carnot 1887 *(assassinated*, 1894)	
Jean Casimir-Périer	1894–1895
François Félix Faure	1895–1899
Émile Loubet	1899–1906
Armand Fallières	1906–1913
Raymond Poincaré	1913–1920
Paul Deschanel	1920
Alexandre Millerand	1920–1924
Gaston Doumerguc	1924–1931
Paul Doumer 1931 *(assassinated*, 1932)	
Albert Lebrun	1932–1940

(Re-elected, 1939. *Deposed*, 1940)

FRENCH STATE
Chief of State
Marshal Pétain 1940–1944

FRENCH RESISTANCE
Leader
Charles de Gaulle 1940–1946

FOURTH REPUBLIC
Presidents

Vincent-Auriol	1947–1954
René Coty	1954–1958

FIFTH REPUBLIC
Presidents

Charles de Gaulle	1958–1969
Georges Pompidou	1969–1974
Valéry Giscard d'Estaing	1974–1981
François Mitterand	1981–

Roman Emperors

	Reigned
Augustus (Octavian)	27 BC–AD 14
Tiberius	14–37
Caligula (Gaius)	37–41
Claudius	41–54
Nero	54–68
Galba	68–69
Otho	69
Vitellius	69
Vespasian	69–79
Titus	79–81
Domitian	81–96
Nerva	96–98
Trajan	98–117
Hadrian	117–138
Antoninus Pius	138–161
Lucius Aurelius Verus	161–169
Marcus Aurelius	161–180
Commodus	180–192
Pertinax	193
Didius Julian	193
Septimius Severus	193–211
Caracalla	211–217
Macrinus	217–218
Elagabalus	218–222
Alexander Severus	222–235
Maximinus	235–238
Gordian I	238
Gordian II	238
Pupienus	238
Balbinus	238
Gordian III	238–244
Philip 'the Arab'	244–249
Decius	249–251
Gallus	251–253
Aemilian	253
Valerian	253–259
Gallienus	259–268
Claudius II	268–270
Aurelian	270–275
Tacitus	275–276
Florian	276
Probus	276–282
Carus	282–283
Numerian	283–284
Carinus	284–285
Diocletian	284–305
Maximian	286–305
Constantius I	305–306
Galerius	305–311
Constantine I, the Great	311–337
Constantine II	337–340
Constantius II	337–361

A cameo portrait of the first Roman Emperor Augustus Caesar (27 BC–AD 14).

Constans	337–350
Julian, the Apostate	361–363
Jovian	363–364
Valentinian I (in the West)	364–375
Valens (in the East)	364–378
Gratian (in the West)	375–383
Valentinian II (in the West)	375–392
Theodosius, the Great (in the East, and after 394, in the West)	379–395
Maximus (in the West)	383–388
Eugenius (in the West)	392–394
Arcadius (in the East)	395–408
Honorius (in the West)	395–423
Constantius III (co-emperor in the West)	421
Theodosius II (in the East)	408–450
Valentian III (in the West)	425–455
Marcian (in the East)	450–457
Petronius (in the West)	455
Avitus (in the West)	455–456
Majorian (in the West)	457–461
Leo I (in the East)	457–474
Severus (in the West)	461–465
Anthemius (in the West)	467–472
Olybrius (in the West)	472
Glycerius (in the West)	473
Julius Nepos (in the West)	473–475
Leo II (in the East)	473–474
Zeno (in the East)	474–491
Romulus Augustulus (in the West)	475–476

Major Wars

Peloponnesian War (431–404 BC) In ancient Greece, the Spartans, Corinthians, and other members of the Peloponnesian League fought the Athenians and their allies of the Delian League. After many battles, the Athenians were starved into surrender.

Punic Wars (264–146 BC) Wars between Rome and Carthage. In the 1st, the Romans gained Sicily. In the 2nd, Hannibal invaded Italy, but the Romans were eventually victorious and gained Spain. In the 3rd, Carthage was destroyed.

The Crusades (1096–1291) A series of wars in which Christian armies from Europe sought to take the *Holy Land* (Palestine) from the Muslims and to prevent the spread of Muslim power. The Crusades caused important changes in society in Europe, but failed to defeat the Muslims in Palestine. One crusading army consisted of about 30,000 children.

Hundred Years' War (1337–1453) Struggle between England and France resulting from the claim of King Edward III of England to the French throne. The English scored some great victories, including Crécy and Agincourt. But in the end the French, rallied by Joan of Arc, were successful, and Calais was the only French territory left to England.

Thirty Years' War (1618–48) A revolt by Bohemia against the rule of the Holy Roman Empire sparked off a war against the Empire by Sweden, France, and some Protestant German states. The war devastated the German lands.

English Civil War (1642–51) King Charles I and his supporters were defeated by the Parliamentarians ('the Roundheads'), and the king was captured and executed. The war resulted in the rise to power of Oliver Cromwell.

The Fronde (1648–53) The Parlement of Paris revolted against the power of the French king, but was defeated. Discontented nobles then rebelled, but were crushed too.

War of the Spanish Succession (1701–14) King Louis XIV of France accepted the Spanish throne on behalf of his grandson, but was opposed by Britain, Austria, and other countries. In the resulting struggle, Prince Eugène and the Duke of Marlborough won notable victories. The war ended in a compromise.

Seven Years' War (1756–63) A struggle for power led to war between Britain and Prussia on one side, and Austria, France, and Russia on the other. There were fierce battles in Europe; and Britain gained Canada and laid the foundations of its Indian empire.

American War of Independence (1775–83) Thirteen British colonies in America declared their independence and defeated the British armies that opposed them. Their victory led to the establishment of the United States.

Napoleonic Wars (1792–1815) The defensive struggle of the French army after the French Revolution later developed into an attempt by France to dominate Europe. Under Napoleon Bonaparte (after 1804, the Emperor Napoleon I) French armies won many brilliant victories. But they suffered major defeats in Spain and Portugal and in Russia. Napoleon was finally overthrown at the Battle of Waterloo in 1815.

Crimean War (1853–56) A dispute between Russia and Turkey developed into a major war because of French and British suspicions of Russia's ambitions. On balance, the French, Turkish, British, and Sardinian armies were victorious, and Russia lost its dominant position in eastern Europe.

HISTORY

Indian Mutiny (1857–58) A mutiny in the Bengal army developed into a full-scale Indian revolt against British rule. The rebels tried to restore the Mughul emperors to power. After the revolt, rule by the British Crown took the place of rule by the East India Company.

American Civil War (1861–65) The first 'modern' war, it was caused by the attempted secession (withdrawal) of 11 southern states from the United States. The northern states (*the Union*) sent armies to prevent the secession. The southern states (*the Confederacy*) fought bitterly, but lost. One issue was slavery, which the southerners wished to retain.

Franco-Prussian War (1870–71) Rivalry between France and Prussia led to war and to humiliating defeat for France. The victorious Prussians established a new German Empire.

Boer Wars (1880–1902) In 1880–81, the Boers (South African Dutch) defeated British forces and established an independent republic in the Transvaal. Fighting started again in1899: after early reverses, the British were victorious.

Sino-Japanese Wars (1894–1945) Three wars between the Chinese and Japanese ended in the defeat of Japan in 1945.

World War I (1914–18) This involved peoples from every continent, though it was centred in Europe. On one side were the *Allies*, chiefly Britain and its Empire, France, Italy, Russia, and the United States. On the other side, the *Central Powers* included Germany, Austria-Hungary, and Turkey. The chief battlegrounds were the *western front* in France and Belgium, the *eastern front* on the Russian borders, and the Atlantic Ocean, where German submarines sank ships carrying food and other supplies to Allied ports. The Central Powers eventually collapsed. More than 15 million people lost their lives in the war.

Two great Allied generals in World War II, Supreme Allied Commander Dwight Eisenhower and Bernard Montgomery.

Spanish Civil War (1936–39) A revolt by army leaders against a left-wing government developed into a violent civil war. Fascist support for one side and communist support for the other gave the conflict world-wide significance. The rebels were victorious.

World War II (1939–45) This began with the invasion of Poland by armies from Nazi Germany. It involved the peoples of more than 50 countries in the most destructive war in history, and cost more than 20 million lives. The *Allies*, on one side, included Britain and the Commonwealth and Empire countries, France, China, Russia, and the United States. The *Axis*, on the other side, included Germany, Italy, and Japan. Fierce land and air battles were fought in Europe, Asia, and Africa, and sea battles in the Atlantic, Pacific, and Indian Oceans.

Korean War (1950–53) After an invasion of South Korea by communist North Korea, the United Nations declared North Korea an aggressor and asked UN members to aid South Korea. A number did so, the chief part being taken by the United States. The Russians and communist Chinese aided North Korea.

Famous Battles

Marathon 490 BC Persian-Greek Wars. Miltiades with 10,000 Greeks routed Darius with 60,000 Persians.

Hastings 1066 Norman Conquest of England. Some 9000 invaders under William of Normandy defeated Harold II and his Saxons.

Agincourt 1415 Hundred Years' War. Henry V and 5700 English, mainly archers, defeated 25,000 French.

Orléans 1429 Hundred Years' War. Joan of Arc defeated an English army besieging the city.

Constantinople 1453 Fall of the Byzantine Empire. The Turks took Constantinople.

Lepanto 1571 Cyprus War. Don John of Austria with 250 Spanish, Venetian, and papal ships destroyed a Turkish fleet of 270 vessels.

Blenheim 1704 War of the Spanish Succession. French and Bavarians defeated by a British-Austrian army under Prince Eugène and the Duke of Marlborough.

First battle of Ypres 1914 German forces trying to reach Calais lost 150,000 men. British and French forces held off attack, losing more than 100,000 men.

Verdun 1916 In a six-month struggle French forces held off a major attack by German armies. French losses were 348,000; German losses 328,000.

Jutland 1916 British Grand Fleet fought German High Seas Fleet. The Germans did not again venture out to sea.

Somme 1916 In a 141-day battle following Verdun, the British and French captured 320 sq km (125 sq miles) of ground, losing 600,000 men. The German defenders lost almost 500,000 men.

Passchendaele 1917 British forces launched eight attacks over 102 days in heavy rain and through thick mud. They

A castle under siege in the Middle Ages. In times of war peasants from the country round a castle would come with their animals to shelter inside its walls.

gained 8 km (5 miles) and lost 400,000 men.

Britain 1940 A German air force of 2500 planes launched an attack lasting 114 days to try and win air supremacy over Britain. The smaller Royal Air Force defeated the attack.

Midway 1942 A fleet of 100 Japanese ships was defeated in the Pacific by an American fleet half the size.

El Alamein 1942 Montgomery's British Eighth Army drove Rommel's German Afrika Korps out of Egypt.

Stalingrad 1942–1943 Twenty-one German divisions tried to capture Stalingrad (now Volgograd) but siege was broken and more than 100,000 German troops surrendered.

Normandy 1944 Allied forces under Eisenhower invaded German-held northern France in biggest-ever seaborne attack. After a month of fighting Germans retreated.

Leyte Gulf 1944 United States 3rd and 7th fleets defeated a Japanese force, ending Japanese naval power in World War II.

Ardennes Bulge 1944–1945 Last German counter-attack in west through Ardennes Forest failed. Germans lost 100,000 casualties and 110,000 prisoners.

117

Historical Assassinations

Victim	Details of assassination	Date
Julius Caesar, Roman dictator	Stabbed by Brutus, Cassius *et al.* in Senate	44 BC
Thomas à Becket, English archbishop	Slain by four knights in cathedral	29.12.1170
Lord Darnley, husband of Mary Queen of Scots	Blow up; plot	10.2.1567
Gustavus III of Sweden	Plot: shot by Johan Ankarström	29.3.1792
Jean Marat, French revolutionary	Stabbed in bath by Charlotte Corday	13.7.1793
Abraham Lincoln, US president	Shot by actor, J. Wilkes Booth, in theatre	14.4.1865*
James Garfield, US president	Shot at station by Charles Guiteau (grudge)	2.7.1881†
Antonio Cánovas del Castillo, Spanish premier	Shot by anarchist	8.8.1897
Humbert I, king of Italy	By anarchist at Monza	29.7.1900
William McKinley, US president	Shot by anarchist, Leon Czolgosz, at Buffalo	6.9.1901‡
Pyotr Stolypin, Russian premier	Shot by revolutionary, Dmitri Bogrov	14.9.1911§
George I, king of Greece	At Salonika	18.3.1913
Francis Ferdinand, archduke of Austria	Alleged Serbian plot: shot in car by Gavrilo Princip at Sarajevo (sparked World War I)	28.6.1914
Jean Jaurès, French socialist	By nationalist, in café	31.7.1914
Rasputin, powerful Russian monk	By Russian noblemen	31.12.1916
Michael Collins, Irish Sinn Fein leader	Ambushed and shot	22.8.1922
Engelbert Dollfuss, Austrian chancellor	Shot by Nazis in chancellery	25.7.1934
Huey Long, corrupt American politician	By Dr Carl Austin Weiss	8.9.1935**
Leon Trotsky, exiled Russian communist leader	Axed in Mexico by Ramon de Rio	21.8.1940
Mahatma Gandhi, Indian nationalist leader	Shot by Hindu fanatic, Nathuran Godse	30.1.1948
Count Folke Bernadotte, Swedish diplomat	Ambushed in Jerusalem by Jewish extremists	17.9.1948
SWRD Bandaranaike, Ceylonese premier	By Buddhist monk in Columbo	25.9.1959
Rafael Trujillo Molina, Dominican Republic dictator	Car machine-gunned	30.5.1961
John F. Kennedy, US President	Shot in car, Dallas, Texas‡‡	22.11.1963
Malcolm X (Little), US Black Muslim leader	Shot at rally	21.2.1965
Hendrike Verwoerd, South African premier	Stabbed by parliamentary messenger, Dimitri Tsafendas (later ruled mentally disordered)	6.9.1966
Rev. Martin Luther King Jr., US Negro Civil Rights leader	Shot on hotel balcony by James Earl Ray, in Memphis, Tennessee	4.4.1968
Robert F. Kennedy, US senator	Shot by Arab immigrant, Sirhan Sirhan, in Los Angeles (Hotel Ambassador)	5.6.1968
Christopher Ewart-Biggs, British ambassador to Republic of Ireland	Car blown up by landmine planted by IRA	21.7.1976
Aldo Moro, president of Italy's Christian Democrats and five times prime minister of Italy	Kidnapped by 'Red Brigade' terrorists (16.3.78) and later found dead	9.5.1978
Airey Neave, British Conservative MP and Northern Ireland spokesman	Explosion under car while leaving House of Commons car park; IRA	30.3.1979
Lord Mountbatten, uncle of Duke of Edinburgh	Explosion in sailing boat off coast of Ireland; IRA	27.8.1979
Park Chung Hee, president of South Korea	Shot in restaurant by chief of Korean Central Intelligence Agency	26.10.1979
Roman Catholic archbishop Oscar Romeroy Galdamez of El Salvador	Shot by right-wing gunmen while saying mass in San Salvador	24.3.1980
John Lennon, musician/songwriter and ex-Beatle	Shot in street in New York by Mark David Chapman	15.12.1980
Anwar al-Sadat, president of Egypt	Shot by rebel soldiers while reviewing military parade	6.10.1981
Mrs Indira Gandhi Indian prime minister	By her own Sikh bodyguards	31.10.1984

*Died next day. †Died 19 Sept. ‡Died 14 Sept. §Died 18 Sept. **Died 10 Sept.
‡‡Accused, Lee Harvey Oswald, himself shot by Jack Ruby (24 Nov.) while awaiting trial.

ANIMALS

Recent Time

Quaternary
Period

Tertiary
Period

CENOZOIC
ERA

Cretaceous
Period

Jurassic
Period

Triassic
Period

MESOZOIC
ERA

Permian
Period

Carboniferous
Period

Devonian
Period

PALAEOZOIC
ERA

Silurian
Period

Ordovician
Period

Cambrian
Period

Geologists divide the millions of years of prehistory into eras. During the Palaeozoic 'old life' Era, until 225 million years ago, life evolved from simple marine creatures and plants to include amphibians and insects. The Mesozoic 'middle life' Era saw the age of the dinosaur; then mammals, birds and flowering plants appeared. From 70 million years ago on is the Cenozoic Era.

Early Life on Earth

Many scientists believe that life on Earth started in the seas. Complex carbon compounds were concentrated there and formed rich 'soup' where simple proteins and nucleic acids could develop. Some of these joined together to form the first living cells. Single-celled plants and animals multiplied, and later more and more complicated forms of life appeared and moved from the seas to land and air.

We gain knowledge of prehistoric plants and animals from their fossils – their remains or impressions in the rocks. Geologists (people who study rocks), and palaeontologists (people who study fossils), divide up the time since the Earth was formed into a number of Periods.

The Earth is believed to be about 4600 million years old. Few traces of life appear in the rocks formed during the first 4000 million years – the so-called Pre-Cambrian Period. The processes of mountain-building, volcanic activity, and erosion destroyed most of the remains there might have been. But at the start of the Cambrian Period sediments began to accumulate on the seabed, together with the remains of living things. In time the sediments became rocks and the remains fossils.

Cambrian period (600 million – 500 million years ago)

Life became abundant in the sea. Algae, seaweed and sponges grew in the shallow waters. There were animals without backbones and often with shells in profusion. They included simple single-celled protozoa. Some, called radiolaria, had spiky shells of silica. Others, called foraminifera, had chalky shells. Countless millions of these shells form the basis of many present-day chalk and limestone formations. There were also jelly-fish, starfish, trilobites, and graptolites. Many fossils remain of the trilobite Agnostus, a minute creature whose hard shells fossilized easily. There were also many crinoids, plant-like animals that were anchored to the sea bed and which are also known as sea lilies.

Ordovician Period (500 million – 440 million years ago)

Most of the Earth was still covered by shallow seas and on the whole the climate was warm. Life was still confined to the seas. Sea-urchins, sea lilies, corals, graptolites, starfishes, and trilobites were still common. But most numerous were varieties of shellfish. There were single-shelled snails and double-shelled lamp-shells, properly called brachiopods. Ancient ancestors of the octopus and cuttle fish called nautiloids became common. The length of the uncoiled shell of some specimens reached 4·5 m (15 ft). The first vertebrate animal, the Aniktozoon – a fish-like creature – appeared in the sea.

Silurian Period (440 million – 400 million years ago)

Low land was repeatedly washed by the seas. Mountains were formed in north-west Europe and elsewhere near the end of the period. The climate was warm. The seas teemed with much the same kind of life as in the previous period, with brachiopods becoming increasingly common. Newcomers were the eurypterids, giant sea scorpions. Large specimens measured about 2·5 m (8–9 ft) long. Primitive jawless fishes called ostracoderms swam in the seas.

A Dictionary of Dinosaurs

Allosaurus was a huge meat-eating dinosaur over 9 m (29 ft) long which ran on powerful hind legs.

Ankylosaurus was one of the most heavily armoured dinosaurs, with bony plates and spikes covering its head, back and tail.

Apatosaurus is another name for Brontosaurus.

Barosaurus was a long-necked dinosaur which browsed on the leaves of trees.

Brachiosaurus resembled Brontosaurus but was even larger. Weighing over 50 tonnes, it was the largest land animal ever to live on Earth.

Brontosaurus was a huge plant-eating dinosaur.

Camptosaurus was an ornithopod about 6 m (20 ft) long which fed mainly on juicy leaves of trees.

Ceratopsians were a group of horned, plant-eating dinosaurs.

Corythosaurus was a duckbill dinosaur, with a helmet-like crest on its head.

Dinosaur is the name given to the great extinct land reptiles belonging to the Saurischian and Ornithischian orders.

Diplodocus was the longest of the dinosaurs. It measured 30 m (98 ft) from head to tail.

Hadrosaurs were a group of dinosaurs with broad, toothless beaks which have earned them the name 'duckbills'.

Iguanadon

9m
(29½ ft)

Heterodontosaurus was a nimble little reptile barely larger than a goose.

Iguanodon was a plant-eating ornithopod about 9 m (30 ft) long which ran on its hind legs.

Ophiacodon was an early meat-eater about 3 m (10 ft) long.

Ornithischians formed one of the two great groups of dinosaurs. All were plant-eaters. The other great group of dinosaurs were the Saurischians.

Ornithomimus was the shape and size of an ostrich. It was a nimble reptile which probably stole eggs from the nests of other reptiles.

Ornithopods were a group of plant-eating dinosaurs which walked on their hind legs.

Pachycephalosaurus was one of the group of dinosaurs nicknamed 'bone-heads'. These dinosaurs had skulls over 25 cm (10 inches) thick.

Parasaurolophus was one of the plant-eating duckbill dinosaurs.

Plateosaurus was an early plant-eater which moved about slowly on all fours.

Saurischians formed one of the two great groups of dinosaurs. They included the gigantic sauropods, such as Brachiosaurus, and the fearsome flesh-eaters, such as Tyrannosaurus. The other great group was the Ornithischians.

Sauropods were a group of gigantic plant-eating dinosaurs with huge bodies, long necks and tiny heads, such as Brontosaurus and Diplodocus. The sauropods must have spent nearly all their time feeding.

Stegosaurus was an armoured dinosaur about 7 m (23 ft) long. It had bony plates on its back and spikes on its tail.

Styracosaurus was a horned dinosaur with a spiked collar around its neck. Styracosaurus was one of the last dinosaurs.

Triceratops was an armoured dinosaur with three long horns on its head and a bony frill round its neck.

Tyrannosaurus was the largest of the fearsome flesh-eating dinosaurs. It stood 6 m high on its powerful hind legs and was 16 m (52 ft) long.

A Bird and some Prehistoric Mammals

Arsinoitherium A 3·5-m (11-ft) long animal rather like a rhinoceros found in what is now Egypt about 30 million years ago.

Baluchitherium The largest known land mammal ever to have lived was about 7 m (23 ft) tall, and lived in Asia about 25 million years ago. Its head was over a metre long.

Daphoenodon This has been called the 'bear-dog', and was about $1\frac{1}{4}$ m (5 ft) long, living about 15 million years ago.

Deinotherium An early ancestor of the elephant which lived about 12 million years ago in Europe and Asia and later in Africa.

Diatryma A flightless bird which lived about 40 million years ago in North America and Europe. It was about 2 m (7 ft) tall, with thick legs, a large head and a powerful beak.

Diprotodon The largest-known marsupial, a plant-eater, lived in Australia about a million years ago. It was $3\frac{1}{4}$ m (11 ft) long.

Eohippus A tiny ancestor of the horse, no bigger than a fox-terrier, lived in North America about 40 million years ago.

Glyptodon Very similar to the modern armadillo, this creature, living in South America about a million years ago, was about 3 m (9 ft) long.

Mastodon An early form of the elephant, this animal was very common for millions of years, dating back to 40 or 50 million years ago.

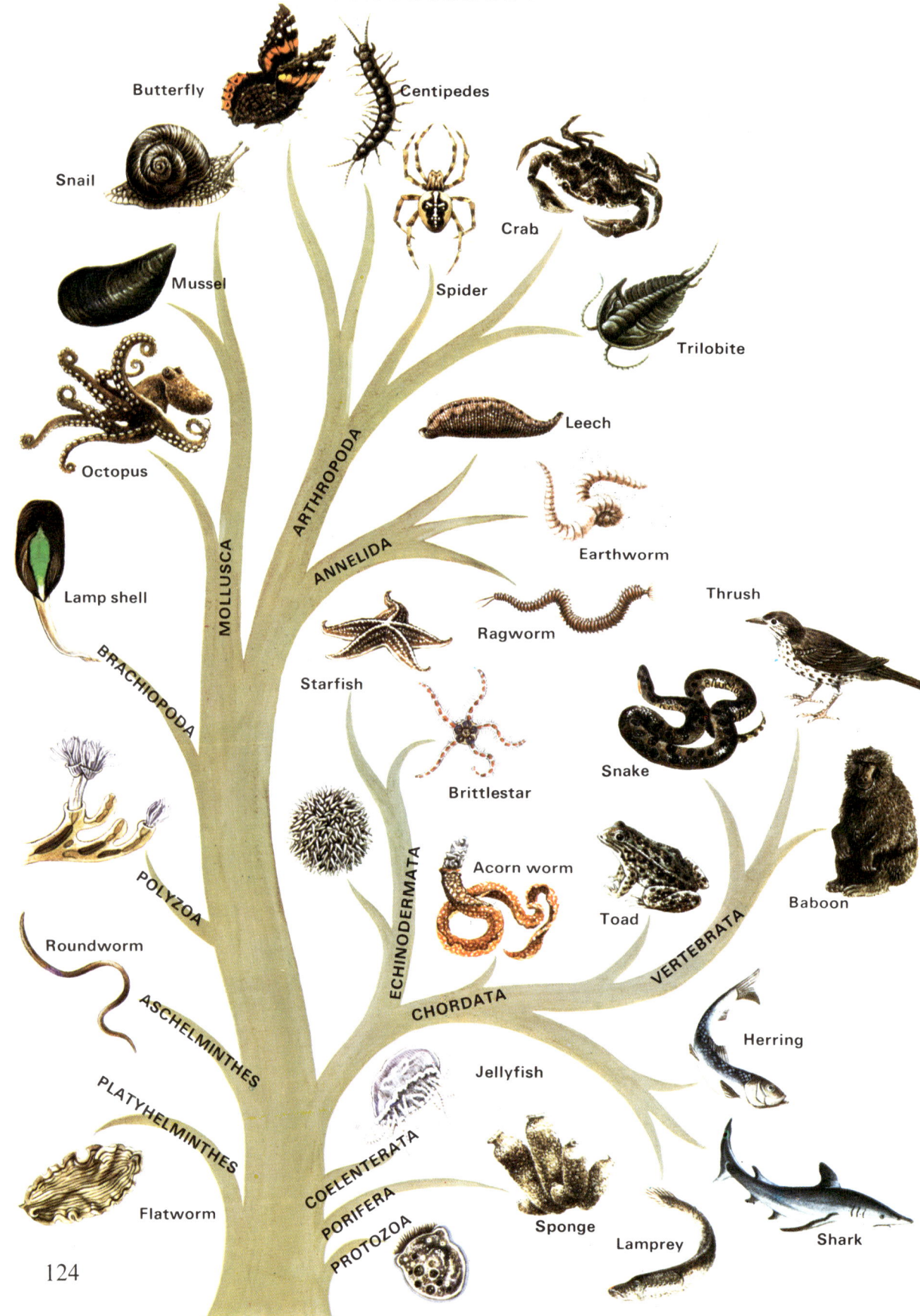

Butterfly
Centipedes
Snail
Spider
Crab
Mussel
Trilobite
Octopus
Leech
Earthworm
Thrush
Lamp shell
Starfish
Ragworm
MOLLUSCA
ANNELIDA
ARTHROPODA
BRACHIOPODA
Snake
Brittlestar
POLYZOA
Acorn worm
Baboon
Roundworm
Toad
ECHINODERMATA
VERTEBRATA
ASCHELMINTHES
CHORDATA
Herring
PLATYHELMINTHES
Jellyfish
COELENTERATA
Flatworm
PORIFERA
Sponge
Shark
PROTOZOA
Lamprey

LARGEST, SMALLEST, FASTEST, OLDEST

Largest animal is the Blue or Sulphur-bottom whale *(Balaenoptera musculus)*. Specimens have been caught measuring more than 30 m (100 ft) long, though Blue whales this size have not been seen for many years.

Smallest animals are some of the protozoa, single-celled creatures. Many of them are around 2 μ (0.00007874 in) long. They can be seen only with a powerful microscope.

Largest animal living on land is the African elephant (*Loxodonta africana*). Bull elephants are about 3.5 m ($11\frac{1}{2}$ ft) tall and weigh up to 7 tonnes.

Longest living animal is the Giant tortoise (*Testudo elephantopus*) known to live up to 177 years.

Fastest animal on land is the cheetah (*Acinonyx jubatus*), which can run at up to 105 km/h (65 mph) over short distances.

Fastest fliers are probably Common swifts which can reach 160 km/h (100 mph) in level flight; peregrine falcons (*Falco peregrinus*) can dive at up to 290 km/h (180 mph).

A Dictionary of Animal Life

adaptation means any characteristic that a species of plant or animal has developed which helps it to survive in its environment. The thick coats, small ears and short tails of Arctic mammals are adaptations to cold living conditions.

aestivation. *Hibernation* means the inactive period that many animals undergo in winter. Certain other animals go through a period of inactivity in hot, dry summer weather. This is called aestivation.

ageing is the process by which an adult animal or plant wears out. An ageing animal cannot make enough new body cells to replace all the old ones that die off. Also wastes collect in the body and affect it.

amoeba is the name given to a group of one-celled jelly-like animals that constantly change shape. They reproduce by simply splitting into two.

amphibians are cold-blooded vertebrates usually with four limbs and soft moist skins. Their shell-less unprotected eggs are generally laid in water, and when the young larvae hatch out they usually spend some time in water before they become adults and live on land. Frogs, toads, salamanders and newts are amphibians.

antelopes are cud-chewing mammals with bony horns. Among them are the eland, the springbok, the hartebeeste and the gnu.

arachnids are the class of *arthropods* (animals with jointed legs and external skeletons) which includes spiders, scorpions, ticks and mites. Most have four pairs of legs.

The tree on the left shows the main groups in the animal kingdom. The smallest branches represent classes (for example, the baboon, a mammal). Some of the classes of worms and other small groups have been omitted.

125

arthropods form the largest group of all the many-celled animals. This group consists of *invertebrates* with jointed legs and an external skeleton. All insects and spiders are arthropods; so are shrimps, crabs and lobsters.

birds are warm-blooded feathered *vertebrates* with light, hollow bones and with their two fore-limbs developed as wings. Most of them can fly, but a few, such as penguins and ostriches, are flightless.

bony fishes are fishes whose skeletons are of real bone (instead of cartilage), such as cod, herring, haddock, pike and salmon.

brachiopods are marine animals with a two-valved shell rather like that of a cockle. As adults they live a fixed life, feeding on food particles brought by currents created by their hair-like cilia. Although they look like bivalve *molluscs*, the brachiopods belong to a very different group of animals.

breathing is the process by which some animals pump air or water in and out of their bodies. All animals extract oxygen from air or water, use it to 'burn' the fuel provided by their food, and then rid themselves of some of the waste products of the burning, such as carbon dioxide.

carnivores are animals that feed wholly or mainly on flesh. Lions, tigers, and sharks are typical carnivores.

cartilaginous fishes are those whose skeletons are made not of bone but of cartilage. Sharks and rays are cartilaginous fishes.

chordates include all animals with at least a very simple rod-like backbone. Most of them, by the time they are adults, have a true backbone and a skull, and these are called vertebrates. The rest never develop a true backbone or a head. They are called protochordates.

coelenterates are a group of water-living *invertebrates*. They have a gut with only one opening, and no blood system. Jellyfish, corals and sea-anemones are coelenterates.

cold-blooded animals are those such as reptiles, whose body temperature changes with the temperature of their surroundings. In very cold surroundings their temperature may fall so low that they are almost completely inactive for a time.

conservation. When any species of animal or plant dies out it can never be replaced. Conservation means taking whatever steps are possible to prevent rare or threatened plants and animals from becoming extinct. It usually involves preserving areas in which the creatures live so that they can survive undisturbed.

crocodilia is the name given to the order of flesh-eating reptiles that includes crocodiles and alligators. Many of these large animals are strong, fast swimmers but spend most of their time just resting in or near the water.

crustaceans are a class of *arthropods*. Most of them, such as crabs, lobsters, shrimps and water-fleas, live in water.

digestion. This is the process by which animals break down the food they eat into simpler substances which they can use for growth, energy and to repair body tissues.

echinoderms are spiny-skinned marine *invertebrates*, such as sea-urchins, starfish, brittle-stars, and sea-cucumbers. The roughness of their skins is due to chalky plates embedded in them.

ecology means the study of all the plants and animals in any particular *habitat*, and the relationships between them. Ecologists are especially interested in *food chains*.

family. An *order* of animals is divided into groups called families. The members of a family are all closely related and usually quite alike. All cats, for example, belong to one family in the order Carnivora.

fertilization is the process by which a male sex cell unites with a female sex cell to form a special cell called a zygote, which gives rise to a new plant or animal.

flatworms include tapeworms and flukes. They are flat and often ribbon-like. Some flatworms live freely in soil and water, but tapeworms and flukes all live as *parasites* inside other animals.

genus Many *families* of animals are divided into a number of genera. The cat family, for example, contains several genera, but all the small cats, including the domestic cat, belong to the genus, Felis. Each genus is made up of very similar animals.

habitat A habitat is a place that provides its own special surroundings and conditions for the creatures that inhabit it. Four very different habitats are a seashore, a hot sandy desert, a coniferous forest, and a grassland.

herbivores are animals that feed entirely on plants. Cows, giraffes and sheep are herbivores.

hibernation means winter sleep. When an animal hibernates, its body temperature falls, slowing down all the chemical changes that go on in the body, and making the animal sleepy and inactive. Some hibernating animals almost cease to breathe and all of them eat little or nothing until spring returns. But a few, such as bats, wake up occasionally to feed.

insects form the largest class of *arthropods*. They have three pairs of legs, and three distinct parts of the body (head, thorax and abdomen). Many of them have wings. Earwigs, bees, ants, fleas and butterflies are insects.

invertebrates are animals without even a rudimentary backbone. Cockles, mussels, snails, insects, spiders, starfish and worms are all invertebrates.

krill are shrimp-like animals, up to about 3 cm (1 inch) long that form part of the zooplankton (small drifting animals) on or near the sea's surface.

larva is the name given to the stage that many animals pass through between hatching from an egg and becoming adult. The larva is very different from the adult, as a tadpole is from a frog, or a caterpillar from a butterfly.

lizards are reptiles that have long, slender, scaly bodies, a tail and usually four five-toed limbs.

mammals are warm-blooded *vertebrates* with hair and a well-developed brain. All feed their young with their own milk. They range in size from the tiny shrew to the giant blue whale.

marsupials are mammals whose young are very undeveloped when born. They spend a period of development in a pouch on the mother's body. Most of the world's marsupials live in Australia, but a few are native to South America. Kangaroos and opossums are marsupials.

metamorphosis is the drastic change that many animals undergo between the stages of being a larva and being an adult, as when a tadpole becomes a frog or a caterpillar becomes a butterfly.

metazoa are many-celled animals. They make up a whole sub-kingdom of the animal kingdom, and range from tiny water-fleas and mice to whales and elephants.

mimicry. Many harmless and otherwise defenceless animals are shaped and coloured very much like poisonous or dangerous ones. This device, which is called mimicry, makes it less likely that predators will attack them.

molluscs are soft-bodied invertebrates, most of which have a hard shell. They include snails, oysters and octopuses.

monotremes are primitive mammals that do not give birth to live young ones but lay eggs instead. The duck-billed platypus and spiny anteater are monotremes.

mutualism is the word used to describe an association between two different kinds of living creature that brings advantages to both. See also *Symbiosis*.

myriapods are long, thin land-living arthropods with many legs. Among them are centipedes and millipedes.

nematodes include eel-worms, round worms and thread-worms. Some nematodes live as parasites in plants or on other animals. But other nematodes live independent lives. There are millions in the soil.

nervous system. This is the system that enables animals to become aware of changing conditions outside their own bodies and to react to what they learn. Special nerve cells carry impulses from all over the body – skin, nose, ears, eyes and mouth – to a central controlling part of the nervous system, which in advanced animals is the brain. Other nerve cells carry appropriate 'action messages' from the central control to the muscles, causing the animal to move in whatever way is appropriate to outside circumstances.

nocturnal animals are those which are most active by night, and rest by day. Owls and bats are almost all nocturnal.

notochord. This is the name given to the very simple rod-like backbone that all *chordates* have at some stage of their development. In *vertebrates* the notochord is replaced by a true backbone with vertebrae at a very early stage in life.

parasites are creatures that live on or in the bodies of other creatures (called their 'hosts'). A parasite obtains food from its host but gives nothing in return.

parasitism – living as a parasite – is very common in nature, and is not always dangerous to the host, though it is often a nuisance. It is not in the parasite's interest to kill its host, for by doing so it would lose its home and its food supply.

phylum. Biologists divide the *Animal Kingdom* and the *Plant Kingdom* into smaller groups called Phyla. All the animals in the same phyla have important features in common. Among the phyla of the Animal Kingdom are *coelenterates, rotifers, molluscs, arthropods, echinoderms* and *chordates*.

phytoplankton consists of all the drifting green plants found on or near the surface of seas and lakes.

placental mammals form by far the greater part of all mammals. They have larger brains than other mammals, such as marsupials, and their young ones become well developed inside the mother's body before they are born.

porifera, or sponges, are many-celled animals usually not included among the *metazoa*. They live a fixed life in water, drawing water into their bodies through small pores and passing it out again through larger pores. The moving water brings them the food particles they live on.

predators are animals that live by preying on other animals. Many birds are predators of caterpillars; sharks are predators of various fishes.

primates are the group of *mammals* that includes monkeys, apes and man. They have large brains, good eye-sight, usually nails instead of claws, and fingers, thumbs and toes that are specially useful for grasping things.

protochordates are animals that have a *notochord* but which, unlike vertebrates, have no true head or heart. One protochordate is the lancelet, which looks fish-like but has no eyes and no true skeleton.

protozoans are animals that consist of

only a single cell with a nucleus. They make up a whole sub-kingdom of the Animal Kingdom.

reptiles are a class of cold-blooded *vertebrates* with tough, horny or scaly skins. Most lay eggs protected by a shell. They include turtles, tortoises, snakes, lizards and crocodiles. Most of them live on land though some, such as crocodiles, turtles and sea snakes, live in water.

rodents are gnawing mammals, such as rats, mice, beavers and squirrels. Rodents have chisel-like front teeth that grow continually, so that they are never worn down.

roundworms are a large group of simple worms that have no sign of rings or segments on their bodies. Many are parasites, living inside other animals.

scavengers are animals that feed on dead plants, dead animals, or animal droppings. By doing so they help to keep a habitat clean. Vultures are useful and important scavengers in many tropical countries.

snakes are long, cylindrical limbless reptiles with scaly skins which they shed from time to time. Snakes can swallow prey larger than their own heads. They do this by 'unhinging' their jaws. Many snakes secrete poison in their salivary glands. The bite of some species can swiftly kill a person.

social insects are insects that live in communities, with different individuals doing different jobs to help the rest. Honeybees are typical. The queen's only job is to lay eggs. The worker bees have many tasks – gathering food, feeding the larvae, tidying the hive, and beating their wings to fan and ventilate it.

species. Every *genus* of animal consists of one or more species. For example, the genus *Equus* includes the horse, three species of zebra and two kinds of wild ass. These six species are alike in their basic structure, but they differ in certain details. Only male and female animals of the same species can produce young capable of breeding.

symbiosis means 'living together', but it is used mainly to describe an association between two different kinds of living creature that brings advantages to both, for example the relationship between oxpeckers and buffalo. See also *Mutualism.*

tadpole is the name given to the fish-like *larva* of an *amphibian* such as a frog or toad. Having no legs or lungs, a tadpole swims in water and breathes through gills. In time it develops legs and lungs; it then loses its tail and gills, and lives on land.

territory. Many animals regard an area around where they live as being especially their own, and will defend it against other animals of their own kind. For example, a dog may bark at another dog that sniffs at the garden gate, but ignore a hedgehog that ambles across the lawn. A robin may chase other robins away from a wide area around its nest, but pay little or no attention to sparrows.

warm-blooded animals are those that control their own body temperatures, so that they do not become too hot in hot surroundings or too cold in cold surroundings.

ungulates are herbivorous (plant-eating) hoofed mammals. Horses, camels and cows are ungulates.

vertebrates are animals with true backbones and skulls. Fishes, amphibians, reptiles, birds and mammals are all vertebrates.

zooplankton is made up of all the tiny animals, larvae and eggs that drift along on or near the surface of the world's seas and lakes.

Many-Legged Creatures

Of all forms of life, the most varied are the insects. More than 700,000 different species are known, and more are being classified each year. The number of individual insects is almost beyond calculation.

An adult insect has six legs, and a body in three sections covered with a hard casing known as an exoskeleton. Most insects have wings. Their eyes are made up of up to 30,000 tiny lenses called facets, each facet contributing a tiny part of the whole view to the insect's brain. Insects have senses of smell and taste, and many kinds can hear, too. They have cold blood which may be colourless, green, or yellow.

Insects are grouped into 33 orders, each containing many families, genera, and species.

Apterygote insects are the simplest kind. They have no wings, and the young are similar in appearance to the adults, except in size.

Exopterygote insects mostly have wings, and pass through three stages of development – egg, nymph, and adult. They include dragonflies (order Odonata), crickets (order Orthoptera), earwigs (Dermaptera), and bugs (Hemiptera).

Endopterygote insects are also winged, and go through four stages – egg, larva, pupa, and adult. They include butterflies and moths (Lepidoptera), flies (Diptera), and beetles and weevils (Coleoptera).

These are not insects. The animals shown here all have jointed limbs like insects, and all belong to the same big group of animals called Arthropods. But they are not insects: all have more than three pairs of legs, and none has any wings.

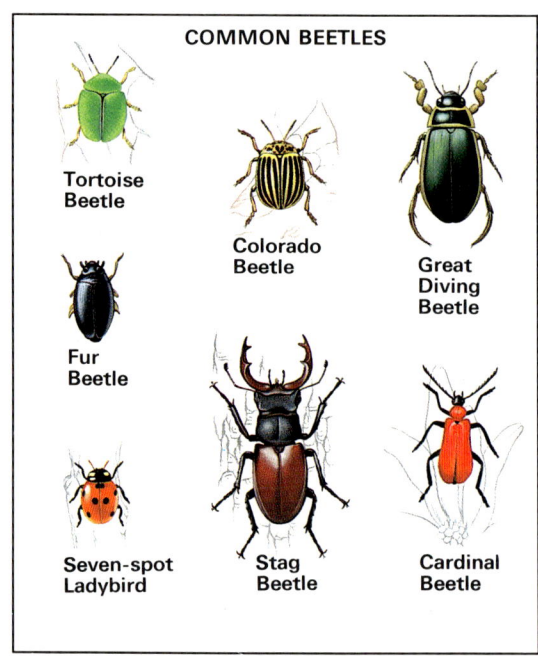

COMMON BEETLES

Tortoise Beetle

Colorado Beetle

Great Diving Beetle

Fur Beetle

Seven-spot Ladybird

Stag Beetle

Cardinal Beetle

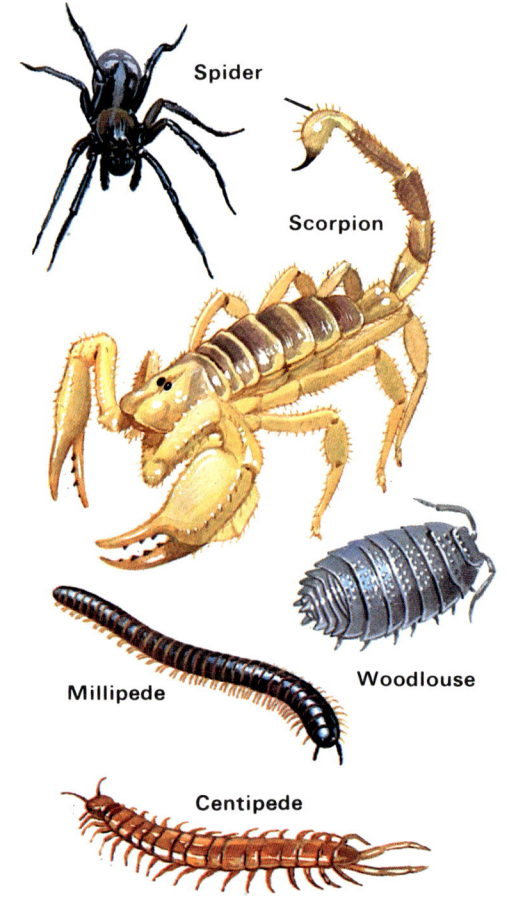

Spider

Scorpion

Millipede

Woodlouse

Centipede

BUTTERFLIES

SOME BUTTERFLIES AND MOTHS

Heath Fritillary

Small Heath

Swallowtail
Butterfly

Meadow Brown
Butterfly

Death's Head
Hawkmoth

Chalkhill Blue

Large White
Butterfly

Peacock
Butterfly

Common Blue
Butterfly

Marbled White

Wall Brown

Puss Moth

Clouded Yellow
Butterfly

Small Copper
Butterfly

Grizzled Skipper

*The patterns and colours on the wings of
butterflies and moths are made from
thousands of tiny scales too small to see
without the help of a microscope.*

Dark Green Fritillary

131

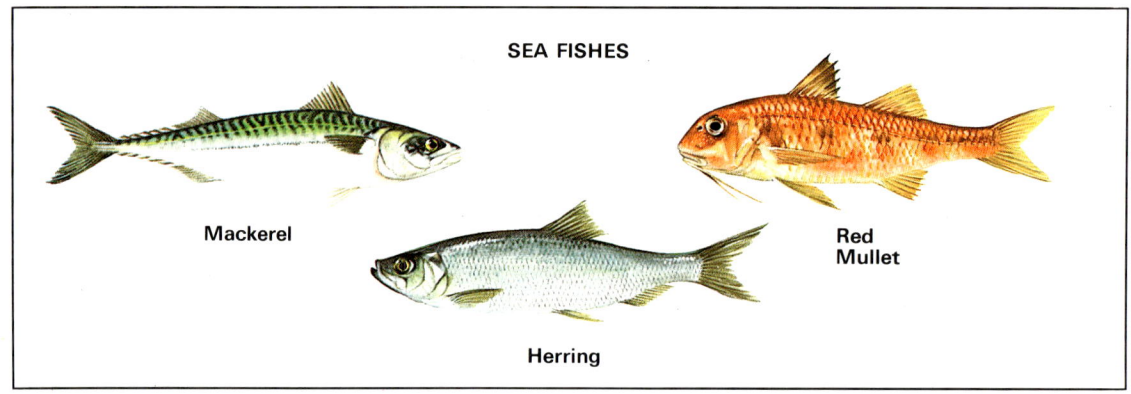

SEA FISHES

Mackerel

Red Mullet

Herring

Migration

Birds find their way over enormous distances with astonishing accuracy. A swallow, for example, can fly from France to South Africa, and return not only to the same country but to the very place it built its nest the year before.

It seems that birds navigate in much the same way as sailors once did, using the Sun, Moon and stars to guide them.

It took people thousands of years to make instruments to do this. But birds apparently have such devices built in.

Birds, however, fly at night and in cloudy weather when there is no Sun to help them. Experiments with birds in a planetarium show that they use star patterns to guide them when the stars are visible. When there is no visible aid they seem to use the Earth's magnetic field as their guide. Tests with birds in metal chambers shielding them from the Earth's magnetism have proved that a bird's brain also has a built-in compass.

Birds also use ordinary vision for finding their way over short distances.

In some ways even more amazing, because of their size, are the journeys made by insects. Monarch butterflies spend the summer in Canada and the northern United States. In autumn they fly south to winter in the southern states and Mexico. Other butterflies and moths make similar journeys every year.

Comparatively few mammals migrate, though many of them lead nomadic lives, wandering in search of food. The caribou of North America wander northward to breed in the tundra, the region of winter ice and summer vegetation that borders the Arctic Ocean. At the end of the brief northern summer they return to the wooded regions further south. Similar migration patterns have been noted for the reindeer of northern Europe and Asia.

Migration is common among fish and other animals that make the sea their home. The European eel, for example, breeds in the Sargasso Sea, in the western Atlantic Ocean. The eel *larvae*, barely 8 cm (3 inches) long, swim to the shores of Europe and North America. During the journey they change into elvers – young eels. The elvers swim up rivers and spend several years in fresh water.

Salmon spawn in fresh water and then die. The young salmon, at the age of about a year, swim down river and out to sea where they travel thousands of miles feeding and growing. They then return to the rivers where they were born.

Whales make regular migrations across the oceans in search of food. Plankton, the main food of most whales, abounds in polar seas in summer, and the whales go there to feed.

FISH RECORDS

The longest bony fish is the beluga (*Huso huso*), a kind of sturgeon found in the USSR. It has been known to grow up to 7.2 m (23 ft 7 in) in length, and reach a weight of 1360 kg (3000 lb).

The heaviest bony fish is the Ocean sunfish (*Mola mola*) which can weigh up to 2 tonnes.

The smallest fish and also the smallest vertebrate is the Dwarf goby, found in fresh water in the Philippines and the Marshall Islands. The maximum size for these tiny fish is 1.25 cm ($\frac{1}{2}$ in).

FRESHWATER FISHES

Pike

Perch

Chub

Carp

The largest group of back-boned animals is the fish. There are about 13,000 species, most of which have bony skeletons. The bony fish include all the familiar fish like eels, herring, minnows, and salmon as well as a large and bewildering variety of little-known species.

The larger group of bony fishes is the ray-finned fishes which includes the primitive sturgeon, one of the largest bony fishes, to the smallest of all fish, the tiny gobies of the Philippines.

The European eel breeds in the Sargasso Sea and the young elvers swim to Europe and North America.

Marine Iguana
(Galapagos Islands)

Anaconda (reptile)

A frog starts as a jelly-covered egg laid and fertilized in water early in the spring. The egg hatches into a tadpole. By summer, legs and lungs appear and tail and gills vanish. The tadpole has become a fully formed but tiny frog.

Reptiles and Amphibians

Reptiles are animals with backbones that live by breathing air. They have cold blood, and in evolution they came after the amphibians and before the mammals. The 5000 species alive today are all that remain of a group of animals that once dominated the Earth – dinosaurs and other giant forms that died out more than 65 million years ago.

Reptiles vary in size from 5 cm (2 inches) long to 9 m (30 ft) or more. They usually have scaly skins, and most of them lay eggs. A few give birth to live young. They have lungs, like mammals, and most reptiles are carnivores.

There are four living orders of reptiles: alligators and crocodiles; tuataras (of which only one kind exists); tortoises, terrapins and turtles; and lizards and snakes.

Amphibians – animals that can live both in water and in air – are the last survivors of the first true land vertebrates that ever existed.

In prehistoric times there were eleven orders of amphibians, and many genera and species. Today there are only three orders left, with a total of about 3000 species. They are: Caecilians (simple worm-like creatures); newts and salamanders; and frogs and toads.

Most amphibians lay their eggs in water. The eggs hatch into a larval form called a tadpole.

Edible Frog

Fire Salamander

Smooth Newt

Frilled lizard
(Australia)

RECORDS

Largest amphibians are the Giant salamanders (genus *Megalobatrachus*) of China and Japan, specimens of which have been known to grow up to 1.5 m (5 ft).

Longest-lived amphibians are probably Japanese Giant salamanders (*Megalobatrachus japonicus*), specimens of which have lived up to 60 years in captivity.

Largest frog is the goliath frog (*Gigantorana goliath*) of Africa. This amphibian habitually grows to a body length of 30 cm (12 in), but many specimens have been reported considerably larger.

Largest reptile is the Estuarine crocodile (*Crocodylus porosus*), which can grow up to 6 m (20 ft).

Largest marine turtle is the Leathery or Leatherback turtle (*Dermochelys coriacea*), whose shell may be 1.8 m (6 ft) long, with a flipper-to-flipper stretch of 3.6 m (12 ft), and a weight of more than 725 kg (1,600 lb).

Largest land tortoise is the Giant tortoise (*Testudo gigantea*), which may have a shell 1.8 m (6 ft) long, and a weight of 225 kg (500 lb) or more.

Largest lizard is the Komodo dragon (*Varanus komodoensis*), a monitor which can grow up to 3 m (10 ft) long and weigh 113 kg (250 lb).

Largest snakes are the anaconda (*Eunectes murinus*) and the reticulated python (*Python reticulatus*), both of which are reported to grow up to 9 m (30 ft) long.

In the air, many birds have unmistakable shapes. The crow and jay belong to the same family and have rounded wings with ragged ends; the dove's wings are broad and pointed; geese have long narrow wings: swifts and swallows, have narrow, swept-back wings for fast flight; the starling, too, moves quickly; hawks and other birds of prey have broad wings for soaring; small birds like chaffinches and sparrows, have short broad wings for changing direction easily; game birds such as pheasants have broad rounded wings for quick take-off.

Birds

Birds are animals with feathers, wings, and beaks. Nearly all of them can fly. They are directly descended from reptiles, and many of them have one obvious link with their ancestors – scales on their legs. The link between reptiles and birds is provided by two prehistoric creatures, *Archaeopteryx* and *Archaeornis*, which lived at the time of the dinosaurs. They had feathers and could fly, but also had many reptilian features including teeth, a long bony tail and wing claws.

There are nearly 11,000 species of birds, and they are grouped into 27 orders. Birds can be classified in many different ways. Water-birds spend their lives on or near water; they include wildfowl – swans, geese, and ducks – and all the various gulls. Perching birds are land-based birds that spend their lives in trees or other high places when not flying. Birds of prey hunt small animals.

Although they look so different from the scales of reptiles, the birds' ancestors, feathers are made of the same substance, keratin – which is also the material of hair. Feathers grow unevenly on a bird's body. Some parts are well covered, others lightly protected.

The silhouettes of these common birds show that each species has a distinct shape. Notice the duck's rounded crown and the woodpeckers's flat one; compare the heron's long graceful neck with the owl's; and see how the robin has thin legs and the duck much thicker ones.

Dove

Hawk

Sparrow

Chaffinch

Pheasant

There are several types of feathers. Flight feathers, those on the wing, are called primary feathers when attached to the 'hand' part, and secondary feathers when on the 'forearm'. Contour feathers cover the body. Other kinds include the fine, downy feathers of the breast. The number of feathers on a bird varies with its size, ranging from 1300 up to 12,000 or more.

In the world of birds the males generally have the brighter plumage. Many birds are dull in appearance; the best singers are often clad in quiet hues. But tropical birds often show a riot of colour. Among the most ornamental are peacocks (*Pavo cristatus*); the female is a dull, brownish creature, but the male has bright blue-green plumage and a great fan of feathers which he displays when courting.

Above: A rough sketch of a bird with labels for colours, markings, bill shape, etc is often more helpful for identification purposes than a long written description.

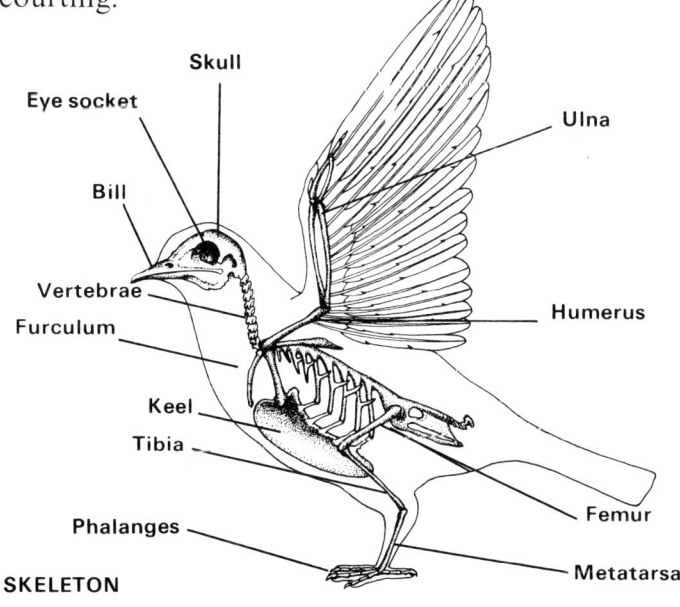

Skull

Eye socket

Bill

Vertebrae

Furculum

Keel

Tibia

Phalanges

SKELETON

Ulna

Humerus

Femur

Metatarsal

Left: A diagram of a bird's skeleton. Note the long flexible neck, the huge breast bone and the strange position of the leg bone.

137

Beak and Claw

Birds' beaks are adapted in many ways. The hawk's hooked beak can tear prey apart, while the pelican's bill acts like a fishing net. The merganser, a duck, has a saw-edged bill to hold slippery fish. The woodpecker can bore holes and the curlew probes the mud. The cardinal, a seed eater, has a short, strong bill. The toucan can pluck food through foliage, while the kingfisher snatches fish as it dives into the water.

Birds' claws are also specially adapted. The osprey, a bird of prey, has talons for grasping. The swift uses its tiny feet only to cling to things. Coots and ducks being water birds have feet adapted for paddling. The ostrich's hoof-like feet help it to run fast. The finch's feet are adapted to perching, three toes pointing forward and one back.

The woodpecker's toes, two forward, two back-pointing, help it to climb tree trunks.

Bird Facts

Largest The male African ostrich grows to a height of about 2·5 m (8 ft). Examples have been found measuring 2·75 m (9 ft) and weighing as much as 155 kg (340 lb). The heaviest flying bird is the Kori bustard of eastern and southern Africa, which may weigh as much as 18 kg (39 lb).

Smallest The bee hummingbird of Cuba measures about 6 cm (2¼ inches) and weighs only about 2 g (0·07 oz). Its nest would fit into half a walnut shell.

Greatest Wingspan The male wandering albatross has an average wingspan of 3·15 m (10 ft). The albatross is not a fast flier, but can stay in the air for days.

Fastest Flier The spine-tailed swift flies at about 100 kph (62 mph). Duck hawks and golden eagles swoop down in dives of up to an estimated 290 kph (180 mph).

Fastest Runner The ostrich can run at 55 kph (34 mph) and reach speeds of 80 kph (50 mph) over short distances.

Right: There is a great range of difference in the colour and size of birds' eggs. The kiwi lays enormous eggs for its size – each egg being one seventh of the bird's weight. Guillemots' eggs have a pointed end, so they always roll in a circle and not off the cliff edges where they are laid.

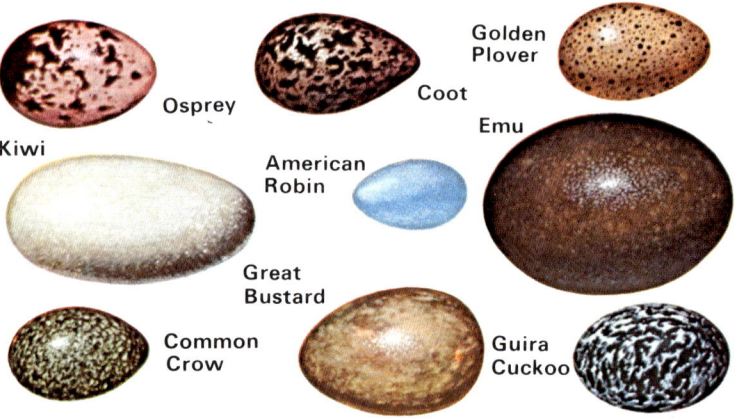

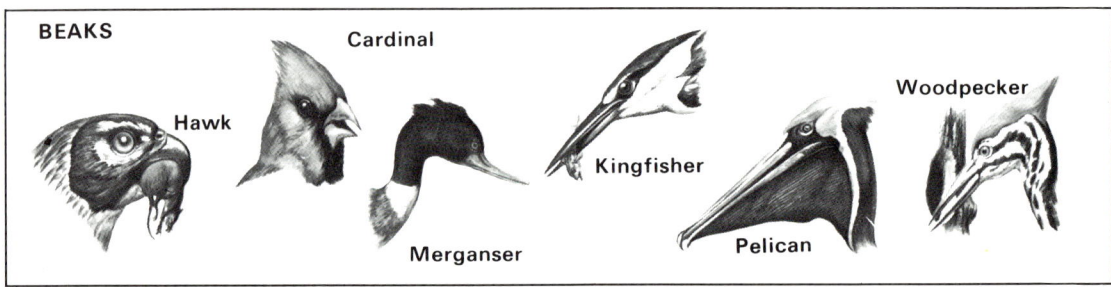

138

Toucan

Crowned Cranes

Hummingbird

Spoonbill

Bluejay

Bird of
Paradise

Crossbill

Blackbird

Pheasant

*Above: Birds from
different parts of the
world. Their beaks have
different shapes to suit the
kind of food they eat.*

ANIMALS

Animal Homes

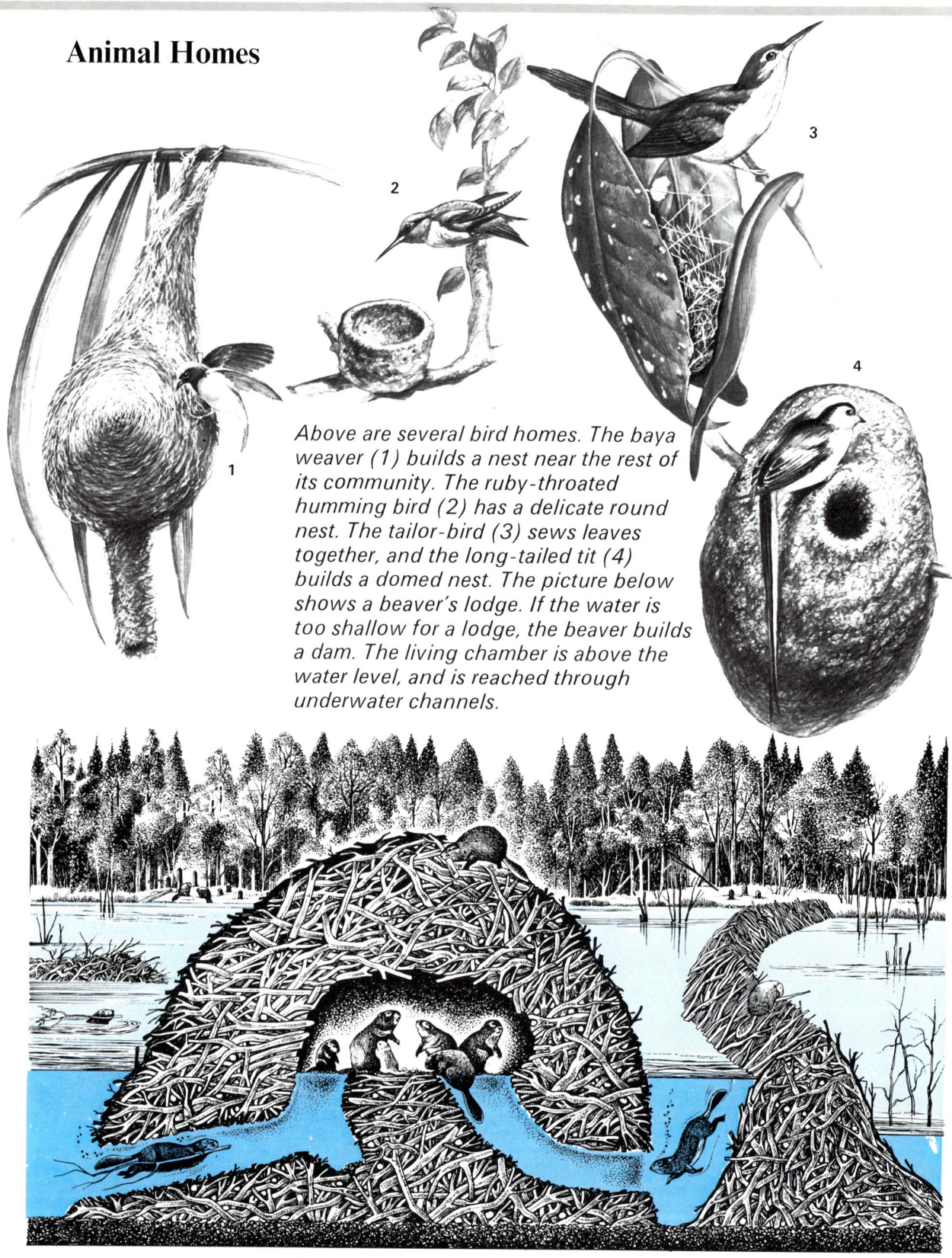

Above are several bird homes. The baya weaver (1) builds a nest near the rest of its community. The ruby-throated humming bird (2) has a delicate round nest. The tailor-bird (3) sews leaves together, and the long-tailed tit (4) builds a domed nest. The picture below shows a beaver's lodge. If the water is too shallow for a lodge, the beaver builds a dam. The living chamber is above the water level, and is reached through underwater channels.

ANIMALS: LONGEVITY AND SPECIALIZED NAMES

Life span (years)		Male	Female	Young	Group
Antelope	10	buck	doe	fawn	herd
Bear	15–50	boar	sow	cub	sleuth
Cat	15	tom	queen	kitten	cluster
Cattle	20	bull	cow	calf	herd
Deer	10–20	buck, hart, stag	doe hind	fawn	herd
Dog	12–15	dog	bitch	puppy	kennel
Donkey	20	jack	jenny	foal	herd
Duck	10	drake	duck	duckling	team
Elephant	60	bull	cow	calf	herd
Fox	10	dog-fox	vixen	cub	skulk
Giraffe	10–25	bull	cow	calf	herd
Goat	10	billy-goat	nanny-goat	kid	herd
Goose	25	gander	goose	gosling	skein, gaggle
Hippopotamus	30–40	bull	cow	calf	herd
Horse	20–30	stallion	mare	foal	herd
Kangaroo	10–20	buck	doe	joey	mob
Lion	25	lion	lioness	cub	pride
Ostrich	50	cock	hen	chick	flock
Pig	10–15	boar	sow	piglet	drove
Rabbit	5–8	buck	doe	kit	warren
Rhinoceros	25–50	bull	cow	calf	crash
Sheep	10–15	ram	ewe	lamb	flock
Tiger	10–25	tiger	tigress	cub	
Whale	20	bull	cow	calf	school, pod
Zebra	20–25	stallion	mare	foal	herd

ANIMAL SPEED RECORDS

	km/h	mph
Spine-tailed swift	170	106
Sailfish	109	68
Cheetah	105	65
Pronghorn antelope	97	60
Racing pigeon	97	60
Lion	80	50
Gazelle	80	50
Hare	72	45
Zebra	64	40
Racehorse	64	40
Shark	64	40
Greyhound	63	39
Rabbit	56	35
Giraffe	51	32
Grizzly bear	48	30
Cat	48	30
Elephant	40	25
Sealion	40	25
Man	32	20
Black mamba	32	20
Bee	18	11
Pig	18	11
Chicken	14	9
Spider	1.88	1.17
Tortoise	0.8	0.5
Snail	0.05	0.03

JOURNEY'S END

Longest bird migration is by the Arctic tern *(Sterna paradisaea)*, which leads a life of perpetual summer. It leaves the Arctic as summer ends and flies 18,000 km (11,000 miles) to Antarctica. At the end of the Antarctic summer it flies back to its breeding ground – so making a round trip of 36,000 km (22,000 miles).

Longest mammal migration is by the Alaska seal *(Callorhinus ursinus)*, which does a round trip of 9600 km (6000 miles).

Most travelled butterfly is the monarch butterfly *(Danaus plexippus)* of North America, which migrates 4000 km (2500 miles) from Hudson Bay to Florida and back.

Mammals

Mammals, like birds, arose from the reptiles. Mammals are even better adapted to life on land than their reptile ancestors. Like birds, mammals are warm blooded – they can keep the temperature of their bodies steady despite variations in the temperature of their surroundings. They do this by several means, including their warm covering of hair.

All mammals feed their young on milk from their mammary glands. Most retain their unborn young inside their bodies for a period of development, although a few mammals, the Monotremes, lay eggs like reptiles.

The basic mammal type is an animal with four legs, breathing air, having warm blood, and giving birth to live young. But there are exceptions to this. In seals, for example, the legs have become flippers. Whales also have flippers, but only one pair: they have no hind limbs at all. But the skeleton of a whale has a definite relationship to other mammals – in the flippers are digital bones similar to those of an ape's hand, though greatly changed in size and proportion. A whale has other features common to all mammals – such as lungs, a four-chambered heart, and a well-developed brain.

The two forms of mammals least like the basic type are the primitive monotremes and marsupials. Monotremes – the duck-billed platypus, for example – lay eggs, like reptiles, but are mammals in all other respects. Marsupials (kangaroos and wallabies, for example) give birth to live young, but only partly developed. The babies spend some time in the pouch on their mother's abdomen.

There are about 4000 species of mammals, grouped into 19 orders.

The feet of mammals vary greatly, largely according to how much they climb, walk, or run. Bears and monkeys stand on the whole foot, from the toes to the heel. Members of the dog and cat families stand and run only on their toes. The foot is greatly elongated, so that the heel appears to come a long way up the leg. All these animals have five toes. But in the last adaptation the number of toes decreases. The ungulates, such as antelopes, pigs, horses, and cows, stand right on the tips of their toes, and often do not have all five. For example, the rhinoceros has three toes, the camel two, and the horse only one. The nail on the horse's single toe has become greatly enlarged to form a hoof. The cloven hoof of pigs and cattle is really two separate toes. The ungulates include all the mammals with horns; they are all plant-eaters.

Man is one of the mammals. He has the scientific name *Homo sapiens*.

Below: How skeletons can differ. Those of man and the dog are not unalike; and of course they belong to the same class, the mammals. The limbs of the dog are adapted for fast running, and those of the fish have turned into fins.

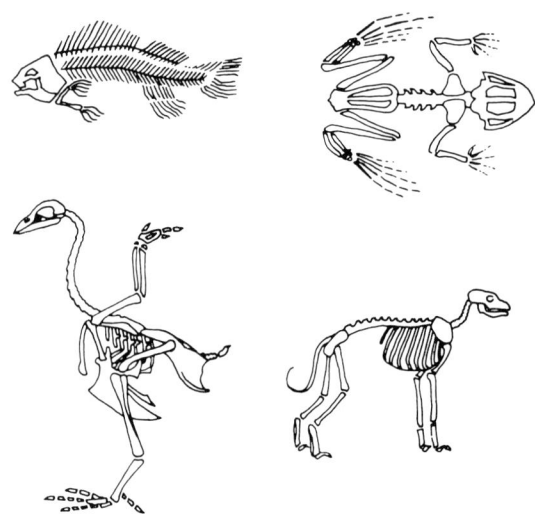

MAMMAL RECORDS

Largest mammal is the Blue whale *(Balaenoptera musculus)*, which can be up to 30 m (100 ft) in length.

Largest land mammal is the African elephant *(Loxodonta africana)*, which can be up to 3·5 m (11½ ft) tall and weigh 7 tonnes.

Smallest mammal is Savi's pygmy shrew *(Suncus etruscus)*, which has a head and body length of 3·8 cm (1½ in) and a tail about 2·5 cm (1 in) long. Its weight is less than 2·8 gm ($\frac{1}{10}$ oz).

Fastest mammal is the cheetah *(Acinonyx jubatus)*, which over a short distance can reach 105 kmh (65 mph).

Tallest mammal is the giraffe *(Giraffa camelopardalis)*, which can be as much as 5·5 m (18 ft) tall, with hooves 15 cm (6 in) high, and weigh up to 1 tonne.

Rarest mammals include several species on the verge of extinction, such as the Tasmanian wolf *(Thylacinus cynocephalus)*, Leadbeater's possum *(Gymnobelideus leadbeateri)*, and the Javan rhinoceros *(Rhinoceros sondaicus)*.

Monkeys and Apes

Primates, as their name implies, form the highest order of mammals. They include lemurs, monkeys, anthropoid apes – and Man.

Higher primates have a supple hand with a thumb that can be opposed to the fingers for grasping, and a complex and highly developed brain. They also have eyes set side by side in the front of the head, giving stereoscopic vision. Many of the primates are able to walk erect or nearly so on their rear feet.

Man is the only primate that does not live at least part of the time in trees, and also the only one that does not have an opposable big toe as well as an opposable thumb.

Apes are the monkey-like animals that are nearest to Man in structure and development. For this reason they are called anthropoid – 'Man-like'. It was once thought that Man was descended from the apes, but scientists now think that apes and men as we know them today had a common ancestor.

Two of the four kinds of apes – the orang utan and the gibbon – live in Africa. Remains of the earliest Hominids – the group that includes both apes and human beings have been found in these two continents.

The apes resemble Man in having no tail, and walking upright some of the time. Their brains are much better developed than those of other primates.

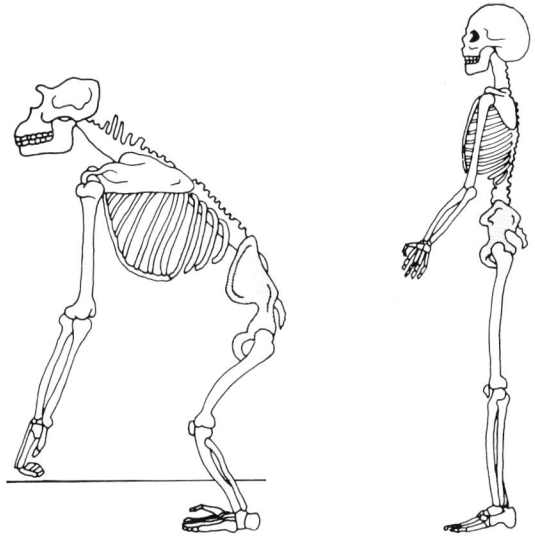

Human and ape skeletons. The ape's arms are longer than its legs and the pelvic girdle (brown) has developed to suit the different postures.

143

Many Kinds of Mammals

Elephants are the largest land animals. African elephants have larger ears than those from India.

Seals are sea mammals, but they do come ashore to lie in the sun.

The chimpanzee is one of the apes, and is found in Africa.

The kangaroo is a marsupial mammal, and carries its young in a pouch.

The European timber wolf lives in the forests of the North.

The hippopotamus is found in Africa, and is nearly as large as an elephant.

Sloths are found in South America, and spend most of their time hanging upside-down in branches of trees.

The aardvark or 'earth pig' lives in southern and central Africa, eating termites and similar insects.

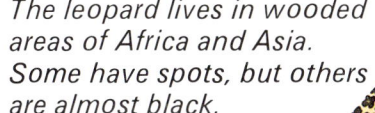

The tallest animals are giraffes, and have long legs and a long neck.

The leopard lives in wooded areas of Africa and Asia. Some have spots, but others are almost black.

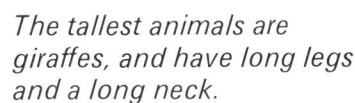

The rhinoceros lives in Africa and south-eastern Asia. It is a distant relative of the horse.

The polar bear lives in the Arctic, and catches seals and fish for food.

Dogs

Of all animals, the dog is probably Man's favourite. For thousands of years the dog has guarded Man's home, has herded his sheep and cattle, and has played with his children.

The dog family (Canidae) is quite large. All the members belong to that group of animals known as *Carnivores* or 'flesh-eaters'. The domestic dog (*Canis familiaris*) is the best-known member of the family. There are more than 100 breeds of domestic dogs, ranging from the huge St Bernard to the tiny Mexican chihuahua.

There are quite a number of wild relations, packs of which still roam throughout large areas of the world. The North American coyote (*Canis latrans*) is related to the dog as are dingoes, foxes, jackals, and wolves. Man has occasionally managed to tame a few of these. But there are some wild dogs, particularly in parts of Asia and South America, that have never been tamed.

Bearded Collie

Bulldog

Toy Poodle

Springer Spaniel

Scottish Terrier

Wolfhound

Pekinese

DOGS

Greyhound

Golden Retriever

Chesapeake
Bay Retriever

Griffon

Yorkshire Terrrier

Flat-coated Retriever

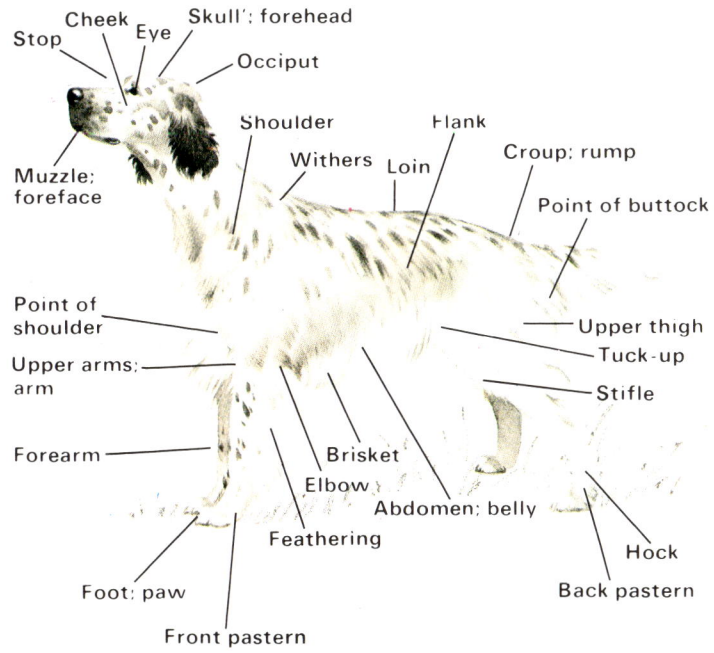

Stop
Cheek
Eye
Skull': forehead
Occiput
Muzzle;
foreface
Shoulder
Flank
Withers
Loin
Croup: rump
Point of buttock
Point of
shoulder
Upper thigh
Upper arms;
arm
Tuck-up
Stifle
Forearm
Brisket
Elbow
Abdomen: belly
Feathering
Hock
Foot: paw
Back pastern
Front pastern

TOP DOGS

Heaviest domestic dog is the
St Bernard, which weighs up to
100 kg (220 lb) and stands 70 cm
(27 in) high at the shoulders.
Tallest domestic dog is the
Irish wolfhound, which is 78 cm
(31 in) high at the shoulders, and
well over 1.8 m (6 ft) when standing on its hind legs.
Smallest domestic dog is the
chihuahua, which weighs 2.7 kg
(6 lb) or less.
Fastest domestic dog is the
saluki, credited with up to
69 km/h (43 mph), and the
greyhound, with speeds over
60 km/h (37 mph).
Largest wild dog species is the
Timber wolf (*Canis lupus*), which
stands 78 cm (31 in) high at the
shoulders and weighs up to 56 kg
(125 lb).

The Cat Family

Cats are the most purely carnivorous of carnivores. They have teeth for stabbing and slicing, but not for chewing. Their lithe bodies are built for speed, and their sharp claws are further formidable weapons. Except for differences in size, all kinds of cats are very similar animals indeed. The lioness roaming through the African shrubland is only a larger version of the small cat playing in the back garden. Because of these similarities all cats belong to one family, Felidae, and as they are all meat-eaters they belong to the order Carnivora.

The cat family also includes tigers, the jaguar, leopards, the cheetah, the puma, the caracal, lynxes, the serval, the ocelot, Scottish wild cats, and several other small wild cats among which are the ancestors of our domestic cat.

Among the known ancestors of the domestic cat is the Caffer cat of Africa, although the Scottish wild cat may also be an ancestor.

Domestic cats fall into two main groups – short-haired and long-haired. Short-haired cats include Burmese, Manx, Abyssinian, and Siamese. Siamese were originally bred in Thailand where they were royal sacred cats. The

Eight Cat Breeds and four Wild Cats

Red Long-hair

Seal Point Siamese

Tortoiseshell Short-hair

Dilute Calico American Short-hair

White Long-hair

Blue-cream American Short-hair

penalty for stealing one was death. Long-haired cats include the different kinds of Persian and Angora cats. With their long silky hair these magnificent creatures vary in colour from pure white to grey.

Although so similar in fundamental body plan, cats are distinguished by their various ways of life and their calls. Five of the larger cats, the tiger, lion, jaguar, leopard, and snow leopard, are called big cats not just because of their size but also because of their ability to roar.

The Americas are particularly rich in cat species, some of which are found nowhere else in the world. The jaguar (*Panthera onca*) of South America is the largest and fiercest of the American cats. It is quite untameable and can attack humans. The puma (*Felis concolor*), also called cougar or mountain lion, is another cat found only in America. Smaller than these two is the ocelot (*Felis pardalis*) of South America.

Cats cannot see in total darkness, but they can see far better in the dark than Man. At the back of their eyes there is a reflecting layer which sends light back through the sensitive cells so increasing the effect of minute amounts of light to the brain. The layer also makes the cat's eyes shine.

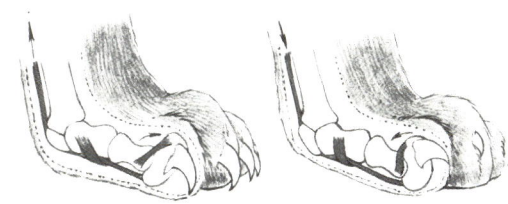

Cats can retract their claws by contracting the muscles to which they are attached.

Russian Blue

Tiger

Caracal

Lynx

Black Panther

CAT RECORDS

Largest member of the cat family is the tiger (*Panthera tigris*). Males have been found up to 3.2 m (10½ ft) in length, standing 0.9 m (3 ft) high at the shoulder.

Rarest of the cats is probably the Javan tiger, a race of *Panthera tigris* which is now only known in two restricted areas of the island of Java. About a dozen are thought to survive.

Longest lived of all big cats is probably the lion (*Panthera leo*), which is known to live up to 25 years or more in captivity.

Dictionary of the Horse

aids The signals used by a rider to convey instructions to the horse. The *natural* aids are those produced by use of the body, legs, hands, and voice; the *artificial* aids include the use of spurs, whips, martingales etc.

balance A horse without a rider has no problems with its balance, but this is immediately upset once the horse is mounted. The rider's skill and experience in sitting correctly and making necessary adjustments will assist the horse to be better balanced.

bit The metal, vulcanite or rubber device which is attached to the bridle and placed in the horse's mouth in order to give the rider control over the pace and direction.

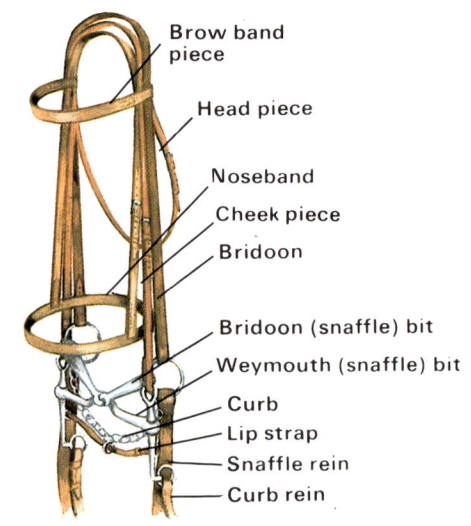

Brow band piece
Head piece
Noseband
Cheek piece
Bridoon
Bridoon (snaffle) bit
Weymouth (snaffle) bit
Curb
Lip strap
Snaffle rein
Curb rein

This picture shows the parts of a bridle (the harness that fits over the horse's head and mouth). Saddles and bridles are known as 'tack'.

Ear
Forelock
Poll
Mane
Eye
Withers
Back
Flank
Loins
Croup
Dock
Tail
Cheek
Thigh
Muzzle
Shoulder
Chest
Sheath
Forearm
Belly
Hock
Knee
Chestnut
Fore Cannon
Hind Cannon
Pastern
Fetlock
Ergot
Hoof
Heel

The bit is also used to control and regulate the position of the horse's head.

bridle The part of the saddlery that is placed over the horse's head, to which are attached the bitting device and reins. There are several different types of bridle; all have a headpiece, throat lash, browband, noseband and cheekpiece. Among the better-known bridles are the Double bridle, Pelham bridle, Kimblewick and Snaffle bridle.

brood mare A female horse used for breeding.

canter One of the paces or gaits of the horse.

colt An ungelded male horse which has not reached the age of four years.

conformation The build of a horse. This word describes the way a horse has been 'put together'.

dam The female parent of a foal.

draught horse A horse that is used to draw a vehicle of any size, though normally this expression is used for horses which come under the heading of heavy horses, including the Shires, the Suffolk Punch, Clydesdale, Breton, Percheron, Ardennes etc.

farrier The craftsman who makes and fits horseshoes.

Federation Equestre Internationale The governing body of international equestrian sport founded in 1921 with its headquarters in Brussels.

filly Female foal.

flash Broad white stripe running down a horse's face.

foal The young horse up to the age of twelve months referred to either as a colt foal or a filly foal, depending on its sex.

forehand The part of a horse which is in front of the rider, i.e. the head, neck, shoulders, withers and forelegs.

gait The movement or pace of a horse or pony. The four basic gaits or paces are the walk, trot, canter and gallop.

gallop One of the paces or gaits of a horse.

girth The circumference of the horse measured behind the withers around the deepest part of the body, or the band usually made of leather, webbing or nylon fixed to the saddle which passes under the belly of the horse to keep the saddle in position.

halter A rope headpiece which usually has a lead rope attached.

hand The measurement equalling four inches (10 cm) used when giving the height of a horse. In Europe the hand, though still used, is now being replaced by a metric measure.

hogging A term used for removing the mane.

livery stable At which privately owned horses are kept, groomed, exercised and are looked after for agreed charges.

mare A female horse.

native breeds Are those which are native to a particular country or region, for example there are nine known British native pony breeds: the Connemara, Dales, Dartmoor and Exmoor, Fell, Highland, New Forest, Shetland and the Welsh.

numnah A pad placed under the saddle, made from sheepskin, felt or a man-made fibre.

quarters The area of the horse's body which extends from the rear of the flank to the root of the tail and downwards on either side to the top of the gaskin.

stallion An ungelded male horse aged four years or over.

star A white mark of any shape or size on the forehead of a horse.

stock A word used in America for a stock horse, so called because they were originally used for working with cattle or stock.

stud The place or establishment at which horses are bred.

Prehistoric Man

Prehistoric Man lived long ago before there were any written records of history. We know about these early times from the tools, weapons and bodies of ancient people, which are dug out of the ground. Prehistory is divided into the Stone Age, the Bronze Age and the Iron Age. The ages are named after the materials that people used to make their tools and weapons.

The Stone Age lasted for a long time. It began around $2\frac{1}{2}$ to 3 million years ago when human-like creatures began to appear on the Earth. They were different from the ape-like animals which lived at the same time. They had larger brains, used stone tools and could walk upright. They lived by hunting animals and collecting plants.

Around 800,000 years ago, a more human-like creature appeared. Scientists call this kind of early Man *Homo erectus*. This means 'upright man'. *Homo erectus* is probably the ancestor of more advanced types of humans, called *Homo sapiens*. This means 'intelligent man'. One kind of *Homo sapiens* was Neanderthal Man, who appeared about 100,000 years ago. Neanderthal Man finally died out and was replaced by modern Man, who is called *Homo sapiens sapiens*. Modern Man appeared in Europe and Asia 35,000 years ago.

Fossil remains of our primitive ancestors have been found in Africa and Asia. These early human-like creatures walked on two legs, and their skulls and teeth were quite like our own. But their brains were much smaller, about the same size as an ape's. After these 'ape-men', however, came creatures much more like modern human beings. They had bigger brains and they could use tools. Having a bigger brain made it possible for primitive people to develop until *Homo sapiens* appeared.

The human brain gave human beings the power to hunt, kill, capture and tame other animals. Human beings developed skills far greater than those of any other creature. This made it possible for them to control the environment in which they lived. They learned to make and use fire, to grow food and to make simple tools.

Towards the end of the long Stone Age, prehistoric people first began to use metals. The first metal they used was copper. They made copper tools about 10,000 years ago. About 5000 years ago, people invented bronze. Bronze is a hard alloy of copper and tin. This was the start of the Bronze Age, when the earliest civilizations began. The Bronze Age ended about 3300 years ago, when people learned how to make iron tools. Iron is much harder than bronze. With iron tools, people could develop farming and cities more quickly than ever before.

Homo erectus

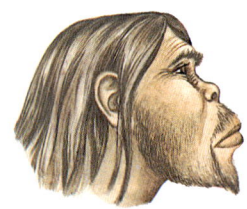

Homo habilis

Neanderthal man

Homo sapiens

PLANTS

The Plant Kingdom

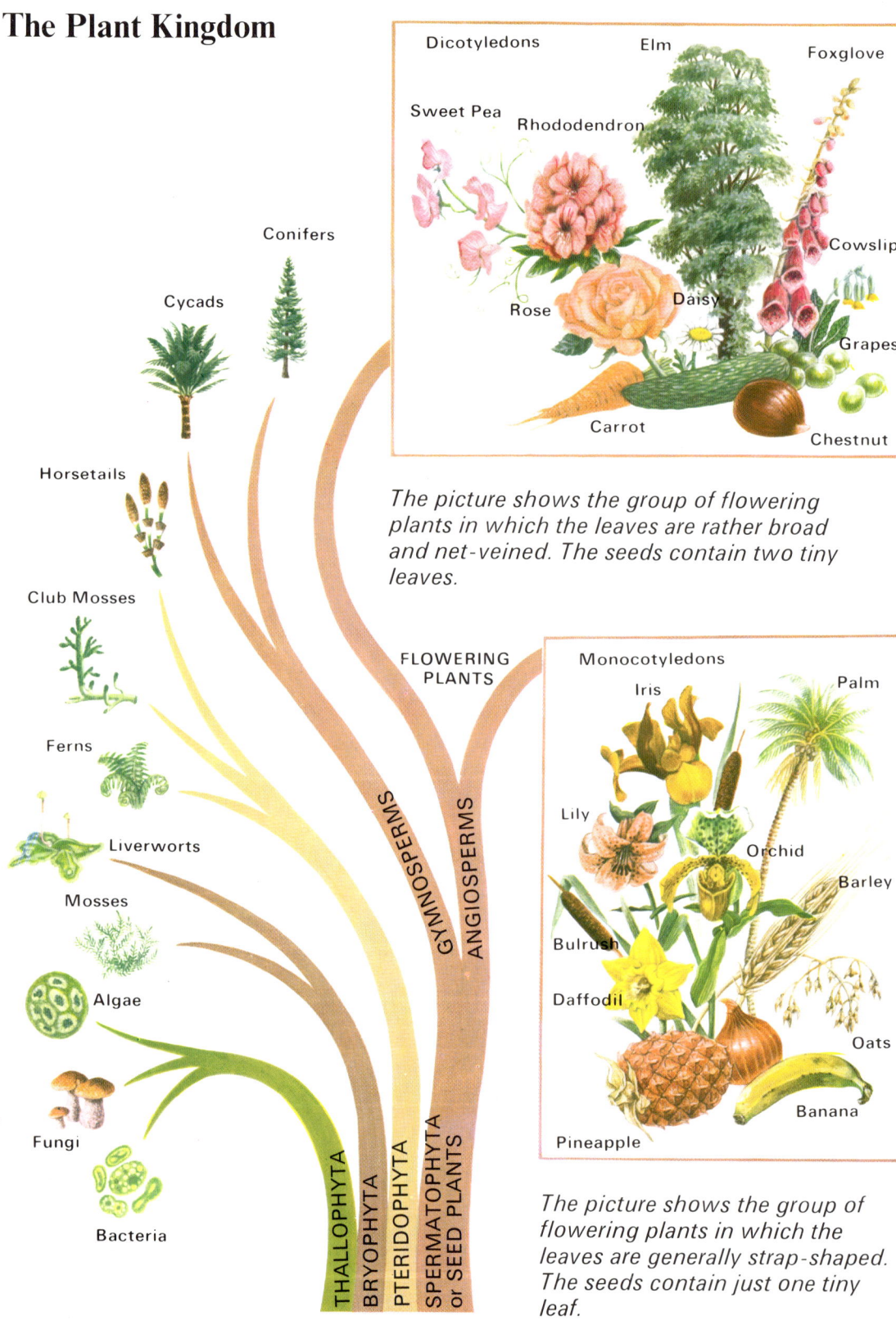

Dicotyledons

Sweet Pea, Rhododendron, Elm, Foxglove, Rose, Daisy, Cowslip, Carrot, Grapes, Chestnut

The picture shows the group of flowering plants in which the leaves are rather broad and net-veined. The seeds contain two tiny leaves.

Monocotyledons

Iris, Palm, Lily, Orchid, Barley, Bulrush, Daffodil, Oats, Banana, Pineapple

The picture shows the group of flowering plants in which the leaves are generally strap-shaped. The seeds contain just one tiny leaf.

Conifers, Cycads, Horsetails, Club Mosses, Ferns, Liverworts, Mosses, Algae, Fungi, Bacteria

FLOWERING PLANTS

GYMNOSPERMS

ANGIOSPERMS

THALLOPHYTA

BRYOPHYTA

PTERIDOPHYTA

SPERMATOPHYTA or SEED PLANTS

Dictionary of Plants

annual A plant which completes its life cycle in one season, and then dies.

anther The part of the stamen that contains the pollen.

asexual reproduction Any form of reproduction that does not involve the fusing of male and female sex cells (gametes).

bark The outer layer of a woody stem.

berry A fleshy fruit with no hard inner layer and usually with several seeds (e.g. orange, gooseberry).

biennial A plant which completes its life cycle in two seasons, and then dies.

bud An undeveloped shoot.

bulb An enlarged underground bud with fleshy leaves in which food is stored.

calyx The name for the sepals of a flower.

carbohydrate A food (e.g. sugar and starch) made up of carbon, hydrogen and oxygen, produced in a plant by photosynthesis. Carbohydrate is 'burned' to provide energy.

carpel The female reproductive organ of a flower, made up of stigma, style and ovary.

cell Minute living unit. All living matter is made up of cells.

chlorophyll The green pigment which enables green plants to use the energy from light to make food (photosynthesis).

chromosome Minute thread-like structure in the nucleus of a cell containing the genes (hereditary instructions).

clone A group of plants with identical chromosomes and features (produced by vegetative reproduction, e.g. clusters of bulbs).

compound leaf One in which the blade is divided into separate leaflets.

corm A short fleshy underground stem in which food is stored.

cotyledon A seed leaf. The first leaf (or pair of leaves) of the embryo plant in a seed, often providing a food store.

deciduous Shedding all leaves at the end of each growing season.

dicotyledon (or dicot). A member of the class of flowering plants with two cotyledons (seed leaves) in each seed.

drupe A fruit with a fleshy outer layer and a hard inner layer (the stone).

ecology The study of the relations between living things and their environment.

embryo The young plant in the seed.

fruit A ripened carpel (or group of carpels). It protects and helps in the dispersal of seeds.

gene Part of a chromosome, containing the coded hereditary information for a particular characteristic. In fact most characteristics involve many genes.

germination The beginning of growth of a seed or spore.

glucose The simple sugar produced in photosynthesis, and stored as a food reserve by some plants.

herb or herbaceous plant A non-woody seed plant in which the aerial parts die (or die down) at the end of each growing season.

This diagram shows the parts of a typical flower. Some flowers have only one ovule. Others have hundreds. After they are fertilized, ovules develop into seeds.

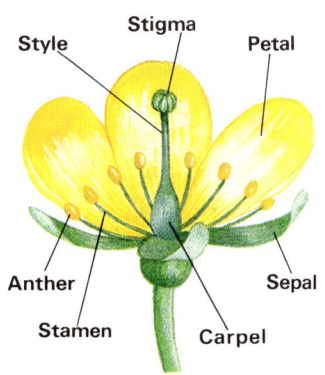

humus Decaying organic matter in the soil.

hybrid A plant produced when pollen from one species fertilizes the flower of different (but usually very closely related) species. Hybrids are usually sterile – they cannot reproduce sexually.

legume (or pod). A type of dry fruit formed from a single ovary, which splits down two sides when ripe (e.g. pea).

nectar The sweet liquid, produced in glands called nectaries, that attracts insects to a flower.

nucleus The part of a cell containing the chromosomes.

nut A one-seeded fruit with a hard woody wall.

osmosis The process whereby a solvent (such as water) diffuses through a semi-permeable membrane in an attempt to equalize the strengths of the solutions on each side of the membrane.

ovary The hollow part of the carpel which contains the ovules. It may also be formed from the cavities of several joined carpels.

ovule A structure inside the ovary which contains the female reproductive cell and which after fertilization develops into the seed.

parasite A living thing which lives on or in another living thing (the host), and which obtains all its food from the host.

perennial A plant that lives on from year to year.

photosynthesis The process by which green plants use the energy of light to make glucose from carbon dioxide and water.

pistil Another word for the female part of the flower – the carpel or group of carpels.

pollen Mass of grains produced in the stamens of a flower, carrying the male reproductive cells.

pollination The transfer of pollen from stamen to stigma.

rhizoid Hair-like structure which an-

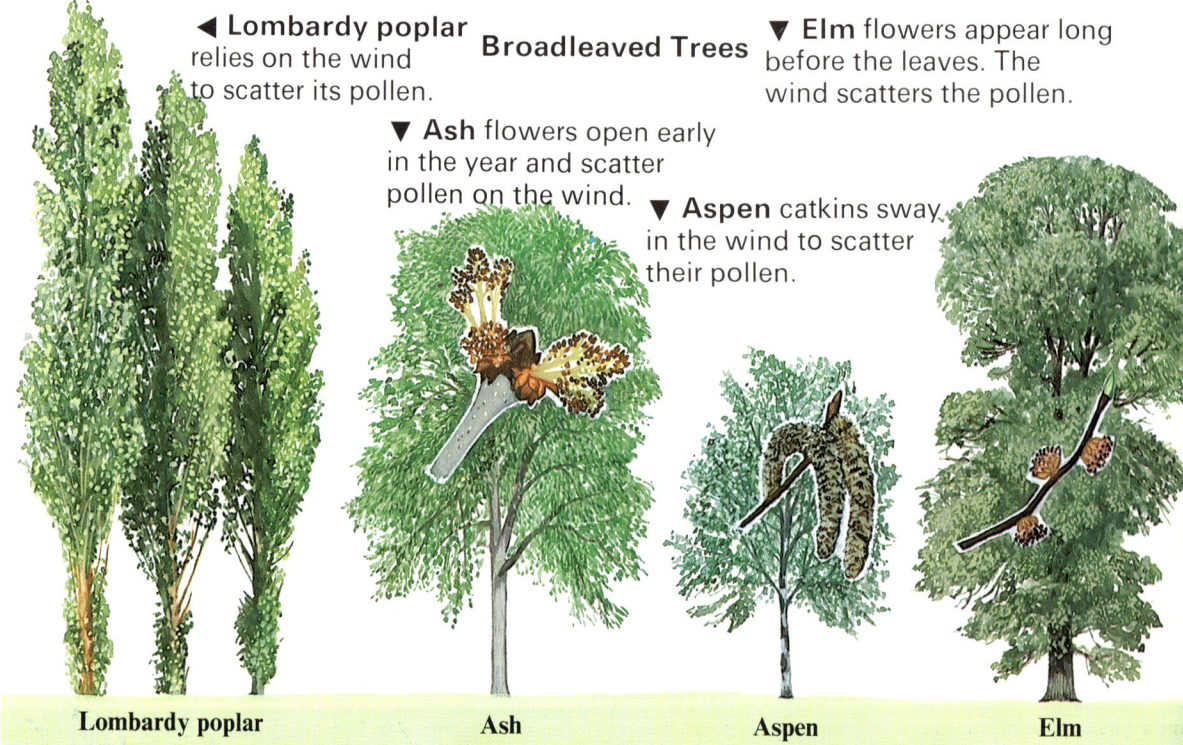

◀ **Lombardy poplar** relies on the wind to scatter its pollen.

Broadleaved Trees

▼ **Elm** flowers appear long before the leaves. The wind scatters the pollen.

▼ **Ash** flowers open early in the year and scatter pollen on the wind.

▼ **Aspen** catkins sway in the wind to scatter their pollen.

Lombardy poplar   Ash   Aspen   Elm

chors mosses in the ground.

rhizome A horizontal underground stem, sometimes containing stored food.

runner A creeping stem by which plants such as the strawberry reproduce vegetatively.

self pollination Transfer of pollen from the stamens to the stigma of the same flower.

sepals The outermost parts of a flower. They are usually green and protect the petals before the flower opens.

shrub A fairly short woody plant with many branches and no main trunk.

spore A single-celled reproductive body which grows into a new plant without any form of sexual union.

stamen Male reproductive part of a flower, made up of the pollen-producing anther and filament.

starch A type of carbohydrate food often stored in plants.

stigma The tip of the carpel which receives the pollen.

style Stalk-like part of the carpel with the stigma at its tip.

symbiosis A close association between two organisms in which both organisms benefit.

taproot The main root of the plant.

tendril A modified stem, leaf or leaflet used by some climbing plants. It is very thin, and is sensitive to touch. When it meets a support it coils round it.

tuber A swollen stem (potato) or root (dahlia) used to store food.

RECORD TREES

Tallest are the California coast redwoods, which grow over 91 m (300 ft) high.

Thickest trunk is that of a Montezuma cypress in Mexico, with a diameter of 12 m (40 ft).

Oldest are the bristlecone pines of Nevada, California, and Arizona, nearly 5,000 years old.

Earliest surviving species is the maidenhair tree or ginkgo of China; it first appeared about 160 million years ago.

▼ **Common lime** is pollinated by insects but its seeds are dispersed by the wind.

▼ **Hornbeam** is pollinated by the wind and its seeds are wind-dispersed.

▼ **Crack willow** is insect-pollinated but its seeds are scattered by the wind.

▼ **Silver birch** catkins open with the leaves. Male catkins hang down, whereas the female catkins are upright.

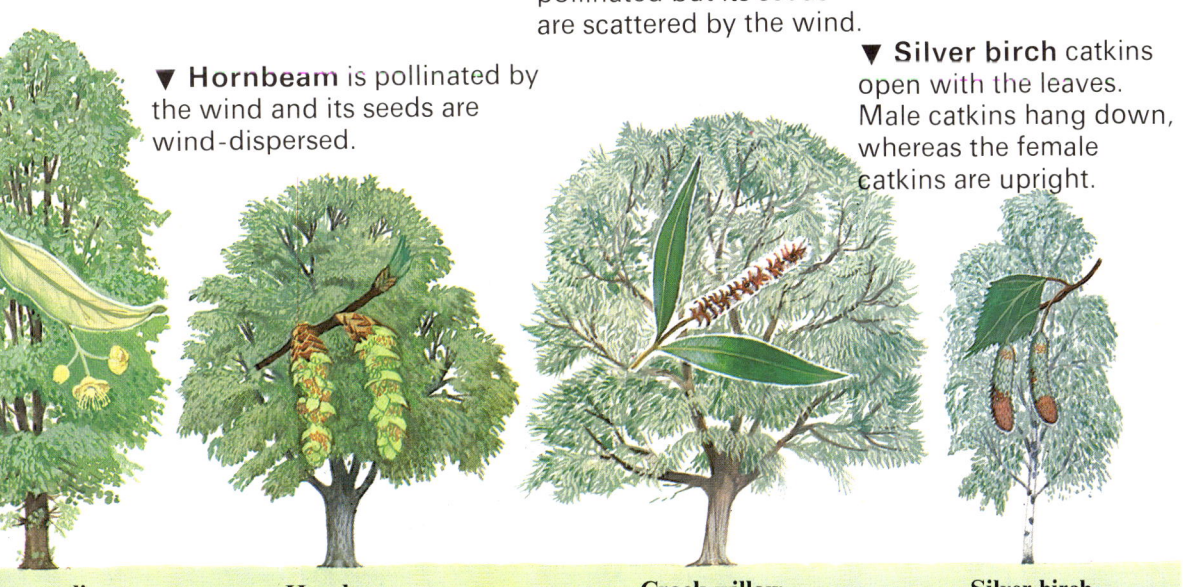

mmon lime   Hornbeam   Crack willow   Silver birch

Some Coniferous Trees

Aleppo pine

Stone pine

Grand fir

Douglas fir

Western hemlock

Corsican pine

Scot s pine

Trees

Trees are the largest of all plants. They are woody plants with a thick central stem, or trunk. Most trees grow to more than 7·6 m (25 ft) high.

Above the ground is the *crown* of the tree. This is made up of the trunk, branches, twigs and leaves. The *roots* are below the ground. They are the fastest growing part of the tree. They support the crown like a giant anchor. The roots take in water from the soil. The water is drawn up through the trunk to the leaves.

There are two main kinds of trees. Conifers are trees with needle-like leaves, such as pines and spruces. In place of flowers, they produce their seeds in cones. Most conifers are evergreens. This means they do not lose their leaves in autumn. Conifers grow in cold or dry regions.

The other kind of tree is the flowering, or broad-leaved tree. Many of them, such as elms and oaks, are *deciduous*, that is, they lose their leaves in autumn. But some broad-leaved trees, such as holly and many tropical forest trees, are evergreen. Broad-leaved trees have flowers which develop into fruits that completely surround the seeds. These trees are often called hardwoods, because of their tough, hard wood. It is harder than that of the softwood conifers.

Cereals

Cereals are important food crops. They belong to the grass family. The fruit or seed of the plant is called a grain.

In tropical lands the most important cereals are rice, maize and millet. In cooler climates the chief cereals are wheat, oats, barley and rye.

Rice is the main food for over half the people in the world. It grows in warm and wet climates and needs plenty of water.

Much of the world's wheat is grown on the plains of Canada, the USA, Australia and the USSR. The grain is ground into flour and used to make bread, pasta and breakfast foods.

Silver fir
Yew

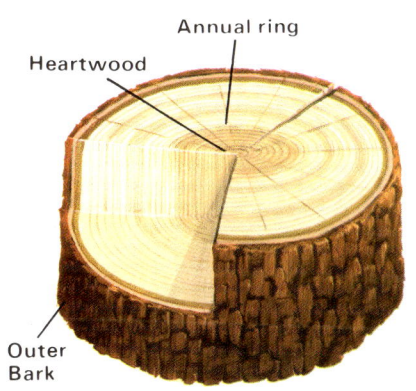

Annual ring
Heartwood
Outer Bark

The world's chief cereals.

Maize
Millet
Rice
Wheat
Rye
Barley

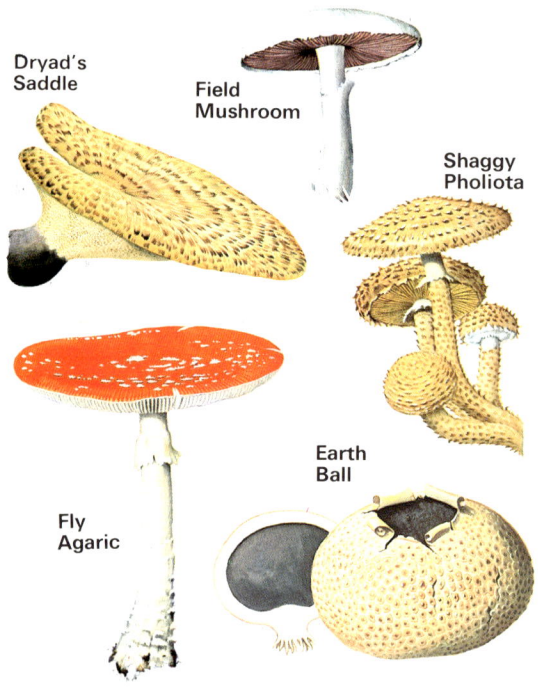

Mushrooms and Toadstools

Mushrooms and toadstools are the fruit bodies of fungi that consist mainly of white strands in the soil or under the bark or in the wood of trees. These fruit bodies appear only when the fungus is ready to produce spores which are simple 'seeds'. Their function is to carry the spores above the ground so that they will be carried by air currents to new places. There are many different kinds of fungus fruit bodies, but the most commonly seen have a cap which opens out to expose gills or tubes (pores) underneath. These produce large quantities of minute spores. The cap is borne on a stalk and there may be a ring at the top of the stalk where the cap has broken away from it to open. Most fungi produce fruit bodies in the autumn, so September and October are the best months to look for them.

The edges of woodlands and fields are particularly good places to look for a wide variety of species. **Never pick or eat a mushroom until you are quite certain that it is not poisonous.**

Make spore prints of toadstools by carefully cutting the ripe caps from the stalks and laying them, gills down, on paper. Cover the caps with a basin to keep out draughts, and leave them for a few hours. Lift the caps up carefully to see the gill pattern 'painted' in spores. Use coloured paper for white-gilled species. If you spray the prints lightly with artists' fixative spray you can keep them permanently.

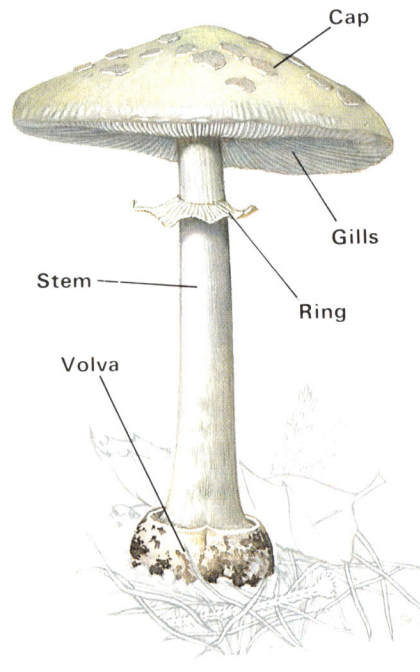

Fruits

Fruits, all shapes and sizes, can contain just one seed, but most have more. They are usually divided into two groups, dry fruits and fleshy fruits. Dry fruits are ones which dry out as they ripen, like pea pods, acorns and sycamore keys. They often have some method of scattering their seeds: the pea pod, for instance, bursts open and shoots out its seeds while the winged sycamore key is carried away by the wind. In fleshy fruits, such as tomatoes, grapes, bananas and cucumbers, the case enclosing the seeds is soft and pulpy. Animals and birds eat this juicy part but drop the seeds – often away from the parent plant.

Apple

Grapes

Pear

Pome
The true fruit is the core, the edible part is the swollen receptacle.

Tomato

Orange

Gooseberry

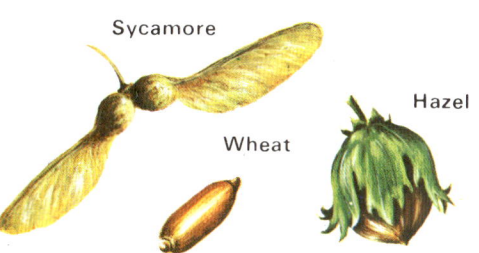

Sycamore

Hazel

Wheat

Indehiscent
Indehiscent fruits do not split open when ripe. They therefore cannot germinate until the ovary wall (the woody or leathery 'coat') rots or is broken.

Dandelion

Cherries

Peach

Drupes
The fruit has a fleshy outer layer, and a hard inner layer (the stone). The actual seed is inside the stone. Blackberries and raspberries consist of several small drupes (drupels) lightly joined together.

Plum

Pea

Poppy

Dehiscent
These split open when ripe. Peas and beans have pods, each formed from one carpel. Poppies have capsules formed from several carpels.

Raspberry

Blackberry

Berries
The entire fruit is fleshy and contains many seeds. It is usually formed from several carpels, each segment of the fruit being formed from one carpel.

PLANTS

The Language of Flowers

Here is a list of flowers, and their supposed meanings, especially if the flowers are given as a present. The list is given only for fun, and should not be taken seriously!

Acacia *Friendship*
Almond blossom *Encouragement*
Aloe *Grief*
Anemone *Soul of Goodness*
Apple blossom *You are preferred*
Arbutus *I love but thee*
Aster *Always gay*
Balm *Sympathy*
Bee Orchid *Industry*
Begonia *Steadfast*
Blackthorn *Courage under trial*
Bluebell *True and tender*
Borage *There are obstacles*
Bramble *Perseverance*
Buttercup *Homeliness*
Calceolaria *Don't be jealous*
Camellia *Beautiful but cold*
Carnation *White purity*
Celandine *Be not downhearted*
Chrysanthemum *Hope springs eternal*
Clematis *Poor but honest*
Clover, white *Think of me*
Clover, red *Sweetness*
Columbine *Bound to win*
Convolvulus *Hearts entwined*
Cornflower *Never despair*
Cowslip *Happiness*
Crocus *Ever glad*
Cypress *Affliction*
Daffodil *Welcome*
Dahlia *Gracious*
Daisy *Innocence*
Eglantine *I am cruel to be kind*
Fennel *Strength*
Fern *Sincerity*
Foxglove *Deceitful*
Fuchsia *Fickleness*
Gentian *Hope*

Geranium *Warm regard*
Gorse *Constancy*
Harebell *Short lived joy*
Hawthorn *Courage in adversity*
Heather *I am lonely*
Holly *Rejoice together*
Honeysuckle *Devotions*
Hyacinth *Hard fate*
Iris *Have faith in me*
Ivy *I cling*
Jasmine *Friends only*
Laburnum *Forsaken*
Lavender *Sweets to the Sweet*
Lilac *Unadorned beauty*
Lily *Austere beauty*
Lily of the valley *Doubly dear*
Lime *Domestic bliss*
Lobelia *Unselfishness*
London Pride *Unassuming*
Magnolia *Magnanimity*
Musk Rose *You charm me*
Myrrh *Happiness*
Myrtle *Unforgotten joys*
Nasturtium *Optimism*
Olive *Peace*
Orange blossom *Happiness in Marriage*
Palm *Victory*
Pansy *Thoughts*
Passion Flower *Comfort in affliction*
Petunia *I believe in thee*

Greater
Celandine

Pimpernel *Consolation*
Polyanthus *Unreasoning pride*
Poppy *Forgetfulness*
Primrose *Do not be bashful*
Primrose, evening *Duplicity*
Rose, red *Love*
Rose, white *Worthy of Love*
Rosemary *Remembrance*
Sage *Virtuous and wise*
St John's Wort *Real Nobility*
Shepherd's Purse *Pride of worth*
Snowdrop *Goodness unalloyed*

Strawberry blossom *Patience and fore-sight*
Sunflower *Adoration*
Sweet Pea *I long for thee*
Sweet William *Pleasant dreams*
Thistle *Defence not defiance*
Thyme *Affection*
Tulip *Unrequited love*
Verbena *You have my confidence*
Violet *Modesty*
Wallflower *Loyalty in friendship*
White heather *Good luck*

Some Flowers of Fields and Meadows

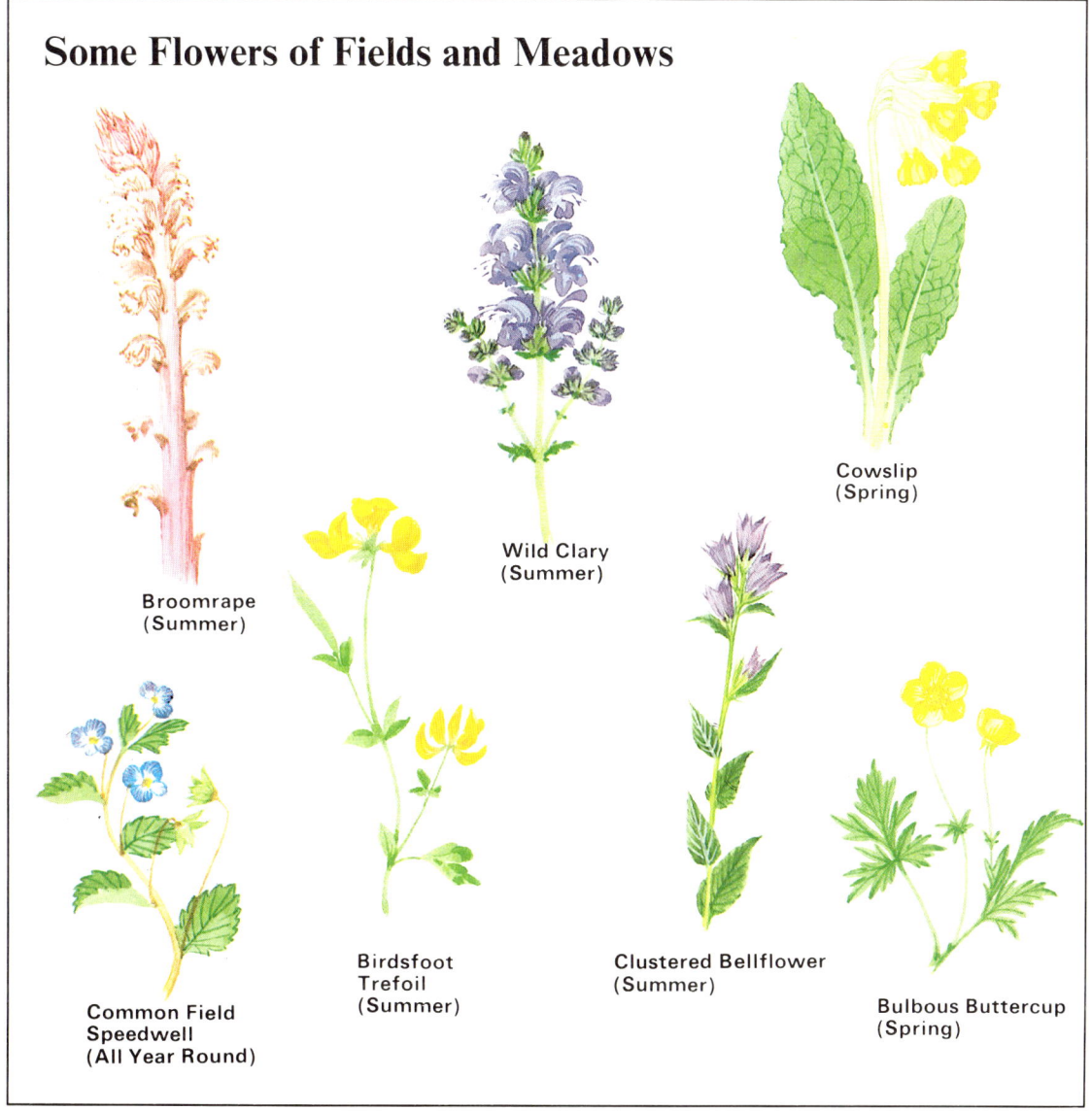

Broomrape
(Summer)

Wild Clary
(Summer)

Cowslip
(Spring)

Common Field
Speedwell
(All Year Round)

Birdsfoot
Trefoil
(Summer)

Clustered Bellflower
(Summer)

Bulbous Buttercup
(Spring)

Common Vetch (Spring to Autumn)

Red Clover (Spring to Autumn)

Eyebright (Spring to Autumn)

Black Knapweed (Summer)

Wood Anemone (Spring)

Centaury (Summer)

White Helleborine (Summer)

Scarlet Pimpernel (Spring to Autumn)

These wild flowers all grow in fields and meadows, or along the roadsides. Fields in which animals graze do not contain many wild flowers. Only the grasses and a few tough plants can stand the constant nibbling. Meadows, in which the grasses are allowed to grow higher for hay, contain more flowers. But the best places for grassland flowers are open hillsides and roadside banks. A few flowers , such as the poppy, like soil that has been ploughed. They often grow as weeds in corn fields.

Common Poppy (Spring to Autumn)

Bistort (Summer to Autumn)

Wild Strawberry (Spring)

Dog's Mercury (Early Spring)

Field Scabious (Summer and Autumn)

Fumitory (Spring to Autumn)

World of Science

Right: In a solid, the atoms or molecules that make it up are packed tightly together. So solids are strong enough to support themselves and sometimes other objects too. In a liquid the atoms or molecules have a looser arrangement. The liquid can flow. In gases the atoms or molecules are not arranged in any way. They can move apart until the gas fills its container.

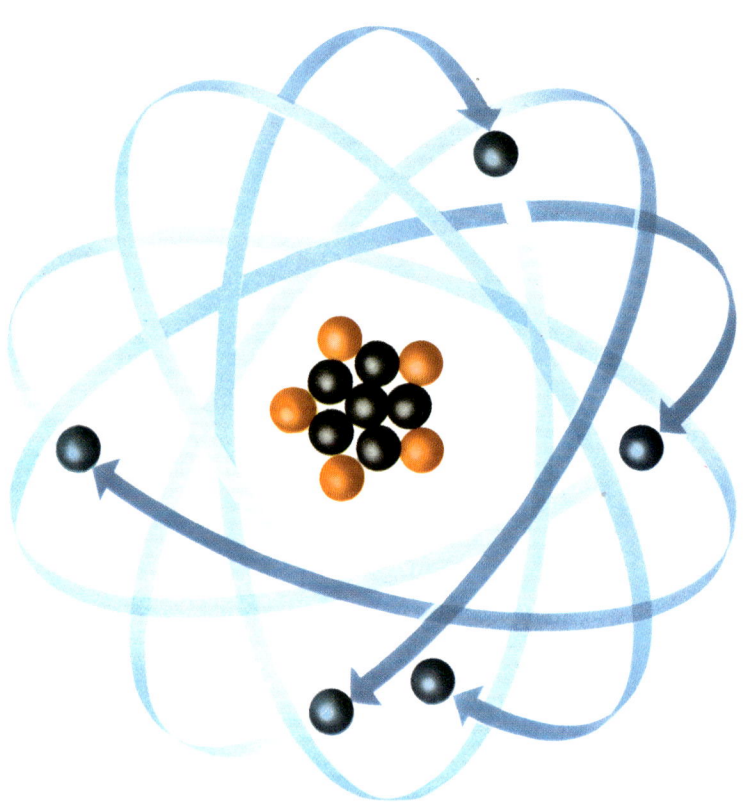

Key Dates in Science

c.400 BC Hippocrates devised the code of medical ethics – now the 'Hippocratic oath'.

1543 Nicolaus Copernicus argued that the Sun is at the centre of the Solar System.

c.1600 Galileo Galilei developed and used the scientific method.

1687 Sir Isaac Newton published his book – the *Principia* – setting out the laws of mechanics.

1770s Antoine Lavoisier founded modern chemistry; he disproved the phlogiston theory when he explained combustion.

1839 Matthias Schleiden and Theodor Schwann suggested that living things are made up of cells.

1858 Charles Darwin set out his theory of evolution.

1869 Dmitri Mendeleyev classified the elements into the Periodic Table.

1900 Max Planck put forward the quantum theory.

1905 Albert Einstein advanced his Special Theory of Relativity.

1911 Ernest Rutherford discovered the nucleus and formulated the atomic theory.

1942 Enrico Fermi and others achieved the first successful nuclear chain reaction.

1957 Arthur Kornberg grew DNA – the molecule of life – in a test-tube.

1969 Neil Armstrong and Edwin Aldrin landed on the Moon.

1976 First successful soft landing on Mars of an unmanned spaceship.

Branches of Science

Science	Study of

EARTH SCIENCES

Geology	rocks, earthquakes, volcanoes, and fossils
Meteorology	the atmosphere and weather
Mineralogy	minerals, their location and mining
Oceanography	waves, tides, currents, trenches, and ocean life
Palaeontology	plant and animal fossils
Petrology	formation and structure of rocks; their chemical content

LIFE SCIENCES

Agronomy	land management of crops and cultivation
Anatomy	structure, form, and arrangement of the body
Bacteriology	bacteria, their growth and behaviour
Biology	animals and plants; origin, morphology, and environment
Botany	the plant world
Cytology	structure, function, and life of cells
Ecology	relationship between living things and environment
Medicine	cause, prevention, and cure of disease
Nutrition	supply of adequate and correct foods to satisfy the body's requirements
Pharmacology	drugs; their preparation, use, and effects
Physiology	the function of living things
Psychology	behaviour of humans and animals; working of the brain
Zoology	animals

MATHEMATICAL SCIENCES

Logic	reasoning by mathematics: used by computers
Mathematics	the application of geometry, algebra, and arithmetic, etc.; application of these to concrete data
Statistics	numerical information which is to be analysed

PHYSICAL SCIENCES

Aerodynamics	the properties and forces of flowing air on solid objects
Astronomy	heavenly bodies and their motions
Chemistry	properties and behaviour of substances
Electronics	behaviour of electrons in a vacuum, in gases, and semiconductors
Engineering	application of scientific principles to industry.
Mechanics	the invention and construction of machines, their operation, and the calculation of their efficiency
Metallurgy	the working of metals; smelting and refining
Physics	nature and behaviour of matter and energy

SOCIAL SCIENCES

Anthropology	origin, culture, development, and distribution of human beings
Archaeology	remains, monuments left by prehistoric people
Economics	use of natural resources to the best advantage
Geography	location of Earth's features and our relation to them
Linguistics	languages and their relationship to each other
Political Science	function of states and governments
Sociology	Relationship between groups and individuals

The Human Body

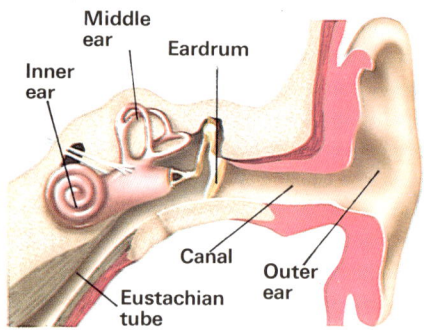

Ear Each ear has three main parts. These are the outer ear, middle ear and inner ear. Sounds reach the outer ear as vibrations, or waves, in the air. The cup-like shape of the ear collects these sound waves and sends them into the tube.

Next, the sound waves reach the middle ear. Here, the waves make the eardrum move to and fro. This is a thin 'skin' across the entrance of the middle ear. The moving eardrum sets tiny bones vibrating in the middle ear.

The vibrations travel on into the inner ear. Here they set liquid moving in the *cochlea*. The nerves inside it turn vibrations into messages that travel to the brain. The inner ear also has three hollow loops containing liquid. These loops send signals to the brain to help the body keep its balance.

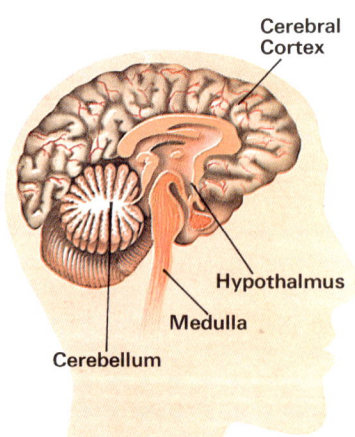

Lungs Your lungs are two large, sponge-like masses in the chest. They fill with air and empty as you breathe in and out.

You breathe in air through the nose. The air flows down the windpipe, or *trachea*. Where the lungs begin, the trachea divides into two hollow branches called bronchial tubes, or *bronchi*. Each divides into smaller tubes called *bronchioles*. These end in cups called air sacs, or *alveoli*. This is where the lungs give oxygen to the blood and take away carbon dioxide.

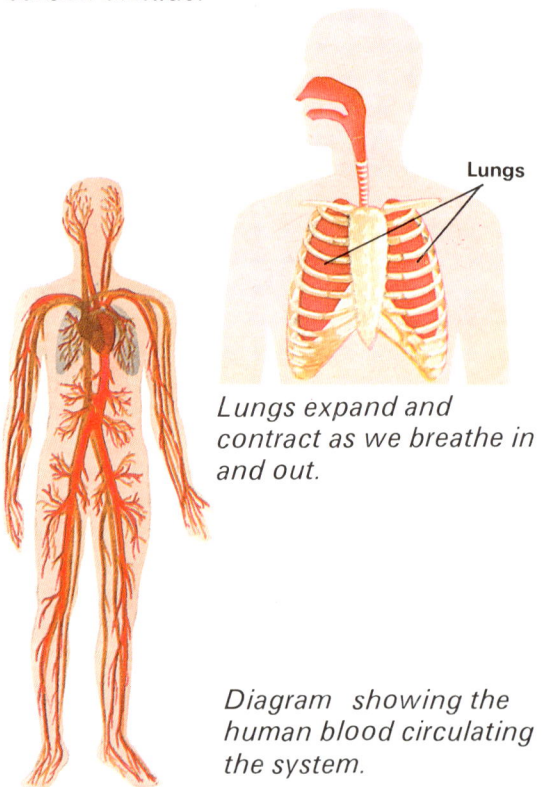

Lungs expand and contract as we breathe in and out.

Diagram showing the human blood circulating the system.

Brain The human brain is largely made up of grey and white matter. Grey matter is nerve cells, and white matter is the nerve fibres that carry messages from the nerve cells to the body. These nerve fibres leave the brain in large bundles like telephone cables and reach out to all parts of the body. Messages from the body are travelling back along the fibres to the brain all the time.

Teeth Humans have all three kinds of teeth because we eat all kinds of food. These are cutting teeth (incisors), tearing teeth (canines) and crushing or chewing teeth (molars). There are two parts to a tooth. The root, which has one, two or three prongs, is fixed in the jawbone. Tooth decay happens when bacteria mix with sugar. Together, they dissolve tooth enamel, making holes that let infection get inside the tooth.

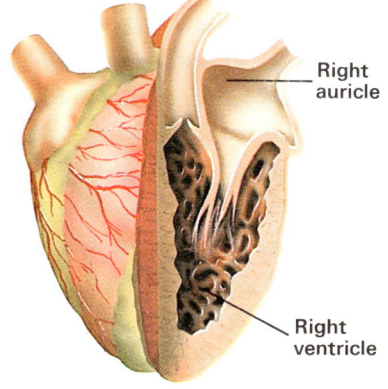

A diagram of the heart.

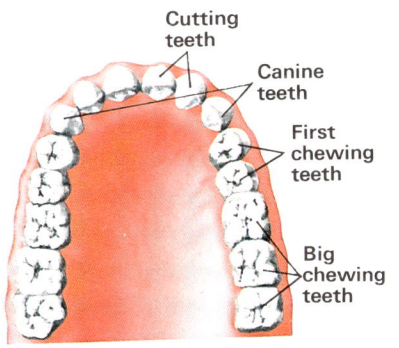

The three kinds of human teeth.

Heart The heart is a muscle in the body. It pumps blood round the body through veins and arteries. In an adult person, the heart goes on working at between 70 and 80 beats a minute until death.

The blood carries oxygen from the lungs and energy from the food we eat. Arteries carry this rich red blood to feed the body. Veins carry away waste products and return the dark 'tired' blood to the heart.

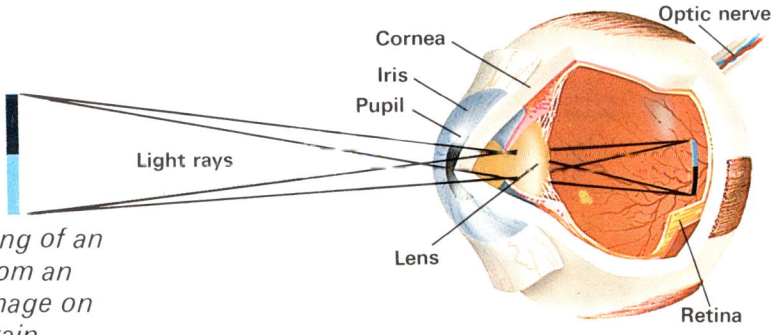

A cutaway drawing of an eye. Light rays from an object form an image on the retina. The brain arranges it into a picture.

Eye A human eye is a ball bigger than a marble. It works much like a camera: both bend light rays to form a picture of the object that the rays come from.

Light rays enter the eye through a layer of transparent skin called the *conjunctiva*. The rays pass through a hard, transparent layer called the *cornea*. This bends the rays. The lens brings them

into focus on the *retina* at the back of the eye. But you do not 'see' the picture formed here until light-sensitive nerve endings on the retina send the brain a message along the *optic nerve*. The *iris* (the coloured part of the eye) can open and close to let more or less light through the *pupil*. This is the dark opening in front of the lens.

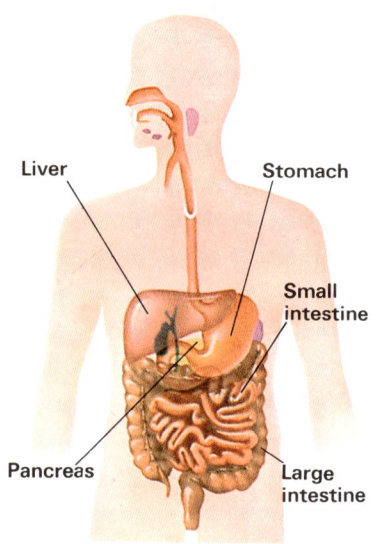

Diagram of the digestive system.

Great Advances in Medicine

Discovery	Discoverer	Date
Microscope	Zacharias Janssen	1590
Blood Circulation	William Harvey	1628
Vaccination	Edward Jenner	1796
Anaesthetic	William Morton	1846
Antiseptic surgery	Joseph Lister	1865
Germs cause disease	Louis Pasteur	1877
Psychoanalysis	Sigmund Freud	1895
X-rays	Wilhelm Roentgen	1895
Radium	Pierre and Marie Curie	1898
Penicillin	Alexander Fleming	1928

Drugs and Medicine

anaesthetic A substance producing total unconsciousness (general), or loss of sensation in a part of the body (local).

analgesic Any pain-killing preparation that does not produce unconsciousness if taken as directed.

antibiotic Drugs, such as penicillin, prepared from fungi; used to combat bacteria.

aspirin Analgesic that also reduces fever; chemical name *acetylsalicylic acid*.

barbiturate A sedative used in sleeping pills.

morphine An analgesic derived from opium; is addictive.

penicillin An antibiotic obtained from *Penicillium*, a fungus mould.

sedative Medicine acting on the nervous system to sooth or make drowsy.

soporific Any drug that induces sleep.

stimulant Any drug that stimulates the rate of the mental or bodily processes.

sulfa drugs The sulphonamides; used against bacterial infections.

tranquillizer Drug that calms the emotions without causing much drowsiness.

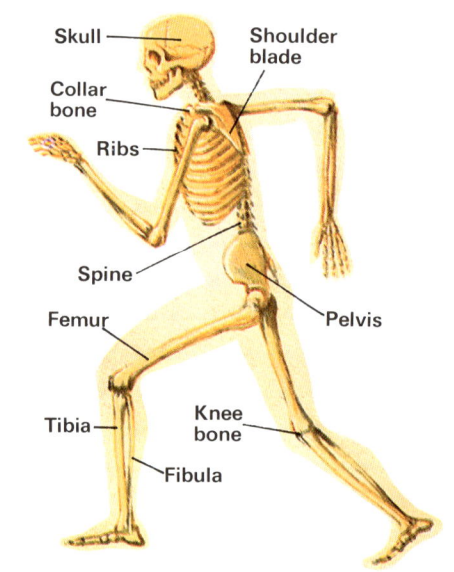

Bones The human skeleton is built of more than 200 bones. The 26 bones of the spine are linked to one another, and form the main framework of the body. They support the skull, the ribs, and the two bone 'girdles' that support the limbs – the shoulder blades and the pelvis. The arms are connected to the shoulder blade; the legs to the pelvis.

Men of Medicine

Banting, Sir Frederick (1891–1941), Canadian physiologist who isolated insulin for the treatment of diabetes. Banting's research colleague was Charles Best.

Barnard, Christiaan (born 1922), South African surgeon, performed the first successful heart transplant operation, in 1967.

Fleming, Sir Alexander (1881–1955), Scottish bacteriologist, discovered penicillin. He shared the 1945 Nobel prize in medicine for its development.

Freud, Sigmund (1856–1939), Austrian psychiatrist, proposed the idea of the conscious and subconscious mind. He introduced psychoanalysis.

Galen (c.130–c.200), Greek physician, studied the anatomy of animals; wrote some 400 books. He discovered that arteries contain blood.

Harvey, William (1578–1657), an English physician, studied the heart and blood vessels. He discovered the one-way circulation of the blood in the body. His book *An Anatomical Treatise on the Motion of the Heart and Blood in Animals* (1628) is regarded as the most important work in the history of physiology.

Jenner, Edward (1749–1823), a British physician, has been called the 'father of immunology'. He discovered vaccination as a means of preventing smallpox. He developed the smallpox vaccine from cowpox germs.

Lister, Lord Joseph (1827–1912), a British surgeon, was the first to introduce antiseptic surgery. Initially he used a carbolic-acid spray to kill germs in the air, but he later realized that germs were also present on instruments and on the surgeon's hands. He introduced the use of antiseptics on everything that came into contact with the patient.

Pavlov, Ivan Petrovich (1849–1936), a Russian physiologist, introduced the idea of conditioned reflexes with his experiments on dogs. He was awarded the Nobel prize in 1904 for his research on digestion and the nervous system.

Schweitzer, Albert (1875–1965), a remarkable man in several fields of endeavour, became a brilliant philosopher, musician (organist), and writer on theology. He was inspired to become a medical missionary, and studied medicine from 1905 to 1913. After raising money to build a Leper hospital in Gabon, at Lambaréné, he cared for the sick there.

Vesalius, Andreas (1514–64), a Flemish anatomist, has been described as the 'father of anatomy'. His book *Concerning the fabric of the Human Body* (1543) gave the first complete description of the human body.

Edward Jenner

Body Facts

Blood takes about one minute to go from the heart, around the body, and back to the heart again.

The skin covering the body measures almost 2 square metres (21 sq. ft).

We have between 90,000 and 140,000 hairs on our heads.

The lungs can hold between 3 to 5 litres (5 to 9 pints) of air. About half a litre is taken in at each breath.

An average adult drinks about 1.5 litres (3 pints) of liquid and eats about 1.5 kilogrammes (3 lb) of food every day.

If all the blood vessels in a human body were laid end to end they would stretch for nearly 100,000 kilometres (62,000 miles).

Mind and Body

What happens to your eyes in the dark? Look in a mirror and close your eyes until they are nearly shut. Your pupils get bigger so that they let in more light. This is what happens when you go out at night. Open your eyes quickly, and you'll see your pupils shrinking. This means that less light is being let in, because in bright light the eyes need less light.

Are you right-eyed or left-eyed? Point your finger at an object in the distance. Then close your left eye and see whether your finger is still pointing at the object. Now do the same thing with your right eye. If your finger moved while your left eye was closed, then your right eye is stronger, and *vice versa*.

Blind spot: One part of the eye, the optic nerve head, does not contain any nerve endings and so cannot actually see anything. You can find this blind spot by holding this book in front of you, closing your right eye and staring at the spot with your left eye. Slowly move the book towards your eye, and eventually the cat will disappear.

Testing the sense of smell: Take one teaspoonful each of ginger, cinnamon, mustard, pepper, peppermint essence and lemon juice. Then get your friends to come in one by one blindfolded, and see if they can tell which is which just by smelling them. Then mix two of the smells together – perhaps the mustard and pepper – and see if your friends can still distinguish them.

Testing the sense of taste: Take one teaspoonful each of flour, icing sugar, sherbet, cocoa powder and a flavoured milkshake powder. Get your friends to come in blindfolded, give them a bit of each to taste and see if they can guess what each is. Then make them hold their noses and see if they can still guess correctly.

Two-point touch: You can discover how sensitive different parts of the body are by touching them with a pair of dividers. Set the points 5 mm ($\frac{1}{4}$ in) apart and try touching various parts of your body with them. Only your fingertips, nose and tongue will register that there are two points. The rest of the body will feel them as one. The middle of the tongue is the most sensitive part of the body, the middle of the back the least.

Find out About Your Personality

Look at the eight colours. Decide which one you like best. Write down the colour and then cover its circle. Which of the remaining colours do you like best? Write it down and cover it up. Repeat until you have covered all of the colours. Write 1st pair beside the first two colours you chose, 2nd pair beside the next two, and so on. You should have four pairs. Now let's find out what your colours mean. The meanings given have been very simplified and must not be taken seriously.

Interpreting the Colour Test

Each colour means something different according to whether it is in the first pair of colours you chose, or in the second pair, the third pair, or the fourth pair.

The following tells you the 'meaning' of each colour for each position.

BLUE in the 1st pair means seeking peace and quiet. In 2nd pair: acts calmly. In 3rd pair: not closely involved. In 4th pair: won't relax.

GREEN in 1st pair: wants to be independent. In 2nd pair: persistent, demanding. In 3rd pair: feels should make the best of things. In 4th pair: unwilling to take steps to overcome stress.

RED in 1st pair: seeking activity and enjoyment. In 2nd pair: active but feels is not making enough progress. In 3rd pair: in need of peace and quiet. In 4th pair: feels helpless.

YELLOW in 1st pair: seeking a change for the better. In 2nd pair: attracted by anything new. In 3rd pair: hopeful but needs reassurance. In 4th pair: has unfulfilled hopes and disappointments.

GREY in 1st pair: unwilling to join in or feels exhausted. In 2nd pair: having difficulty in getting desires. In 3rd pair: willing to join in but avoids conflict. In 4th pair: impatient.

VIOLET in 1st pair: yearns for romantic tenderness. In 2nd pair: needs to express himself or herself sensitively. In 3rd pair: quick to take offence. In 4th pair: controlled and demands sincerity.

BROWN in 1st pair: seeks freedom from problems and wants relaxation. In 2nd pair: feels uneasy and insecure. In 3rd pair: sensual. In 4th pair: demands esteem from others.

BLACK in 1st pair: considers existing circumstances are disagreeable and demanding. In 2nd pair: dissatisfied. In 3rd pair: feels that things stand in the way. In 4th pair: wants to be independent.

Perfect Numbers

The ancient Egyptians and Greeks were not only interested in using sums to help them build their houses and temples, or to work out the positions of the Sun and stars, they were also keen to know about the properties of particular numbers themselves. Some numbers were thought to bring good or bad luck.

The ancient Greeks discovered that some numbers have a most peculiar property. Take the number 6, for example. The numbers which are lower than 6 and divide exactly into it without leaving a remainder are 1, 2, and 3. (It is true that 6 divides exactly into 6, but we have not counted it because it is not lower than 6!) Now the peculiarity of 6 is that these numbers add up to 6 ($1+2+3=6$). The same thing does not work with the number 10, for instance. 1, 2, 5, all divide exactly into 10, but they add up to only 8.

You might not think that this property of the number 6 is very surprising, but guess how many numbers less than 10,000 have the same property. The answer is four, and it would take you many hours of hard work to find out which they are.

The ancient Greeks were so impressed with these few rare numbers – the numbers which are equal to the sum of all the lower numbers which divide exactly into them – that they called them *perfect numbers*. The next three perfect numbers after 6 are 28, 496, and 8128. It took another fifteen hundred years after the days of ancient Greece before the fifth perfect number was discovered. It turned out to be 33,550,336. How long do you think it would have taken you to reach that, using pencil and paper?

Today mathematicians can use electronic computers to take the hard work out of doing their sums. Even so, only another twelve perfect numbers have been discovered. Perhaps this is not so surprising when you consider that the largest perfect number – the seventeenth – is so big that you have to string together 1373 digits to write it down. (A digit is a whole number less than ten.) See if you can prove that 28 and 496 are perfect numbers.

Numerals

Arabic	Roman	Binary
1	I	1
2	II	10
3	III	11
4	IV	100
5	V	101
6	VI	110
7	VII	111
8	VIII	1000
9	IX	1001
10	X	1010
11	XI	1011
12	XII	1100
13	XIII	1101
14	XIV	1110
15	XV	1111
16	XVI	10000
17	XVII	10001
18	XVIII	10010
19	XIX	10011
20	XX	10100
21	XXI	10101
29	XXIX	11101
30	XXX	11110
40	XL	101000
50	L	110010
60	LX	111100
64	LXIV	1000000
90	XC	1011010
99	XCIX	1100011
100	C	1100100
500	D	111110100
1000	M	1111101000

Inventions

4000–3000 BC	Bricks – in Egypt and Assyria
c.3000 BC	Wheel – in Asia
c.3000 BC	Plough – in Egypt and Mesopotamia
c.500 BC	Abacus – the Chinese
c.300 BC	Geometry – Euclid (Gk.)
200s BC	Screw (for raising water) – Archimedes (Gk.)
AD 105	Paper (from pulp) – Ts'ai Lun (China)
AD 230	Algebra – Diophantus (Gk.)
c.1000	Gunpowder – the Chinese
c.1100	Rocket – the Chinese
c.1440	Printing press (movable type) – Johannes Gutenberg (Ger.)
1520	Rifle – Joseph Kotter (Ger.)
1589	Knitting machine – William Lee (Eng.)
c.1590	Compound microscope – Zacharias Janssen (Neth.)
1593	Thermometer – Galileo (It.)
1608	Telescope – Hans Lippershey (Neth.)
1642	Calculating machine – Blaise Pascal (Fr.)
1643	Barometer – Evangelista Torricelli (It.)
1650	Air pump – Otto von Guericke (Ger.)
1656	Pendulum clock – Christian Huygens (Neth.)
1665–75	Calculus – Sir Isaac Newton (Eng.) and Gottfried Leibniz (Ger.) independently
1675	Pressure cooker – Denis Papin (Fr.)
1698	Steam pump – Thomas Savery (Eng.)
1712	Steam engine – Thomas Newcomen (Eng.)
1714	Mercury thermometer – Gabriel Fahrenheit (Ger.)
1733	Flying shuttle – John Kay (Eng.)
1735	Chronometer – John Harrison (Eng.)
1752	Lightning conductor – Benjamin Franklin (US)
1764	Spinning jenny – James Hargreaves (Eng.)
1765	Condensing steam engine – James Watt (Scot.)
1783	Parachute – Louis Lenormand (Fr.)
1785	Powerloom – Edmund Cartwright (Eng.)
1793	Cotton gin – Eli Whitney (US)
1796	Lithography – Aloys Senefelder (Ger.)
1800	Electric battery – Count Alessandro Volta (It.)
1800	Lathe – Henry Maudslay (Eng.)
1804	Steam locomotive – Richard Trevithick (Eng.)
1815	Miner's safety lamp – Sir Humphry Davy (Eng.)
1816	Bicycle – Karl von Sauerbronn (Ger.)

Bicycle 1816

1817	Kaleidoscope – David Brewster (Scot.)
1822	Camera – Joseph Niepce (Fr.)
1823	Digital calculating machine – Charles Babbage (Eng.)
1824	Portland cement – Joseph Aspdin (Eng.)
1825	Electromagnet – William Sturgeon (Eng.)
1826	Photograph (permanent) – Joseph Niepce (Fr.)
1827	Match – John Walker (Eng.)

1828	Blast furnace – James Neilson (Scot.)
1831	Dynamo – Michael Faraday (Eng.)
1834	Reaping machine – Cyrus McCormick (US)
1836	Revolver – Samuel Colt (US)
1837	Telegraph – Samuel F. B. Morse (US)
1839	Vulcanized rubber – Charles Goodyear (US)
1844	Safety match – Gustave Pasch (Swed.)
1846	Sewing machine – Elias Howe (US)
1849	Safety pin – Walter Hunt (US)
1852	Gyroscope – Léon Foucault (Fr.)
1853	Passenger lift – Elisha Otis (US)
1855	Celluloid – Alexander Parkes (Eng.)
1855	Bessemer converter – Henry Bessemer (Eng.)
1855	Bunsen burner – Robert Bunsen (Ger.)
1858	Refrigerator – Ferdinand Carré (Fr.)
1858	Washing machine – Hamilton Smith (US)
1859	Internal combustion engine – Etienne Lenoir (Fr.)
1862	Rapid-fire gun – Richard Gatling (US)
1866	Dynamite – Alfred Nobel (Swed.)
1867	Typewriter – Christopher Sholes (US)
1868	Lawn mower – Amariah Hills (US)
1870	Margarine – Hippolyte Mège-Mouriés (Fr.)
1873	Barbed wire – Joseph Glidden (US)
1876	Telephone – Alexander Graham Bell (Scot.)
1876	Carpet sweeper – Melville Bissell (US)
1877	Phonograph – Thomas Edison (US)

Revolver 1836

Safety match 1844

1878	Microphone – David Edward Hughes (Eng./US)
1879	Incandescent lamp – Thomas Edison (US)
1884	Fountain pen – Lewis Waterman (US)
1884	Linotype – Ottmar Merganthaler (US)
1885	Motorcycle – Edward Butler (Eng.)
1885	Vacuum flask – James Dewar (Scot.)
1885	Electric transformer – William Stanley (US)
1886	Electric fan – Schuyler Wheeler (US)
1887	Gramophone (disc) – Emile Berliner (Ger./US)
1887	Monotype – Tolbert Lanston (US)
1887	Motor-car engine – Gottlieb Daimler and Karl Benz (Ger.), independently

Telephone 1876

1888	Pneumatic tyre – John Boyd Dunlop (Scot.)
1888	Kodak camera – George Eastman (US)
1890	Rotogravure – Karl Klic (Czech.)
1892	Zip fastener – Whitcomb Judson (US)
1895	Wireless – Guglielmo Marconi (It.)
1895	Safety razor – King C. Gillette (US)
1897	Diesel engine – Rudolf Diesel (Ger.)
1898	Submarine – John P. Holland (Ire./US)
1899	Tape recorder – Valdemar Poulsen (Den.)
1901	Vacuum cleaner – Cecil Booth (Eng.)
1902	Radio-telephone – Reginald Fessenden (US)
1903	Aeroplane – Wilbur and Orville Wright (US)
1908	Bakelite – Leo Baekeland (Belg./US)
1908	Cellophane – Jacques Brandenberger (Switz.)
1911	Combine harvester – Benjamin Holt (US)
1913	Geiger counter – Hans Geiger (Eng.)
1914	Tank – Ernest Swinton (Eng.)
1915	Tungsten filament lamp – Irving Langmuir (US)
1918	Automatic rifle – John Browning (US)
1925	Television (working system – John Logie Baird (Scot.) and others
1925	Frozen food process – Clarence Birdseye (US)
1926	Rocket (liquid fuel) – Robert H. Goddard (US)
1928	Electric shaver – Jacob Schick (US)
1930	Jet engine – Frank Whittle (Eng.)
1934	Launderette – J. F. Cantrell (US)

Television 1920s

Radio 1895

1935	Nylon – Wallace Carothers (US)
1935	Parking meter – Carlton Magee (US)
1935	Photographic colour film – Leopold Godonsky (US)
1939	Electron microscope – Vladimir Zworykin and others (US)
1942	Aqualung – Jacques Cousteau & Emile Gagnan (Fr.)
1944	Automatic digital computer – Howard Aiken (US)
1946	Electronic computer – J. Presper Eckert and John W. Mauchly (US)
1947	Polaroid camera – Edwin Land (US)
1948	Transistor – John Bardeen, Walter Brattain and William Schockley (US)
1948	Xerography – Chester Carlson (US)
1948	Long-playing record – Peter Goldmark (US)
1959	Fork-lift truck – Coventry-Climax Co. (Eng.)
1960	Laser – Theodore Maiman (US)
1965	Holography (an idea conceived in 1947 and subsequently developed using laser) – T. Gabor (Hung./GB)
1971	EMI-Scanner – Godfrey Hounsfield (Eng.) (developed from his invention of computed tomography in 1967)

SCIENCE AND TECHNOLOGY

The Elements and their Atomic Numbers

Name	Symbol	No.	Name	Symbol	No.	Name	Symbol	No.
Actinium	Ac	89	Hafnium	Hf	72	Praseodymium	Pr	59
Aluminium	Al	13	Helium	He	2	Promethium	Pm	61
Americium	Am	95	Holmium	Ho	67	Protactinium	Pa	91
Antimony	Sb	51	Hydrogen	H	1	Radium	Ra	88
Argon	Ar	18	Indium	In	49	Radon	Rn	86
Arsenic	As	33	Iodine	I	53	Rhenium	Re	75
Astatine	At	85	Iridium	Ir	77	Rhodium	Rh	45
Barium	Ba	56	Iron	Fe	26	Rubidium	Rb	37
Berkelium	Bk	97	Krypton	Kr	36	Ruthenium	Ru	44
Beryllium	Be	4	Lanthanum	La	57	Samarium	Sm	62
Bismuth	Bi	83	Lawrencium	Lr	103	Scandium	Sc	21
Boron	B	5	Lead	Pb	82	Selenium	Se	34
Bromine	Br	35	Lithium	Li	3	Silicon	Si	14
Cadmium	Cd	48	Lutetium	Lu	71	Silver	Ag	47
Caesium	Cs	55	Magnesium	Mg	12	Sodium	Na	11
Calcium	Ca	20	Manganese	Mn	25	Strontium	Sr	38
Californium	Cf	98	Mendelevium	Md	101	Sulphur	S	16
Carbon	C	6	Mercury	Hg	80	Tantalum	Ta	73
Cerium	Ce	58	Molybdenum	Mo	42	Technetium	Tc	43
Chlorine	Cl	17	Neodymium	Nd	60	Tellurium	Te	52
Chromium	Cr	24	Neon	Ne	10	Terbium	Tb	65
Cobalt	Co	27	Neptunium	Np	93	Thallium	Tl	81
Copper	Cu	29	Nickel	Ni	28	Thorium	Th	90
Curium	Cm	96	Niobium	Nb	41	Thulium	Tm	69
Dysprosium	Dy	66	Nitrogen	N	7	Tin	Sn	50
Einsteinium	Es	99	Nobelium	No	102	Titanium	Ti	22
Erbium	Er	68	Osmium	Os	76	Tungsten	W	74
Europium	Eu	63	Oxygen	O	8	Uranium	U	92
Fermium	Fm	100	Palladium	Pd	46	Vanadium	V	23
Fluorine	F	9	Phosphorus	P	15	Xenon	Xe	54
Francium	Fr	87	Plantinum	Pt	78	Ytterbium	Yb	70
Gadolinium	Gd	64	Plutonium	Pu	94	Yttrium	Y	39
Gallium	Ga	31	Polonium	Po	84	Zinc	Zn	30
Geranium	Ge	32	Potassium	K	19	Zirconium	Zr	40
Gold	Au	79						

Chemical Names of Everyday Substances

Substance	Chemical Name
Baking Powder	Sodium Bicarbonate
Boracic Acid	Boric Acid
Borax	Sodium Borate
Chalk	Calcium Carbonate
Common Salt	Sodium Chloride
Epsom Salts	Magnesium Sulphate
Lime	Calcium Oxide
Magnesia	Magnesium Oxide
Plaster of Paris	Calcium Sulphate
Red Lead	Triplumbic Tetroxide
Saltpetre	Potassium Nitrate
Sal Volatile	Ammonium Carbonate
Vinegar	Dilute Acetic Acid
Washing Soda	Crystalline Sodium Carbonate

Chemical Indicators

Indicators show whether a substance is alkaline or acid. The following list gives the effect of adding an indicator.

Indicator	Litmus	Methyl Orange
Alkaline	turns blue	turns yellow
Acid	turns red	turns pink

A to Z of Science

absolute zero Lowest temperature possible in theory; zero on absolute scale is $-273 \cdot 15°C$.

absorption Penetration of a substance into the body of another; e.g. a gas dissolving in a liquid.

acceleration Rate of change of velocity; measured in distance per second per second.

acid Chemical substance that when dissolved in water produces hydrogen ions, which may be replaced by metals to form salts.

alkali *Base* consisting of a soluble metal hydroxide. Alkali metals, such as sodium and potassium, form *caustic alkalis*.

alloy Metal composed of more than one element; e.g. dentist's amalgam is an alloy of mercury (70%) and copper (30%).

alternating current Electric current that rapidly decreases from maximum in one direction, through zero, and then increases to maximum in the other direction.

ampere (A) Unit of electric current equivalent to flow of 6×10^{18} electrons per sec (i.e. 6 million million million electrons). It is named after André Marie Ampère.

amplifier An electronic device that increases the strength of a signal (e.g. radio waves) fed into it by using power from another source.

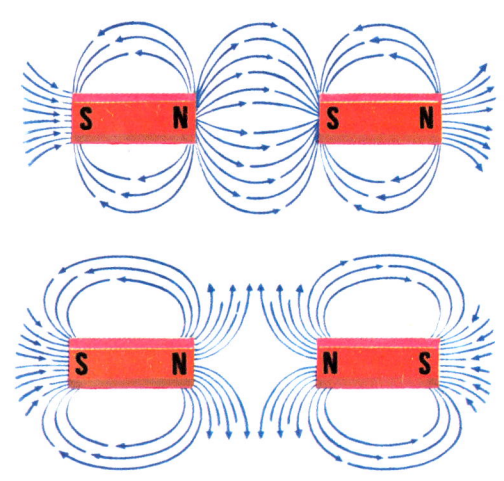

Around magnets are fields of force. These can be seen by sprinkling iron filings on a card resting on a bar magnet. The filings arrange themselves into a series of curved lines linking the north and south poles. These lines follow the so-called lines of magnetic force round the magnet, which make up its magnetic field.

anode Positive electrode through which current enters an electrolytic cell or a vacuum tube.

Archimedes' principle When a body is immersed or partly immersed in a fluid, the apparent loss in weight is equal to the weight of the fluid displaced.

atom Smallest fragment of an element that can take part in a chemical reaction. Consists of central *nucleus* (made up of *protons* and *neutrons*) surrounded by orbiting *electrons*. Number of protons (equal to number of electrons) is called the *atomic number*. Total mass of all the atomic particles is called the *relative atomic mass*. See also *isotope*.

base Substance that reacts chemically with an *acid* to form a *salt* and water.

boiling point Temperature at which liquid turns into vapour throughout its bulk; the vapour pressure of the liquid then equals the external pressure on it.

Boyle's law At constant temperature, the volume of a gas is inversely proportional to its pressure; i.e. the higher the pressure, the smaller the volume.

calorie Unit of heat equal to amount needed to raise the temperature of 1 gram of water through 1 degree C.

catalyst Substance that markedly alters the speed of a chemical reaction, without appearing to take part in it.

cathode Negative *electrode* through which electric current leaves an electrolytic cell or a vacuum tube.

Celsius Temperature scale on which 0°C is the melting point of ice and 100°C is boiling point of water; same as centigrade.

centigrade See *Celsius*.

centrifugal force Force that appears to act on an object moving in a circular path.

Charles's law At constant pressure, the volume of a gas is proportional to its absolute temperature; i.e. the higher the temperature, the greater the volume.

chloride Salt of hydrochloric acid.

circuit, electrical The complete path taken by an electric current.

combustion (burning) Chemical reaction in which a substance combines with oxygen and gives off heat and light, and burns with a flame.

compound Substance consisting of two or more *elements* in chemical combination in definite proportions; e.g. water (hydrogen and oxygen) and salt (sodium and chlorine).

concave Curving inwards. A concave lens is thinner at the middle than at the edges.

condensation Change of vapour into liquid that takes place when pressure is applied to it or the temperature is lowered.

conductor, electric Substance that permits the flow of electricity; e.g. metals.

convection Transfer of heat by means of the movement of heated matter from one place to another. It takes place in liquids and gases through the actual movement of the fluid.

convex Curving outwards. A convex lens is thinner at the edges than at the middle.

corrosion Slow chemical breakdown, often by oxidation of metals, by the action of water, air, or chemicals such as acids.

cosmic rays High-energy radiation, mainly in the form of charged particles striking the Earth from outer space.

crystal Substance that has been solidified in a definite geometrical form. Some solids do not form crystals, and are said to be *amorphous*. The geometrical patterns are called *lattices*. Crystals are classified according to the structure of their lattices and the bonds holding them together.

current, electric Flow of electrons along a conductor; measured in *amperes*.

decibel Unit for comparing power levels or sound intensities; tenth of a *bel*.

density Mass per volume.

diffraction The spreading out of light by passing it through a narrow slit or past the edge of an obstacle.

diode Electronic valve with two electrodes – an *anode* and a *cathode*.

distillation A technique for purifying or separating liquids by heating to boiling point and condensing the vapour produced back to a liquid.

dry ice Solid carbon dioxide.

dynamo Device for converting mechanical energy into electrical energy; in simple form it consists of an armature rotating between the poles of a powerful electromagnet.

elasticity Property of a material that makes it go back to its original shape after a force deforming it is removed; if stressed beyond the *elastic limit*, the material does not return to its original shape.

electrode Metal plate through which electric current enters or leaves an electrolytic cell, battery, or vacuum tube. See *anode* and *cathode*.

electrolysis Conduction of electricity between two electrodes, through solution or molten mass (electrolyte) containing ions; accompanied by chemical changes at the electrodes.

electromagnet Magnet consisting of an iron core surrounded by a coil of wire carrying an electric current. The core is magnetized only when the electric current is flowing.

electron Negatively charged atomic particle; every neutral atom has as many orbiting electrons as there are protons in the nucleus. See also *current, electric*.

electron microscope Instrument that uses a beam of electrons to produce magnified images of objects that are too small even to be seen with ordinary optical (light) microscopes.

element Substance made up entirely of exactly similar atoms (all with the same atomic number). The elements are listed, with their chemical symbols and atomic numbers, on p.178.

energy Capacity for doing work; examples include: *chemical energy* (possessed by a substance in its atoms or molecules, and released in a chemical reaction); *electrical energy* (associated with electric charges and their movements); *heat* (possessed by a body because of the motion of its atoms or molecules – a form of kinetic energy); *kinetic energy* (possessed by a body because of its motion); and *potential energy* (possessed by a body because of its position).

erg Absolute unit of work in the cgs system, defined as the work done by a force of 1 dyne acting through 1 cm.

evaporation Phenomenon in which liquid turns into vapour without necessarily reaching the boiling point. It occurs because fast-moving molecules escape from the surface of the liquid.

Fahrenheit Temperature scale on which the melting point of ice is 32°F and the boiling point of water is 212°F.

fermentation Chemical reaction of organic substances brought about by living organisms such as yeasts and bacteria.

fission (splitting) In atomic or nuclear fission, the nuclei of heavy atoms split and release vast quantities of energy; this is the energy-generating process that takes place in atomic bombs and nuclear reactors.

fluid Substance (liquid or gas) that takes the shape of part or all of the vessel containing it.

focus The point at which converging rays of light meet.

force Anything that can act on a stationary body and make it move, or make a moving body change speed or direction.

freezing point Temperature at which a liquid changes to a solid. It is the same as *melting point* of the solid.

frequency Of a wave motion, the number of oscillations, cycles, vibrations, or waves per second.

friction Force that resists sliding or rolling of one surface in contact with another.

fulcrum The point of support of a lever.

fusion, nuclear The joining of nuclei of light atoms together with the release of vast amounts of energy; this is the process that occurs in hydrogen bombs and in stars. Also known as a *thermonuclear reaction*.

gas Substance that no matter how little there is always takes up the whole of the vessel containing it. See also *vapour*.

Geiger counter Instrument for detecting

and measuring radioactivity.

gravitation Force of attraction between any two objects because of their masses. *Newton's law of gravitation* states that the force between two particles is directly proportional to the product of their two masses, and inversely proportional to the square of the distance between them.

hydrocarbon Chemical compound containing only hydrogen and carbon.

inclined plane Simple machine consisting of smooth plane sloping upwards; used for moving heavy loads with relatively small force.

indicator Substance that changes colour to indicate the end of a chemical reaction or to indicate the pH (acidity or alkalinity) of a solution. See *pH*.

inert gases A group of chemically inactive gases – helium, neon, argon, krypton, xenon, radon; also called the noble, or rare, gases.

inertia Property of an object that makes it resist being moved or its motion being changed.

infra-red rays Electromagnetic radiation of wavelengths just longer than those of visible light; invisible heat radiation.

insulation Use of an insulator, a substance that is a poor conductor of heat, sound, or electricity, to prevent their passing through.

isotope One of two or more forms of an element with the same atomic number (i.e. number of protons in the nucleus), but different relative atomic masses (due to different numbers of neutrons in the nucleus). See also *atoms*.

laser Type of *maser* that produces an intense beam of light that is monochromatic (single colour) and coherent (all its waves are in step); abbreviation for *light amplification by stimulated emission of radiation*.

latent heat Heat absorbed, without a rise in temperature, when a substance is

This toy figure always springs up right no matter how much it is tilted. The centre of gravity is so low that it always remains to one side of the point on which the toy pivots and gravity pulls it back upright.

changed from solid to liquid or liquid to gas.

lens Device that affects light passing through it by converging (bringing together) or diverging (spreading apart) the rays.

lever Simple machine consisting of a rigid beam pivoted at one point, called the *fulcrum*; effort applied at one point on the beam can lift a load at another point.

liquid Substance that without changing its volume takes up the shape of all, or the lower part of, the vessel containing it.

litmus Vegetable dye used as a chemical indicator; it is red in acid solutions and blue in alkaline solutions.

magneto High-voltage electric generator in which a permanent magnet is spun inside a coil; it gives only short pulses of current and is used for starting petrol engines. See also *dynamo*.

maser Microwave amplifier that uses energy changes within atoms or molecules; abbreviation for *microwave ampli-*

fication by *stimulated* *emission* of *radi-ation*.

mass Amount of matter in an object; property of an object that gives it inertia.

melting point Temperature at which solid turns to liquid; equal to *freezing point* of the liquid.

metal Element or alloy that is a good conductor of heat and electricity, has a high density, often has a characteristic lustre, and can generally be worked by beating or drawing into wire.

mixture More than one element or compound together, but not in chemical combination; components can be separated by physical means.

molecule Smallest amount of chemical substance that can exist alone; it is made up of one or more atoms.

momentum The product of the mass and velocity of a moving body.

motion, Newton's laws of (1) A stationary object remains still or a moving object continues to move in a straight line unless acted on by an external force. (2) The force producing acceleration in an object is proportional to the product of the object's mass and its acceleration. (3) Every action has an equal and opposite reaction.

neutron Uncharged atomic particle found in the nuclei of all atoms except hydrogen.

nucleus, atomic The positively charged centre of an atom; consists of one or more protons and, except for hydrogen, one or more neutrons. See also *atom*.

oxide Chemical compound of oxygen and another element.

ozone Form of oxygen containing three atoms in each molecule; O_3.

Pascal's law In a fluid, the pressure applied at any point is transmitted equally throughout it.

pendulum Device consisting of a mass (bob) swinging at the end of a rigid or flexible support; *period* (time of one swing) of a simple pendulum, which has a flexible support such as a length of cord, is independent of the mass of the bob, depending only on the length of the cord and the acceleration due to gravity.

proton Positively charged atomic particle found in the nuclei of all atoms. The number of protons in an atom is the *atomic number*.

pulley Grooved wheel round which rope or chain runs; used for lifting weights.

radiation, heat Transfer of heat by means of waves; infra-red rays.

radioactivity Emission of radiation, such as *alpha-particles, beta-particles,* and *gamma-rays,* from unstable elements by the spontaneous splitting of their atomic nuclei.

reaction Chemical process involving two or more substances (*reactants*) and resulting in a chemical change.

refraction Bending of a light ray as it crosses the boundary between two media of different optical density.

By bending light rays, refraction causes images to be displaced, as when objects are seen through water. Lenses work by refraction, causing light rays to converge or diverge, producing magnified or diminished images accordingly.

relativity Einstein's theory that it is impossible to measure motion absolutely, but only within a given frame of reference.

salt Chemical compound formed, with water, when a *base* reacts with an *acid*; a salt is also formed, often with the production of hydrogen, when a metal reacts with an acid. *Common salt* is sodium chloride.

saturated solution Solution that will take up no more of the dissolved substance.

SI units (Système International d'Unités) Internationally agreed system built round seven basic units, with several derived units, replacing other systems for scientific purposes.

solder Alloy with a low melting point, used for joining metals; alloys of tin and lead in varying proportions are used as soft solders; alloys of copper and zinc are used for brazing.

solid State of matter that has a definite shape and resists having it changed; a crystalline solid melts to a liquid on heating above its melting point.

solubility Quantity of a substance (solute) that will dissolve in a solvent to form a solution.

solvent Liquid part of a solution.

speed Distance travelled by a moving object divided by the time taken. Speed in a particular direction is *velocity*.

surface tension Property of the surface of a liquid that makes it behave as though it were covered with a thin elastic skin.

suspension System consisting of very fine solid particles evenly dispersed in a liquid.

temperature Degree of hotness of an object referred to a selected zero (see *Celsius, Fahrenheit*).

thermometer Device for measuring temperature; common mercury thermometer is based on the expansion of mercury with rises in temperature, a thin thread of mercury rising up a tube as the temperature rises.

thermostat Control device, sensitive to changes in temperature, that maintains the temperature in an enclosure within a narrow, predetermined range.

UHF Ultra-high frequency radio waves.

ultrasonic waves 'Sound' waves beyond the range of human hearing.

ultraviolet rays Electromagnetic radiation of wavelengths just shorter than those of visible light. Sun's radiation is rich in ultraviolet rays; they may be produced artificially with a mercury vapour lamp.

volt (V) Unit of electromotive force. (emf).

volume Measurement of the space occupied by an object.

watt (W) Unit of electrical power, defined as the rate of work done in joules per second; equal to the product of current (A) in amperes and potential difference in volts (V). $W = AV$.

wavelength Of a wave motion, the distance between crests (or troughs) of two consecutive waves; equal to the velocity of the wave divided by its frequency.

waves Regular disturbances that carry energy. Particles of a medium may vibrate; e.g. air molecules vibrate when sound waves pass, and water molecules vibrate when ripples cross water. Light and radio travel as electromagnetic waves.

vacuum In practice, region in which pressure is considerably less than atmospheric pressure.

vapour Gas that can be turned into a liquid by compressing it without cooling.

velocity Rate of change of position equal to *speed* in a particular direction.

VHF Very high frequency radio waves.

X-rays Very short wavelength electromagnetic waves.

White light splits into the seven colours of the rainbow, the spectrum, when it is shone through a prism.

Grow Your Own Crystals

Blue copper sulphate

Boiling water

Under the right conditions minerals grow into beautiful crystals of many different shapes and sizes and colours. You can grow crystals easily yourself, using common minerals found in the home and garden, such as washing soda, table salt and Epsom salts.

Pour hot water into a heat-proof dish or beaker and add the mineral little by little, stirring all the time until it dissolves. Eventually you will find that the solution becomes saturated – no more mineral will dissolve. Now allow the solution to cool. As it does so the mineral will start to come out of solution as crystals. To encourage crystals to form dangle a thread in the solution, and the crystals will form on the end.

SCIENCE AND TECHNOLOGY

Master Builders

Isambard Kingdom Brunel (1806–59) was a British civil engineer, the son of Marc Isambard Brunel (1769–1849), who built the Thames (Rotherhithe) Tunnel. He helped his father on this project. He also designed and built bridges, including the Clifton suspension bridge over the River Avon, near Bristol, and the first transatlantic steamships. He built the Hungerford bridge over the Thames, and the Tamar bridge in Cornwall. His works also include long stretches of railway, with all the tunnels and bridges. And he introduced a larger railway gauge to allow faster speeds.

Ferdinand de Lesseps (1805–94), a French diplomat, designed both the Panama and the Suez canals. The Suez Canal was dug between 1859 and 1869. Lesseps started on the Panama Canal in 1882, but seven years later his company went bankrupt with only a quarter of the work done. The failure was caused largely by terrible loss of life due to yellow fever and accidents. The Panama Canal was eventually completed after Lesseps' death.

Louis Henry Sullivan (1856–1924) was an American architect who, with his partner, Dankmar Adler, designed over 100 buildings in the United States between 1881 and 1895. He was the man who adapted modern methods to building, applying ideas in architecture to skyscrapers such as the Prudential Building in Buffalo, New York. His pupil was Frank Lloyd Wright.

Joseph Baermann Strauss (1870–1938) was an American engineer, who, after founding his own firm in 1904, built over 400 bridges in the United States, including the Golden Gate Bridge in San Francisco and the George Washington Bridge in New York City.

Dams – Highest and Largest

Highest	Location	Type	(m)	(ft)	completed
Nurek	USSR	earthfill	317	1040	1980
Grande Dixence	Switzerland	gravity	284	932	1962
Inguri	USSR	arch	272	892	*
Vaiont	Italy	multi-arch	262	858	1961
Mica	Canada	rockfill	242	794	1973
Mauvoisin	Switzerland	arch	237	777	1958

Largest†	Location	(cub. m)	(cub. yd)	completed
New Cornelia Trailings	Arizona, USA	209,506,000	274,026,000	1973
Tarbela	Pakistan	142,000,000	186,000,000	1979
Fort Peck	Montana, USA	96,000,000	125,000,000	1940
Oahe	S Dakota, USA	70,000,000	92,000,000	1963
Mangala	Pakistan	65,650,000	85,740,000	1967
Gardiner	Canada	65,550,000	85,740,000	1968
Oroville	California, USA	60,000,000	78,000,000	1968

*Under construction.

†All earthfill except Tarbela (earth- and rock-fill).

Largest Bridge Spans

Arch:
Coalbrookdale, Britain

	Location	Longest span (m)	(ft)	Opened
Suspension				
Akashi-Kaikyo	Japan	1750	5840	*
Humber Estuary	England	1410	4626	1980
Verrazano Narrows	NY, USA	1298	4260	1964
Golden Gate	Calif., USA	1280	4200	1937
Cantilever				
Quebec Railway	Canada	549	1800	1917
Forth Rail	Scotland	518	1700	1890
Steel Arch				
New River Gorge	W. Va., USA	518	1700	1977
Bayonne	NJ, USA	504	1652	1931
Sydney Harbour	Australia	503	1650	1932
Cable-Stayed				
Second Houghly	Calcutta, India	457	1500	*
St-Nazaire	Loire, France	404	1325	1975
Duisburg-Neuenkamp	W. Germany	350	1148	1970
Continuous Truss				
Astoria	Oregon, USA	376	1232	1966
Concrete Arch				
Gladesville	Australia	305	1000	1964
Longest bridge (total length)				
Pontchartrain Causeway	Louisiana, USA	38·4km	23·9	1969

*Under construction.

Suspension:
Golden Gate,
San Francisco, USA

Tallest Structures

The world's tallest building is the 110-storey 443 m (1454 ft) Sears Tower in Chicago, USA. With TV antennae, it reaches 475·2 m (1559 ft). The world's tallest structure is the 646 m (2120 ft) mast of Warszawa Radio at Konstantynow, near Plock, in Poland. Made of galvanized steel, it was completed in July 1974.

The highest structures of ancient times were the pyramids of Egypt. The Great Pyramid of Cheops, at el-Gizeh, built in about 2580 BC, reached a height of 146·6 m (480·9 ft). It was another 4000 years before this was surpassed – by the central tower of Lincoln Cathedral, England, which was completed in 1548 and stood 160 m (525 ft) before it toppled in a storm.

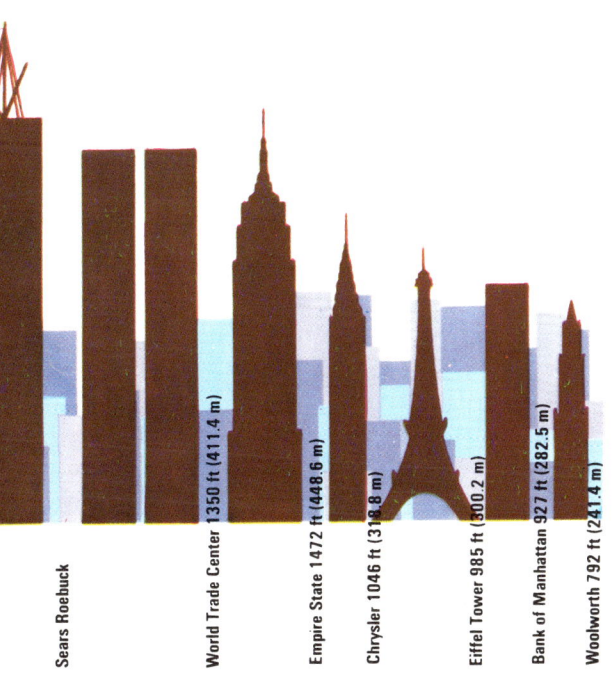

Sears Roebuck

World Trade Center 1350 ft (411.4 m)

Empire State 1472 ft (448.6 m)

Chrysler 1046 ft (318.8 m)

Eiffel Tower 985 ft (300.2 m)

Bank of Manhattan 927 ft (282.5 m)

Woolworth 792 ft (241.4 m)

187

SCIENCE AND TECHNOLOGY

The Great Wall of China *was built over 2000 years ago to keep out enemies. It is 3460 km (2130 miles) long, and is built from earth and stone. A watch-tower was built every 180 metres (200 yards) along the wall. It stretches from the Yellow Sea in the east to Asia in the west. The top of the wall is flat and resembles a roadway.*

Aqueducts *are man made conduits for carrying water, and can be made in the form of pipes underground, or as a kind of overhead canal built on arches like the one being built in the picture by Roman engineers. Examples of Roman aqueducts are the Aqua Claudia in Rome, the Pont du Gard at Nîmes in France, and that at Segovia in Spain, all of which exist in good condition. The Pont du Gard is 48 metres (160 ft) high, and has three tiers of arches.*

The Krak des Chevaliers *is a walled citadel or castle in Jordan, in the Middle East, built in 1131 by the Knights Hospitallers, and still in fine condition. It stands near the town of El Kerak, and although conquered by Saladin in 1188, was a Christian centre until 1910.*

Great Artists

Botticelli, Sandro (1444–1510; Italian), was a painter who spent most of his life in Florence. Most of his work consisted of religious pictures, with clear, delicate lines.

Braque, Georges (1882–1963; French), a painter and sculpter, was one of the founders of Cubism.

Brueghel, Pieter (1520?–1569; Flemish), is renowned for lively pictures of village life. Many of his paintings have hundreds of people in them.

Cézanne, Paul (1839–1906; French), is famous for his landscapes and still-lifes. He used strong colours applied with firm, bold strokes of the brush.

Constable, John (1776–1837; English), was one of the greatest landscape painters. He loved to paint quiet country scenes, full of warm sunlight and sombre, rich colours.

Degas, Edgar (1834–1917; French), an artist of the Impressionist period, is noted for his pictures of ballet dancers.

Dürer, Albrecht (1471–1528; German), He made many fine woodcuts and engravings for book illustrations. He excelled at portrait paintings in oils, and landscapes in water-colours.

Fra Angelico (1387–1455; Italian) A Dominican friar, he decorated the walls of his friary with frescoes. His paintings are sharp and clear, and tranquil in feeling.

Gauguin, Paul (1848–1903; French), escaped from European civilization to paint in the peaceful Pacific island of Tahiti.

Giotto (1266?–1337; Italian), greatly influenced renaissance art. His style was more realistic than that of the formal painters of his time.

Goya, Francisco (1746–1828; Spanish), painted the people of the court as he saw them rather than flatteringly.

Greco, El (1548?–1614; Greek/Spanish), was born Domenikos Theotocopoulos in Crete, but worked in Venice and Spain. His nickname means 'the Greek'.

Hogarth, William (1697–1764; English), satirized the cruelty and vice which he saw around him in London. His engravings of moral subjects are full of minute detail.

Holbein, Hans, the Younger (1497?–1543; German), was a portrait painter who created realistic likenesses of his subjects. One of his best-known portraits is that of King Henry VIII of England.

Klee, Paul (1879–1940; Swiss), He described the method he used in his many drawings, etchings, and paintings as 'taking a line for a walk'.

Leonardo da Vinci (1452–1519; Italian), was a painter, architect, sculptor, and musician, as well as a brilliant inventor and scientist. His notebooks are full of sketches showing details of the anatomy of people and animals, and studies of rock formations.

Michelangelo Buonarroti (1475–1564; Italian) His finest work was painted on the ceiling of the Sistine Chapel, in the Vatican. In his last years he turned to architecture, designing the dome of St Peter's Basilica in Rome.

Picasso, Pablo (1881–1973; Spanish), He spent most of his life in France. His early paintings showed poor and suffering people and were dominated by the colour blue. In 1907 he introduced the style of painting known as Cubism, and from this gradually evolved a distortion of form that changed the whole course of art.

Raphael (1483–1520; Italian), was greatly influenced when young by Michelangelo and Leonardo. His pictures are notable for their peaceful beauty and perfect composition.

Rembrandt van Rijn (1606–1669; Dutch), was one of the finest portrait painters. He was a master at capturing the character of his subjects, and in the dramatic use of light and shade (*chiaroscuro*).

Renoir, Pierre Auguste (1841–1919; French), used rich colours; pinks and reds tend to dominate most of his paintings.

Rubens, Peter Paul (1577–1640; Flemish). After spending eight years in Italy he became court painter in Antwerp. Assistants helped him complete his many large canvases of religious and mythological subjects.

Titian (1477–1576; Italian), was the greatest Venetian painter. His full name was Tiziano Vecelli. He painted many religious works for churches.

Toulouse-Lautrec, Henri de (1864–1901; French), is best remembered for his Parisian cabaret posters and his pictures of music-hall performers.

Turner, Joseph Mallord William (1775–1851; English), is especially noted for his water-colours and his magnificent sunsets.

Van Eyck, Jan (1370?–1440; Flemish), was one of the earliest painters to use oil colours. His richly coloured paintings show great attention to detail.

Van Gogh, Vincent (1853–1890; Dutch). His early pictures were sombre, but in his later work he used bright, swirling colours. During a fit of insanity he cut off part of one ear.

Velazquez, Diego Rodriguez de Silva (1599–1660; Spanish), became court painter at Madrid in 1623. He is renowned for his portraits of Philip IV and the courtiers.

Watteau, Jean Antoine (1684–1721; French), painted delicate, softly coloured pictures, with a dream-like melancholy air.

Painting Terms

abstract art Art form that represents ideas (by means of geometric and other designs) instead of natural forms.

baroque Style that flourished from late 1500s to early 1700s. Characterized by exaggerated shapes, with rich, flowing curves.

Byzantine Style practised in Eastern Roman Empire (400s–1453); figures are stiff and formal, with rich colours.

cubism Important movement in modern French painting started by Picasso and Braque in 1907. Cubists aimed to reduce objects to basic shapes of cubes, spheres, cylinders, and cones.

fresco Method of great antiquity but perfected during Italian Renaissance; uses pigments ground in water applied to a fresh lime-plaster wall or ceiling.

impressionism Important movement that developed among French painters just after mid-1800s. Impressionists were particularly concerned with light and its effects. They put down on canvas their immediate impressions of nature. Monet, Renoir, Pissaro, Sisley, Cézanne, and Degas were leading impressionists.

Pre-Raphaelite Brotherhood Group mainly of painters who advocated return to spirit and manner of art before time of Raphael (1483–1520). Founded in England (mid-1800s) by Rossetti, Holman Hunt, and Millais, members practised truthful adherence to natural forms and effects.

Renaissance Rebirth in arts and learning that took place in Europe (especially Italy) from 1300s to 1500s. In painting it was typified by original styles, underived from antiquity. Among the masters of this period were Leonardo da Vinci, Michelangelo, Titian, and Raphael.

rococo European art style (about 1735–1765) characterized in painting by lavish decoration and ornament.

surrealism 20th-century art movement that aimed at escaping control of reason and tried to express subconscious mind pictorially.

ART AND ENTERTAINMENT

Madonna and Child by the Italian Renaissance artist Raphael.

A self-portrait painted around 1660 by the Dutch artist Rembrandt Van Rijn.

A scene of country life painted by the Flemish painter, Pieter Brueghel in the 1500s.

The Fighting Téméraire by the British painter J. M. W. Turner.

Le Repas *(the meal) – a scene of life in Tahiti by the French artist Gauguin.*

Lady with Umbrella *by the French impressionist artist, Claude Monet.*

Far right: A statue by the Spanish artist Pablo Picasso, outside the Chicago Civic Center.

Below: A painting by the French 'primitive' artist Henri Rousseau.

Light Red over Black, *an abstract painting by the American artist Mark Rothko (1950s).*

ART AND ENTERTAINMENT

Above: A stone figure from Guatemala where the Mayan civilization flourished from AD 300 to 900. Right: Intricate pottery figurines from Nigeria.

Drawing and Perspective

The human body can be divided up into sections to keep proportions right.

Vanishing point

Wall

Horizon

Road

Vanishing point

Straight lines appear to converge at one place, called the vanishing point.

Tall building

Above: A figure by the great modern sculptor Henry Moore. It is in the Tate Gallery, London.

A Greek bronze horse and jockey dating from the 2nd century. It was found in the sea near Athens.

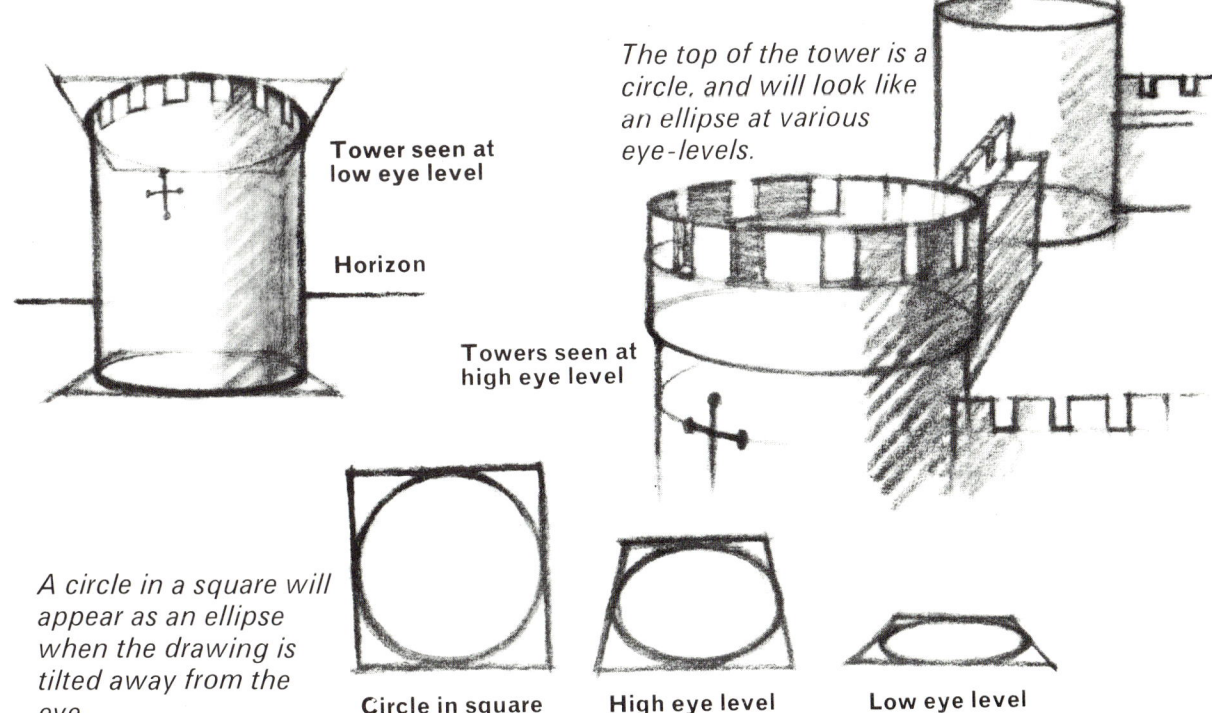

Tower seen at low eye level

Horizon

The top of the tower is a circle, and will look like an ellipse at various eye-levels.

Towers seen at high eye level

A circle in a square will appear as an ellipse when the drawing is tilted away from the eye.

Circle in square

High eye level

Low eye level

ART AND ENTERTAINMENT

Renaissance: Florence Cathedral, Italy.

Byzantine: Sancta Sophia, Istanbul.

Greek Doric: Temple of Neptune, Greece.

Periods of Architecture

Greek	600s–100s *BC*
Roman	100s *BC–AD* 400s
Byzantine	*AD* 400s–1453
Romanesque (N Europe)	mid-900s–late 1100s
Norman (England)	late 1000s–1100s
Gothic	mid-1100s–1400s
Renaissance (Italy)	1400s–1500s
French Renaissance	1500s
Baroque (Italy)	1600–1750
Georgian (England)	1725–1800
Rococo	mid-1700s
Regency (England)	1800–1825
Art Nouveau (Europe)	1890–1910
Expressionism (Germany)	1910–1930s
Functionalism	1920s–
International Style	1920s–
Brutalism	1950s–

Above: Gothic: Bourges Cathedral, France; Left: Modern: Empire State Building, New York, USA (1920s) and below: Sydney Opera House, Australia (1960s).

Roman: Arch of Constantine, Rome, Italy

Some Historic Pottery and Porcelain Factories

Belleek (Ireland)	1857–
Bennington (US)	1793–1894
Bow (England)	1744–1776
Bristol (England)	1749–1781
Caughley (England)	1754–1814
Chantilly (France)	1725–1800
Chelsea (England)	1745–1784
Coalport (England)	1796–
Copenhagen (Denmark)	1774–
Derby (England)	1750–1848
Derby, Royal Crown	1876–
Frankenthal (Germany)	1755–1799
Greenpoint (US)	1848–
Hoechst (Germany)	1750–1798
Limoges (France)	1771–
Liverpool (England)	1710–c. 1800
Ludwigsburg (Germany)	1758–1824
Meissen (Germany)	1710–
Mennecy (France)	1735–1785
Nymphenburg (Germany)	1753–
Sèvres (France)	1756–
Spode (England)	1770–
Tucker (US)	1826–1838
Vincennes (France)	1738–1756
Wedgwood (England)	1759–
Worcester (England)	1751–

Architects

Aalto Alvar (1898–1976), Finnish
Adam, Robert (1728–92), Scottish
Alberti, Leone Battista (1404–72), Italian
Bernini, Gianlorenzo (1598–1680), Italian
Bramante, Donato (1444–1514), Italian
Bruneheschi, Pilippo (1377–1446), Italian
Cortona, Pietro da (1596–1669), Italian
Fischer von Erlach, Johann (1656–1723), Austrian
Guadi, Antonio (1852–1926), Spanish
Gropius, Walter (1883–1969), German
Jefferson, Thomas (1743–1826), American
Jones, Inigo (1573–1652), English
Le Corbusier (1887–1965), French-Swiss
Mansart, François (1598–1666), French
Michelangelo, Buonarroti (1475–1564), Italian
Mies van der Rohe, Ludwig (1886–1969), Ger./US
Nash, John (1752–1835), English
Nervi, Pier Luigi (1891–1979), Italian
Niemeyer, Oscar (1907–   ), Brazilian
Palladio, Andrea (1518–80), Italian
Saarinen, Eero (1910–1960), Finnish-American
Vitruvius Pollo, Marcus (1st Cent. BC), Roman
Wren, Sir Christopher (1632–1723), English
Wright, Frank Lloyd (1869–1959), American

Ionic

Doric

Corinthian

There were three main styles of Greek capital, the Doric, Ionic and Corinthian styles. The Doric style was severe and simple; the Ionic order was carved and scrolled. The Corinthian style, popular from the 5th century BC onwards, was elaborately decorated with scrolls and acanthus leaves.

The Ballet

arabesque Position in which dancer stands on one leg with arms extended, body bent forward from hips, while other leg is stretched out backwards.

attitude Position in which dancer stretches one leg backwards, bending it a little at the knee so that lower part of leg is parallel to floor.

ballerina Female ballet dancer.

barre Exercise bar fixed to classroom wall at hip level; dancers grasp it when exercising.

battement Beating movement made by raising and lowering leg, sideways, backwards, or forwards.

choreography Art of dance composition.

corps de ballet Main body of ballet dancers, as distinct from soloists.

entrechat Leap in which dancer rapidly crosses and uncrosses feet in air.

fouetté Turn in which dancer whips free leg round.

glissade Gliding movement.

jeté Leap from one foot to another.

pas Any dance step.

pas de deux Dance for two.

pas seule Solo dance.

pirouette Movement in which dancer spins completely round on one foot.

Two long-favourite ballets are Swan Lake *(above) and* Sleeping Beauty. *These two ballets are as famous for their music as for their dancing, Below: Louis XIV's dance master, Pierre Beauchamp, devised the five basic ballet positions.*

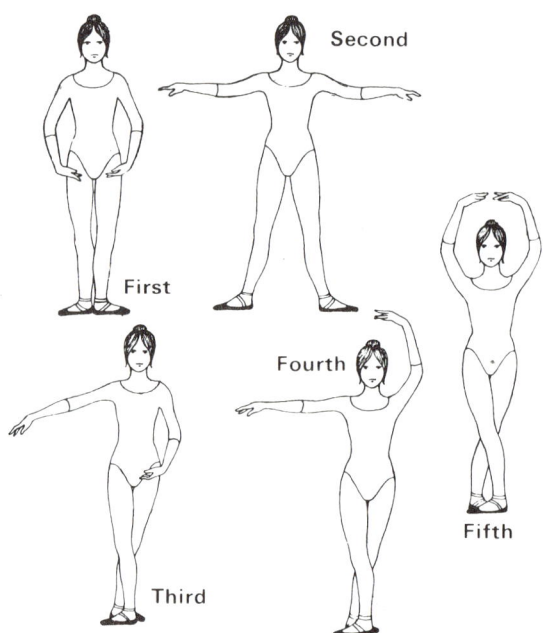

pointes Tips of dancer's toes, on which many movements are executed.

positions Five positions of feet on which ballet is based (see illustrations).

tutu Short, stiff, spreading skirt worn in classical ballet.

Glossary of Musical Terms

adagio At a slow pace.
allegro At a fast pace.
alto Highest adult male voice (artificially produced).
andante At a quiet, peaceful pace.
arpeggio Notes of chord played in rapid succession, one after the other.
bar Metrical division of music bounded by vertical bar-lines.
baritone Male voice higher than bass and lower than tenor.
bass Lowest male voice.
chord Three or more notes sounded together.
choir A body of singers.
chorus Main body of singers in choir; words and music repeated after each stanza of song.
clef Sign in music notation that fixes pitch of each note written on the stave.
concerto Substantial work for one or more solo instruments and orchestra.
contralto Lowest female voice.
counterpoint Two or more melodies combined to form a satisfying harmony.
crescendo Increasing in loudness.
flat Conventional sign showing that pitch of a certain note has been lowered by a semitone.
forte Played or sung loudly.
fortissimo Very loud (loudest).
harmony Combining of chords to make musical sense.
key Classification of the notes on a scale.
largo At a slow pace.
lied German word for 'song' (plural *Lieder*).
major One of the two main scales, with semitones between 3rd and 4th and 7th and 8th notes.
melody A tune, series of musical sounds following each other, as distinct from harmony.
mezzo Half or medium.
mezzo-soprano Female voice between contralto and soprano.
microtone Interval smaller than a semitone: used in Asian music.
minor One of the two main scales. Harmonic minor scales have a semitone between 2nd and 3rd, 5th and 6th, and 7th and 8th notes.
octave Interval made up of 8 successive notes of scale, from one note to note of the same name, above or below.
oratorio Religious musical composition for soloists, chorus, and orchestra, but without costume or scenery.
pianissimo Very soft (softest).
piano Played or sung softly; shortened to p.
plainsong Unaccompanied vocal melody used in medieval church music.
scale Progression of successive notes ascending or descending.
score Written music showing all parts (vocal and instrumental) of composition on separate staves.
semitone A half-tone; smallest interval commonly used in Western music.
sharp Conventional sign indicating that note referred to has been raised in pitch by a semitone.
solo Piece for a solo performer.
sonata Musical piece, usually for one or two players, consisting of three or four movements in contrasting rhythms and speeds.
soprano Highest female voice; also the voice of boys before it breaks.
stave or staff Framework of lines and spaces on which music is usually written.
suite Orchestral piece in several movements.
symphony Large orchestral piece of a serious nature, usually in four movements; also a sonata for orchestra.
tempo Pace or speed of piece of music.
tenor High male voice; also the viola.
treble Upper part of a composition; a high voice.

Musical Instruments

There are four kinds of musical instruments. In wind instruments, air is made to vibrate inside a tube. This vibrating air makes a musical note.

All *woodwind* instruments such as clarinets, bassoons, flutes, piccolos, and recorders have holes that are covered by the fingers or by pads worked by the fingers. These holes change the length of the vibrating column of air inside the instrument. The shorter the column the higher the note. In *brass* wind instruments, the vibration of the player's lips makes the air in the instrument vibrate. By changing the pressure of the lips, the player can make different notes. Most brass instruments also have valves and pistons to change the length of the vibrating column of air, and so make different notes.

Stringed instruments work in one of two ways. The strings of the instrument are either made to vibrate by a bow, as in the violin, viola, cello and double bass; or the strings are plucked, as in the guitar, harp or banjo.

The word orchestra *once meant 'dancing place'. In ancient Greek theatres, dancers and musicians performed on a space between the audience and the stage. When Italy invented opera, Italian theatres arranged their musicians in the same way. Soon, people used the word* orchestra *to describe the group of musicians.*

In *percussion* instruments, a tight piece of skin or a piece of wood or metal is struck to make a note. There are lots of percussion instruments – drums, cymbals, gongs, tambourines, triangles and chimes.

Electronic instruments such as the electric organ and the synthesizer make music from electronic circuits.

Drums   Trumpet

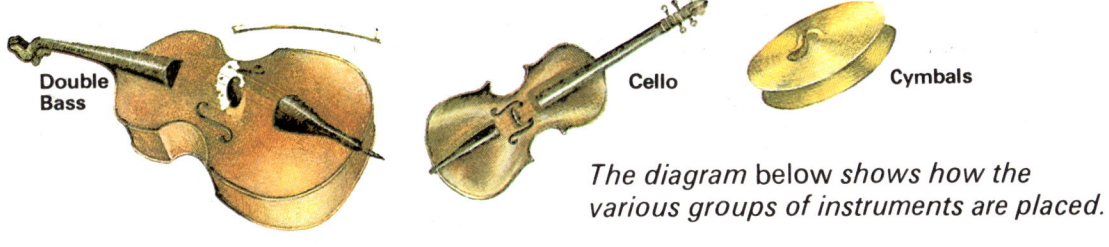

Double Bass

Cello

Cymbals

The diagram below *shows how the various groups of instruments are placed.*

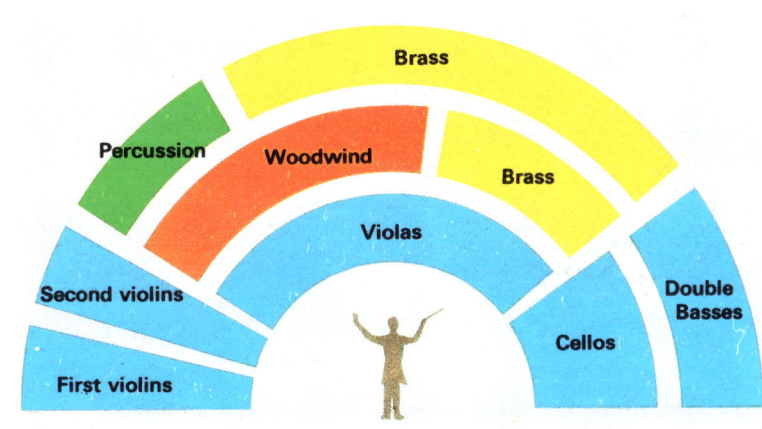

Brass

Percussion

Woodwind

Brass

Violas

Second violins

Double Basses

First violins

Cellos

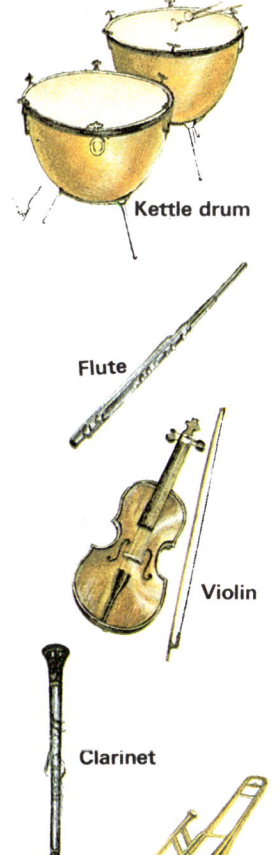

Kettle drum

Flute

Violin

Clarinet

Trombone

French horn

Famous Composers

Antonio Vivaldi, Italian (1678?–1741)
Johann Sebastian Bach, German (1685–1750)
Wolfgang Amadeus Mozart, Austrian (1756–1791)
Ludwig van Beethoven, German (1770–1827)
Franz Schubert, Austrian (1797–1828)
Hector Berlioz, French (1803–1869)
Fréderic Chopin, Polish (1810–1849)
Robert Schumann, German (1810–1856)
Franz Liszt, Hungarian (1811–1886)
Giuseppe Verdi, Italian (1813–1901)
Richard Wagner, German (1813–1883)
Johannes Brahms, German

(1833–1897)
Peter Ilyich Tchaikovsky, Russian (1840–1893)
Anton Dvorak, Czech (1841–1904)
Edvard Grieg, Norwegian (1843–1907)
Giacomo Puccini, Italian (1858–1924)
Gustav Mahler, Austrian (1860–1911)
Claude Debussy, French (1862–1918)
Jean Sibelius, Finnish (1865–1957)
Sergei Rachmaninov, Russian (1873–1943)
Igor Stravinsky, Russian (1882–1971)
Dmitri Shostakovich, Russian (1906–1975)
Benjamin Britten, British (1913–1976)

Pop Music has moved through many vogues during the 20th century, from its beginnings in jazz and country-and-western music to the modern groups using electronic instruments, microphones and strongly amplified sounds of today. Pop has become a kind of international language, with people from many countries performing in any land, west or east.

A to Z of Pop Music

acoustic Non-electric, with reference usually to guitars.

backing group Group of singers who sing in support of a soloist.

bebop, bop Type of jazz that started in 1940s in attempt to break monotonous rhythm of earlier jazz.

big bands Dance bands of *swing* era (late 1930s and early 1940s), featuring many musicians and one or more vocalists.

bluegrass Folk music with overdrive; folk and country music played with a distinctive beat; line-up includes some or all of the following: acoustic guitar, banjo, mandolin, fiddle, dobro, auto-harp, string bass.

blues Form of jazz using 12-bar melodic section; essentially vocal, the music is often slow and sad.

boogie woogie A jazz barrelhouse style of piano playing, with repetitive bass in left hand and stylized melodic variations in right.

calypso Folk music of West Indies, usually sung, in 4/4 time.

combo Small group of musicians.

country and western Topical and traditional rural music, mainly vocal and American, evolved from folk, blues, and hillbilly music.

dixieland jazz Originally, early Negro jazz; later applied to music of white imitators.

folk music, folk song Music and ballads of the people, usually handed down from one generation to another.

gig One-night stand or engagement.

gospel music Country version of the spiritual, heavily commercialized from the 1930s onwards.

jitterbugging Improvised, all-in, athletic dancing, originating in late 1930s with development of boogie woogie.

jive A later, slightly more respectable form of jitterbugging.

mainstream jazz Middle-of-the-road jazz that avoids extremes of trad or progressive jazz; expertly played by experienced professionals.

new wave Movement beginning in the 1970s which included punk rock and offbeat arrangements, and also heavy rock.

progressive jazz Attempt to fuse jazz with other musical elements and thus break away from more traditional aspects.

punk rock Rock music with outrageous, often obscene, words, accompanied by equally outrageous behaviour by its performers.

ragtime Essentially Negro piano music based on rigidly syncopated pattern; had some influence on jazz.

reggae A gay, West Indian type of rock jazz with simple 2-beat rhythm.

rhythm and blues Urban blues performed mainly by black musicians; traditional blues were hotted up with infusions of rock and roll and later developments.

rock and roll, rock 'n roll, rock Rhythmic development of blues and skiffle, with undisguised emphasis on the beat, and body movements of dancers.

skiffle Makeshift jazz music (in vogue mid-1950s) that included guitars, banjos, mandolins, and a number of home-made instruments such as washboard, tea-chest bass, and paper-and-comb.

soul music Popular, often religious music written and performed by Negroes; used for dancing.

steel bands West Indian percussion bands, originating in Trinidad, that use as instruments the tops of oil drums, tuned to various pitches.

swing Commercialized jazz featured by the *big band*; period 1935–46 known as swing era.

traditional jazz, trad Jazz that adheres to old traditional New Orleans highly improvised, contrapuntal sounds.

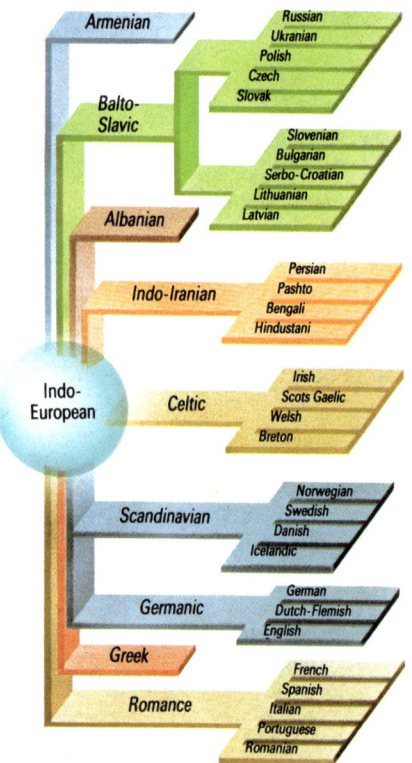

The World's Languages

Experts who study languages have grouped different tongues into families. These families of languages consist of those which are related to each other. Some while ago, it was noticed that although languages are different from each other, there are many words which actually resemble others in another tongue.

For instance, the English words *mother, father, brother* in German are *Mutter, Vater, Bruder.* In Swedish they are *moder, fader, broder,* and in Dutch they are *moeder, vader, broeder.* The spelling sometimes makes the words look quite different, but when they are pronounced, they will sound remarkably alike.

This is because English, Swedish, German and Dutch are all related languages, and with Danish, Norwegian, and Icelandic, are called Teutonic ton-gues. Many centuries ago, they were all one language, and over the years, they have developed into separate ones.

Other languages, in turn, are also related to each other. In French, the same three words are *mère, père, frère,* and in Italian, the words are *madre, padre, fratello,* in Spanish they are *madre, padre, hermano,* and in Portuguese they are *madre, padre, irmão.* All very similar, except the words for 'brother', which have altered quite a lot. However, all these four languages are members of the same family, which, together with a few others, like Romanian and Latin, are called the Romance tongues.

Another group is called the Slavonic, and this includes languages like Russian, Polish, Serbian, Czech and Bulgarian, all of which are quite like each other in many ways.

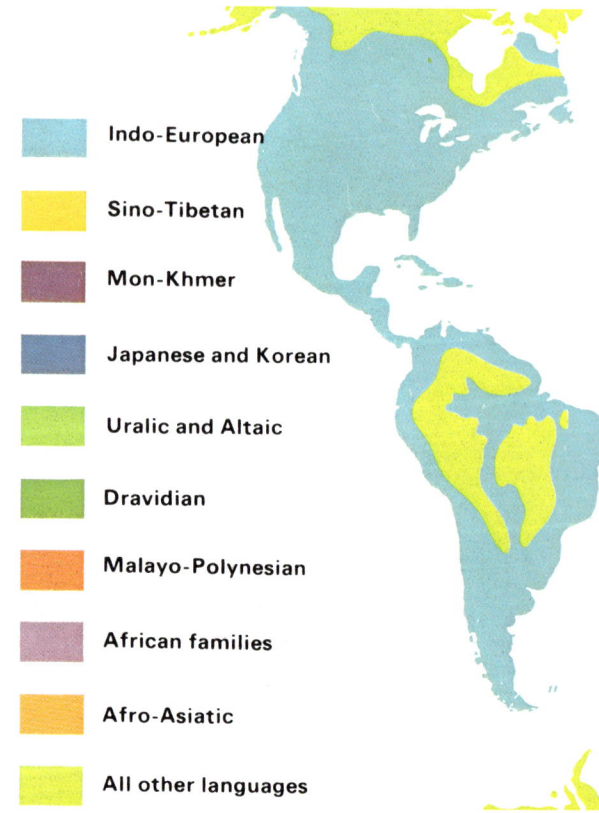

Indo-European

Sino-Tibetan

Mon-Khmer

Japanese and Korean

Uralic and Altaic

Dravidian

Malayo-Polynesian

African families

Afro-Asiatic

All other languages

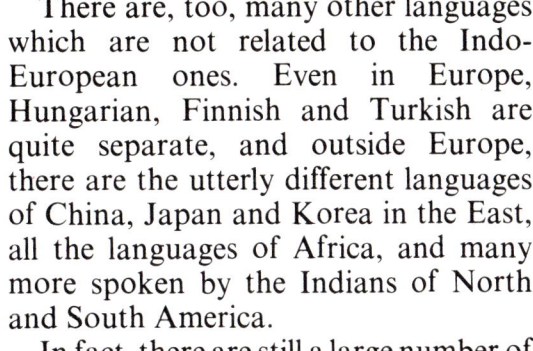

Now, although the three families we have described are each composed of similar tongues, each *family* is also related to each other. The Romance, Teutonic, and Slavonic languages are all part of the Indo-European language group, and are in turn related to Indian languages like Sanskrit. Sanskrit is now a dead language, but it is well understood, and many modern Indian languages are related to it.

If you look at the chart on the left of these pages, you will see how all the Indo-European languages are related to each other through a kind of family tree. Of course, the various tongues have changed so much over thousands of years that they have become quite foreign to each other. One has to take special language classes to learn any of the others, even though they are distantly related to one's own.

There are, too, many other languages which are not related to the Indo-European ones. Even in Europe, Hungarian, Finnish and Turkish are quite separate, and outside Europe, there are the utterly different languages of China, Japan and Korea in the East, all the languages of Africa, and many more spoken by the Indians of North and South America.

In fact, there are still a large number of languages spoken by only a few people, and the actual number of different ones numbers many hundreds.

Not only do the languages themselves vary, but in many cases, the language is written in a different alphabet. Even in Europe, we have three main alphabets: the Roman, or Latin alphabet, which is used in printing this book, the Russian or Cyrillic alphabet, used in Russian, Ukrainian, Bulgarian and Serbian, and the Greek alphabet, still used for writing the Greek language.

In the Far East, Chinese is written in special characters, each one representing a word, the Japanese use a system of syllable-writing, and the Koreans have a special alphabet. In South East Asia, there are many other alphabets used for writing the various Indo-Chinese languages, and those in India and Pakistan.

Nearer at home, we have the Arabic and Hebrew alphabets, both of which, although they look quite different, are related to each other, and historically to the Roman alphabet.

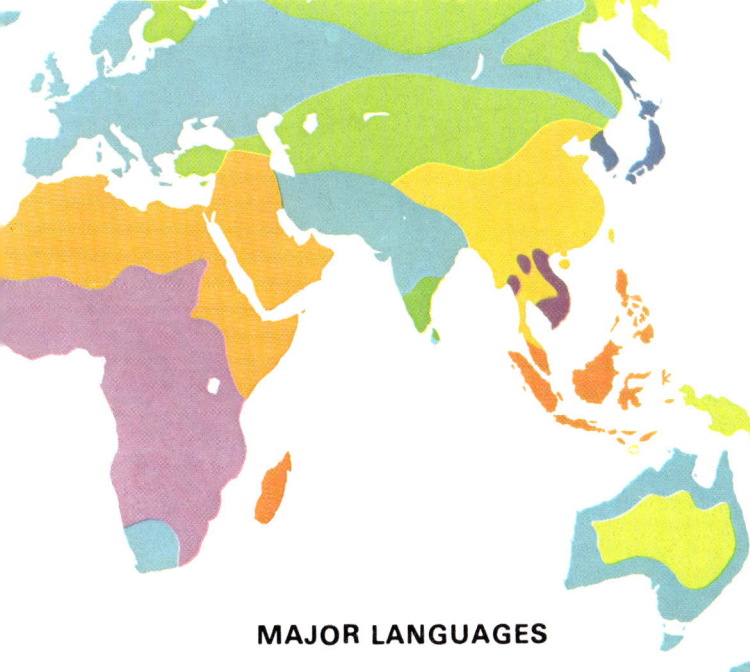

MAJOR LANGUAGES

Special Terms in Literature

allegory A story in which the obvious meaning also symbolizes a hidden meaning.

alliteration Beginning two or more consecutive words with the same letter or sound.

ballad A poem describing a historical or legendary event or deed. Ballads were very popular in the late Middle Ages.

blank verse A form of poetry based on unrhyming ten-syllable lines with alternate syllables stressed.

bound verse Poetry with a pattern of metre.

comedy A play with a happy ending and sometimes with comic events and characters.

couplet Two successive lines of verse that rhyme with one another.

detective fiction Novels in which the detection of crime is the main theme.

drama A story written in *dialogue*, or conversation, form so that it can be spoken and acted.

elegy A poem mourning a death or on some other solemn theme.

epic A long narrative poem about heroic historical or legendary events and people. An example is Homer's *Odyssey*.

epigram Neat, brief, witty saying; e.g. The vain have only one to please.

essay A short composition, generally in prose, in which the writer expresses his ideas on a chosen subject.

fable A short tale with a moral lesson in which animals act and talk like people.

fiction Any narrative which is not pure fact.

folk tale A traditional story passed on by word of mouth from generation to generation.

free verse A form of poetry without metre but with natural stresses dependent on the ideas being expressed.

idyll An ancient kind of poem set against a background of idealized shepherd life and often dealing with such themes as friendship, love, and youth. Examples are Virgil's *Eclogues*.

limerick A kind of comic, nonsense poem in five lines, usually rhyming *a a b b a*. Edward Lear wrote many limericks.

lyric poem A poem mainly concerned with expressing the poet's feelings or thoughts.

narrative poem One that tells a story.

ode A medium-length poem, usually in praise of something. It has various forms.

parable A tale with a moral lesson.

parody Comic imitation of a serious piece of writing, often satirical and exaggerated.

rhyme Agreement in sound of two syllables, but with differing preceding consonants.

romance A form of adventure story popular in ancient and medieval times.

romantic Belonging to the Romantic period, the early 1800s, when writers stressed liberty and chose exotic themes and settings.

saga A medieval Icelandic or Scandinavian tale about the historical or mythical deeds of a hero.

science fiction Stories of fantastic adventures based, sometimes loosely, on scientific fact and often dealing with space, time, and other worlds.

sonnet A 14-lined poem with various rhyming schemes. Italian sonnets rhyme *abba abba cdc dcd*. Elizabethan sonnets rhyme *abab cdcd efef gg*.

synonym Word having the same general meaning as another, but often with subtle distinction.

tragedy Generally a play with an unhappy ending.

verse Originally a line of poetry; now generally a stanza, or a complete poem.

An engraving by Gustave Doré for the Spanish classical novel Don Quixote *by Miguel de Cervantes.*

Famous Writers

Andersen, Hans Christian (1805–75), Danish writer, best known for his fairy tales. Best loved are *The Tinderbox, The Emperor's New Clothes,* and *The Snow Queen.*

Austen, Jane (1775–1817), English novelist, wrote about comfortably off country people, who lead lives bound by strict rules of behaviour. They include *Sense and Sensibility, Pride and Prejudice* and *Emma.*

Balzac, Honoré de (1799–1850), French novelist, wrote a series of 90 realistic stories about everyday life in France called the *Human Comedy.*

Blake, William (1757–1827), English poet and artist. His *Songs of Innocence* and *Songs of Experience* show the same world from the viewpoints of innocence and disillusioned experience.

Brontë Family name of three English novelist sisters: **Charlotte** (1816–55), **Emily Jane** (1818–48), and **Anne** (1820–49). Charlotte included many personal experiences in her most famous novel, *Jane Eyre. Wuthering Heights,* a dramatic love story is Emily's best work.

Bunyan, John (1628–88), English preacher and religious writer, best known for his allegory *The Pilgrim's Progress.*

Burns, Robert (1759–96), Scottish poet who wrote poems in Scottish dialect, and composed many songs, including *Auld Lang Syne.*

Byron, Lord George (1788–1824), English Romantic poet, wrote several long narrative poems. The finest is *Don Juan.*

Carroll, Lewis (Charles Lutwidge Dodgson) (1832–98), is best remembered for his stories *Alice's Adventures in Wonderland* and *Through the Looking Glass.*

Cervantes, Miguel de (1547–1616), Spanish novelist, playwright, and poet, author of the novel *Don Quixote,* story of a gentleman who imagines he can put right all the evil in the world.

Chaucer, Geoffrey (1340?–1400), English poet, famous for his *Canterbury Tales,* a collection of stories told by travellers on a journey.

Coleridge, Samuel Taylor (1772–1834), English Romantic poet and friend of Wordsworth, wrote the famous poem *The Rime of the Ancient Mariner.*

Dante, Alighieri (1265–1321), Italian poet, wrote *Divine Comedy,* a poem in three parts about a man's role on Earth.

Dickens, Charles (1812–70), English novelist, wrote stories about the harsh lives of ordinary people in industrial England. The best include *Great Expectations, David Copperfield, Oliver Twist.*

Dostoevsky, Fyodor (1821–81), Russian novelist, wrote powerful stories. Among the finest are *Crime and Punishment, The Idiot* and *The Brothers Karamazov.*

Eliot, George (Marian Evans) (1819–80), English novelist, wrote *The Mill on the Floss* and several other novels including *Middlemarch,* a story about country people.

Eliot, T.S. (Thomas Stearns) (1888–1965), American-born British poet, dramatist, and critic, first wrote poetry expressing his frustration and despair.

Hemingway, Ernest (1898–1961), American novelist, wrote stories about adventurous and violent lives. Best known include *A Farewell to Arms* and *For Whom the Bell Tolls.*

Homer (700s BC), great and influential Greek poet, wrote the *Iliad* which tells the story of the siege of Troy, while the *Odyssey* describes the wanderings of the hero Odysseus after the war.

Johnson, Dr Samuel (1709–84), English poet and essayist, wrote on English poetry, and compiled a *Dictionary of the English Language.*

Joyce, James (1882–1941), Irish novelist, wrote stories about people in conflict with their surroundings.

Keats, John (1795–1821), English Romantic poet, composed narrative poems. The finest include *Ode to Autumn* and *Ode to a Nightingale.*

Kipling, Rudyard (1865–1936), an Indian-born English novelist, wrote of the British Empire, and adventure stories for children which include *Kim, The Jungle Book* and the *Just So Stories.*

Lawrence, D. H. (David Herbert) (1885–1930), English novelist; His best work is about working-class life, including growing up, and natural love. *Sons and Lovers* and *Lady Chatterley's Lover.*

Milton, John (1608–74), English poet and religious and political writer. His most important works were the long poems *Paradise Lost* and *Paradise Regained.*

Poe, Edgar Allan (1809–49), American short-story writer, poet and critic, is best known for his tales of mystery.

Rabelais, François (1494?–1553?), French priest and doctor, poked fun at life in his day in his four books about Gargantua and Pantagruel.

Scott, Sir Walter (1771– 1832), Scottish novelist and poet, author of romantic adventures often set in the Middle Ages. They include *Waverley* and *Ivanhoe.*

Shelley, Percy Bysshe (1792–1822), English Romantic poet, wrote idealistic poems including *Ode to a Skylark* and *The Cloud.*

Stevenson, Robert Louis (1850–94), Scottish novelist, wrote *Treasure Island* and *Kidnapped,* both adventure stories, and *Dr Jekyll and Mr Hyde,* a mystery.

Swift, Jonathan (1667–1745), Irish clergyman, wrote satirical pamphlets on religion and politics, but is best known for his story *Gulliver's Travels.*

Tennyson, Alfred, Lord (1809–92), English poet, wrote *Break, Break, Break, The Charge of the Light Brigade* and *Idylls of the King.*

Tolstoy, Count Leo (1828–1910), Russian novelist and playwright, wrote one of the world's greatest novels, *War and Peace.* It traces the lives of several families during Napoleon's invasion of Russia.

Twain, Mark (Samuel Langhorne Clemens) (1835–1910), American novelist, wrote many books about American life. His best describe life along the Mississippi River, *The Adventures of Huckleberry Finn.*

Virgil (Publius Vergilius Maro) (70–19 BC), the great Roman poet, wrote the *Aeneid,* a long epic poem about the founding of Rome.

Wordsworth, William (1770–1850), an English poet, expressed his deep love of nature in poems often written in beautiful, simple language.

Famous Dramatists

Beckett, Samuel (born 1906), Irish dramatist and novelist, became famous for plays that express the absurdity of human existence. The most important are *Waiting for Godot,* and *Endgame.*

Chekhov, Anton (1860–1904), Russian dramatist, whose plays include *Uncle Vanya, The Three Sisters* and *The Cherry Orchard.*

Coward, Sir Noël (1899–1973), English dramatist, musical composer, and actor, became famous as a playwright in the 1920s. His best plays included *Hay Fever, Private Lives, Blithe Spirit* and *Present Laughter.*

Goethe, Johann Wolfgang von (1749–1832), German poet, dramatist, and novelist, wrote several plays, including *Egmont* and his most famous work, *Faust,* a long poetic drama in two parts. It tells the legendary story of the man who sells his soul to the Devil.

Ibsen, Henrik (1828–1906), Norwegian dramatist, known for his realistic, poetic and increasingly symbolic, plays about problems of modern life. They include *Ghosts, A Doll's House* and *Hedda Gabler.*

Molière (Jean Baptiste Poquelin) (1622–73), French writer of comedies and actor, ran a theatre company for which he wrote many plays. The best include *The Miser, Tartuffe, The Misanthropist.*

O'Neill, Eugene (1888–1953), American dramatist wrote a series of successful plays between 1920 and 1934, of which *Mourning Becomes Electra* is the best known. His later plays included *The Iceman Cometh.*

Osborne, John (born 1929), English dramatist, became known for his play *Look Back in Anger,* an attack on contemporary Britain.

Shakespeare, William (1564–1616), Britain's greatest dramatist, was also an actor and a writer of beautiful sonnets. His 36 plays include historical dramas, such as *Henry V* and *Julius Caesar;* comedies, *A Midsummer Night's Dream* and *The Taming of the Shrew;* tragedies, *Hamlet, King Lear,* and *Romeo and Juliet;* and fantasy romances, *The Tempest.*

Shaw, George Bernard (1856–1950) Irish-born dramatist, wrote popular plays that expressed his own bold ideas in brilliant, witty dialogue. The best-known include *Arms and the Man, Man and Superman, Pygmalion, Heartbreak House* and *Saint Joan.*

Wilde, Oscar (1856–1900), Irish dramatist and novelist, is best remembered for his witty social plays about the upper classes. They include *Lady Windermere's Fan, An Ideal Husband,* and his best play, *The Importance of Being Earnest.*

The Globe Theatre London, where many of Shakespeare's plays were first performed.

ART AND ENTERTAINMENT

Some Theatrical Terms

burlesque Play that parodies another; in the United States, a vulgar variety performance aimed chiefly at male audiences.

cabaret Entertainment performed while audience dines

epilogue A speech made at the end of a play by one of the characters or by an actor representing the author.

farce A kind of comic play based on a series of hilariously improbable events. Examples: the farces of Georges Feydeau and Arthur Wing Pinero.

kitchen-sink drama Realistic plays of the mid-1950s about the lives of working-class people. Example: Arnold Wesker's *Chicken Soup with Barley*.

melodrama A kind of play with a sensational plot and exaggerated emotion. Example: *The Bells* by Leopold Lewis.

mime The art of acting without words. Marcel Marceau is a famous mime artist.

music hall A kind of theatre from the 1850s to World War I, which presented variety entertainment consisting of comic acts, acrobats, songs, and dances.

mystery play A religious play of the 1300s and 1400s presenting a scene from the Bible. Also called a *miracle play*.

pantomime A Christmas entertainment based loosely on a fairy story, such as *Cinderella*, but with modern songs and topical jokes.

passion play A religious play about the Crucifixion performed on Good Friday in Middle Ages. A famous passion play is still performed every ten years at Oberammergau in southern Germany.

prologue A speech made at the beginning of a play by one of the characters or by an actor representing the author.

props, or **properties** The small objects needed on the stage to make a play realistic, such as cups, flowers, newspapers, but not furniture or scenery.

repertory A collection of plays that a company performs in a season.

revue A theatre entertainment popular since the 1890s and consisting of a series of songs, short acted scenes, and dances.

son et lumière An open-air entertainment at a place of historical interest. The history of the place is told over loudspeakers while relevant parts are lit up.

theatre-in-the-round Theatre in which the stage is surrounded by the audience.

theatre of the absurd A kind of drama of the 1950s portraying the absurd human existence on Earth. Such as plays by Samuel Beckett, Harold Pinter, and Eugene Ionesco.

thriller A play with an exciting plot, usually including crime with murder.

tragedy Generally a play with an unhappy ending.

vaudeville American word for *music hall*.

Poets Laureate

Ben Johnson	1619–1637
Sir William Davenant	1638–1668
John Dryden	1668–1688
Thomas Shadwell	1689–1692
Nahum Tate	1692–1715
Nicholas Rowe	1715–1718
Laurence Eusden	1718–1730
Colley Cibber	1730–1757
William Whitehead	1757–1785
Thomas Warton	1785–1790
Henry James Pye	1790–1813
Robert Southey	1813–1843
William Wordsworth	1843–1850
Lord Tennyson	1850–1892
Alfred Austin	1896–1913
Robert Bridges	1913–1930
John Masefield	1930–1967
Cecil Day Lewis	1968–1972
Sir John Betjeman	1972–1984
Ted Hughes	1984–

THEATRE RECORDS

Longest continuous run of any play at one theatre ended on March 23, 1974, after 8860 performances of *The Mousetrap,* by Agatha Christie. Having spent 22 years at the Ambassador's Theatre, London, it moved to the St Martin's next door.

The oldest indoor theatre still in use is Palladio's Teatro Olimpico, in Vicenza, Italy. Completed in 1585, it was designed according to the principles of the Roman writer Vitruvius.

First theatre in Britain was built by James Burbage in 1576, and called simply 'The Theatre'. Later, it was dismantled and its timbers used to build Shakespeare's Globe.

Oldest national theatre in the world is the Comédie Française, established in 1680 by order of Louis XIV. It was formed by combining the three most important companies then playing in Paris.

JAPANESE THEATRE

Japanese drama includes *noh plays, bunraku,* and *kabuki.* Noh plays are a slow-moving combination of chanting, dancing, and music telling a simple story. Bunraku is a play performed with puppets. Kabuki grew out of a combination of noh, bunraku, and dancing. It developed in Japan when Shakespeare was writing his plays in England. In both countries, women's parts were played by male actors. Kabuki is highly dramatic. Warriors die protecting their feudal lords or, having offended against tradition, commit *hara-kiri* (suicide) by their swords. A true kabuki performance lasts for days. Masks, which are generally elaborate, are often worn by the actors in both noh and kabuki. There can be up to fifteen such masks each representing a different emotion. There is usually little scenery.

FILM-MAKING TERMS

close-up A picture taken near the subject.
dolly Mobile carriage to carry a camera.
dubbing Adding sound to a film.
freeze Holding one shot so that the action seems to stop.
flash-back An interruption in the story of a film to recall a past event.
intercut shots Two related series of shots shown alternately, such as the heroine tied to the railway lines and the train approaching.
library shot Film taken from material already made and in stock.
long shot A shot taken from a distance.
pan Short for panoramic shot – a sideways sweep by the camera.

prop Short for property – an object used by an actor, such as a gun or a telephone.
rushes The day's shots, before editing.
scenario A scene-by-scene outline of a film script.
set An area prepared for a film scene, either in a studio or out of doors.
shoot To photograph a scene.
take Part of a scene shot without interruption.
track in, track back To move a camera on its dolly towards or away from the subject.
zooming Using a variable lens to give the effect of tracking in or back.

Left: A scene from William Wyler's Award-winning epic Ben Hur; *it won 'Oscars' (as Academy awards are nicknamed) for best picture, best actor (Charlton Heston as Ben Hur), and best director. Centre: In 1968 the musical* Oliver, *based on the British stage musical which was adapted from Charles Dickens's world-famous book Oliver Twist, won the Academy award for best picture. Right:* The Godfather, *'best picture' for 1972.*

Some Famous Film-Makers

Astaire, Fred (Frederick Austerlitz) (1899–); American dancer and actor (stage and film). Often teamed with Ginger Rogers. *Top Hat* (1935).

Bogart, Humphrey De Forest (1899–1957); American film star, usually as the tough guy. *Dead End* (1937), *Casablanca* (1943), *The African Queen* (1952). A film *Bogie*, was made of his life in 1980.

Boyer, Charles (1899–1978); French film star, famous as the 'great lover'. *Caravan* (1934), *The Garden of Allah* (1936), *Algiers* (1938), *Gaslight* (1944).

Brando, Marlon (1924–); American stage and film star. *The Men* (1950), *A Streetcar Named Desire* (1951), *The Young Lions* (1958).

Burton, Richard (Richard Jenkins) (1925–1984); British film and stage star. *Look Back in Anger* (1959), *Cleopatra* (1962), *Anne of a Thousand Days* (1970).

Cagney, James (1899–); American film star, famed for his cocky personality. *The Public Enemy* (1931), *Angels With Dirty Faces* (1938), *Yankee Doodle Dandy* (1942).

Chaplin, Sir Charles Spencer (Charlie Chaplin) (1899–1977); British film actor, director and producer. Famed for his role in silent films as the 'Little Tramp'. *The Gold Rush* (1924), *City Lights* (1931), *The Great Dictator* (1940). A film, *The Life Story of Charles Chaplin*, was made in Britain in 1926, but was never shown because of a threat of legal action.

Chevalier, Maurice (1887–1972); French singer, entertainer and film star. *The Love Parade* (1930), *Le Silence d'Or* (1947), *Gigi* (1958).

Cooper, Gary (Frank James Cooper) (1901–61); American film star with a slow, deliberate manner. *A Farewell to Arms* (1932), *City Streets* (1932), *Mr Deeds Goes to Town* (1936), *For Whom the Bell Tolls* (1943).

Crawford, Joan (Lucille le Sueur) (1906–77); American film star. *Grand Hotel* (1932), *Rain* (1932), *Mildred Pierce* (1945).

Crosby, Harry Lillis (Bing) (1903–78);

American singer, a leading crooner of the 1930s and 40s, radio and film star. *Anything Goes* (1936), *Road to Singapore* (1940), *Going My Way* (1944).

De Mille, Cecil Blount (1881–1959); American film director, a pioneer in Hollywood. *The Squaw Man* (1913), *The Ten Commandments* (1923, 1956), *The Sign of the Cross* (1932), *The Plainsman* (1936).

Dietrich, Marlene (Maria Magdalena von Losch) (1901–); German-born film star of glamorous legend. *The Blue Angel* (1930), *Shanghai Express* (1932), *Destry Rides Again* (1939), *Witness for the Prosecution* (1957).

Disney, Walter Elias (Walt) (1901–66); American cartoon animator and film producer. Creator of Mickey Mouse, who first appeared in *Steamboat Willie* (1928). Other cartoon successes include *Snow White* (1937), *Pinocchio* (1939), *Fantasia* (1940).

Douglas, Kirk (Issur Danielovitch Demsky) (1918–); American film star. *The Strange Love of Martha Ivers* (1946), *Lust for Life* (1956), *Spartacus* (1960), *Cast a Giant Shadow* (1966).

Fields, W.C. (Wiliam Claude Dukinfield) (1879–1946); American comedian, film star and eccentric. *It's a Gift* (1934), *David Copperfield* (1934), *My Little Chickadee* (1940). A film, *W.C. Fields and Me* was made in 1976, with Rod Steiger in the part.

Flynn, Errol (1909–59); Tasmanian-born film star. *Captain Blood* (1935), *The Charge of the Light Brigade* (1936), *The Sea Hawk* (1940), *Gentleman Jim* (1942).

Fonda, Henry Jaynes (1905–82); American film and stage star. *Young Mr Lincoln* (1939), *The Grapes of Wrath* (1940), *Twelve Angry Men* (1957).

Gable, (William) Clark (1901–1960); American film star of strongly masculine roles. *It Happened One Night* (1934),

Mutiny on the Bounty (1935), *San Francisco* (1936), *Gone With the Wind* (1939). A film based on his life, *Gable and Lombard*, was made in 1976.

Garbo, Greta (Greta Lovisa Gustafsson) (1905–); Swedish film star who became one of the Hollywood 'greats'. *Flesh and the Devil* (1927), *Anna Christie* (1930), *Ninotchka* (1939).

Garland, Judy (Frances Gumm) (1922–69); American film star and entertainer. *The Wizard of Oz* (1930), *Babes in Arms* (1939), *Meet Me in St Louis* (1944), *A Star is Born* (1954).

Goldwyn, Samuel (Samuel Goldfish) (1884–1974); Polish-American film producer; *Wuthering Heights* (1939), *The Kid from Brooklyn* (1946), *The Secret Life of Walter Mitty* (1947).

Grant, Cary (Archibald Leach) (1904–); British-born debonair film actor; *I'm No Angel* (1933), *I Was a Male War Bride* (1949).

Griffith, D.W. (David Wark Griffith) (1874–1948); American film producer, the first major producer-director. He introduced many now familiar techniques with spectacular films: *The Birth of a Nation* (1915), and *Intolerance* (1916).

Harlow, Jean (Harlean Carpentier) (1911–1937); American blonde film star of the early '30s. *Hell's Angels* (1930), *Red Dust* (1932). Two films based on her life have been made: both called *Harlow*, and made in 1965.

Hayworth, Rita (Margarita Carmen Cansino) (1918–); American actress and dancer, often in fiery roles. *Gilda* (1946).

Hepburn, Katharine (1907–); American stage and film actress. Many of her best films were made with Spencer Tracy. She has won three Academy Awards. Films: *Morning Glory* (1933), *Guess Who's Coming to Dinner* (1967),

The Lion in Winter (1968).

Heston, Charlton (John Charlton Carter) (1924–   ); American film actor, particularly in Biblical and mediaeval epics. *Ben Hur* (1959), *El Cid* (1961).

Hitchcock, Alfred (1899–1984); British film and TV director of suspense thrillers. *Blackmail* (1929), *The Thirty-Nine Steps* (1935), *Psycho* (1960), *The Birds* (1963).

Hope, Leslie Townes (Bob) (1903–   ); American comedian for forty years. Famous for troop shows and films with Bing Crosby and Dorothy Lamour, especially ''The Road'' series.

Keaton, Buster (Joseph Francis Keaton) (1895–1966); American film actor and comedian, mainly in silent comedies. Called 'Old Stoneface' for his unsmiling appearance. *The Navigator* (1924), *The General* (1926), *Steamboat Bill Junior* (1927). Two films have been made based on his life: *The Buster Keaton Story* (1957), and *The Comic* (1969).

Korda, Sir Alexander (Sandor Corda) (1893–1956); British film producer and director, born in Hungary. He revived the British film industry with *The Private Life of Henry VIII* (1933), and *Rembrandt* (1936).

Laughton, Charles (1899–1962); British-born, later American stage and film actor. *The Private Life of Henry VIII* (1933), *Rembrandt* (1936), *The Hunchback of Notre Dame* (1939).

Laurel, Stan (Arthur Stanley Jefferson) (1890–1965); British-born film comedian, famed for his partnership with Oliver Hardy. *Way Out West* (1936), *A Chump at Oxford* (1940).

Lloyd, Harold Clayton (1893–1971); American film comedian of the silent and early sound era, famous for his timid character but dangerous stunts. *Safety Last* (1923), *The Freshman* (1925), *The Kid Brother* (1927).

Mayer, Louis Burt (1885–1957); American founder (with Sam Goldwyn) of Metro-Goldwyn-Mayer, the Hollywood film-makers.

Powell, William (1892–1984); American film actor, famed for his 'Thin Man' character 1934–47. *The Great Ziegfeld* (1936), *My Man Godfrey* (1936), *Mister Roberts* (1955).

Robinson, Edward G. (Emanuel Goldenburg) (1893–1973); American film star of Romanian origin. Often played villains or policemen. *Little Caesar* (1930), *The Woman in the Window* (1944), *Double Indemnity* (1944), *Key Largo* (1948).

Rogers, Ginger (Virginia Katharine McMath) (1911–   ); American actress and dancer, especially with Fred Astaire. *Top Hat* (1935), *Lady in the Dark* (1943).

Stewart, James Maitland (1908–   ); American leading man in films, usually comedies. *You Can't Take it With You* (1938), *Destry Rides Again* (1939), *Philadelphia Story* (1940), *Harvey* (1950).

Tracy, Spencer (1900–67); American film actor, usually appearing as the tough, honest hero. Often played opposite Katharine Hepburn. *Captain Courageous* (1937), *Boys' Town* (1938), *Adam's Rib* (1949), *Guess Who's Coming to Dinner* (1967).

Wayne, John (Marion Michael Morrison) (1907–79); One of the most successful of all American film actors, usually in action films, especially Westerns. *Stagecoach* (1939), *The Quiet Man* (1952), *True Grit* (1969). He appeared in 153 films in all, playing the lead in all but 11.

Zanuck, Darryl Francis (1902–79); American production chief in the film industry. Helped to found 20th Century Productions, which later merged with Fox, when he became chief executive.

Track and Field

Greek girl winning race at the women's Olympics at Hera.

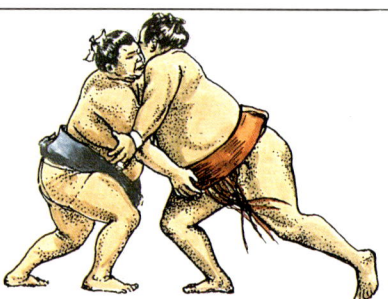

Sumo wrestling in Japan dates from 1624 and is still practised today.

Hunters on skis from Lapland, 1539. Today shooting and skiing is represented by an Olympic sport—the biathlon.

Ball Games

Greek game of 'hockey'.

Mayan ball game. You had to hit the ball through the hole using knee, hip or elbow.

Playing bowls, 1640. Earlier, King Edward III had banned bowls fearing that it might jeopardize the practice of archery.

Animal Sport

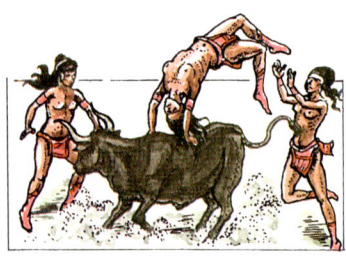

Bull-leaping, Crete 1900 BC. Teams of three men and women somersaulted between the horns of a charging bull.

Chariot racing, Constantinople AD 500. Different political parties raced against each other. The losing party often caused a riot.

The Start of Ball Games

Football was played in medieval England. A monk wrote that it was 'abominable' and 'more common, undignified and worthless than any other kind of game'. 1823 was destined to be a landmark in sporting history. At Rugby School a boy named William Webb Ellis 'with fine disregard for the rules of football as played in his time, first took the ball in his arms and ran with it.'

That was the beginning of Rugby Football, handling the ball, as distinct from 'soccer', so called from the Football Association founded in 1863. Both games have spread to many other countries.

Boxing is another old sport. Prize fighting started in London in the 18th century. The fighters wore no gloves.

Left: Woman throwing the discus. Right: Jesse Owens wins the long jump with a leap of 8.06 m at the 1936 Olympics.

Mark Spitz powering to a win in the 100 metres butterfly in 1972. That year he won 9 gold medals.

Cricket in 1743. The wicket keeper has removed his wig. Over-arm bowling began in 1864.

Women playing tennis at Wimbledon in the 1880s.

Pelota is a very fast game that originated in northern Spain.

Jousting, 1400. To train for war, knights fought mock battles.

Hunting the hare was a sport for gentlemen, 16th century.

Hawking, 1600, was popular all over Europe.

Cricket began in England and was played all over the British Empire in the 19th century. It is still played in many of those countries, particularly in India, Pakistan, Ceylon, the West Indies, Australia, New Zealand and South Africa. The name comes from *cricc*, or crook, and the game started in Saxon times as a diversion for bored shepherds, defending the wicket gate of their sheep-pen from an improvised ball. The curved wood continued until about 1770, when the straight bat was adopted to cope with more accurate bowling. The MCC (Marylebone Cricket Club) was founded in 1787 and still controls the sport. The sedate, innocent-looking but very crafty game of bowls was banned under

Richard II in 1388, but played by Drake while wating for the Spanish Armada precisely 200 years later. It is still a most popular pastime. So, in France, is its equivalent *boule*, played on the hard-trodden earth under the plane-trees on some small-town boulevard.

Baseball, America's own special game, developed from cricket and the children's game of rounders, was first played in 1845.

Tennis was forbidden as 'dangerous' at Narbonne College in France in 1379. But the modern form, lawn tennis, dates only from 1875, when rules were drawn up for a game to be played on grass instead of in expensive covered 'courts'. The famous Wimbledon championship started only two years afterwards and the new game swiftly gained world-wide popularity.

Golf was born in Scotland. It was banned there as early as 1457 – often the first date we know for a sport is the year some one disapproved of it! – but a century later it was played by Mary Queen of Scots herself. Her son took it south when he became James I of England, but it long remained a Scottish game. The first tournament was held in 1744, the first 18-hole course laid out at St Andrews in 1764.

Personalities in Sport

Ali, Muhammad (Cassius Clay) (1942–   ); American boxer, the first to hold the heavyweight title three times (1964–67, 1974–78, 1978–79). A leader in the Black Muslim religion.

Anquetil, Jacques (1934–   ); French cyclist, who in 1964 won the 5000 kilometre (2700 mile) race for the fifth time.

Bannister, Sir Roger Gilbert (1929–   ); British athlete; the first man to run the mile in under 4 minutes (1954).

Best, George (1946–   ); British association footballer, born in Northern Ireland. His brilliant career came to an end due to pressure from hero-worshipping fans and media.

Borg, Björn (1956–   ); Swedish tennis player, who won the Wimbledon singles title five times running (1976–80).

Botham, Ian (1955–   ); British cricketer, famed as both batsman and bowler. Has achieved over 4000 runs and has taken more than 300 wickets in Test cricket. In 1984, he took 8 wickets in the Test against the West Indies.

Brabham, Jack (1926–   ); Australian motor-racing driver, the first to win the world championship in his own car. Retired in 1970.

Bradman, Sir Donald (1908–   ); Australian cricketer, considered to be the most outstanding batsman of all time. Averaged 99·94 in 52 Tests (1928–48) and 95·14 in all matches.

Budge, Donald (1915–   ); American tennis player, the first to complete the Grand Slam of the four major titles in one year (1938).

Busby, Sir Matt (1909–   ); Scottish international association footballer who became manager of Manchester United, and who survived the Munich air crash.

Charlton, Robert (Bobby) (1937–   ); British association footballer, captain of Manchester United, who scored a record 49 goals in 106 internationals.

Clark, Jim (1936–1968); Scottish racing driver, one of the greatest of all, who drove for Lotus. He won 25 grands prix.

Cobb, John Rhodes (1899–1952); British racing motorist, who set up world land speed records at Bonneville salt flats, USA in 1938, 1939 and 1947 (394·2 mph/634·4 kph). Killed while making water speed record in Loch Ness, Scotland.

Coe, Sebastian Newbold (1956–); British athlete, who as a runner, set up three world records in 1981 (800 metres (1:41·72), the 1000 metres (2:12·18) and the mile (3:47·33). He won gold and silver medals in the 1980 and 1984 Olympics in the 1500 metres and 800 events.

Compton, Denis (1918–); British cricketer and association footballer. Cricket record of 3816 runs and 18 centuries in 1947 and fastest 300 (181 minutes). Played in 78 Tests.

Connolly, Maureen ('Little Mo') (1934–1969); American tennis player, who won the tennis Grand Slam in 1953. Her career ended after a horse-riding accident in 1954.

Connors, Jimmy (1952–); American tennis player; US singles champion 1974, 1976, 1978. Wimbledon champion 1974.

Court, Margaret (b. Margaret Smith) (1942–); Australian tennis player, the second woman (after Maureen Connolly) to win the Grand Slam (1970). Won a record 22 major singles and 58 titles in all.

Crapp, Lorraine (1938–); Australian swimmer, who in 1956 was the first woman to break the 5 minutes 500 metres freestyle record.

Cruyff, Johan (1947–); Netherlands association footballer, and a leading goal-scorer for both the Ajax team and the national Netherlands side.

Davis, Joe (1901–78); British billiards and snooker player, who was the only man to hold both world billiards and snooker titles simultaneously. He won the world professional title 15 times.

Davis, Steve (1957–); British snooker player (unrelated to Joe Davis), who won the world title in 1981, and who made his first televised maximum break (147) in 1982.

Dempsey, Jack (1895–1983); American heavyweight boxer, a powerful puncher, who won the world title in 1919, losing it in 1926 to Gene Tunney.

Di Stefano, Alfredo (1926–); Argentinian association footballer, who played for Spain and Real Madrid as well as the Argentine.

DiMaggio, Joe (Joseph Paul DiMaggio) (1914–); American baseball player, outfielder (1936–51) with the New York Yankees team. Married to Marilyn Monroe 1954–55.

Fangio, Juan Manuel (1911–); Argentinian motor racing driver, who has been world champion five times.

Finney, Tom (1922–); British association footballer; a brilliant winger for Preston and England. Record score of 30 goals in 76 games.

Fraser, Dawn (1937–); Australian swimmer, who won Olympic gold medals in 1956, 1960 and 1964.

Fry, Charles Burgess (1872–1956); British sportsman; a cricketer (Sussex, Hampshire and England); association footballer (England) and athlete. Regarded as greatest batsman of his time, making over 30,866 runs, with 94 centuries.

Goolagong, Evonne (Mrs Roger Cawley) (1951–); Australian tennis player, champion at Wimbledon, 1971.

Grace, Dr William Gilbert (1848–1915); British physician and cricketer, an all-rounder who dominated the game at the end of the 19th century. Made 54,904 runs, with 126 centuries. His brother, Edward Mills Grace, was also a famed cricketer.

Hagen, Walter (1892–1969); American golfer, who was PGA champion 1921 and 1924–27, and British Open champion 1922. 1924, 1928 and 1929.

Henie, Sonja (1912–1969); Norwegian-born American ice-skater and Hollywood film star. Winner of 10 successive world titles (1927–36) and 3 Olympic gold medals (1928, 1932, 1936). Films: *One in a Million* (1936), *Sun Valley Serenade* (1941).

Hill, Graham (1929–1975); British motor-racing driver, who began as a mechanic. World champion 1962 (BRM) and 1968 (Lotus). Killed in an air crash.

Hobbs, Sir John Berry (Jack) ('the Master') (1882–1963); British cricketer, and one of the century's leading world's batsmen. Scored 61,237 runs with 197 centuries.

Hogan, William Benjamin (Ben) (1912–); American golfer, winner of the US Open 1948, 1950, 1951, and 1953. Master's championship 1951 and 1953; PGA champion 1946 and 1948.

Hutton, Sir Leonard (1916–); British cricketer, who made the highest Test score against Australia, 364 (Oval, 1938) in 13 hours 17 minutes, the record lasting for 20 years.

James, Alex (1902–1953); British association footballer, Scottish-born, but famed for his prowess with the English Preston and Arsenal teams.

John, Barry (1945–); Welsh rugby union fly-half (Llanelli, Cardiff, Wales and British Lions). Scored record 90 points for Wales in 25 games.

Killy, Jean-Claude (1943–); French ski-racer, and Olympic champion in downhill, slalom, and giant slalom, 1968. World Cup champion 1967, 1968.

King, Billie Jean (Billie Jean Moffitt) (1943–); American tennis player; US singles champion 1967, 1971–72, 1974, and Wimbledon champion 1966–68, 1972–73, 1975.

Knievel, Evel (Robert Craig Knievel) (1938–); American stunt motorcyclist.

Laker, James Charles (Jim) (1922–); British cricketer (Surrey, Essex and England), a renowned right-arm off-spin bowler. World record 19 wickets for 90 in a Test against Australia, 1956.

Lauda, Niki (1949–); Austrian motor-racing driver, and winner of the World Grand Prix 1977.

Laver, Rodney George (1938–); Australian tennis player, and the only man to achieve the Grand Slam of major singles titles twice, as an amateur and as a professional (1962 and 1969). First player to win $1 million.

Law, Denis (1940–); British association footballer, for Huddersfield Town Manchester City, Turin, Manchester United and Scotland.

Lenglen, Suzanne (1899–1938); French tennis player, virtually unbeatable 1919–26. A professional from 1926 after winning 6 Wimbledon singles.

Lillee, Dennis (1949–); Australian cricketer, a devastatingly fast bowler, setting a new record after he took his 310th wicket in 1981.

Longden, Johnny (1907–); British jockey, who rode over 6032 winning horses, the first man to exceed 5000.

Lonsdale, 5th Earl (Hugh Cecil Lowther) (1857–1944); British sportsman, with interests in hunting, racing, yacht-racing and boxing. Created Lonsdale Belts in 1909 as rewards to champion boxers winning titles at the National Sporting Club in London.

Louis, Joe (Joseph Louis Barrow), 'The Brown Bomber' (1914–1981); American heavyweight boxer who won the world championship in 1937, defending his title successfully 25 times. Retired undefeated 1949. Was knocked out by Rocky

Marciano in 1951 after unsuccessful comeback.

Lunn, Sir Arnold (1888–1974); British pioneer in skiing and authority on mountaineering, son of Sir Henry Lunn. Methodist missionary and travel agent. Sir Arnold organized the first world skiing championships. *History of Ski-ing* (1953).

McBride, Willie John (1940–); Irish rugby second-row forward, who captained the British Lions to success in South Africa in 1974.

McEnroe, John P. (1959–); American tennis player, US and Wimbledon championship winner since 1979. A controversial player with a quick and caustic tongue.

Marciano, Rocky (Rocco Francis Marchegiano) (1923–1969); American heavyweight boxer, who won the world title in 1952, retiring unbeaten in 1956 after 49 fights. Killed in an aircraft crash.

Matthews, Sir Stanley (1915–); British association footballer for Stoke City, Blackpool and England. A right winger, known as the 'Wizard of the Dribble' for his wonderful ball control.

Meads, Colin Earl (1936–); Rugby union lock forward for New Zealand. Was sent off in 1967 while playing Scotland at Murrayfield. Retired 1972.

Moody, Helen Newington Wills (1905–); American tennis player, who dominated the game from 1922–38, winning 19 major singles.

Moore, Robert Frederick (Bobby) (1941–); British association footballer for West Ham United and England. Captained England to World Cup victory in 1966. Capped a record 108 times.

Moss, Stirling (1929–); British motor-racing driver who won 16 grands prix but never a world championship. Nearly died after a crash at Goodwood in 1962, ending his racing career.

Naismith, Dr James A. (1861–1939); Canadian-born American physical educator, the originator of basketball in 1891.

Nastase, Ilie (1946–); Romanian tennis player, renowned for tennis court tantrums. US singles champion, 1972.

Navratilova, Martina (1956–); Czechoslovakian-born American tennis player; Wimbledon champion 1978 and 1979; French championships and Grand Slam, 1983–4.

Nepia, George (1905–); New Zealand rugby union fullback player, a Maori. Visited England and France with the All-Blacks 1924–25, when the team won every one of 30 matches.

Nicklaus, Jack William (1940–); American golfer, considered by many to be the greatest golfer of all time. US

Pelé of Brazil, perhaps the greatest footballer of all time.

amateur champion 1959, 1961; US Open champion 1962, 1967, 1972; Open champion 1966, 1970. Has won more titles than any other golfer in history.

Nurmi, Paavo (1897–1973); Finnish athlete, foremost of 'Flying Finns'. Almost unbeatable over 1500–10,000 metres. He won 9 Olympic medals (1920–28).

Ovett, Steven Michael James (1955–); British athlete, who won the 800 metres title in the 1980 Olympics, but who was unsuccessful in the 1984 events. Set up world record for 1500 metres in 1983 (3:30·77).

Owens, Jesse (James Cleveland Owens) (1913–1980); American athlete who set up five world records: the 100 yards (equal), long jump, 220 yards/200 metres, and 220 yards hurdles in one afternoon (25 May 1935). A black man, he embarrassed the Nazis at the 1936 Olympics by winning four gold medals.

Palmer, Arnold (1929–); American golfer, winner of the Master's championship in 1958, 1960, 1962 and 1964, and the US Open championship in 1960.

Pelé, (Edson Arantes do Nascimento) (1940–); Brazilian association footballer, regarded as the world's greatest. He starred in two world cup championships, leading the Brazilian team in 1958 and 1970. With Santos team, and then with New York Cosmos soccer team 1975–77.

Perry, Frederick John (Fred) (1909–); British lawn tennis and table tennis player; the only man in the world to lead at both. World table tennis champion 1929. At Wimbledon, he won the men's singles for three year's running (1934–36).

Piggott, Lester (1935–); British jockey, acclaimed by many as all-time No. 1. Has won 25 English classics (including 8 Derbys).

Player, Gary (1935–); South African golfer; British Open champion 1959, 1968; US Open champion 1965; Master's champion 1961; US PGA champion 1962, 1972.

Puskas, Ferenc (1927–); Hungarian association footballer for Kispest, Honved, Real Madrid and Hungary. Played for Real Madrid when they won the European Cup in 1960. Retired as a player, becoming a coach and manager.

Ramsey, Sir Alfred E. (Alf) (1920–); British association footballer for Southampton, Tottenham Hotspur and England. As manager, he masterminded the progress of the England team to victory in the World Cup in 1966.

Rhodes, Wilfred (1877–1973); British cricketer for Yorkshire and England, who took a record 4187 wickets (slow left arm), and scored 32,722 runs. Played in 58 Tests.

Richards, Sir Gordon (1904–); British champion jockey, who was champion in England 26 times 1925–53. Won record 4870 races, including 269 in the year 1947. He rode 14 classic winners.

Rimet, Jules (1873–1956); French association football administrator, who was president of the French Football League 1919–1949, and president of FIFA 1921–56. The World Cup trophy is named after him.

Robinson, 'Sugar' Ray (Walker Smith) (1920–); American welterweight boxing champion 1946–51. A middleweight champion five times 1951–60. Regarded by many as the greatest boxer of the past 40 years.

Rono, Henry (1952–); Kenyan athlete, who in 1978 won four major events: 3000 metres, 5000 metres, 10,000 metres and the 3000 metres steeplechase. He broke world records in three of these.

Ruth, Babe (George Herman Ruth) (1895–1948); American baseball player for the Boston Red Sox, New York Yankees and Boston Braves. Famed mainly for his time (1920–34) with NY Yankees, setting up many hitting records, including 60 home runs in the 1927 season and 714 during his career. In 1919 he hit a home run of 587 feet (178·9 metres).

Sobers, Sir Garfield St Aubin (Gary) (1936–   ); West Indian cricketer, who played for the West Indies, Barbados, South Australia and Nottinghamshire. One of the world's finest all-rounders, who scored a record 8032 runs in 93 Tests.

Spitz, Mark Andrew (1950–   ); American swimmer, who won 7 gold medals in the 1972 Olympics, and 2 in the 1980 Games.

Stengel, Casey was one of baseball's great managers. He led the New York Yankees to seven world championships, including five straight from 1949 to 1953, and again in 1956 and 1958. Stengel's Yankees were also American League champions from 1955 to 1958, and in 1960. In 1962, Stengel became manager of the New York Mets.

Stewart, John Young (Jackie) (1939–   ); Scottish motor-racing driver, who won three world championships and 27 grands prix before retiring in 1973.

Surtees, John (1934–   ); British racing motor-cyclist and motor-racing driver, the only man to win world championships in both fields.

Thorpe, Jim (James Francis) (1888–1953); American athlete, probably the most outstanding all-round sportsman of all time. He won the pentathlon and decathlon in the 1912 Olympics, but was denied the medals on a technicality. Half Indian, he played major league American football and professional baseball.

Tilden, William Tatem ('Big Bill')

Gary Sobers, the West Indian cricketer who scored six sixes in an over.

(1893–1953); American tennis player, who dominated men's tennis in the 1920s. Voted the greatest tennis player of the first half of the 20th century in 1950.

Trueman, Frederick Sewards (1931–   ); British cricketer for Yorkshire and England. A popular fast bowler, he took a record 307 Test wickets.

Wade, Virginia (1945–   ); British tennis player who was Wimbledon champion in 1977.

Weissmuller, Peter John (Johnny) (1903–1984); American swimmer and film star, famed for his portrayal of Tarzan in 19 films. Voted the greatest swimmer of the half-century.

Zatopek, Emil (1922–   ); Czechoslovak athlete and runner who achieved 18 world records and won 4 Olympic titles, including the 5000 metres, 10,000 metres and marathon in 1952.

The Olympic Games

The first recorded Olympic Games were held in 776 BC on the plains of Olympia in south-western Greece. The games honoured Zeus, the most powerful of all the Greek gods, but their more practical purpose was to promote friendship between the independent Greek states taking part and so lessen the danger of war between them. At first the events were mainly foot races. Then the Greeks added discus and javelin throwing, jumping and wrestling. Later still came chariot racing and boxing. Winning competitors were crowned with sacred olive wreaths. In time, Greece fell under Roman rule, and the high standards of sportsmanship declined. Rome's Christian Emperor Theodosius finally abolished the games after AD 393.

THE MODERN OLYMPICS
In 1896 the Olympic Games were revived as an international event for the world's best amateur athletes. Like the ancient Greeks, some Europeans thought the Games would lessen the danger of war. Also, interest in the ancient Games had been revived because the original Olympic stadium had been excavated by archaeologists in 1878.

Thirteen countries were represented in the 1896 Games, which were held in Athens. Since then the Games have been held at four year intervals, interrupted only by the two World Wars, at the following places:

1896 Athens, Greece
1900 Paris, France
1904 St Louis, United States
1906 Athens, Greece
1908 London, England
1912 Stockholm, Sweden
1920 Antwerp, Belgium
1924 Paris, France
1928 Amsterdam, Netherlands
1932 Los Angeles, United States
1936 Berlin, Germany
1948 London, England
1952 Helsinki, Finland
1956 Melbourne, Australia
1960 Rome, Italy
1964 Tokyo, Japan
1968 Mexico City, Mexico
1972 Munich, West Germany
1976 Montreal, Canada
1980 Moscow, USSR
1984 Los Angeles, United States
1988 Seoul, South Korea

WINTER OLYMPICS
1924 Chamonix, France
1928 St Moritz, Switzerland
1932 Lake Placid, USA
1936 Garmisch, Germany
1948 St Moritz, Switerland
1952 Oslo, Norway
1956 Cortina, Italy
1960 Squaw Valley, USA
1964 Innsbruck, Austria
1968 Grenoble, France
1972 Sapporo, Japan
1976 Innsbruck, Austria
1980 Lake Placid, USA
1984 Sarajevo, Yugoslavia
1988 Calgary, Canada

ATHLETICS

Ruling body – International Amateur Athletic Federation (IAAF)

Men's World Records

100 metres	9·95 s	Jim Hines (USA)	14.10.68
200 metres	19·72 s	Pietro Mennea (Italy)	12.9.79
400 metres	43·86 s	Lee Evans (USA)	18.10.68
800 metres	1 m 41·72 s	Sebastian Coe (GB)	10.6.81
1000 metres	2 m 12·18 s	Sebastian Coe (GB)	11.7.81
1500 metres	3 m 30·77 s	Steve Ovett (GB)	27.8.83
1 mile	3 m 47·33 s	Sebastian Coe (GB)	27.8.81
2000 metres	4 m 51·4 s	John Walker (NZ)	30.6.76
3000 metres	7 m 32·1 s	Henry Rono (Kenya)	27.6.78
5000 metres	13 m 00·42 s	David Moorcroft (GB)	7.7.82
10,000 metres	27 m 22·4 s	Henry Rono (Kenya)	11.6.78
Marathon*	2 hr 8 m 13 s	Alberto Salazar (USA)	25.10.81
110 metres hurdles	12·93 s	Renaldo Nehemiah (USA)	19.8.81
400 metres hurdles	47·13 s	Ed Moses (USA)	3.7.80
3000 metres steeple-chase	8 m 5·37 s	Henry Rono (Kenya)	13.5.78
4 × 100 metres relay	37·83 s	United States	11.8.84
4 × 400 metres relay	2 m 56·16 s	United States	20.10.68
High jump	2·36 m (7 ft 8¾ in)	Gerd Wessig (E. Germany)	1.8.80
Pole vault	5·81 m (19 ft 0¾ in)	Vladimir Poliakov (USSR)	27.6.81
Long jump	8·90 m (29 ft 2½ in)	Bob Beamon (USA)	18.10.68
Triple jump	17·89 m (58 ft 8½ in)	João de Oliveira (Brazil)	15.10.75
Shot putt	22·15 m (72 ft 8 in)	Udo Beyer (E. Germany)	6.7.78
Discus throw	71·16 m (233 ft 5 in)	Wolfgang Schmidt (E. Germany)	9.8.78
Hammer throw	81·80 m (268 ft 4 in)	Yuriy Sedykh (USSR)	31.7.80
Javelin throw	96·72 m (317 ft 4 in)	Ferenc Paragi (Hungary)	23.4.80
Decathlon	8649 points	Guido Kratchmer (W. Ger.)	14/15.6.80

Women's World Records

100 metres	10·88 s	Marlies Oelsner† (E. Germany)	1.7.77
200 metres	21·71 s	Marita Koch (E. Germany)	10.6.79
400 metres	48·60 s	Marita Kock (E. Germany)	4.8.79
800 metres	1 m 53·43 s	Nadyezhda Olizarenko (USSR)	27.7.80
1500 metres	3 m 52·47 s	Tatyana Kazankina (USSR)	13.8.80
1 mile	4 m 20·89 s	Lyudmila Veselkova (USSR)	13.9.81
3000 metres	8 m 27·12 s	Lyudmila Bragina (USSR)	7.8.76
5000 metres	15 m 14·51 s	Paula Fudge (GB)	13.9.81
10,000 metres	32 m 17·9 s	Yelena Sipatova (USSR)	19.9.81
Marathon*	2 h 25 m 29 s	Allison Roe (New Zealand)	25.10.81
100 metres hurdles	12·36 s	Grazyna Rabsztyn (Poland)	13.6.80
400 metres hurdles	54·28 s	Karin Rossley (E. Germany)	18.5.80

Continued

SPORT

Womens World Records

4 × 100 metres relay	41·60 s	East Germany	1.8.80
4 × 400 metres relay	3 m 19·23 s	East Germany	31.7.76
High jump	2·01 m (6 ft 7 in)	Sara Simeoni (Italy)	4.8.78
Long jump	7·09 m (23 ft $3\frac{1}{4}$ in)	Vilma Bardauskiene (USSR)	29.8.78
Shot putt	22.45 m (73 ft 8 in)	Ilona Slupianek (E. Germany)	10.5.80
Discus throw	71.80 m (235 ft 7 in)	Maria Petkova (Bulgaria)	13.7.80
Javelin throw	71.88 m (235 ft 10 in)	Antoaneta Todorova (Bulgaria)	15.8.81
Pentathlon	5083 points	Nadyezhda Tkachenko (USSR)	24.7.80
Heptathlon	6717 points	Ramona Neubert (E. Ger.)	27/28.6.81

*World best time (no official world record because of variation in courses).
‡Now Marlies Göhr.

ASSOCIATION FOOTBALL

European Cup Finals

1956	Paris	Real Madrid (Spain)......4	Stade de Reims (France).......3
1957	Madrid	Real Madrid (Spain)......2	Fiorentina (Italy).............0
1958	Brussels	Real Madrid (Spain)......3	AC Milan (Italy) 2
1959	Stuttgart	Real Madrid (Spain)......2	Stade de Reims (France).......0
1960	Glasgow	Real Madrid (Spain)......7	Eintracht Frankfurt (W. Ger.)..3
1961	Berne	Benfica (Portugal).......3	Barcelona (Spain) 2
1962	Amsterdam	Benfica (Portugal).......5	Real Madrid (Spain) 3
1963	Wembley	AC Milan (Italy).........2	Benfica (Portugal) 1
1964	Vienna	Internazionale (Italy) 3	Real Madrid (Spain) 1
1965	Milan	Internazionale (Italy) 1	Benfica (Portugal) 0
1966	Brussels	Real Madrid (Spain)......2	Partizan Belgrade (Yug.).......1
1967	Lisbon	Celtic (Scotland) 2	Internazionale (Italy)..........1
1968	Wembley	Manchester U (England)..4	Benfica (Portugal) 1
1969	Madrid	AC Milan (Italy).........4	Ajax (Netherlands) 1
1970	Milan	Feynoord (Netherlands)...2	Celtic (Scotland)..............1
1971	Wembley	Ajax (Netherlands).......2	Panathinaikos (Greece)........0
1972	Rotterdam	Ajax (Netherlands).......2	Internazionale (Italy)..........0
1973	Belgrade	Ajax (Netherlands).......1	Juventus (Italy) 0
1974	Brussels	Bayern Munich (W. Ger.) .1	Atlético Madrid (Spain) 1
	Replay	4	0
1975	Paris	Bayern Munich (W. Ger.) .2	Leeds United (England) 0
1976	Glasgow	Bayern Munich (W. Ger.) .1	St Etienne (France) 0
1977	Rome	Liverpool (England)......3	B Mönchengladbach (W. Ger.) .1
1978	Wembley	Liverpool (England)......1	FC Bruges (Belgium)..........0
1979	Munich	Nottingham Forest (Eng.) .1	Malmö (Sweden) 0
1980	Madrid	Nottingham Forest (Eng.) .1	SV Hamburg (W. Ger.).........0
1981	Paris	Liverpool (England)......1	Real Madrid (Spain) 0
1982	Rotterdam	Aston Villa (England).....1	Bayern Munich (W. Ger.) 0
1983	Athens	Hamburg (W. Ger.) 1	Juventus (Italy) 0
1984	Rome	Liverpool (England)......4	A.S. Roma (Italy) 2

ASSOCIATION FOOTBALL

World Cup Finals

1930	Montevideo, Uruguay (100,000)	Uruguay	4	Argentina	2
1934	Rome, Italy (55,000)	Italy	2	Czechoslovakia	1
1938	Paris, France (65,000)	Italy	4	Hungary	2
1950	Rio de Janeiro, Brazil (199,850)	Uruguay	2	Brazil	1
1954	Berne, Switzerland (55,000)	W. Germany	3	Hungary	2
1958	Stockholm, Sweden (49,737)	Brazil	5	Sweden	2
1962	Santiago, Chile (69,068)	Brazil	3	Czechoslovakia	1
1966	Wembley, England (93,000)	England	4	W. Germany	2
1970	Mexico City, Mexico (110,000)	Brazil	4	Italy	1
1974	Munich, W. Germany (75,000)	W. Germany	2	Netherlands	1
1978	Buenos Aires, Argentina (77,000)	Argentina	3	Netherlands	1
1982	Madrid, Spain (90,000)	Italy	3	W. Germany	1

FOOTBALL ASSOCIATION (ENGLAND) CUP WINNERS

1930 Arsenal	1954 West Bromwich Albion	1971 Arsenal
1931 West Bromwich Albion	1955 Newcastle United	1972 Leeds United
1932 Newcastle United	1956 Manchester City	1973 Sunderland
1933 Everton	1957 Aston Villa	1974 Liverpool
1934 Manchester City	1958 Bolton Wanderers	1975 West Ham United
1935 Sheffield Wednesday	1959 Nottingham Forest	1976 Southampton
1936 Arsenal	1960 Wolverhampton Wanderers	1977 Manchester United
1937 Sunderland	1961 Tottenham Hotspur	1978 Ipswich Town
1938 Preston North End	1962 Tottenham Hotspur	1979 Arsenal
1939 Portsmouth	1963 Manchester United	1980 West Ham United
1946 Derby County	1964 West Ham United	1981 Tottenham Hotspur
1947 Charlton Athletic	1965 Liverpool	1982 Tottenham Hotspur
1948 Manchester United	1966 Everton	1983 Manchester United
1949 Wolverhampton Wanderers	1967 Tottenham Hotspur	1984 Everton
1950 Arsenal	1968 West Bromwich Albion	
1951 Newcastle United	1969 Manchester City	
1952 Newcastle United	1970 Chelsea	
1953 Blackpool		

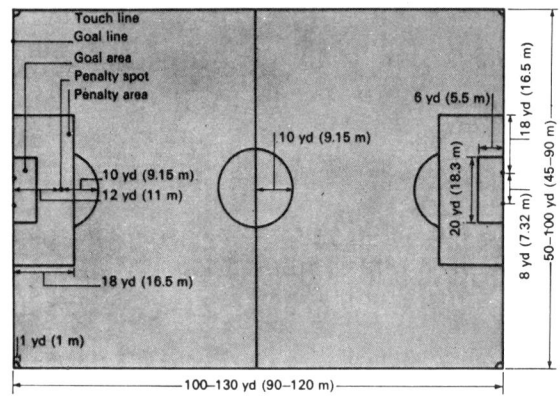

The layout of a football pitch

ASSOCIATION FOOTBALL

Ball – circum. 68–71 cm (27–28 in), weight 400–450 gm (14–16 oz).

Duration of game– 90 min (2 × 45 min) plus 2 × 15 min extra in certain cup games.

Number per side – 11 (1 or 2 substitutes, depending on competition.)

Ruling body – Fédération Internationale de Football Association (FIFA)

BADMINTON

Court – 13·4 × 6·1 m (44 × 20 ft). Singles – 13·4 × 5·2 m (44 × 17 ft).

Height of net – 1·55 m (5 ft 1 in).

Weight of shuttlecock – 4·73–5·50 gm.

Scoring – best of 3 or 5 15-pt. games, men; best of 3 11-pt. games, women.

Ruling body – International Badminton Federation (IBF).

World team championships – Thomas Cup (men); Uber Cup (women).

Major individual competitions – World championships; All-England Championships.

BASEBALL

Pitching distance – 18·4 m (60 ft 6 in).

Side of 'diamond' – 27·4 m (90 ft)

Max. length of bat – 1·07 m (3 ft 6 in).

Diameter of ball 7 cm ($2\frac{3}{4}$ in).

Weight of ball – 149–156 gm (5–$5\frac{1}{4}$ oz).

Number per side – 9 (substitutes allowed).

No. of innings – 9 or more (played to finish).

BILLARDS AND SNOOKER

Table – 3·50 × 1·75 m (12 ft × 6 ft $1\frac{1}{2}$ in.)

Diameter of balls – 5·25 cm ($2\frac{1}{16}$ in.)

Billiards – red, white, spot white.

Billiards scoring – pot or in-off red 3, white 2; cannon 2.

Snooker balls (value) – black (7), pink (6), blue (5), brown (4), green (3), yellow (2), 15 reds (1 each), white (cue-ball).

Ruling body – Billiards and Snooker Control Council

Major competitions – World championships (for both snooker and billiards, professional and amateur).

CHESS

Ruling body International Chess Federation.

World Champions

1866–94	Wilhelm Steinitz (Austria)
1894–1921	Emanuel Lasker (Germany)
1921–27	Jose R. Capablanca (Cuba)
1927–35	Alexander A. Alekhine (USSR*)
1935–37	Max Euwe (Netherlands)
1937–46	Alexander A. Alekhine (USSR*)
1948–57	Mikhail Botvinnik (USSR)
1957–58	Vassily Smyslov (USSR)
1958–59	Mikhail Botvinnik (USSR)
1960–61	Mikhail Tal (USSR)
1961–63	Mikhail Botvinnick (USSR)
1963–69	Tigran Petrosian (USSR)
1969–72	Boris Spassky (USSR)
1972–75	Bobby Fischer† (USA)
1975–	Anatoli Karpov (USSR)

*Took French citizenship.
†Karpov won title when Fischer defaulted.

CRICKET

Pitch – wicket to wicket 20 m (22 yd, bowling crease 2·64 m (8 ft 8 in).

Stumps –71·1 cm (28 in) high, 22·9 cm (9 in) overall width.

Bat (max.) – 96·5 cm (38 in) long, 10·8 cm ($4\frac{1}{4}$ in) wide.

Ball – circum. 22·4–22·9 cm, ($8\frac{13}{16}$–9 in), weight 156–163 gm ($5\frac{1}{2}$–$5\frac{3}{4}$ oz).

No. per side – 11 (subs. only for fielding).

Ruling body – International Cricket Conference (ICC).

CYCLE RACING

Ruling body – Union Cycliste Internationale.

Major competitions: ROAD RACING – Tour de France, Olympic 100-km (62-mile) race.

TRACK RACING – Olympics and world championships (sprint, pursuit, 1-km time trial, motor-paced).

Other cycle sports – six-day racing, cyclo-cross, cycle speedway, bicycle polo, time trials.

Cricket records –Test matches

Highest innings – 365* G. S. Sobers, W. Indies (v Pakistan, Kingston, 1958).

Most runs in series – 974 D. G. Bradman. Australia (v England, 1930) in career – 8090 G. Boycott, England.

Most hundreds – 29 D. G. Bradman, Australia.

Best bowling in match – 19–90 J. C. Laker, England (v Australia, Old Trafford, 1956) in innings – 10–53 J. C. Laker. England (v Australia, Old Trafford, 1956).

Most wickets in series – 49 S. F. Barnes, England (v S. Africa, 1913–14) in career – 315 D. Lillie, Australia.

Highest partnership – 451 (2nd Wkt) W. H. Ponsford (266) and D. G. Bradman (244), Australia (v England, Oval, 1934)

Highest total – 903 (for 7) England (v Australia, Oval, 1938)

Most wicket-keeping dismissals in career – 290 R. W. Marsh, Australia.

Most Test appearances – 114 M. C. Cowdrey, England.

Cricket records – all matches

Highest innings – 499 Hanif Mohommad, Karachi (v Bahawalpur, 1958–59).

Most runs in season – 3816 D. C. S. Compton, England and Middlesex, 1947; in career – 61,237 J. B. Hobbs, England and Surrey.

Most hundreds in career – 197 J. B. Hobbs, England and Surrey.

Most runs in over – 36 G. S. Sobers, Notts (v Glamorgan, Swansea, 1968).

Best bowling in innings – 10–10 H. Verity, Yorks (v Notts, Leeds, 1932).

Most wickets in season – 304 A. P. Freeman, England and Kent, 1928; in career – 4187 W. Rhodes, England and Yorks.

Highest partnership – 577 (4th wkt) V. S. Hazare (288) and Gul Mahomed (319), Baroda (v Holkar, Baroda, 1947).

Highest total – 1107 (all out) Victoria (v NSW Melbourne, 1926).

Most wicket-keeping dismissals in career – 1526 J. T. Murray, England and Middlesex.

*not out

EQUESTRIAN SPORTS

Ruling body – Fédération Equestre Internationale (FEI)

Major competitions: SHOW JUMPING – world championships (men's and women's) every 4 years, alternating with Olympics; President's Cup (world team championship) based on Nations Cup results; 2-yearly European Championships (men's and women's); King George V Gold Cup; Queen Elizabeth II Gold Cup.

THREE-DAY EVENT (1 Dressage, 2 Endurance or Cross-country, 3 Show jumping) – 4-yearly world championships and Olympics; 2-yearly European Championships; Badminton Horse Trials.

DRESSAGE – Olympics and world championships.

GOLF

Ball – max. weight 46 gm (1·62 oz), min. diam. UK 4·11 cm (1·62 in), US 4·27 cm (1·68 in).

Hole – diam. 10·8 cm ($4\frac{1}{4}$ in).

No. of clubs carried – 14 maximum.

Ruling body – Royal and Ancient Golf Club of St Andrews; United States Golf Association.

Major competitions: Individual – Open, US Open, US Masters, US PGA.

Team – World Cup (international teams of 2, annual), Eisenhower Trophy (world amateur, teams of 4, 2-yearly), Ryder Cup (US v GB, 2 yearly).

GYMNASTICS

Ruling body – Fédération Internationale de Gymnastique.

Events: Men's – floor exercises, rings, parallel bars, pommel horse, vault (lengthwise), horizontal bar; overall; team; women's – floor exercises (to music), vault, asymmetrical bars, beam; overall; team.

Major competitions – World and Olympic championships, alternately every 4 years.

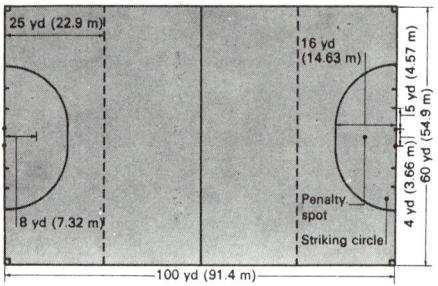

The layout of a hockey pitch

HOCKEY

Goals – 3·66 m (12 ft) wide, 2·13 m (7 ft) high.

Ball – circum. 23 cm (9 in), weight 156–163 gm ($5\frac{1}{2}$–$5\frac{3}{4}$ oz), made of cork and twine covered in leather.

Duration of game – 70 min (2 × 35).

No. per side – 11 (2 subs. in men's game).

Ruling bodies: men's – Fédération Internationale de Hockey (FIH); women's – Women's International Hockey Rules' Board.

Major competitions – Olympic Games and World Cup (4-yearly).

LACROSSE

Pitch – 100 × 54 m (110 × 60 yd) men; 110 × 64 m (120 × 70 yd) preferred for women's international matches.

Goals – 1·8 × 1·8 m (6 × 6 ft).

Olga Korbut, the Russian gymnast.

Ball – circum. 19·7–20·3 cm ($7\frac{3}{4}$–8 in), weight 141–149 gm (5–$5\frac{1}{4}$ oz men; 135–149 gm ($4\frac{3}{4}$–$5\frac{1}{4}$ oz) women.

Duration 60 min (4×15) men, 50 min (2×25) women.

No. per side – 10.

MODERN PENTATHLON

Order of events – riding, fencing, shooting, swimming, running.

Ruling body – Union Internationale de Pentathlon Moderne et Biathlon.

Major competitions – annual world championships (including Olympics).

MOTOR SPORT

Ruling body – Fédération Internationale de l'Automobile (FIA).

Major events and competitions: Formula One – World Drivers Championship (based on points gained in individual grands prix: 9, 6, 4, 3, 2, 1 for first 6.)

Sports car racing – Le Mans.

Rally driving – Monte Carlo Rally.

Other motor sports – drag racing, karting, hillclimbing, trials, autocross, rallycross, autotests, stock-car racing, vintage-car racing.

World Champions

1950 Giuseppe Farine (Italy)
1951 Juan Manuel Fangio (Argentina)
1952 Alberto Ascari (Italy)
1953 Alberto Ascari (Italy)
1954 Juan Manuel Fangio (Argentina)
1955 Juan Manuel Fangio (Argentina)
1956 Juan Manuel Fangio (Argentina)
1957 Juan Manuel Fangio (Argentina)
1958 Mike Hawthorn (England)
1959 Jack Brabham (Australia)
1960 Jack Brabham (Australia)
1961 Phil Hill (USA)
1962 Graham Hill (England)
1963 Jim Clark (Scotland)
1964 John Surtees (England)
1965 Jim Clark (Scotland)
1966 Jack Brabham (Australia)
1967 Denis Hulme (New Zealand)
1968 Graham Hill (England)
1969 Jackie Stewart (Scotland)
1970 Jochen Rindt (Austria)
1971 Jackie Stewart (Scotland)
1972 Emerson Fittipaldi (Brazil)
1973 Jackie Stewart (Scotland)
1974 Emerson Fittipaldi (Brazil)
1975 Niki Lauda (Austria)
1976 James Hunt (England)
1977 Niki Lauda (Austria)
1978 Mario Andretti (USA)
1979 Jody Scheckter (South Africa)
1980 Alan Jones (Australia)
1981 Nelson Picquet (Brazil)
1982 Keke Rosberg (Finland)
1983 Nelson Picquet (Brazil)
1984 Niki Lauda (Austria)

MOTORCYCLING SPORT

Ruling body – Fédération Internationale Motorcycliste (FIM).

Classes – 50 cc, 125 cc, 250 cc, 350 cc (junior), 500 cc (senior), 750 cc, unlimited, sidecar.

Major competitions – world championships (based on points gained in individual grands prix), including Isle of Man TT.

Other motorcycle sports – scrambling (motorcross), trials, grasstrack racing.

NETBALL

Court – $30·5 \times 15·2$ m (100×50 ft).

Net – 3·05 m (10 ft) high; ring diam. 38 cm (15 in).

Ball – as for soccer.

Duration of game – 60 min (4×15).

No. per side – 7 (subs. for injuries).

Ruling body – Internationale Federation of Netball Associations.

World championships – every 4 years.

ROWING

Ruling body –Fédération Internationale des Sociétés d'Aviron (FISA).

International events: men – eights, fours and pairs (both coxed and coxless), single, double, and quadruple sculls; women – eights, coxed fours, single, double, and quadruple sculls.

Major competitions – World championships every 4 years, alternating with Olympics; Henley Regatta (including Grand Challenge Cup and Diamond Sculls).

Standard course – men 2000 m (2187 yd), boys 1500m (1640 yd), women 1000 m (1094 yd).

RUGBY LEAGUE

Pitch (max.) – 69 m (75 yd) wide, 100 m (110 yd) between goals, 6–11 m (6–12 yd) behind goals.

Goal posts – as for rugby union.

Ball – length 27–29 cm (10½–11½ in), short circum. 58–61 cm (22¾–24 in).

Duration of game – 80 min (2 × 40).

No. per side – 13 (2 substitutes).

Scoring – TRY 3 pts., CONVERSION 2, PENALTY GOAL 2, DROPPED GOAL 2 (1 in internationals).

Ruling body – Rugby Football League International Board.

Major competition – World Cup.

RUGBY UNION

Pitch (max.) – 69 m (75 yd) wide, 100 m (110 yd) between goals, 22 m (25 yd) behind goals.

Goal posts – 5·6 m (18½ ft) wide, no height limit, crossbar 3 m (10 ft) above ground.

Ball – length 28 cm (11 in), short circum. 58–62 cm (22¾–24½ in), weight 400–440 gm (14–15½ oz).

Duration of game – 80 min (2 × 40).

No. per side – 15 (2 subs. for injury only).

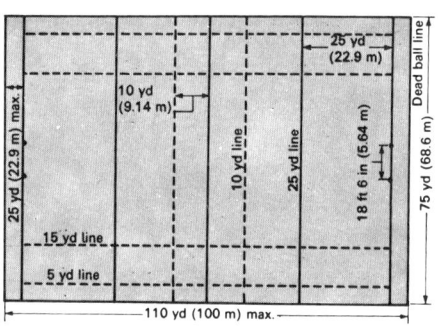

The layout of a rugby pitch

Scoring – TRY 4 pts., CONVERSION 2, PENALTY GOAL 3, DROPPED GOAL 3

Ruling body – International Rugby Football Board.

Major competitions – Five Nations Championship (England, France, Ireland, Scotland, Wales), Ranfurly Shield (New Zealand), Currie Cup (South Africa).

Touring sides – Lions (GB), All Blacks (New Zealand), Springboks (South Africa), Wallabies (Australia), Tricolors (France).

SPEEDWAY

Track – 4 laps of 274–411 m (300–450 yd), surface – red shale or granite dust.

Meeting – 20 races, 4 riders in race, each getting 5 rides.

Scoring – 1st 3 pts., 2nd 2, 3rd 1.

Machines – Brakeless 500 cc motorcycles.

Ruling body – Fédération Internationale de Motorcycliste (FIM).

Major competitions – World Championship (individual), World Team Cup, World Pairs Championship.

SQUASH

Ball – diam. 39·5–41·5 mm (1·56–1·63 in), weight 23·3–24·6 gm (0·82–0·87 oz), made of matt surface rubber.

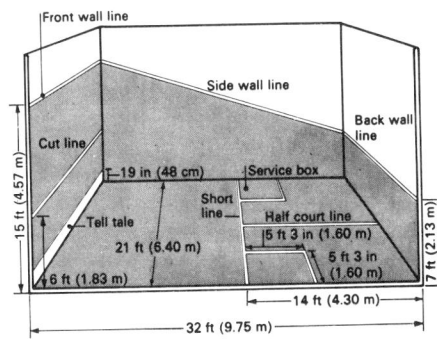

The layout of a squash court

Racket (max.) – length 68·6 cm (27 in), head 21·6 cm ($8\frac{1}{2}$ in) long by 18·4 cm ($7\frac{1}{4}$ in) wide.

Scoring – best of 5 9-up games.

Ruling body – International Squash Rackets Federation.

Major competitions – World Open, Women's Open.

SWIMMING AND DIVING

Standard Olympic pool – 50 m (54·7 yd) long, 8 lanes.

Ruling body – Fédération Internationale de Natation Amateur (FINA).

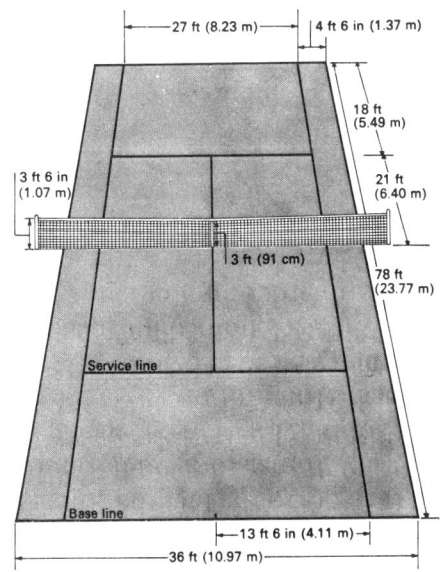

The layout of a tennis court

Competitive strokes – freestyle (usually front crawl, backstroke, breaststroke, butterfly; individual medley (butterfly, backstroke, breaststroke, freestyle), medley relay (backstroke, breaststroke, butterfly, freestyle).

Diving events – men's and women's springboard at 3 m ($9\frac{3}{4}$ ft), highboard at 10 m (33 ft) (lower boards also used).

Major competitions – Olympics and world championships.

Major long-distance swims – English Channel, Cook Strait (NZ), Atlantic City Marathon (US).

TABLE TENNIS

Table – 2·74 × 1·52 m (9 × 5 ft), 76 cm ($2\frac{1}{2}$ ft) off floor.

Net – height 15·2 cm (6 in), length 1·83 m (6 ft).

Ball – diam. 37–38 mm (1·46–1·50 in), weight 2·40–2·53 gm (0·085–0·089 oz), made of celluloid-type plastic, white or yellow.

Bat surface – max. thickness 2 mm (8·08 in) pimpled rubber or 4 mm (0·16 in) sandwich rubber.

Scoring – best of 3 or 5 21-pt games.

Ruling body – International Table Tennis Federation.

Major competitions – world championships, Swaythling Cup (men's team), Corbillion Cup (women's teams), all two-yearly.

TENNIS

Ball – diam. 6·35–6·67 cm ($2\frac{1}{2}$–$2\frac{5}{8}$ in), weight 56·7– 58·5 gm (2–$2\frac{1}{16}$ oz), made of wool-covered rubber, white or yellow.

Rackets – no limits, wood or metal frames, strung with lamb's gut or nylon.

Scoring – best of 3 or 5 6-up sets, with tiebreaker at 6–6 (or first to lead by 2);

games of 4 pts. (15, 30, 40, game), 40–40 being DEUCE and 2-pt. lead required; tiebreaker game usually first to 7 pts. with 2-pt lead.

Ruling body – International Lawn Tennis Federation (ILTF).

Major competitions – Wimbledon, Australian Open, US Open, French Open (the four constituting 'Grand Slam') Davis Cup (world team championship), Federation Cup (Women's World Cup), Wightman Cup.

WIMBLEDON CHAMPIONS (since 1946)

	men	women
1946	Yvon Petra (Fra)	Pauline Betz (US)
1947	Jack Kramer (US)	Margaret Osborne (US)
1948	Bob Falkenburg (US)	Louise Brough (US)
1949	Fred Schroeder (US)	Louise Brough (US)
1950	Budge Patty (US)	Louise Brough (US)
1951	Dick Savitt (US)	Doris Hart (US)
1952	Frank Sedgman (Aus)	Maureen Connolly (US)
1953	Victor Seixas (US)	Maureen Connolly (US)
1954	Jaroslav Drobny (Cz)	Maureen Connolly (US)
1955	Tony Trabert (US)	Louise Brough (US)
1956	Lew Hoad (Aus)	Shirley Fry (US)
1957	Lew Hoad (Aus)	Althea Gibson (US)
1958	Ashley Cooper (Aus)	Althea Gibson (US)
1959	Alex Olmedeo (Peru)	Maria Bueno (Brazil)
1960	Neale Fraser (Aus)	Maria Bueno (Brazil)
1961	Rod Laver (Aus)	Angela Mortimer (GB)
1962	Rod Laver (Aus)	Karen Susman (US)
1963	Chuck McKinley (US)	Margaret Smith (Aus)
1964	Roy Emerson (Aus)	Maria Bueno (Brazil)
1965	Roy Emerson (Aus)	Margaret Smith (Aus)
1966	Manuel Santana (Sp)	Billie Jean King (US)
1967	John Newcombe (Aus)	Billie Jean King (US)
1968	Rod Laver (Aus)	Billie Jean King (US)
1969	Rod Laver (Aus)	Ann Jones (GB)
1970	John Newcombe (Aus)	Margaret Court* (Aus)
1971	John Newcombe (Aus)	Evonne Goolagong (Aus)
1972	Stan Smith (US)	Billie Jean King (US)
1973	Jan Kodes (Cz)	Billie Jean King (US)
1974	Jimmy Connors (US)	Chris Evert (US)
1975	Arthur Ashe (US)	Billie Jean King (US)
1976	Bjorn Borg (Swed)	Chris Evert (US)
1977	Bjorn Borg (Swed)	Virginia Wade (GB)
1978	Bjorn Borg (Swed)	Martina Navratilova (Cz)
1979	Bjorn Borg (Swed)	Martina Navratilova (Cz)
1980	Bjorn Borg (Swed)	Evonne Cawley† (Aus)
1981	John McEnroe (USA)	Chris Evert-Lloyd (US)
1982	Jimmy Connors (US)	Martina Navratilova (Cz)
1983	John McEnroe (US)	Martina Navratilova (Cz)
1984	John McEnroe (US)	Martina Navratilova (Cz)

WINTER SPORTS

Skiing was once a way of travelling in Scandinavia. It is now a quickly learned sport but requires professional instruction. Basically, the skier speeds over snow on *skis* – two long, narrow wooden, plastic or metal strips with frontal points curving upwards. The skier uses a pair of sticks to support his weight in turning and other movements.

Ski-jumping is for experts. Jumpers speed down a steep slope and over a platform which they leave at about 80 km (50 miles) an hour to land perhaps 50 m (164 ft) ahead and below.

Ski-bobbing is a new sport in which skiers race over the snow on 'ski-bikes'. These have handle-bars and two short skis. The skier wears small foot-skis with clawed heels to brake.

Tobogganing (An American Indian word) is a sport for one person who lies face downwards on a toboggan that speeds down snow or ice slopes.

Bobsleighing is for two, four or five seated persons. One steers, another brakes the sleigh, which speeds along a man-made ice slope between ice walls.

Ice skating is a most graceful sport. Top skaters perform intricate 'figures' on the ice and make spectacular leaps and spins. There are championships for pairs skating, ice dancing and for singles.

234

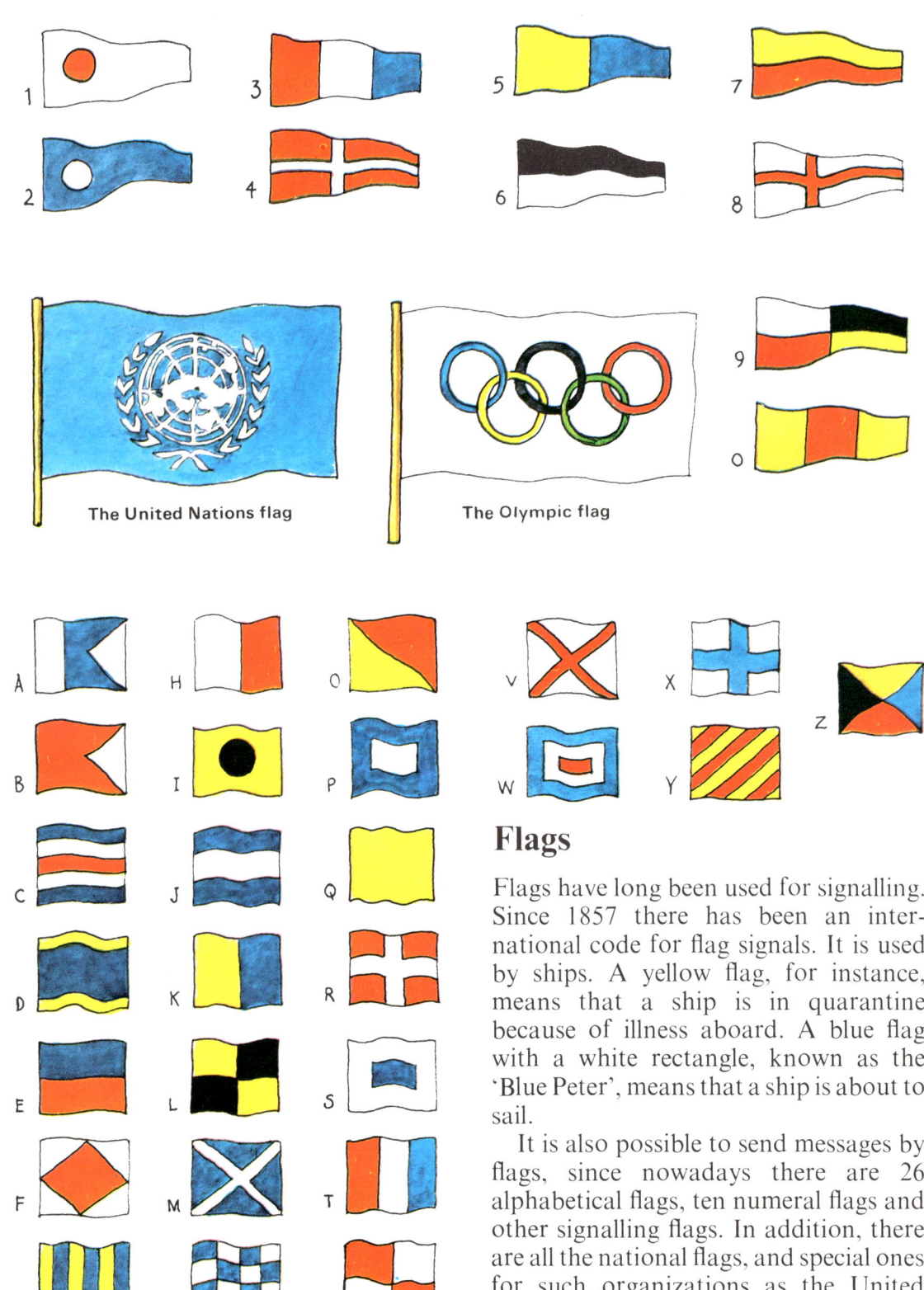

The United Nations flag

The Olympic flag

Flags

Flags have long been used for signalling. Since 1857 there has been an international code for flag signals. It is used by ships. A yellow flag, for instance, means that a ship is in quarantine because of illness aboard. A blue flag with a white rectangle, known as the 'Blue Peter', means that a ship is about to sail.

It is also possible to send messages by flags, since nowadays there are 26 alphabetical flags, ten numeral flags and other signalling flags. In addition, there are all the national flags, and special ones for such organizations as the United Nations and the Olympic Games.

236

Television

Inside a colour television camera are tinted mirrors (called dichroic mirrors), which split up the light from the scene into three colours blue, green, and red. Each of these images is then scanned separately by a special camera tube. The three signals are combined and sent along a single cable to be transmitted.

Inside a colour television receiver, the three colour components are separated out again, and each one controls the strength of an electron beam. The beams scan the screen, which is coated with minute phosphor dots, which glow blue, green, or red, and make up the full colour picture.

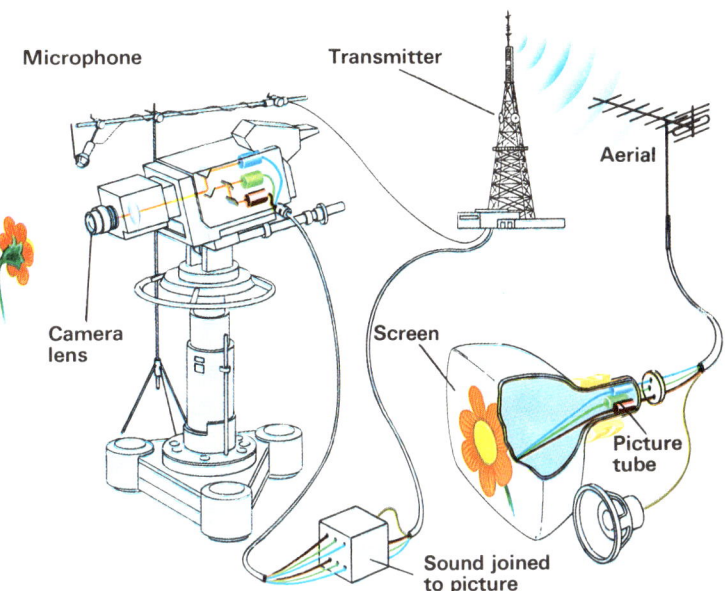

Microphone

Transmitter

Aerial

Camera lens

Screen

Picture tube

Sound joined to picture

The Telephone

The first electric telephone was made by Alexander Bell in 1876. This produced only a very weak sound over long distances, but many other types of telephones soon followed. In 1892, Ericsson designed the magneto telephone. It looked much more like the telephone we know today than Alexander Bell's first telephone.

The first telephone calls could only be sent through wires. Now a telephone call may travel by wire, or by radio, sometimes bounced off satellites. When you dial a number, the telephone sends out electrical pulses. They go to an exchange, which automatically connects you to the number you dialled.

When you speak into the mouthpiece, sound waves hit a diaphragm, making it vibrate against carbon granules. Their electrical resistance changes according to the pressure applied on them, causing a varying electric current. This current is transmitted along a telephone wire to the earpiece of another telephone. There it flows through an electromagnet attached to a diaphragm, which re-creates the original sounds. See diagram at right.

THE TELEPHONE HANDSET

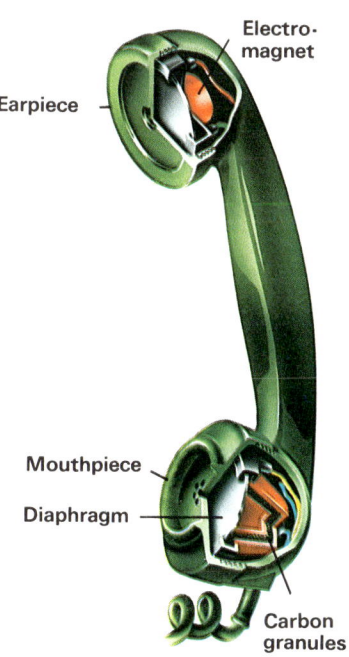

Electro-magnet

Earpiece

Mouthpiece

Diaphragm

Carbon granules

Key Dates in radio and TV

1895 Guglielmo Marconi makes a radio transmission over a range of 1 km (0·6 miles).

1897 Ferdinand Braun invents the cathode-ray tube.

1901 Marconi transmits a coded radio signal across the Atlantic Ocean.

1904 John Fleming invents the diode valve, used in radio transmitters.

1906 Reginald Fessenden makes the first speech and music transmissions.

1907 Rotating mirror scanner invented by Boris Rosing.
Lee de Forest invents the triode valve, used in radio receivers.

1908 A. A. Campbell-Swinton experiments with cathode-ray tubes as television receivers.

1915 Speech transmitted by radio across the Atlantic.

1919 Experimental broadcasting begins in Britain and the United States.

1923 Vladimir Zworykin invents the iconoscope television camera tube.

1925 BBC begins regular radio broadcasts from London.
John Logie Baird demonstrates mechanical television.

1930 First simultaneous sound-and-vision transmission by BBC.
Radio Corporation of America makes experimental transmissions.

1932 BBC begin regular transmissions.

1936 All-electric television transmissions begun by BBC.
EMI introduce their 'Emiscope' electronic television tube.

1939 Electronic television transmissions start in USA.

1940 CBS introduces first experimental colour broadcast, in New York.

1956 Colour television transmissions begin, in USA.

1957 British colour television system demonstrated.

1962 First television transmission by satellite via Telstar.

1967 Colour television transmissions begin in Britain, France, West Germany and USSR.

Radio and TV Terms

amplifier An apparatus for strengthening an electric signal.

camera tube Found in a television camera, and on which the image forms.

cathode ray tube A kind of valve used in a television set on the end of which the picture appears.

electron A very small particle in the atom, charged negatively.

electron gun The part of a cathode-ray tube which fires a stream of electrons.

frequency The number of radio waves per second.

image orthicon tube Television camera tube which converts an optical image into a varying electric current.

photo-electric cell Device that converts light into electrical impulses.

phosphor Used to coat the inside of a television tube.

radio wave Radiated waves of electromagnetic energy.

scanning Movement of a light beam or beam of electrons across a picture in a series of lines.

telecine Machine for showing cinema films on television.

video-tape recorder Machine for recording television pictures on magnetic tape.

wavelength The length of one complete radio wave.

zoom lens A camera lens which can take long-shots or close-ups on the same camera.

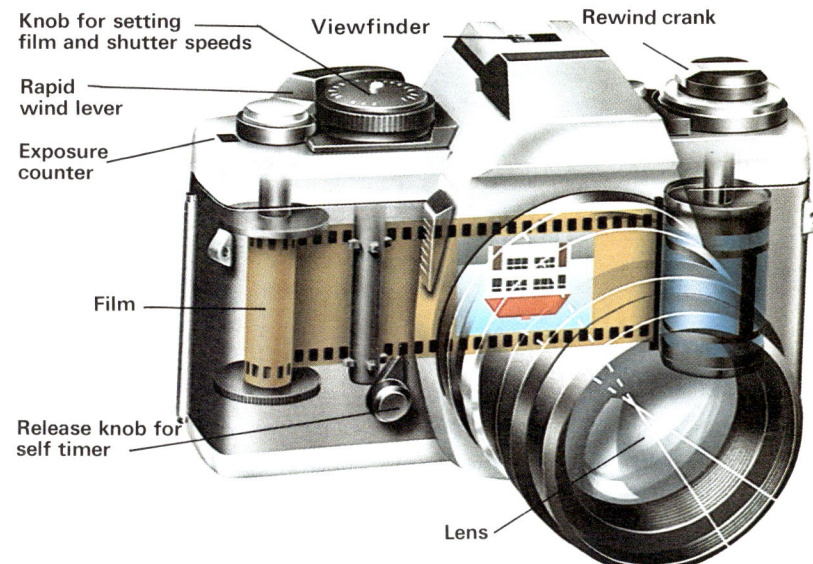

Knob for setting
film and shutter speeds

Viewfinder

Rewind crank

Rapid
wind lever

Exposure
counter

Film

Release knob for
self timer

Lens

The lens of a camera allows light to fall on to the film inside. When this happens, an upside-down image of the scene in front of the lens (in this case a house) is formed on the film.

Photography A to Z

aperture Size of the opening in the lens diaphragm. Controls light entering the camera.

developer Chemical that converts an invisible latent image into a visible form.

diaphragm The adjustable blades inside the lens which determine the aperture.

double expose Exposing the same piece of film, or photographic paper, twice.

filter Transparent material (usually glass) which is specially coated to affect the light passing through it.

fish-eye lens Extreme wide angle lens.

fixing Processing stage where the film, or print, is stabilized and no longer affected by white light.

flare Light scattered by reflections within the lens or camera.

f-number (or f-stop) Denotes size of opening of the lens aperture as marked on the lens; equivalent to focal length divided by aperture diameter.

hypo Common name for a fixing agent.

iris diaphragm Adjustable lens aperture made up of metal leaves.

negative An image made on an emulsion by exposure and development. Tones appear reversed, ie, light as dark, dark as light.

panchromatic Emulsion sensitive to all colours of the visible spectrum and to certain ultra-violet light.

plate camera Camera that uses glass photographic plates.

polarized light Rays of light that vibrate in one plane only.

rangefinder Coupled focusing system found in some 35mm cameras.

reflex camera Camera that features an internal mirror to reflect light coming in through-the-lens onto a viewing screen.

shutter Mechanical system used to control the amount of light reaching the film, thus affecting exposure.

telephoto lens A long focal length lens.

transparency A positive image made on transparent film.

tripod Camera support with extending legs and adjustable head.

viewfinder Used for viewing, and sometimes focusing on the subject.

wide-angle lens A lens with wide viewing angle. It has a focal length shorter than the diagonal of the film format in use.

zoom lens A lens with an adjustable focal length.

A mainframe computer consists of several large units – the input station, central processor, memory stores, and output units such as printers.

Computer Terms

acoustic coupler Equipment which turns computer signals into telephone signals and back again.

artificial intelligence Ways of trying to get computers to think for themselves. This technology is in its early stages.

basic *B*eginners *A*ll-purpose *S*ymbolic *I*nstruction *C*ode; simple computing language, widely adopted for home computing and in schools.

binary Microcomputers use a two-state, or binary, code to represent the ons and offs of electrical voltages.

bit The space needed for a binary 0 or 1.

byte Eight bits (usually enough space for a letter or number).

bugs Mistakes in your program.

central processing unit (CPU) The part of a computer that does all the information processing.

Compiler An automatic translator that turns programs into the micro-computer's binary code.

data The information you feed into your computer.

disk Floppy disks and hard disks can be used for storing data when your computer's main memory is full.

flowchart A useful way of breaking a problem down into the steps a computer will have to follow to solve it.

graphics Drawing pictures and diagrams.

hardware Everything you can see and touch about your microcomputer.

Input Putting things in to your micro-computer. Input devices are machines that feed information into your micro-computer.

interface If you want to connect two pieces of equipment together, they must use the same code. Another way of saying this is that the interface must match.

K An abbreviation for kilo, which means a thousand. It usually stands for kilobyte when used in connection with computers. One kilobyte equals around a thousand bytes.

keyboard The most common input unit. It looks like a typewriter, but is much quieter in operation.

lightpen This looks like a pen but has a light-sensitive tip. It can be used with a screen to draw pictures.

LSI Stands for Large Scale Integration, and is used in connection with silicon chips. It refers to the fact that there are a lot of tiny transistors built on to the surface of a chip. VLSI means Very Large Scale Integration.

main memory Needed by the CPU to deal quickly with its immediate needs. The CPU of a microcomputer can't hold on to any information without the main memory.

mega Short for million. A megabyte, for example, is a million bytes.

microelectronics The variety of products that come on silicon chips.

microprocessor A type of silicon chip built to act as a CPU.

output Getting things out of your microcomputer. Output can include words on paper, pictures on a screen, and even sound.

packages Ready-made software programs.

peripheral Any device that you can connect to your microcomputer.

printers Devices used for getting your output on to paper as words or numbers.

program Software instructions that tell a microcomputer how to solve a problem.

programmer Someone who writes computer programs.

RAM Short for Random-Access Memory. It is a type of chip used for main memories. A 1K RAM holds one kilobyte of main memory.

ROM Read-Only Memory. A ROM chip holds information, such as operating systems, which does not need to be changed.

semiconductor A material which is normally a poor conductor of electricity but, when treated, allows current to flow. Silicon is the most common semiconductor used in microelectronics.

silicon chips Tiny pieces of silicon designed to hold the electronic circuits that store and process the information passing through your microcomputer.

software The ideas and instructions that tell your microcomputer what to do. Software is built up of programs.

tape Used as a storage device with microcomputers. Information is recorded on the magnetic surface of the tape.

terminal When the keyboard and screen are together in a single unit, this is usually called a terminal.

VDU Your screen, or (short for) visual display unit.

viewdata System which connects ordinary television sets to computers via telephone lines to gain access to information.

A kitchen of the future with banks of computers running all the systems in the house. Outside a Mowbot mows the lawn following a set programme of directions.

Stamp Collecting Terms

The practice of collecting postage stamps first became popular in the early 1860s. Since then it has mushroomed into perhaps the most widespread hobby in the world.

cancellation Any mark, such as a post-mark, applied to a stamp on a letter to prevent its re-use.

A red cancellation on a block of British twopenny blues of 1840.

commemorative A stamp or set of stamps issued to celebrate an event or anniversary.

control Letters or numbers printed in the margin of a sheet of stamps to identify the printing or year of issue.

cover Envelope or wrapper.

cylinder number A control number in the margin of a sheet of stamps printed from rotary cylindrical plates. See *control* and *plate number*.

die The plate or block used for printing stamps.

embossing Printing of a stamp with the design or part of it raised.

error Stamp issued with accidental alteration from the normal, such as a missing colour or perforation. See also *variety*.

first-day cover A cover with stamp or stamps postmarked on the first day of issue.

fiscal A stamp issued for tax or revenue purposes, rather than for postage.

imperforate Having no perforation.

mint An unused stamp in perfect condition with full original gum is described as *mint*, or more properly *unmounted mint*. *Mounted mint* refers to a similar stamp but with a hinge-mark on the back where it has once been attached to the page of an album. See *unused*.

mounted mint See *mint*.

perforation The rows of holes punched in a sheet of stamps to make it easy to detach stamps from the sheet.

philately The collection and study of postage stamps. A stamp collector is a *philatelist*.

phosphor Colourless fluorescent band printed on stamps in some countries for 'recognition' by electronic sorting machines. Can be seen if stamp is held to the light almost horizontally.

plate number The number of the printing plate from which a sheet of stamps was printed. In many early stamps of Great Britain, for example, this number was engraved on the plate and appeared on the stamps.

postmark A mark stamped on mail by the postal authorities to cancel the stamp. Usually has the time, date, and place of stamping, sometimes with a design or an advertisement, or perhaps an indication of 'first day of issue'.

unmounted mint See *mint*.

unused A stamp that has not been used; in particular one with face unmarked but with perhaps some of the original gum removed. See *mint*.

variety Stamp with a minor variation from the normal printing. This usually occurs now in a particular stamp on a sheet and is found on the same stamp on each sheet printed from the same cylinder. See also *error*.

watermark A device, such as a crown or letters, formed in the paper on which stamps are printed.

Milestones in Transport

BC

c. 3500 First wheeled vehicles used in Mesopotamia.

1875 A canal built by King Sesostris in Egypt.

1800 War chariots developed by the Hittites.

312 Romans construct the Appian Way, which ran 260 km from Rome to Capua.

AD

c. 1100 Magnetic compass developed.

1400s Advent of versatile three-masted ship.

1662 First omnibus (horse-drawn), invented by Blaise Pascal (France).

1769 First steam-powered road vehicles, built by Nicolas Cugnot.

1783 First balloon ascent by Joseph and Jacques Montgolfier.

1783 First successful experiment with steamboats.

1804 Invention of the first successful steam locomotive by Richard Trevithick.

1815 Macadam paving for roads developed by John L. McAdam.

1819 First ship employing steam power crossed the Atlantic Ocean.

1822 First iron steamship.

1825 Stockton and Darlington Railway opened.

1839 First pedal-driven bicycle, invented by Kirkpatrick Macmillan (GB).

1852 First airship (France).

1862 First petrol engine made by Alphonse Beau de Rochas.

1863 First underground railway opened in London.

1869 Opening of the Suez Canal. Completion of the first trans-continental railroad in the United States.

A penny farthing from the 1880s.

A racing bicycle used today

1876 Nikolaus Otto improves the 4-stroke petrol engine.

1885 Gottlieb Daimler and Carl Benz make the first petrol engine motor cars.

1890 First electric tube.

1894 First ships driven by steam turbine.

1897 First diesel engine built.

1903 First successful powered aeroplane flight by Wilbur and Orville Wright.

1908 First Model-T Ford.

1914 Completion of Panama Canal.

1919 First non-stop transatlantic flight made by John Alcock and Arthur Brown.

1925 First diesel locomotive in regular service (US).

1930 Design for a jet aircraft patented by Frank Whittle.

1936 Prototype helicopter successfully tested.

1939 Construction and flight of the first jet aircraft by the Heinkel Company of Germany.

1949 The De Havilland *Comet* was the first commercial jet airliner to enter service.

1952 First commercial jet airliner.

1954 The submarine *Nautilus,* the world's first atomic-powered ship, launched by the US Navy.

1957 First artificial satellite in space.

1959 First hovercraft.

1961 First man in space.

1962 First nuclear-powered merchant ship.

1968 First supersonic airliner.

Dug-out canoes (above) were fairly easy to paddle. Log rafts were usually pushed along with the aid of a long pole.

Egyptian ships had no keel and were kept rigid by a hogging line tied tightly from bow to stern. The ship was steered by oars.

Sailing Terms

aft Towards the rear of a vessel.
amidships Near the centre of a vessel.
barque Sailing vessel with three or more masts, all but the last square-rigged; the third mast is rigged fore-and-aft.
beam Width of vessel's hull.
bow The front of a vessel.
bowsprit Long projection from the bow that supports rigging and possibly a jib or spritsail.
crow's nest Look out position near the top of a mast.
deck The planked or plated-over 'floor' across a ship's hull. A small vessel has only one deck.
displacement Weight of water (generally expressed in tonnes) displaced by a floating vessel.
draught Amount of a ship's hull below the waterline, i.e. the minimum depth of water in which a vessel will float.
fo'c'sle (forecastle) Raised deck at the front of a vessel.
fore (or for'ard) Towards the front of a vessel.
foremast Mast at the front of a vessel.
foresail Lowermost sail on foremast.
jib Triangular sail between the foremast and the bowsprit.

keel The main structural member running lengthwise along the bottom of a ship's hull.
knot Unit of speed for boats and ships. One knot equals 1 nautical mile per hour.
lateen A triangular sail suspended from a sloping yard attached to a mast.
mainmast Mast second from the front; the middle mast on a three-masted vessel.
mainsail Lowermost sail on mainmast.
mizzen Lateen sail on mizzen mast.
mizzen mast Third mast towards the rear of a vessel.

A paddle steamer (below) of the 1800s. Early steamships had sails as well as engines, because they could not carry enough coal.

A carrack of the 1400s still had the raised stern and forecastle originally used as fighting platforms.

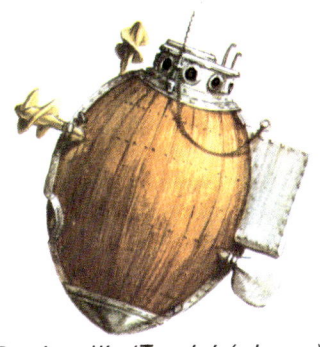

David Bushnell's 'Turtle' (above) was the first military submarine. In 1776 the tiny screw-propelled one-man craft tried to sink a British warship by screwing explosive charges into the wooden hull.

overall length Length of a vessel's hull.
poop Raised deck towards the stern of a vessel.
rudder Vertical control surface in the water at the rear of a vessel, by means of which it is steered.
royal Sail above the topgallant.
schooner Two-masted sailing vessel with mainly fore-and-aft sails.
sheet Rope or cable attached to the end of a yard for controlling the angle of the sail to the mast.
spanker Fore-and-aft sail on rearmost mast.

spritsail Square sail on yard suspended from the bowsprit.
stay Thick cable sloping down from a mast, generally to the base of the mast in front of it.
staysail Triangular sail between two masts.
stern The rear of a vessel.
topgallant Sail above the topsail.
topsail Sail above the foresail or mainsail, etc.
yard Length of timber, generally horizontal and pivoted to a mast, from which a sail is suspended.

Right: The hovercraft's flexible 'skirt' traps compressed air beneath the hull and increases the lift. The SRN4 ferry can travel over land or water, at speeds of up to 60 knots.

Below: The 'United States' (1952) was the last holder of the Blue Riband for trans-Atlantic liners.

Famous Voyages

1487 Bartolomeu Diaz (*c.* 1457–1500) sailed from Portugal and discovered the Cape of Good Hope after rounding southern Africa and entering the Indian Ocean.

1492 Christopher Columbus (1451–1506) set sail from Portugal with three small ships – the *Santa Maria, Pinta,* and *Niña* – to seek a westward passage to the Indies. Instead, after more than six months, he reached North America, landing at San Salvador, in the Bahamas.

1497 Vasco da Gama (*c.* 1469–1524) set sail from Portugal, rounded the Cape of Good Hope at the tip of Africa, and sailed across the Indian Ocean to Calicut in India.

1642 Abel Tasman (1603–59) sailed southwards from Java and discovered Tasmania and New Zealand.

1768 Captain James Cook (1728–79) travelled southwards, round Cape Horn at the tip of South America, and across the Pacific Ocean to New Zealand. He arrived home three years later after crossing the Indian Ocean and sailing round the Cape of Good Hope. On his second voyage (1772) he discovered South Georgia island in Antarctica. His third voyage (1776–79) took him eastwards around the Cape of Good Hope and back to New Zealand. He carried on across the Pacific Ocean and discovered Hawaii.

1831 Charles Darwin (1809–82) sailed as a naturalist on HMS *Beagle* on a five-year voyage to study the plants and animals of South America and various Pacific islands. As a result of his observations, he wrote the famous book *On the Origin of Species* (1859).

1947 Thor Heyerdahl (born 1914) sailed a balsa-wood raft, the *Kon-Tiki,* from Peru in South America across the Pacific Ocean to the Tuamotu Islands in Polynesia, so providing evidence that some Polynesians may be descended from South American Indians.

1966 Sir Francis Chichester (1901–72) sailed his 16-metre (32½ ft) ketch *Gypsy Moth IV* single-handed, at the age of 64, from Plymouth eastwards and completely round the world – in 226 days.

Notable Disasters

AT SEA

Birkenhead (1852), British troopship, ran aground off Port Elizabeth (S Africa) and broke in two on rocks; 455 perished, 193 survived.

Sultana (1865), Mississippi river steamer, blew up (boiler explosion); 1450 died.

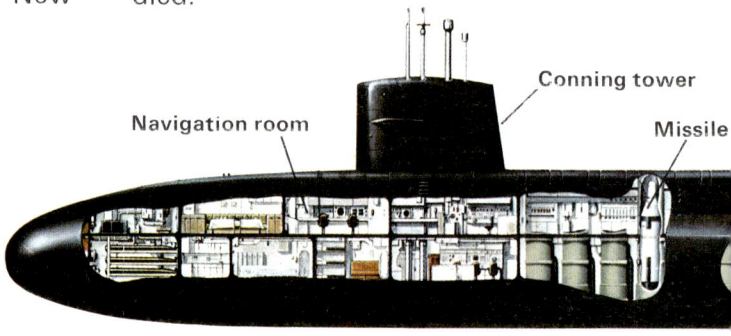

This cutaway drawing of a nuclear submarine shows the navigation room beneath the conning tower and the nuclear reactor and steam turbine engine in the stern.

Navigation room Conning tower Missile

Mary Celeste (1872), American half-brig, found abandoned in Atlantic with no sign of life; great mystery of the sea.

General Slocum (1904), an excursion steamer, burned in New York harbour; 1021 died.

Titanic (1912), British liner, struck iceberg in N Atlantic; about 1500 died, 705 survived.

Empress of Ireland (1914), Canadian steamer, sank after collision in St Lawrence River; 1024 died.

Lusitania (1915), British liner, torpedoed by German submarine off Ireland; 1198 died.

Thetis (1939), British submarine, sank in Liverpool Bay; 99 perished.

Curacao (1942), British cruiser, sank after collision with liner Queen Mary; 335 died.

Wilhelm Gustloff (1945), German liner, torpedoed by Russian submarine off Danzig; about 700 died.

Truculent (1950), British submarine, sank in Thames Estuary after collision with tanker; 64 died.

Affray (1951), British submarine, sank in English Channel; 75 died.

Toya Maru (1954), Japanese ferry, sank in Tsugaru Strait; 1172 died.

Andrea Doria (1956), Italian liner, collided with Swedish liner Stockholm off Nantucket (NY) in fog, 51 died, about 1,655 rescued.

Thresher (1963), American nuclear submarine, sank in N Atlantic; 129 died.

TRAINS

1876 Dec. 29: Passenger train derailed as iron bridge collapsed in snowstorm, Ashtabula River, Ohio, USA; 91 died.

1879 Dec. 28: Tay Bridge, Dundee, Scotland, blown down, taking passenger train with it; 73 drowned.

1881 June 2: Train fell into river near Cuartla, Mexico; about 200 died.

1915 May 22: Two passenger trains and troop train collided at Quintins Hill, Dumfriesshire, Scotland; 227 died.

1917 Dec. 12: Troop train derailed near mouth of Mt Cenis tunnel, Modane, France; 543 died.

1944 Jan. 16: Train wrecked inside tunnel, Leon Province, Spain; 500–800 died.

1944 Mar. 2: Train stalled in tunnel near Salerno, Italy; 521 suffocated.

1953 Dec. 24: Wellington-Auckland express plunged into stream near Waiouru, New Zealand; 155 died.

1955 Apr. 3: Train plunged into canyon near Guadalajara, Mexico; about 300 died.

1957 Sept 1: Train plunged into ravine near Kendal, Jamaica; about 175 died.

1957 Sept. 29: Express train crashed into stationary oil train near Montgomery, W. Pakistan; 300 died.

1962 May 3: Three trains collided in Tokyo; 163 died.

1963 Nov. 9: Two passenger trains hurtled into derailed freight train near Yokohama, Japan; over 160 died.

1970 Feb. 4: Express train crashed into stationary commuter train near Buenos Aires, Argentina; 236 died.

1970 Feb 16: Train crashed in northern Nigeria; about 150 killed in crash and another 52 injured survivors killed in road crash on way to hospital.

1972 Oct 6: Train carrying religious pilgrims derailed and caught fire near Saltillo, Mexico; 204 died.

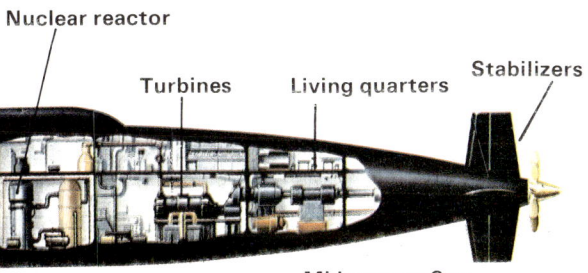

Nuclear reactor
Turbines
Living quarters
Stabilizers
Midsummer Sun

Track Terms

APT Advanced Passenger Train.

arrester Trackside device to slow or stop shunted vehicles.

brake van Van manned by a guard and containing a screw brake, marshalled at the rear of a goods train.

buffers Sprung metal 'studs' at the ends of a vehicle to absorb the shocks of minor collisions in shunting.

bufferstop Set of buffers mounted at the end of a length of track.

chair U-shaped metal casting that holds rail to sleepers.

connecting rod Metal rod joining the driving wheels of a locomotive.

coupling Hooking device for joining railway vehicles to a train.

double-heading Using two locomotives to pull one train.

fishplate Metal plate used to join rails end to end.

footplate Part of locomotive on which the crew work.

frog X-shaped casting that allows rails to 'cross' at points.

gauge Width of track, measured between the inside edges of the rails.

goods train Train of vans or wagons for carrying freight.

hump shunting Using a downgrade after a hump in the track to move railway vehicles.

light engine Locomotive travelling without pulling a train.

loading gauge Maximum permitted height of a railway vehicle.

marshalling Sorting vehicles into the correct order for a train.

permanent way Railway track.

points Special part of the track laid where trains need to switch from one set of rails to another.

shoe Steel collector on electric train for collecting electricity from a third rail.

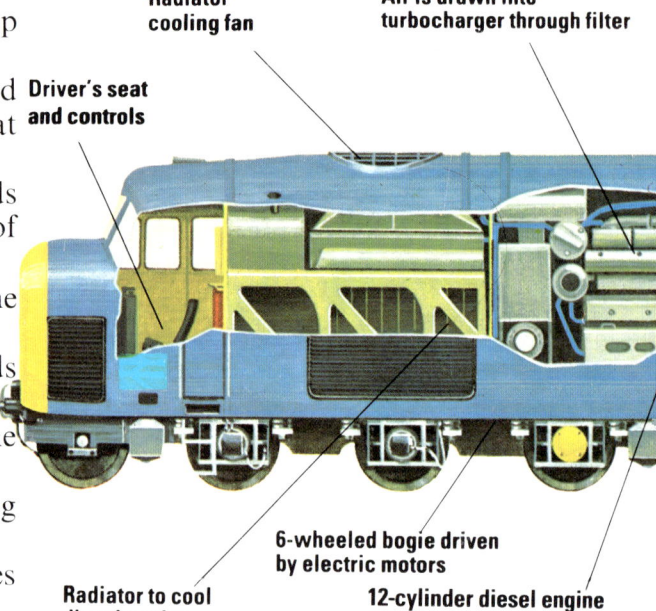

Radiator cooling fan

Air is drawn into turbocharger through filter

Driver's seat and controls

6-wheeled bogie driven by electric motors

Radiator to cool diesel engine

12-cylinder diesel engine drives electric generator

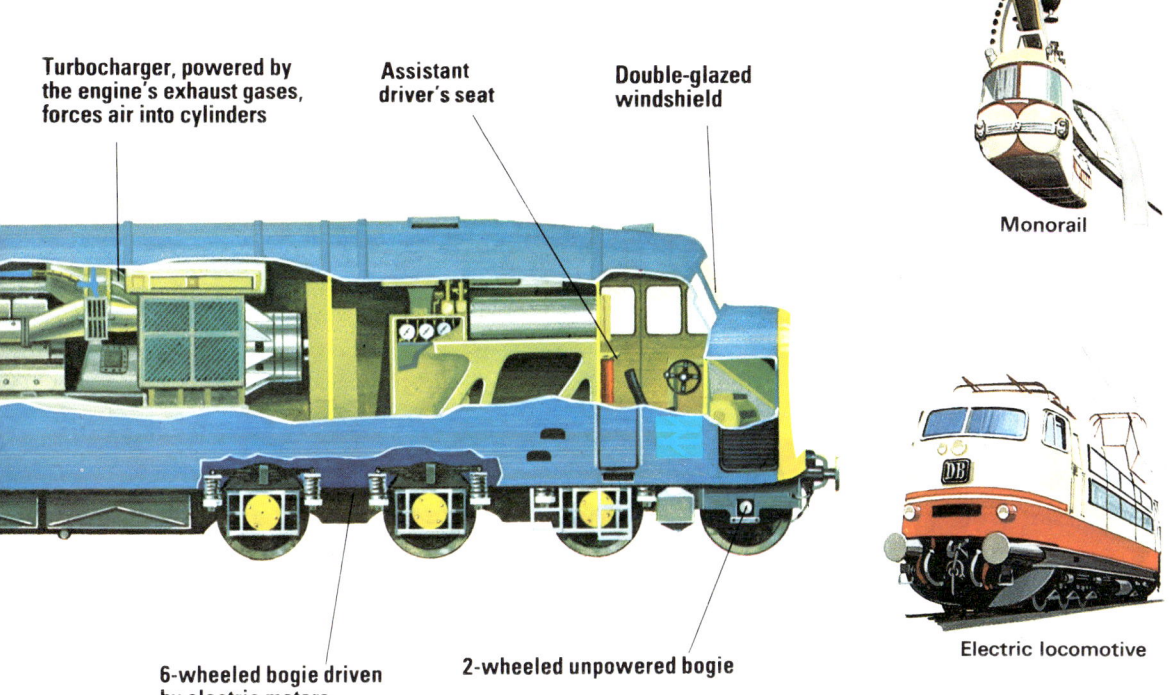

Turbocharger, powered by the engine's exhaust gases, forces air into cylinders

Assistant driver's seat

Double-glazed windshield

Monorail

Electric locomotive

6-wheeled bogie driven by electric motors

2-wheeled unpowered bogie

Steam locomotive

Diesel locomotive

shunting Pushing uncoupled vehicles along the track.

siding Branch track for holding stationary vehicles.

sleeper Wood or concrete tie across and beneath the rails to form the track.

tender Container for coal and water drawn by a steam locomotive.

vacuum brake Type of railway vehicle brake held *off* by low air pressure (vacuum).

welded rail Rail made continuous by welding together shorter lengths.

The Canadian Pacific Railway

When the west coast province of British Columbia became part of Canada in 1871, a trans-continental railroad was promised. It was no easy task to span vast rocky wastes and empty prairie and to climb the mighty Rocky Mountains, and money kept running out. The final spike was not hammered in until 7 November 1885. Today's CPR, with 27,500 km (17,000 miles) of track, its ships and airlines, is the world's largest transport system.

249

TRANSPORT AND COMMUNICATION

Railway Dates

1801 Richard Trevithick (GB) makes full-size steam-carriage.

1803 First public freight railway: Surrey Iron Railway, engineered by William Jessop and James Outram (GB).

1804 Trevithick constructs locomotive to haul 10-tonne load from Pen-y-darran to Glamorganshire Canal.

1805 World's first passenger railway service opened in Surrey with horse-drawn carriages.

1812 World's first steam railway began at the Middleton colliery, Yorkshire, using locomotives on a racked rail designed by John Blenkinsop.

1813 William Hedley (GB) builds two smooth-wheeled engines, *Puffing Billy* and *Wylam Billy*.

1814 First locomotive, *Blücher*, designed by George Stephenson began work at the Killingworth colliery near Newcastle upon Tyne.

1825 Opening of Stockton & Darlington Railway (27 Sept.) first regularly operated steam railway in world.

1829 Stephensons' *Rocket* impressively wins Rainhill Trials, Liverpool.

1829 First steam locomotive in America, British-built *Stourbridge Lion*, ran at Honesdale, Pennsylvania.

1830 Opening of Liverpool & Manchester Railway (15 Sept.), first regular public passenger service. South Carolina Railroad opened, first in United States.

1837 First sleeping car came into operation, in Pennsylvania (USA).

1863 First dining cars, between Baltimore and Philadelphia (USA).

1863 Opening of world's first underground railway, in London.

1867 First elevated railway, experimental overhead track in Manhattan, New York.

1869 Completion of Pacific Railroad, coast-to-coast across United States.

1879 First electric railway opened, 274-m (300-yd) electric tramway, in Berlin.

1883 Orient Express (Paris-Vienna-Istanbul) comes into operation.

1885 Canadian Pacific line completed.

1890 First tube railway, in London.

1893 World's first 100 mph run, by *Locomotive 999*, Grimesville, NY.

1893 First electric traction overhead railway, along Mersey shore, Liverpool.

1895 First main-line electrification, in tunnel under Baltimore, USA.

1925 First diesel-electric locomotive tried out, in Canada.

1932 German State Railways introduce the diesel-electric *Flying Hamburger*.

1948 First gas-turbine electric locomotive tested.

1955 World's first 200 mph run, achieved by French locomotive: 330 km/h (205 mph).

1966 Japanese National Railways open New Tokaido Line: with average speed of 163 km/h (101 mph).

1974 World rail speed record of 410 km/h (254·70 mph) set up on 14 August over 9·97 km (6·2 miles) of test track in Colorado by US Federal Railroad.

1976 British Rail inaugurate their daily High Speed Train services. It covers 151·2 km (94 miles) in 50 minutes 31 seconds.

An aerial cableway view of Alpine scenery. The car hangs from a trolley which runs on grooved wheels along the upper cable.

● The world's largest station is Grand Central Terminal, New York. It has 44 platforms, 67 tracks, covers an area of 19 hectares (48 acres) and is used by over 180,000 people and 550 trains daily. It was built between 1903 and 1913.

● The station with the longest name was *Llanfairpwllgwyngyllgogerych wyrndrobwllllantysiliogogogoch* in North Wales. The name means 'Mary's church by the white hazel pool near the fierce whirlpool with the church of Tysilio by the red cave'.

The Trans-Siberian Railway

Most of this 9300 km (5800 mile) line was built between 1891 and 1899 across frozen wastes and in sub-zero temperatures. By 1901, rail travel from Moscow to Vladivostok on the Sea of Japan was broken only by the ferry trip across Lake Baikal. A line skirting the lake along its mountainous shore, one of the world's great engineering feats, was completed in 1916. Nowadays, the journey takes nine days, including 5200 km (3230 miles) of electrified line, the longest stretch in the world. In bad weather before the railway opened, it had been known to take travellers two years.

Motor-Car Terms

accelerator Pedal that regulates engine speed by controlling the flow of fuel.

accumulator Battery that can be recharged.

air-cooled engine Engine cooled by air drawn into the engine compartment by a fan and directed over the cylinders.

alternator Electric generator producing alternating current.

battery Group of two or more cells connected together for storing electricity.

big end Larger end of a connecting rod, attached to the crankshaft.

brake Mechanism that slows down or stops a car by means of friction applied at the wheels.

chassis Steel framework 'foundation' of a car.

choke Means of enriching the petrol/air mixture going to the cylinder. It is needed for cold starting.

clutch Device for disconnecting the drive from the engine to the gear-box.

coil Device for stepping up the low-voltage current supplied by the battery to the high-voltage current necessary to produce sparks at the sparking plugs.

combustion Burning of the petrol/air mixture in the cylinders thus releasing power.

combustion chamber Space in the internal combustion engine where combustion takes place. It may be in the cylinder head or in the top of the piston.

compression Reducing the volume of a gas in order to increase its pressure. During the compression stroke, the piston compresses the petrol/air mixture.

crankshaft Shaft that is turned by the connecting rods from the pistons. The up-and-down motion of the pistons is converted into rotary motion.

cylinder Broad tube in the engine in which each piston moves up and down.

dipstick Rod for measuring the amount of oil in the sump or gear-box.

This drawing is not of any particular make, but it shows all the more important parts that you will find on almost any modern car.

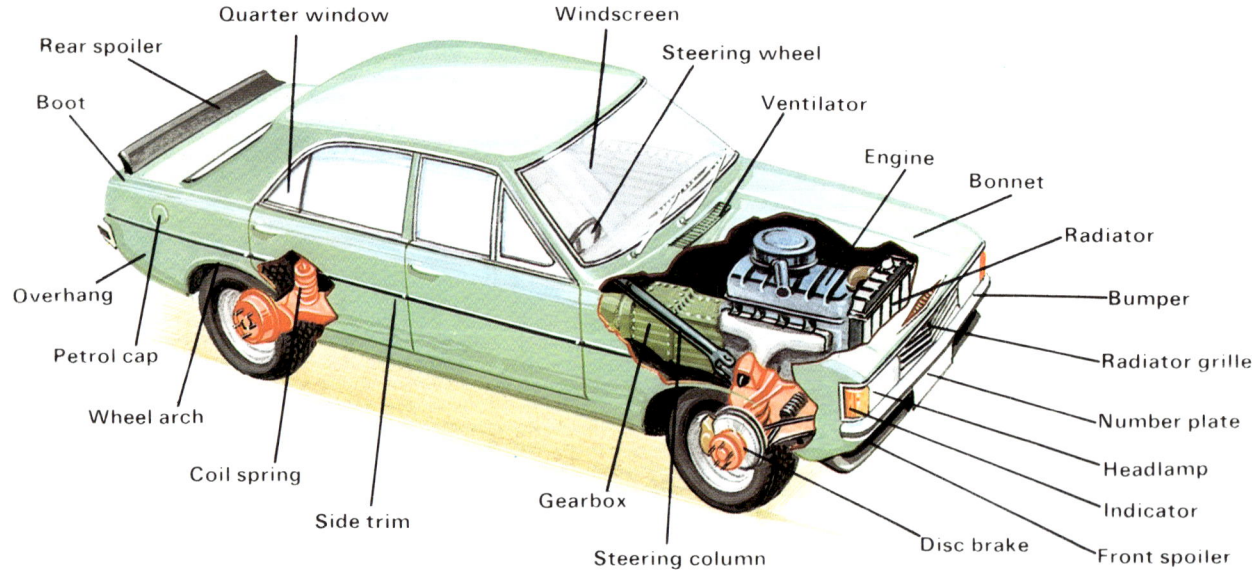

disc brakes Brakes operated by friction pads pressing against a metal disc that revolves with the wheel.

distributor Unit that distributes high-voltage current from the coil to each of the sparking plugs in turn.

drum brakes Brakes operated by lined brake shoes pressing against a drum that revolves with the wheel.

dynamo Generator that produces direct current.

exhaust system Pipes and silencers that carry exhaust gases away from the engine.

fan belt Belt that drives the cooling fan from a pulley on the crankshaft.

four-stroke cycle Operating cycle of the internal combustion engine. The strokes (up or down movements of the piston) are induction, compression, power and exhaust. See page 254.

gear-box Grouping of gears that transmits power from the engine to the propeller shaft, making it possible to change the ratio between speed and torque.

horsepower Unit of measurement for an engine's power output.

idling Way the engine runs when no pressure is being applied to the accelerator.

ignition Firing of the petrol/air mixture in the combustion chambers of the engine.

independent suspension System in which each wheel has its own suspension.

induction First stroke in the 4-stroke cycle, when the inlet valve opens and the piston descends drawing the petrol/air mixture into the cylinder.

internal combustion Engine in which power produced by the combustion engine of fuel is converted into movement. See page 254.

radial-ply tyre Tyre in which the cords or the piles are at right angles to the direction of travel. Strengthening bands of fabric circle the tyre under the tread.

radiator Device for cooling the water in the car's cooling system. Hot water from the engine jacket circulates through thin-walled tubes in the radiator, and loses heat to the air rushing through.

silencer Unit in the exhaust system that reduces the noise made by exhaust gases by decreasing their energy.

spark plug Device that, using high-voltage current from the distributor, generates a spark to ignite the petrol/air mixture in the cylinder.

speedometer Instrument that indicates a vehicle's speed. It is usually operated by a cable from a road wheel or from the output shaft of the gear-box.

steering column Metal supporting tube inside which steering shaft rotates.

sump Oil reservoir at the bottom of the crankcase. The oil lubricates the engine. A dipstick is used to measure the oil level.

suspension System, usually based on springs, that minimizes the effect of road irregularities on the way a car rides.

synchromesh Device for preventing gear crashing. It synchronizes the speeds of the required two gear wheels before they engage with each other.

tachometer or rev. counter. Instrument for indicating engine speed by recording the rate at which the camshaft rotates.

torque The effort or power exerted by anything that revolves. An engine's power is essentially torque.

two-stroke cycle Engine operating cycle in which each second stroke is a power stroke.

valve Device that allows the flow of a gas or a liquid. In the engine cylinders, valves allow the induction of the petrol/air mixture and the exhaust of the burnt gases.

water pump This speeds up the flow of water through the engine cooling system.

Motor-Car Firsts and feats

● The world's first traffic lights were set up in Detroit (USA) in 1919. Britain's three-colour traffic-lights were first used in 1928.

● The first car fitted with a reversing light was a Wills Sainte Claire (USA), in 1921.

● In 1924 the world's first motorway was opened. It ran from Milan to Varese in Italy. Germany's first (1935) was from Damstadt to Frankfurt. America's first dual-carriageway turnpike (the Pennsylvania Turnpike) opened in 1940, and Britain's first motorway (the Preston Bypass) opened in 1958.

● Russia made her first private car, the Nami 1, in 1926. 'The People's Car', China's first, appeared in 1951.

● The first car heaters fed from the cooling system were introduced in the USA in 1926. Pioneers of the early days had 'Motor Hot Water Bottles' which were upholstered to match the car – except for owners of German Daimlers (built between 1897 and 1900), who had foot-warmers run from the cooling system.

● White lines running down the middle of the road were first used in Britain, in 1927.

● The world's first production car with a synchromesh gearbox was a 1929 Cadillac. Vauxhall and Rolls Royce followed in Britain in 1932.

● The first parking meter appeared in 1935 (in Oklahoma City, USA); and in the same year the first factory-fitted windscreen washers (on a Triumph). It was also the year of the world's longest marathon car run. Driving 19 hours every day from 23 June 1935 to 22 July 1936, Francois Lecot covered 402,336 kilometres (250,000 miles) at an average speed of 64 km/h (40 mph).

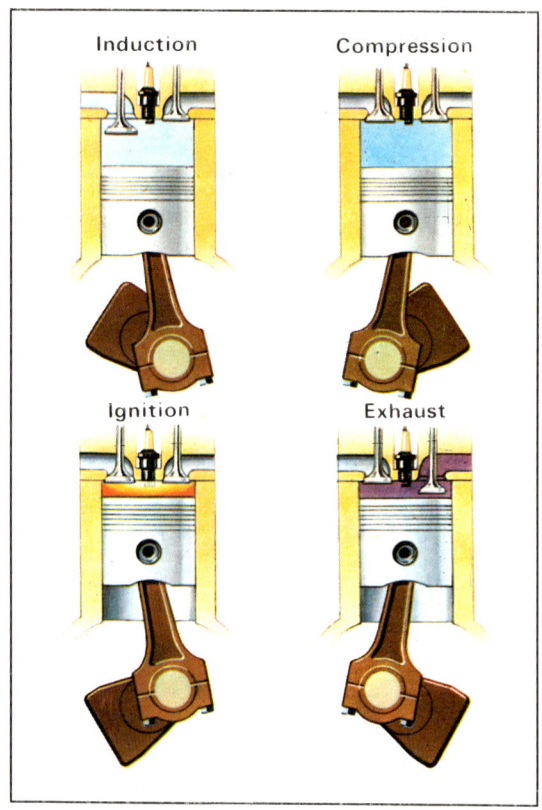

The cylinder action of a petrol internal combustion engine. Induction: *The piston moves downwards and the petrol/air mixture is drawn into the cylinder.* Compression: *The piston rises, compressing the mixture.* Ignition: *The sparking plug sparks, igniting the compressed mixture. The gases produced force the piston downwards.* Exhaust: *As the piston moves upwards again the burnt gases are forced out.*

Dates in Car History

1901 A car with front-wheel drive, the Korn & Latil Voiturette, is built in France.
A car fitted with a speedometer is made in London.

1902 The Belgian-made Dechamps car is built with a standard electric self-starter.

Engine Layouts

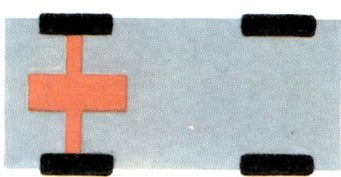
Front-wheel drive and front in-line engine.

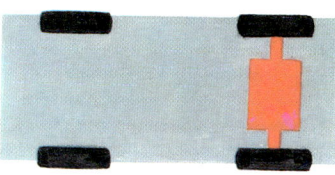
Rear-wheel drive and rear engine. A short bonnet so you can see forward, but handling can be tricky.

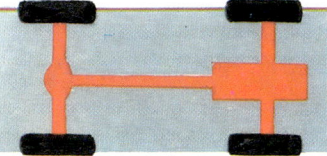
Four-wheel drive gives the car a good grip on rough ground, but it has to have drive shafts going forward and back.

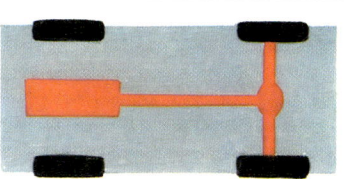
Rear-wheel drive and front engine. Easy to work on, but the drive shaft sticks up inside the car.

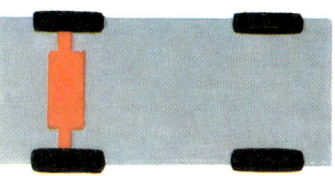
Front-wheel drive and front transverse engine.

A 9 hp Napier car is built in London with an all-metal body.

A Pan-American motor-car is built in the United States with a silencer.

1904 The first car to travel at over 100 mph (160 km/h) runs at Ostend, Belgium, driven by Louis Rignolly.

1916 The first automatic windscreen wipers are fitted to a Willys Knight car in the USA.

1919 The first servo-assisted four-wheel brakes are fitted to the H6 Hispano-Suiza.

1920 The Duesenberg Model A car is built with hydraulic brakes in the USA.

1926 Safety-glass windscreens are fitted as standard to Stutz and Rickenbacker cars in the USA.
Power-steering is fitted to a Pierce Arrow car in the USA.

1950 The first gas-turbine private car is built in Britain for a Rover two-seater.

1967 The rotary Wankel-engined car is built in Germany.

Car Shapes

Notchback

Fastback

Estate

Hatchback

Convertible

These are the most common shapes of car. Family cars can be notchbacks, fastbacks, hatchbacks, or estates.

Badges and Mascots

Badges and mascots are not as common as they used to be. Radiator grilles are smaller, and mascots standing on top of bonnets can cause injury in an accident. Car makers do not always put a badge on every model they build, and sometimes there are special badges for special models. Here are some of the better known badges which you will find on almost every car of their make with some of the history of each.

Alfa Romeo
The serpent comes from the arms of Milan, the Italian city where the cars are made. This badge has been used for over fifty years.

Cadillac
The heraldic Cadillac badge is one of the best known of all automobile insignias. The heyday of the giant 16-cylinder models was in the early 1930s.

Fiat
This laurel wreath badge is used on their sports cars, in memory of their successful Grand Prix racing team of the 1920s.

Ford
The Ford script has always been used on their cars, though the blue background dates from 1927. Older Fords have the script on their radiators.

Peugeot
The lion, which used to be on an enamelled radiator badge, comes from the arms of the Peugeot family's home city, Belfort in France.

Renault
This diamond badge has been used since 1924: before, Renaults had their name on a round badge at the front.

Rolls-Royce
The entwined Rs spell the names of the make's two founders. The letters have been black instead of red since 1933.

Aston Martin
Another one that's been used for many years – the maker's initials with wings attached, a favourite shape on cars.

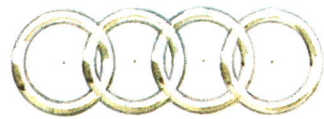

Audi
The four rings stand for the four companies (Audi, DKW, Horch and Wanderer) that originally made up the Auto Union company.

Chevrolet
The Chevrolet badge is probably the best known of all automobile insignias. Chevrolet has long been known as the world's best-selling automobile.

Lancia
The name 'Lancia' means a lance in Italian. The badge is made up of a flag, a lance, and the steering wheel of a car.

M.G.
This eight-sided badge with brown letters on a cream background was first used on M.G. radiators as long ago as 1927.

Mercedes-Benz
The three-pointed 'rising star' was the house emblem of Gottlieb Daimler, whose Mercedes company merged with Benz in 1926.

Vauxhall
The griffin is from the arms of Fulk Le Bréant, Norman lord of the manor of Vauxhall in London, where the cars were first made.

Volkswagen
The initial letters of a name which means 'people's car' in German. The first VW was designed to a German government order.

Volvo
Like the bar across the grille, the badge is a symbol for iron, for which Sweden, where the car comes from, is famous.

Motor Cars: International Identification Letters

A	Austria	GCA	Guatemala	RC	Taiwan
ADN	Yemen PDR	GH	Ghana	RCA	Central African R.
AFG	Afghanistan	GR	Greece	RCB	Congo
AL	Albania	GUY	Guyana	RCH	Chile
AND	Andorra	H	Hungary	RH	Haiti
AUS	Australia	HK	Hong Kong	RI	Indonesia
B	Belgium	HKJ	Jordan	RIM	Mauritania
BD	Bangladesh	I	Italy	RL	Lebanon
BDS	Barbados	IL	Israel	RM	Malagasy Rep.
BG	Bulgaria	IND	India	RMM	Mali
BH	Belize	IR	Iran	RO	Romania
BR	Brazil	IRL	Ireland,	ROK	South Korea
BRN	Bahrain		Republic of	ROU	Uruguay
BRU	Brunei	IRQ	Iraq	RP	Philippines
BS	Bahamas	IS	Iceland	RSM	San Marino
BUR	Burma	J	Japan	RU	Burundi
C	Cuba	JA	Jamaica	RWA	Rwanda
CDN	Canada	K	Kampuchea	S	Sweden
CH	Switzerland	KWT	Kuwait	SCV	Vatican
CI	Ivory Coast	L	Luxembourg	SD	Swaziland
CL	Sri Lanka	LAO	Laos	SF	Finland
CO	Colombia	LAR	Libya	SGP	Singapore
CR	Costa Rica	LB	Liberia	SME	Surinam
CS	Czechoslovakia	LS	Lesotho	SN	Senegal
CY	Cyprus	M	Malta	SU	USSR
D	West Germany	MA	Morocco	SY	Seychelles
DDR	East Germany	MAL	Malaysia	SYR	Syria
DK	Denmark	MC	Monaco	T	Thailand
DOM	Dominican Rep.	MEX	Mexico	TG	Togo
DY	Benin	MS	Mauritius	TN	Tunisia
DZ	Algeria	MW	Malawi	TR	Turkey
E	Spain	N	Norway	TT	Trinidad and
EAK	Kenya	NA	Netherlands		Tobago
EAT	Tanzania		Antilles	USA	United States
EAU	Uganda	NIC	Nicaragua	VN	Vietnam
EC	Ecuador	NIG	Niger	WAG	Gambia
ES	El Salvador	NL	Netherlands	WAL	Sierra Leone
ET	Egypt	NZ	New Zealand	WAN	Nigeria
F	France	P	Portugal	WD	Dominica
FJI	Fiji	PA	Panama	WL	St Lucia
FL	Liechtenstein	PAK	Pakistan	WS	Western Samoa
FR	Faroe Islands	PE	Peru	WV	St Vincent
GB	Great Britain	PL	Poland	YU	Yugoslavia
GBA	Alderney C. I.	PNG	Papua	YV	Venezuela
GBG	Guernsey C. I.		New Guinea	Z	Zambia
GBJ	Jersey C. I.	PY	Paraguay	ZA	South Africa
GBM	Isle of Man	RA	Argentina	ZRE	Zaire
GBZ	Gibraltar	RB	Botswana	ZW	Zimbabwe

1770 Cugnot

1886 Daimler

1899 Renault

1910 Model T Ford

1935 Hispano Suiza

1961 E Type Jaguar

1981 Mini Metro

The Story of Cars and Motorcycles

Two German engineers, Karl Benz and Gottlieb Daimler, built the first cars in 1885 and 1886. These had a petrol engine, like most modern cars. Later, some cars like Cugnot's, were built with steam engines; others were driven by electricity from batteries. But in the end the petrol engine proved to be the most successful.

At first, cars were hand-made and expensive. It was not until 1908 that they began to be made cheaply. In that year Henry Ford started to mass produce his Model T, called the 'Tin Lizzie'. It marked the beginning of the modern car industry, which now produces over 25 million cars a year throughout the world.

A modern car is a collection of 10,000 or more separate parts. These parts make up several basic units: the body, the engine and the transmission are the main units.

The first motorcycles were built at the end of the 1800s when men such as Edward Butler, an Englishman, and Gottlieb Daimler, a German, began making powered bicycles and tricycles. The first motorcycle races in 1907 encouraged improvements in design which soon brought the motorcycle to something like its present form with electric ignition, variable gears and the engine mounted low down between the two wheels.

1894 Hildebrand and Wolfmuller

1980s Honda 500

259

Plane Facts

World speed record 3529 km/h (2193 mph) by US Lockheed SR-71A in 1976. This aircraft took off from the ground.

World altitude record (aircraft) 37,650 m (123,523 ft) by USSR Mikyon E226 in 1977. This aircraft took off from the ground.

Fastest round-the-world flight Made by three US Boeing *Stratofortresses* in 1957, which flew 39,147 km (24,325 miles) in under $45\frac{1}{2}$ hours.

Biggest aircraft Heaviest plane is the US Boeing 747-200B weighing 372 tonnes. Largest was the US Hughes H2 *Hercules* flying-boat (1947) with a wing-span of 97·5 metres (319 ft).

Lightest aeroplane Birdman TL-1 monoplane, with unladen weight of 45 kg (100 lb), first flown in Florida, USA, 1975.

Largest airport Dallas/Fort Worth, in Texas, which covers an area of 70·8 sq km (27 sq. miles).

Boeing 747 *This airliner can carry up to 490 passengers. But the basic passenger model shown here usually carries only 374 people. The spacious cabins provide plenty of room for all the passengers.*

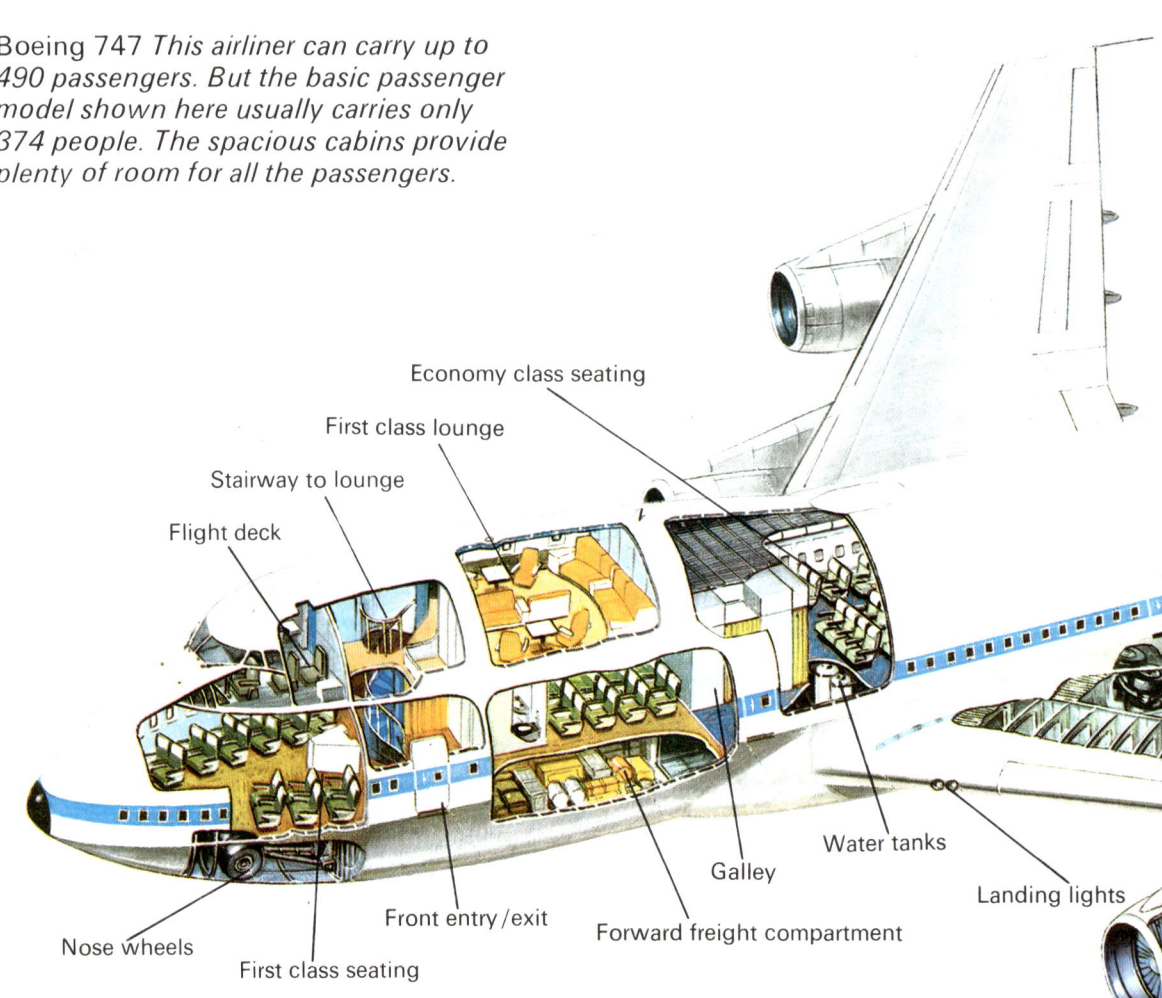

Economy class seating

First class lounge

Stairway to lounge

Flight deck

Water tanks

Landing lights

Galley

Nose wheels

First class seating

Front entry/exit

Forward freight compartment

Busiest airport Chicago International Airport (O'Hare), which has an aircraft movement every 45 seconds on average. London's Heathrow handles more international flights than any other airport.

Fastest jet plane US Lockheed SR-71, with speed of about 3540 km/h (2200 mph).

Fastest airliner BAC-Aérospatiale *Concorde*, which can fly at 2330 km/h (1450 mph) (Mach 2·2) carrying 128 passengers. The USSR Tupolev Tu-144 has a similar speed.

Largest helicopter USSR Mil Mi-12, weighing 105 tonnes, which lifted a payload of 40·2 tonnes in 1969. It has a 67 metre (219 ft) span over its rotor tips.

Balloon distance record 3053 km (1900 miles) in 1914 by a German, H. Berliner, who flew from Berlin to Russia.

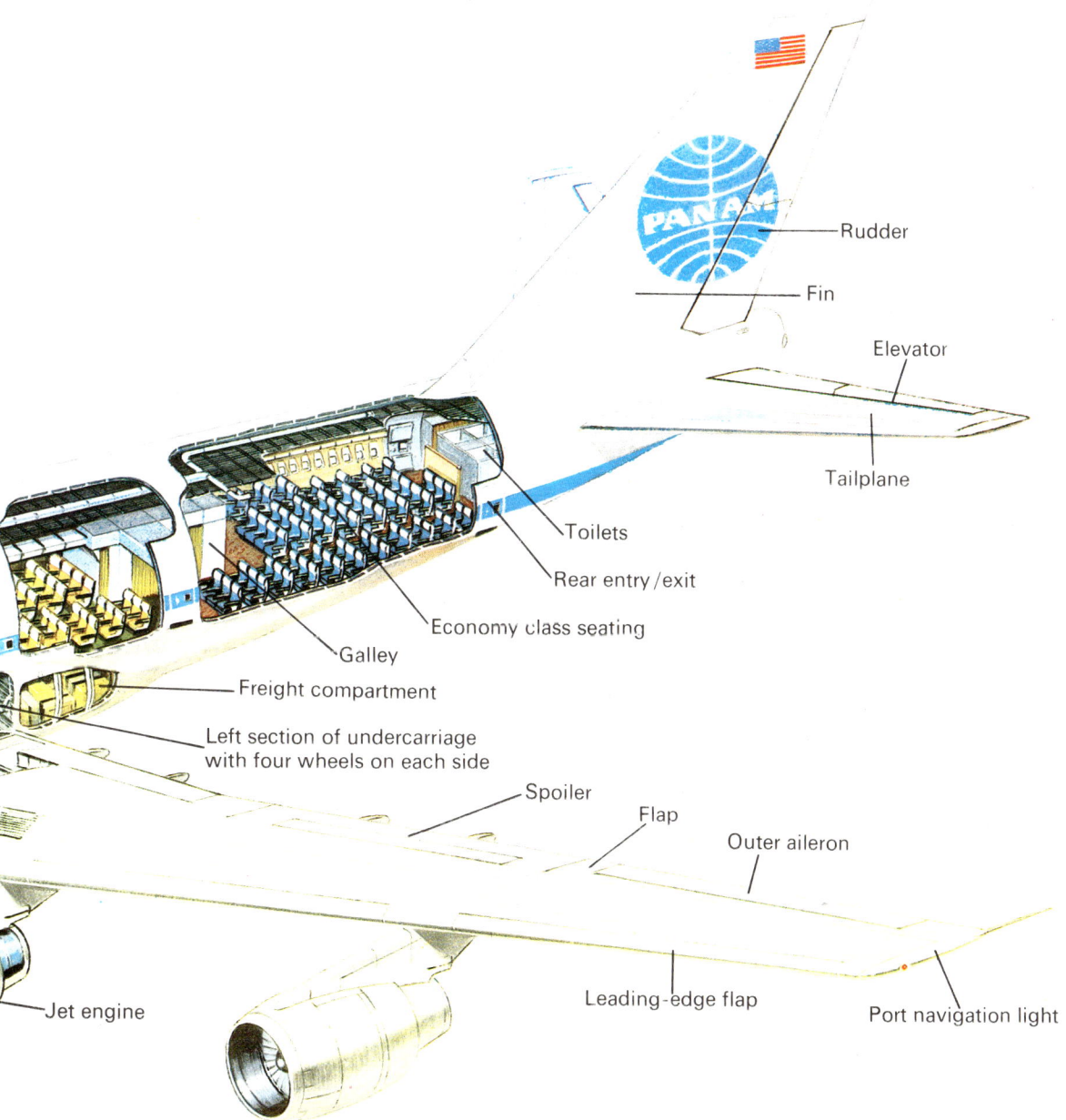

Rudder

Fin

Elevator

Tailplane

Toilets

Rear entry/exit

Economy class seating

Galley

Freight compartment

Left section of undercarriage with four wheels on each side

Spoiler

Flap

Outer aileron

Jet engine

Leading-edge flap

Port navigation light

TRANSPORT AND COMMUNICATION

Different Types of Aircraft

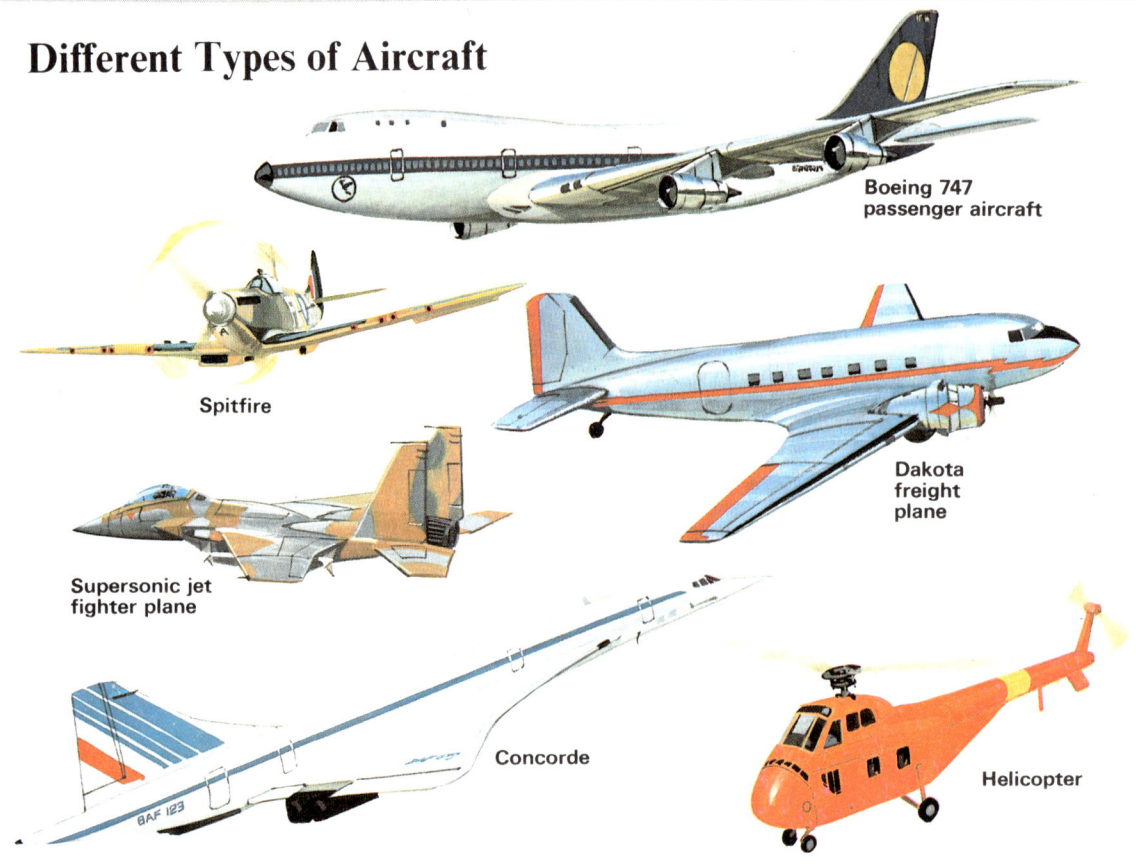

Boeing 747
passenger aircraft

Spitfire

Dakota
freight
plane

Supersonic jet
fighter plane

Concorde

Helicopter

Notable Air Disasters

Date		Deaths
4.4.33	*Akron* dirigible (US) crashed, New Jersey coast	73
6.5.37	*Hindenburg* zeppelin (Ger.) burned at mooring, Lakehurst, NJ	36
23.8.44	US Air Force B-24 hit school, Freckelton, England	76*
24.6.50	DC-4 airliner (US) exploded in storm over Lake Michigan	58
20.12.52	US Air Force C-124 fell and burned, Washington	87
18.6.53	US Air Force C-124 crashed and burned near Tokyo	129
30.6.56	Super-Constellation and DC-7 airliners collided over Grand Canyon	128
6.2.58	Elizabethan airliner (GB) crashed on take-off at Munich, W Germany	23‡
16.12.60	DC-8 and Super-Constellation airliners collided over New York	134*
15.2.61	Boeing 707 (Belgian) crashed near Brussels	73§
3.6.62	Boeing 707 (French) crashed on take-off, Paris	130
22.6.62	Boeing 707 (French) crashed in storm, Guadeloupe	113
20.5.65	Boeing 720B (Pak.) crashed at Cairo airport	121
24.1.66	Boeing 707 (Indian) crashed on Mont Blanc (France)	117
4.2.66	Boeing 727 (Jap.) plunged into Tokyo Bay	133
5.3.66	Boeing 707 (GB) crashed on Mt Fuki (Japan)	124
20.4.67	Britannia turboprop (Swiss) crashed at Nicosia (Cyprus)	126
16.3.69	DC-9 (Venez.) crashed on take-off, Maracaibo	155*
30.7.71	Boeing 727 (Jap.) collided with F-86 fighter, Japan	162

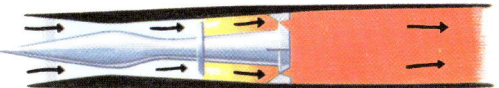

The simplest sort of jet engines are ramjets. They have no fans or turbines and air is just squeezed into the tube as it moves through the air. V-1 'doodlebugs' used ramjets.

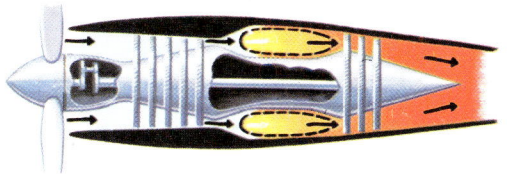

Turboprop engines produce jet thrust like turbojets, but their turbines also drive a propeller. They are more economical but slower than pure jets, and were popular for transport aircraft.

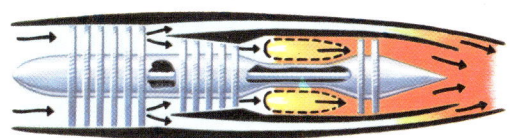

Bypass (or turbofan) jet engines have huge fans at the front to suck in vast amounts of air. Some of this bypasses the combustion chamber and then re-joins the exhaust gases. The result is much greater thrust.

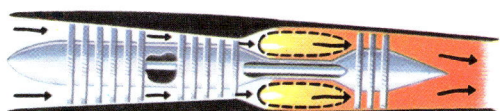

Turbojets are noisier and less powerful than turbofans but they were long preferred for warplanes because they are smaller and easy to fit with afterburners.

14.8.72	Ilyushin-62 (E Ger.) crashed on take-off, Berlin	156
13.10.72	Ilyushin-62 (USSR) crashed near Moscow	176
4.12.72	Spanish charter jet airliner crashed on take-off, Canary Is.	155
22.1.73	Boeing 707 (chartered) crashed on landing at Kano, Nigeria	176
3.3.74	DC-10 (Turk.) crashed in forest, Ermenonville, France	346
10.9.76	British Trident 3 and Yugoslavian DC-9 collided in mid-air near Zagreb (Yugoslavia)	176
27.3.77	Two Boeing 747s (American and Dutch) collided on ground at Tenerife Los Rodeos airport (Canary Islands)	582
1.1.78	Boeing 747 (Indian) crashed into the sea off Bombay (India)	213
15.11.78	DC-8 (Iceland) crashed while attempting to land, Sri Lanka	262
14.3.79	Trident (China) crashed near Peking	200
24.5.79	DC-10 (US) crashed near Chicago	273
25.4.80	British chartered Boeing 727 crashed in Canary Islands	146
7.7.80	Airliner (USSR; type unspecified) crashed on take-off, Alma-Ata	163
19.8.80	Lockheed Tristar (Saudi) destroyed by fire after emergency landing, Riyadh	301
1.12.81	DC-9 (Yugoslav.) crashed in Corsica	174

* Total includes deaths on ground or buildings.
‡ Mostly players (8) and officials (3) of England football champions Manchester United, and 8 journalists.
§ Including skaters (17) and officials of US world championships team.

TRANSPORT AND COMMUNICATION

Airline Insignia

Each aeroplane or helicopter you see that is flown by an airline company will have a painted symbol. This can usually be seen on the tail.

Each country has special registration letters. Every aircraft from that country has to show these letters on the fuselage. British aircraft have the letter G. A typical British registration is G-BGJE.

Aer Lingus
(Eire EI)

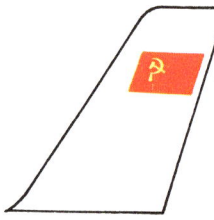

Aeroflot
(Soviet Union CCCP)

Qantas
(Australia VH)

Swissair
(Switzerland HB)

British Airways
(United Kingdom G)

Kuwait Airways
(Kuwait 9K)

British Caledonian
(United Kingdom G)

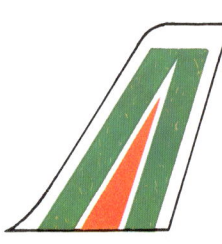

Alitalia
(Italy I)

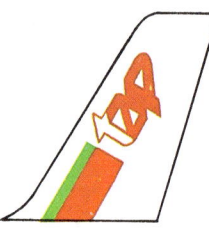

TAP
(Portugal CS)

THY
(Turkey TC)

Varig
(Brazil PP)

El Al
(Israel 4X)

Viasa
(Venezuela YV)

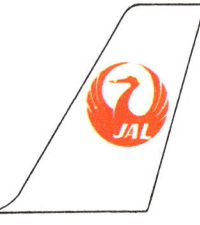

Japan Air Lines
(Japan JA)

JAT
(Yugoslavia YU)

Saudia
(Saudia Arabia HZ)

Air Algérie
(Algeria 7T)

Air Canada
(Canada C)

Air France
(France F)

Air-India
(India VT)

Austrian Airlines
(Austria OE)

Balkan Bulgarian Airlines
(Bulgaria LZ)

Braathens-SAFE
(Norway LN)

Sabena
(Belgium OO)

BWIA International
(Trinidad & Tobago 9Y)

CP Air
(Canada C)

CSA
(Czechoslovakia OK)

Cyprus Airways
(Cyprus 5B)

Ethiopian Airlines
(Ethiopia ET)

Finnair
(Finland OH)

Gulf Air
(Oman A40)

Iberia
(Spain EC)

LOT
(Poland SP)

Singapore Airlines
(Singapore 9V)

South African Airways
(South Africa ZS)

Olympic Airways
(Greece SX)

Firsts in Flight

1783 First human ascent, made in a captive Montgolfier hot air balloon by J. F. Pilâtre in Paris.

1783 First flight in a hydrogen balloon, made by J. A. C. Charles and M. Roberts.

1785 First air crossing of the English Channel, in a hydrogen balloon, by J. P. Blanchard and J. Jeffries.

1852 First (steam) powered airship, flown by Henri Giffard over Paris.

1853 First successful aeroplane (glider), built by Sir George Cayley.

1890s First successful glider flights, made by Otto Lilienthal of Germany.

1903 First controlled flight in a heavier-than-air machine, made by Wilbur and Orville Wright at Kitty Hawk, USA.

1909 First aeroplane crossing of the English Channel, by Louis Blériot of France in his Blériot XI monoplane.

1910 First commercial airline service by airships, established by Count Ferdinand von Zeppelin of Germany.

1919 First transatlantic flight by flying-boat made by Lieut-Cdr Albert C. Read, of the United States.

1919 First non-stop transatlantic aeroplane flight, made by Capt J. Alcock and Lieut A. W. Brown of Britain.

1923 First autogyro, flown by Juan de la Cierva in Spain.

1927 First non-stop transatlantic solo flight, made by Charles Lindbergh in his *Spirit of St Louis*.

1928 First transatlantic passenger flight, by a German airship.

1930 First patented design for jet aircraft engine, by Frank Whittle in Britain.

1930 Amy Johnson becomes first woman to fly solo from England to Australia.

1933 First solo round-the-world flight, made by Wiley Post in his *Vega* monoplane.

1939 First heavier-than-air trans-atlantic passenger service, begun by Pan American Airways.

1939 First jet-propelled aeroplane, built by the Heinkel Company in Germany.

1939 First flight of a single-rotor helicopter, made by Igor Sikorsky.

1947 First supersonic flight, made by Capt Charles Yeager in a rocket-powered Bell XS-1.

Wilbur (left) and Orville Wright

1949 First non-stop round-the-world flight, made by Capt James Gallagher and crew in a Boeing *Superfortress* bomber.

1952 First jet airliner in regular service, the De Havilland *Comet* on a British Overseas Airways Corporation route.

1965 First conventional aircraft to fly at more than 2000 mph (3200 km/h), a US Lockheed YF-12A.

1976 First supersonic airliner to begin international flight, the BAC-Aérospatiale *Concorde*.

Aviation A to Z

aerobatics Manoeuvres carried out by an aircraft in flight, either singly or in formation.

aerodrome Another word for an airport or airfield.

aerodynamics The study of the forces which act on a flying body, such as an aircraft.

aerofoil Part of an aircraft specially shaped to produce lift – such as the wing or tailplane.

ailerons Flaps on the trailing edge of the wing which make the aircraft bank.

airframe The whole of an aircraft *without* its engines.

air intake Opening through which air is sucked into an aero-engine.

airscrew Another word for a propeller.

airship A lighter-than-air machine powered by an engine.

airspeed indicator Instrument which measures the speed of an aircraft.

air traffic control Control of aircraft in flight from the ground.

altimeter Instrument which measures an aircraft's height above the ground.

amphibian An aircraft capable of operating from land or water.

approach lights Lights marking the approach to an airport runway.

apron Concrete area close to airport buildings for the loading and unloading of aircraft.

autogyro Aircraft which gets its lift from an unpowered rotor, but which has wings and a propeller. The Autogyro was pioneered by Juan de la Cierva.

automatic pilot A device (set by the pilot or ground-controlled) which flies an aircraft automatically.

balloon An unpowered lighter-than-air aircraft.

banking Manoeuvre (used for turning) when aircraft wing is tilted.

biplane Aircraft with two wings, one above the other.

cockpit Area where the pilot of an aircraft sits, (the flight deck).

control column Control which works the elevators and ailerons of an aircraft.

delta wing Triangular-shaped wing used on high-speed aircraft.

dirigible Early steerable airship.

ditching Crash-landing an aircraft at sea.

drag Resistance of the air to the movement of an aircraft through it.

ejector seat System for ejecting the pilot safely from a damaged aircraft and parachuting him or her to the ground.

elevator Hinged horizontal plane on the tail of an aircraft.

ETA Estimated time of arrival.

fin Fixed vertical stabilizer on the tail of an aircraft.

flap Hinged surfaces on the trailing edge of the wing which increase lift or drag and are used to reduce landing speed.

flight recorder or 'black box' Records details of the flight and provides valuable information in the event of a crash.

flying boat Aircraft with watertight hull which lands and takes off from water.

fuel tanks Containers for fuel either within the fuselage or wings, or suspended beneath them as 'drop-tanks'.

fuselage The body of an aircraft.

gas bag Gas container within the envelope of a balloon or airship.

glider Unpowered aircraft.

ground controlled approach (GCA) Radar-controlled system for guiding an aircraft about to land.

ground controller Person who controls aircraft movements by radio and radar from the ground.

guided weapons Missiles carried by military aircraft. Missiles may be air-to-air or air-to-ground.

hangar Building in which aircraft are kept.

helicopter Aircraft which gets its lift from powered rotating blades or 'rotors'.

jet propulsion Propulsion by reaction from the emission of a jet of air at high speed.

Mach number Measurement of airspeed in relation to the speed of sound (known as mach 1).

navigation lights Lights shown by an aircraft at night. Red (port), green (starboard) and white (tail, above and below fuselage) lights flash when the aircraft is in a busy area.

pancake landing A landing from too steep an angle at too low a speed.

parachute Umbrella-shaped device for slowing aircraft on landing and permitting pilots to descend safely to earth.

payload The economic load (passengers, freight) that an aircraft can carry.

pressurization Artificial maintenance of normal air pressure inside an aircraft.

ram jet Simple form of jet engine.

reverse thrust Directing jet thrust *forwards* to slow down an aircraft.

rigid airship Airship in which the envelope is supported by a metal framework.

rotor An aerofoil which produces lift by rotating or spinning. Used by helicopters.

runway Strip of concrete or tarmac on which aircraft land and take-off.

sailplane Glider able to fly for long periods in air currents.

SARAH (Search and rescue and homing.) Radar transmitter on a pilot's life jacket.

seaplane Aircraft able to take-off and land from water, usually fitted with floats.

short-range Under 2215 km.

stall A stall occurs when an aircraft does not have enough lift and loses height rapidly.

sonic boom Noise produced by aircraft travelling at supersonic speed and caused by shock waves.

sound barrier Term coined in the 1940s for buffeting and other phenomena experienced just below supersonic speed.

STOL Short take-off and landing.

test pilot Pilot who flies new aircraft on test.

thermal Current of rising air used by gliders.

three-point landing Normal landing when all wheels touch down at the same time.

thrust Force produced by aero engines which drives aircraft forwards.

triplane Early airplane with three wings, one above the other.

turbojet Typical form of pure jet engine.

turboprop Jet engine in which the hot exhaust gases provide jet thrust and also drive a conventional propeller.

undercarriage Landing gear of an aircraft, usually retracted into the wings and fuselage during flight.

VTOL Vertical take-off and landing.

wind sock Cone-shaped sleeve which shows the direction of wind on an airfield.

wing The main supporting surface of an aircraft.

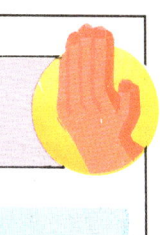

RELIGION

Egyptian Mythology

Amon (Ammon, Amen) A god of Thebes, united with Ra as Amon-Ra, supreme king of the gods.

Anubis Jackal-headed son of Osiris; guided souls of the dead.

Apis Sacred bull of Memphis.

Hathor Cow-headed sky goddess of love.

Horus Hawk-headed god of light, son of Osiris and Isis.

Isis Goddess of motherhood and fertility; chief goddess of Ancient Egypt.

Osiris Supreme god, ruler of the afterlife; husband of Isis.

Ptah The creator, chief god of Memphis.

Ra Sun god; ancestor of the pharaohs.

Serapis God combining attributes of Osiris and Apis.

Set God of evil; jealous brother-son of Osiris, whom he slew and cut into pieces.

Thoth Ibis-headed god of wisdom.

Norse Mythology

Aesir Collectively, the chief Norse gods.

Asgard Home of the gods.

Balder God of summer sun; son of Odin and Frigga; killed by mistletoe twig.

Frey God of fertility and crops.

Freya (Freyja) Beautiful goddess of love and night; sister of Frey; sometimes confused with *Frigga*.

Frigga Goddess of married love; wife of Odin.

Heimdal Guardian of Asgard; he and Loki slew one another.

Hel Goddess of the dead, queen of the underworld; daughter of Loki.

Hödur (Hoth) Blind god of night; unwitting killer of twin brother Balder.

Loki God of evil; contrives Balder's death.

Odin Supreme god, head of Aesir; god of wisdom and of the atmosphere.

Thor God of thunder; eldest son of Odin.

Valhalla Hall in Asgard where Odin welcomed souls of heroes killed in battle.

Valkyries Nine handmaidens of Odin who chose warriors to die in battle and conducted them to Valhalla.

Gods of Greece and Rome

Aphrodite (Venus) Goddess of beauty and love; sprang from foam in sea, but also said to be daughter of Zeus; mother of Eros.

Apollo Son of Zeus and Leto; god of poetry, music, and prophecy; ideal of manly beauty.

Ares (Mars) God of war, son of Zeus and Hera; Roman god *Mars*, father of Romulus and Remus identified with Ares.

Artemis (Diana) Twin sister of Apollo; goddess of moon and famous huntress.

Athene (Minerva) Goddess of wisdom and war, daughter of Zeus and Metis; sprang fully grown and armed from father's head.

Cronos (Saturn) A Titan, god of agriculture and harvests; father of Zeus.

Dionysus (Bacchus) God of wine and fertile crops; son of Zeus and Semele.

Hera (Juno) Queen of heaven, daughter of Cronos and Rhea, wife and sister of Zeus; guardian spirit of women.

Hermes (Mercury) Messenger of gods, son of Zeus and Maia; god of physicians, traders, and thieves.

Hestia (Vesta) Goddess of the hearth, sister of Zeus; her temple held Sacred Fire guarded by Vestal Virgins.

The Lares and Penates Gods of the household. The Penates guarded the family's larder, and the Lares the house.

Poseidon (Neptune) Chief god of sea, brother of Zeus.

Zeus (Jupiter) Chief of the Olympian gods, son of Cronos and Rhea, god of thunder and lightning.

Mythical Characters

When there is a Latin equivalent of a Greek name, the character is listed under the Greek version, with the Latin in parentheses.

Achilles Greek hero of Trojan War; died when Paris wounded vulnerable heel.

Adonis Beautiful youth loved by Aphrodite; killed by boar.

Aeneas A Trojan, son of Venus, carried his father to safety out of Troy; married and deserted Dido, queen of Carthage.

Agamemnon King of Mycenae, Greek leader against Troy; murdered by wife Clytemnestra, avenged by son Orestes.

Ajax Greek warrior; killed himself when Achilles' arms awarded to Odysseus.

Amazons Female warriors from Asia.

Andromeda Chained to rock as prey for monster, rescued by Perseus.

A bronze head of Apollo, the Greek god of poetry, the arts, and prophecy; he was also the healer and sender of plagues.

Argonauts Jason and 50 heroes who sailed on *Argos* in search of Golden Fleece.

Asclepius (Aesculapius) Mortal son of Apollo, later deified as god of medical art; he was killed by Zeus for raising dead.

Atlas A Titan, made war on Zeus, condemned by him to bear heavens on shoulders; later turned into mountain.

Bellerophon Corinthian hero, rode winged horse Pegasus; fell to death trying to reach Olympus.

Centaurs Race of half-horses half-men.

Cerberus Three-headed dog, guarded Hades.

Cyclopes Race of one-eyed giants led by Polyphemus; (singular, *Cyclops*).

Daedalus Athenian craftsman, builder of Labyrinth in Crete; imprisoned there with son Icarus; escaped with home-made wings.

Demeter (Ceres) Goddess of agriculture.

Elysium Paradise of Greek mythology to which heroes passed without dying.

Eos (Aurora) Goddess of dawn.

Eros (Cupid) God of love, son of Aphrodite.

Fates Three sisters, goddesses who determined human destiny.

Graces Three beautiful goddesses, daughters of Zeus, personifying brilliance (Aglaia), joy (Euphrosyne), and bloom (Thalia).

Hades (Dis) Abode of dead, ruled by Pluto; name sometimes used for Pluto.

Hebe (Juventas) Goddess of youth, cupbearer of gods; daughter of Zeus and Hera; wife of Heracles.

Hecate Goddess of witchcraft and ghosts.

Hector Eldest son of Priam; chief hero of Trojans; slain by Achilles.

Helen of Troy Fairest woman in world; daughter of Zeus and Leda; cause of Trojan War.

Hephaestus (Vulcan) God of destructive fire, heavenly blacksmith; husband of Aphrodite; son of Zeus and Hera or just Hera.

Heracles (Hercules) Famous strong man and greatest of deified heroes, performed 12 labours to be free from bondage; son of Zeus and Alcmene.

Hypnos (Somnus) God of sleep.

Janus Roman god of doors and gates, represented by two faces pointing in opposite ways.

Jason Son of Aeson, see *Argonauts*.

Laocoön Priest of Apollo at Troy; he and two sons killed by serpents sent by Athene.

Midas King of Phrygia; touch turned everything to gold.

Muses Nine lesser divinities who presided over arts and sciences; daughters of Zeus and Mnemosyne.

Narcissus Beautiful youth beloved by Echo, fell in love with own image in pool.

Odysseus (Ulysses) Greek hero of Trojan War; king of Ithaca, husband of Penelope, he roamed ten years after fall of Troy.

Oedipus King of Thebes, unwittingly murdered father (Laius) and married mother (Jocasta); tore out own eyes.

Olympus Mountain in north of Greece, abode of gods.

Orpheus Skilled musician, son of Calliope and Apollo, who gave him his famed lyre.

Pan (Faunus) God of woods and fields, flocks and shepherds, part man, part goat.

Pandora First woman on earth; opened box containing all human ills.

Persephone (Proserpine) Daughter of Zeus and Demeter; wife of Pluto and queen of infernal regions.

Perseus Son of Zeus and Danaë; killed Medusa; married Andromeda.

Phoebus see *Apollo*.

Pluto God of Hades, brother of Zeus.

Plutus Greek god of wealth.

Prometheus A Titan, stole fire from heaven, punished by being chained to mountain while vultures ate his liver.

Psyche Princess loved by Eros but punished by jealous Aphrodite; became immortal and united with Eros.

Rhea Greek nature-goddess, wife and sister of Cronos; mother of Zeus, Poseidon, Pluto, Demeter, Hera; later identified with Roman goddesses Ops and Cybele.

Romulus Founder of Rome; suckled with twin brother Remus by she-wolf; killed Remus.

Satyrs Hoofed demigods of forests, fields, and streams.

Selene (Luna) Goddess of the moon.

Thanatos (Mors) God of death.

Titans Offspring of Uranus and Ge; one, Cronos, dethroned Uranus, but his son Zeus in turn hurled Titans from heaven.

Uranus Oldest of Greek gods, personification of heaven, father of Titans.

Twelve Labours of Hercules

1 Killing Nemean lion
2 Killing Hydra (many-headed snake)
3 Capturing hind of Artemis
4 Capturing Erymanthian boar
5 Cleansing Augean stables in a day
6 Killing man-eating Stymphalian birds
7 Capturing Cretan wild bull
8 Capturing man-eating mares of Diomedes
9 Procuring girdle of Amazon Hippolyta
10 Killing the monster Geryon
11 Stealing apples from garden of Hesperides
12 Bringing Cerberus up from Hades

BUDDHISM

Buddhists number 250 million, and live mainly in China and other parts of Asia.

A statue of the Buddha.

A stone cross, symbol of the Christian faith.

CHRISTIANITY

Christians number about 1000 million, though many do not actively practise the religion. More than 500 million are Roman Catholic. Protestants, Anglicans and Episcopalians number more than 300 million. The Orthodox Churches claim 120 million.

An Eastern Orthodox bishop.

ISLAM

Muslims number over 500 million. There are two main branches – Sunni Islam which accepts the *Koran* and traditions of Muhammad; and Shia Islam (mostly in Persia) which accepts only the *Koran*.

The crescent moon, symbol of Islam.

JUDAISM

Jewish people number about 15 million, of whom 6 million live in the USA.

Left: The Menorah, symbol of the Jewish faith.

HINDUISM

Hindus number nearly 500 million and live mainly in India.

A Hindu carving.

Judaism

Judaism is the ancient religion of the Jews. Traditionally it has two founders: Abraham and Moses. Its sacred books include the Hebrew Bible and the Talmud.

Teachings: Faith in one God is the basis of Judaism. Judaism also teaches the coming of a Messiah (God's anointed) who will establish a new life for mankind.

Worship: The synagogue is both the house of worship and a centre for Jewish education. Prayers in synagogues are chanted by a *cantor* or *chazzan*, while worshippers either chant or pray in silence. Prayers may be in Hebrew, Aramaic, or local languages.

Organization: The leader of a Jewish community is the *rabbi* (master) who is chosen by the community. A Jewish court, the *Bet Din* (House of Judgment), has religious authority over a community.

Customs, ceremonies, and festivals are many, but Jews differ in the extent to which they observe them. No Jews eat pork, and many eat only food that is *kosher* (prepared for use according to ancient law). Main feasts and fasts are: Jewish New Year (September or October); Yom Kippur, the Day of Atonement, a fast (September or October); Pesach (Passover) in commemoration of the Biblical exodus from Egypt (March or April).

Christianity

Christianity, founded in Palestine by Jesus nearly 2000 years ago, stemmed partly from Judaism. Its holy book is the Bible, and its symbol is the cross.

Teachings: Acceptance of the teachings of Jesus Christ as given in the New Testament, and belief in Jesus as the Son of God who was crucified to redeem our sins. Christians believe in life after death.

Worship: The Christian centre of worship is the church (or chapel, mission hall, etc.) where services and prayers are usually led by a priest or a minister.

Organization and sects: St Paul (martyred in about AD 67) organized Christianity into an effective religion. Christianity became the main religion of the Roman Empire in the AD 300s. In 1054 the eastern *Orthodox* and western *Roman Catholic* churches separated. In the 1300s came the Great Schism of the West, when rival Popes ruled for 40 years. The Reformation came in the 1500s–1600s when most of northern Europe protested against the Church of Rome. England rejected the Pope's authority but its Church of England kept much of the Roman Catholic ritual. Protestants became further divided into Lutherans, Methodists, Baptists etc.

Customs, ceremonies and festivals: Christian observances normally take place in church. Easter – the commemoration of Christ's resurrection – is the most important time of the Christian year. Christ's birthday is celebrated on Christmas Day. The coming of the Holy Spirit is celebrated at Pentecost.

This fresco by the artist Giotto shows St Francis preaching to the birds. In 1210 St Francis founded the first order of friars, known as the Franciscans. They lived lives of poverty and simplicity, earning a living by working as they preached.

Patron Saints

St Agatha	Nurses
St Andrew	Scotland (30 November)
St Anthony	Gravediggers
St Augustine of Hippo	Brewers
St Benedict	Speleologists
St Cecilia	Musicians
St Christopher	Sailors
St Crispin	Shoemakers
St David	Wales (1 March)
St Dunstan	Goldsmiths and silversmiths
St George	England (23 April)
St Hubert	Hunters
St Jerome	Librarians
St John of God	Booksellers
St Joseph	Carpenters
St Lawrence	Cooks
St Luke	Physicians
St Martha	Dieticians
St Matthew	Tax-collectors
St Michael	Police
St Nicholas	The original Santa Claus
St Patrick	Ireland (17 March)
St Paul	Carpet-weavers and tent-makers
St Peter	Blacksmiths and fishermen
St Valentine	Sweethearts
St Vincent	Wine-growers
St Vitus	Dancers and comedians
St William	Hatters
St Winifred	Bakers

Left: A wall painting depicting one of Jesus' miracles – the healing of the blind man.

Islam

Islam, founded in Arabia by Muhammad in AD 622, derived largely from Judaism and Christianity. Its main sacred book is the Koran and its symbol is the crescent.

Teaching Islam means *submission* and each of its followers is a *Muslim*, one who submits to God (Allah). The starting point of Islam was the Hegira (flight) from Mecca to Medina by Muhammad which took place in AD 622 by the Christian calendar.

Worship: The 'five pillars of Islam' are: *iman* (faith in Allah and in his messenger, Muhammad); *salat* (prayer) five times daily facing Mecca – dawn, noon, afternoon, evening, nightfall; *zakat* (giving of alms) is compulsory; *saum* (fasting) during Ramadan (the holy, ninth month of the Muslim year) – Muslims may not eat, drink or smoke between sunrise and sunset during Ramadan; *hadj* (pilgrimage to Mecca, Saudi Arabia) is commanded by the Koran.

Organization: Islam early divided into sects, the main ones being the *Sunnites*, *Shi'ites*, *Kharijites,* and *Wahabis.* Prayer takes place anywhere, but the religious centre is the *mosque* recognized by its dome and minaret(s). Islam has no priests, but an *imam* leads prayers and a *muezzin* chants the call to prayer.

Customs, ceremonies and festivals: No Muslims eat pork, and many do not drink alcohol. Main feasts include *Id al-Fitr* to end Ramadan, *Id al-Adha* the animal sacrifice that concludes the hadj, and Muhammad's birthday. Most sacred place is the *Kaaba*, a sacred shrine in Mecca that contains the *Black Stone*, said to have been given to Abraham by the Archangel Gabriel.

Buddhism

Buddhism was founded in Nepal in the 500s BC by Siddhartha Gautama, a prince who became Buddha. Its holy books include the Tipitaka and Prajna-paramita.

Teachings: Belief that human suffering is the result of self desire and that relief from suffering can come only by ending such desire. This can be achieved only by living the way of life laid down by the Buddha. The Buddha taught that people are not punished *for* their sins but *by* them. Whatever they do has consequences that come back to them; good acts bring rewards, bad acts bring suffering. Like Hinduism, Buddhism teaches that people may be reborn into many lives. If they reach Nirvana, the final Enlightenment, they are not reborn.

Worship and organization: Buddhism has temples, monks, and nuns. It also has images of the Buddha, but these are not worshipped. Meditation (deep thinking on spiritual matters) can take place anywhere.

Customs, ceremonies and festivals: Strict Buddhists do not eat meat or drink alcohol, but the Buddha prohibited very little, advocating only moderation in all things, and above all tolerance. Festivals include the Buddha's birthday and the four phases of the moon.

Teachings of the Buddha

Respect the self of your fellow men as you respect your own; be compassionate and respect even the lowest forms of life; give and receive freely, but never take by force.

Hindu pilgrims bathing in the Ganges. Since ancient times, Hindus have regarded this river as sacred, and believe that bathing in it will wash away their sins.

The Hindu Caste System

In Hindu society each person is born into a *caste* – a religious and social class or category that he or she can never change. There are thousands of caste distinctions, but the most important are:

Brahmans or **Brahmins,** the highest caste, are the priests and scholars.

Kshatriyas, the second highest, are the warriors, who are also the people considered fit to rule.

Vaisyas are the merchants, farmers and peasants.

Sudrus are the unskilled labourers. Millions of people fit into no caste and are, in religious terms, 'unclean'. In the past, they did the roughest and dirtiest jobs and followed 'unclean' trades, such as butchering or hunting. These 'outcastes', or 'untouchables', lived sordid, poverty-stricken lives, and their touch was considered impure by members of the highest castes. But throughout history many Indian leaders and thinkers have protested against the way they have been treated. In an attempt to improve their lives, Mohandas Gandhi encouraged people to call them *harijans* – that is, 'children of God'. The Indian government has made discrimination based on caste a punishable offence.

Hinduism

Hinduism is a very ancient Indian religion. It has no known founder. It has many gods or aspects of a god, and many holy writings including the *Vedas*, the *Ramayana*, and the *Makabharata*. Its symbol is the sacred word om.

Teachings: Belief in *Brahman* (supreme soul or spirit) which is eternal, absolute, and infinite. Yet Hindus worship thousands (possibly millions) of gods, all of which are aspects of Brahman. The three chief gods are Brahman (the creator), Siva (the destroyer) and Vishnu (the preserver). Hindus believe in reincarnation – that a soul moves from body to body in humans, animals and plants in a long cycle of lives before it is reunited with Brahman.

Worship and organization: Hindus worship in temples. Some of these are grand, others merely village shrines. Religious teachers are called *gurus*, and holy men, *sadhus*.

Customs, ceremonies and feasts. The cow is sacred, so Hindus never eat beef, and most are vegetarians. Important ceremonies include the thread ceremony at which the *twice-born* (higher caste) boys are given a sacred thread by a priest.

A statue of Buddha in a Bangkok temple.

A scene from the Nuremberg Chronicles of 1493 showing Noah building the ark.

Other Religions

Bahá'í Persian religion founded in 1800s; members believe in unity of mankind and peace through religion and science.

Confucianism A philosophical, religious, and political system dating from about 500 BC in China. It spread widely in Japan and Korea.

Jainism Small Indian sect, offshoot of Hinduism in the 6th century BC; teaches that salvation depends on rigid self-effort and non-violence towards all creatures.

Shinto The religion of Japan; adherents worship many gods, including nature and ancestor worship.

Sikhs Adherents of Sikhism, India's fourth largest religion, located mainly in Punjab, founded by Guru Nanak (1469–1538), who rejected formalism of Hinduism and Islam.

Taoism Major Chinese religion founded by Lao Tzu in 500s BC; believers yield to *Tao*, 'the way', in order to restore human harmony.

Zoroastrians Believers in teachings of Persian prophet Zoroaster (600s BC) humility is greatest virtue in battle between good and evil.

RELIGION

Christian Groups

Adventists Protestant sects that sprang from the teachings of William Miller in mid-1800s; they believe in the 2nd and pre-millennial advent of Christ. *Seventh Day Adventists* (founded 1860) form largest group.

Anglicans Members of churches that agree with Church of England.

Anglo-Catholics Those who hold to the catholicity of the Church of England.

Baptists Protestant denomination, one of whose key beliefs is baptism by the total immersion of adults.

Calvinists Followers of teachings of John Calvin, who accept absolute sovereignty of God and supremacy of Bible.

Christian Scientists Followers of religious movement founded in late 1800s by Mary Baker Eddy; stress present perfectibility of God and mankind, and practise spiritual healing.

Church of England The established church in England, springing mainly from fusion of Celtic Church with that of St Augustine; during Reformation, royal supremacy was substituted for that of pope.

Congregationalists Nonconformist Christians who believe that each local congregation is responsible only to God and that all Christians are equal.

Copts Members of an Egyptian Christian church, branch of *Eastern Orthodox Church*; have dietary laws and practise circumcision.

Eastern Orthodox Church Federation of Christian churches (Russian Orthodox, Greek Orthodox, etc) found in eastern Europe and Egypt; faith is expressed in Creed of Constantinople.

Episcopalians Members of church governed by bishops.

Friends, Society of Christian group founded by George Fox in 1640s; they reject creeds, rites, and organized religion in favour of spontaneous worship; popularly known as Quakers.

fundamentalists Protestant Christians who believe that Bible is literally true, without error, and wholly inspired by God.

Lutherans Members of oldest and largest Protestant church, founded by Martin Luther in 1500s; Bible is only authority.

Methodists Members of Protestant movement founded by John Wesley (1703–91); they stress evangelical Christianity and religious experience.

Moravians Members of Protestant church founded in Bohemia and Moravia in 1457; based on teachings of John Huss.

Mormons American religious sect founded by Joseph Smith (1830); officially, Church of Jesus Christ of Latter-day Saints.

Nonconformists Term used originally for Protestants separated from the Church of England; later applied to all dissenting groups

Pentecostal sects Group of fundamentalist sects distinguished mainly by 'speaking with tongues', also called 'Holy Rollers' because some devotees fall to ground in trance.

Presbyterians Members of Protestant churches that follow system of government established by John Calvin during Reformation.

Protestant Any Christian outside Roman Catholic and Eastern Orthodox churches.

Quakers See *Friends, Society of*

Roman Catholics Christians who accept the pope as spiritual leader on earth; they claim to belong to the one Holy and Apostolic Church.

Salvation Army Religious movement founded by William Booth (about 1865); aims to preach evangelical Christianity to the masses normally untouched by religion.

Swedenborgians Followers of the teachings of Emanuel Swedenborg (1688–1722); founded Church of the New Jerusalem, claiming that teachings were new dispensation of Christianity.

Unitarians Believers in doctrine of unity of Godhead and divinity of God the Father only.

Religious Leaders

Booth, William (1829–1912), founder of the Salvation Army, an evangelical mission organized on military lines; he was known as General Booth. Members of his family continued his work.

Buddha, 'the Enlightened One', was born about 563 BC in northern India. The sufferings he saw made him renounce all worldly pleasures. He became a teacher, stressing that right speech, action, living, effort, awareness, and meditation must be followed to attain perfection. He died at 80.

Calvin, John (1509–64), a French scholar, was one of the pioneers of the Protestant Reformation. He set up a Protestant Church in Geneva, and wrote many books, which continued to be influential after his death, particularly *Institute of the Christian Religion*. About a quarter of the world's Protestants are Calvinists.

Confucius (c. 551–479 BC) was a Chinese thinker and philosopher whose 'system' also spread to Korea and Japan. It contained no innovations, and was based on a study of rightness which mankind should follow.

Eddy, Mary Baker (1821–1910), an American, founded the Christian Science movement; believed in spiritual healing.

Jesus Christ (c. 4 BC–AD 29) founded Christianity. He was born in Bethlehem and, growing up, he went from place to place preaching and performing miracles. He is believed by Christians to have been the son of God. He was tried by Pontius Pilate, who did not dare to run counter to popular opinion, and he was convicted, and crucified. Three days later he is said to have risen from his grave.

Lao Tzu (c. 604–531 BC), a Chinese philosopher, is believed by many to be the founder of Taoism.

Luther, Martin (1483–1546), was a German theologian and Protestant leader of the Reformation. He opposed the corruption of the Church of his day in his *Ninety-Five Theses*, which he nailed to the door of Wittenberg church, an act said to have started the Reformation.

Muhammad (Mohammed, Mahomet) (570–632), founder of Islam, the religion of the Muslims, was born in Mecca. After a series of revelations, he preached for 13 years, but underwent persecutions resulting in his flight to Medina in 622. After much fighting, his followers defeated the Meccans in 630 and he returned to Mecca in triumph. The *Koran*, the sacred book of Islam, is God's Message as revealed to him.

Wesley, John (1703–91), founder of the Methodist movement, was the 15th child of a family of dissenters. He trained groups of lay preachers who travelled widely, classes of 12 meeting weekly for prayers, Bible study, and discussion. Differences with the Anglican Church resulted in a separation.

Wycliffe, John (c. 1320–84), an English reformer, began the translation of the Bible into English, as a protest against certain accepted practices. He supported anti-papal policies, and his followers, known as *Lollards*, were persecuted.

RELIGION

People of the Bible

OLD TESTAMENT

Aaron Elder brother of Moses and Miriam; 1st High Priest of Hebrew nation.

Abel Second son of Adam and Eve; shepherd who became the first murder victim when killed by his brother Cain.

Abraham (Abram) Father of Hebrew nation and traditionally head of Judaism, Christianity, and Islam; journeyed from Ur to Canaan with his family, where he received God's promises.

Absalom David's 3rd son; handsome and spoilt, he plotted against his father but was defeated.

Adam The first man, who, with his wife Eve, was expelled from Garden of Eden for disobeying God's laws.

Belshazzar Last Babylonian king who, during a feast, saw handwriting miraculously appear on a wall.

Benjamin Youngest son of Jacob and Rachel and young brother of Joseph; held as hostage by Joseph to guarantee return of his brothers when they went to buy food at Pharaoh's court.

Cain Eldest son of Adam and Eve; world's first farmer, and murderer – killed his brother Abel.

Daniel Jewish prophet at the court of Babylon, where he had been taken by Nebuchadnezzar; had a gift for interpreting dreams; miraculously protected when thrown into den of lions.

David Shepherd boy of Bethlehem who succeeded Saul as King of Israel, ruling for 40 years. Was skilled swordsman and harpist, and as a boy killed the giant Goliath.

Delilah Philistine woman who seduced Samson and betrayed him to foes.

Elijah Fearless Hebrew prophet (flourished about 850 BC) who denounced idolatry and performed many miracles; carried into heaven by fiery chariot and horses.

Elisha Elijah's disciple and successor as prophet of Israel; author of many miracles.

Esau Elder of Isaac's twin sons and his favourite; tricked out of birthright by his brother Jacob with mother's connivance.

Esther Beautiful Jewess brought up captive as orphan ward of her cousin Mordecai in Persia; devoted to her people, risked her life to protect them.

Eve The first woman; with Adam she was expelled from the Garden of Eden after being tempted by serpent to eat forbidden fruit.

Ezekiel A major prophet of Israel; captured by Babylonians in 597 BC.

Gideon Hero and judge of Israel; led famous and successful night attack on Midianite camp with only 300 men.

Goliath Philistine giant killed by David.

Hezekiah 13th king of Judah, one of the greatest; restored temple worship.

Isaac Son of Abraham and Sarah, and father of Jacob and Esau.

Isaiah Greatest of Old Testament prophets, who ministered to Jerusalem and Judah in 700s BC; emphasized God's holiness and greatness of House of David.

Ishmael Son of Abraham and Hagar, handmaiden to Sarah, Abraham's wife; became rival to Isaac, was expelled into desert.

Israel Jacob's new name, given to him after reunion with Esau.

Jacob Second brother of Isaac and Rebekah, and younger twin brother of Esau; tricked Esau out of inheritance and fled from his wrath, but was later reunited with him and changed his name to Israel.

Jeremiah One of the major prophets; foretold destruction of Jerusalem.

Jezebel Wife of Ahab, King of Israel, and worshipper of Baal. Cruel, murderous, and lustful, she was in constant conflict with Elijah.

Job Pious but suffering man who lived in Uz; his drama posed the question: 'Why does God allow suffering?'

Jonah Minor prophet of Israel; after ignoring God's commands was thrown into sea, but rescued by big fish that swallowed him and then cast him ashore.

Jonathan Saul's eldest son and renowned friend of David; brave warrior, he was killed in battle.

Joseph Favourite son of Jacob and Rachel, had 'coat of many colours'. Sold into slavery by 10 jealous brothers; eventually became prime minister of Egypt and reunited with his family.

Joshua Successor to Moses and leader of the Israelites in conquest of Canaan; in his defeat of Jericho, the walls fell down.

Lot Abraham's nephew; accompanied his uncle from Ur to Haran and thence to Canaan; chose fertile Jordan basin for his home; rescued from destruction of Sodom.

Miriam Sister of Moses and Aaron; nursemaid to infant Moses.

Moses Israel's great leader, lawgiver, prophet and priest, and founder of Israel's religious and national life. Rescued from Egyptian murder of male babies, he was brought up in Egyptian court; eventually led Israelites out of Egyptian captivity to promised land of Canaan, receiving Ten Commandments on the way.

Nebuchadnezzar Powerful Babylonian king who reigned in 500s BC; captured Jerusalem twice and deported Jews to Babylon.

Noah Grandson of Methuselah; had 3 sons (Shem, Ham, Japheth) at age of 500. Built ark to save his family, himself, and a male and female of every living thing from great flood.

Rebekah Wife of Isaac and mother of Jacob and Esau; brought to Isaac from Mesopotamia by Abraham's servant.

Ruth Moabite widow who accompanied her widowed mother-in-law, Naomi, to Bethlehem, where she married Boaz.

Samson Judge of Israel, of enormous physical strength; harassed the Philistines until betrayed by Delilah.

Samuel Prophet of Israel and last of the judges; anointed Israel's first two kings.

Sarah Wife of Abraham and, at an advanced age, mother of Isaac.

Saul First king of Israel; given to fits of madness, and jealous of his lieutenant David; eventually killed in battle with the Philistines.

Solomon Son of David and Bathsheba; wisest and wealthiest of Israel's kings; built great temple in Jerusalem.

NEW TESTAMENT

Andrew Peter's brother, one of the 12 apostles; he was a fisherman.

Barabbas Robber and murderer who was freed instead of Jesus.

Barnabas Cypriot who introduced Paul to the Church and was commissioned with him for missionary work; sometimes classed as apostle.

Bartholomew One of the 12 apostles; possibly identical with Nathanael.

Caiaphas High priest of Jews to whom Jesus was first taken after his arrest.

Elizabeth Wife of Zechariah and mother of John the Baptist, as well as cousin of Mary the mother of Jesus.

Gabriel Angel who announced to Zechariah birth of John the Baptist, and to Mary birth of Jesus.

Herod (1) Herod the Great, ruled when Jesus was born; (2) Herod Antipas, his son, ruled when John the Baptist was murdered; (3) Herod Agrippa, who killed James the brother of John; (4) Herod Agrippa II, before whom Paul was tried.

James (1) James the Greater, one of the 12 apostles, son of Zebedee, brother of John; (2) James the Less, one of the 12 apostles, son of Alphaeus; (3) James, 'brother' of Jesus, leader of the Jerusalem Church.

Jesus Founder of Christianity and central figure of New Testament.

John Youngest of the 12 apostles, 'the disciple whom Jesus loved'.

John the Baptist Forerunner of Jesus whom he baptized.

Joseph (1) Husband of Mary the mother of Jesus; (2) Joseph of Arimathaea, secret disciple in whose tomb Jesus was lain.

Judas Iscariot The disciple who betrayed Jesus; committed suicide.

Lazarus Brother of Martha and Mary; raised from the dead by Jesus.

Luke Christian physician and Paul's travelling companion; author of *Luke* and *Acts*.

Mark Author of the 2nd gospel; accompanied Paul and Barnabas and also Peter.

Martha Close friend of Jesus and sister of Mary and Lazarus of Bethany.

Mary (1) Mother of Jesus; (2) Mary of Bethany, sister of Martha and Lazarus, who anointed Jesus; (3) Mary Magdalene, out of whom Jesus cast 7 devils, and who was first to see him after his resurrection.

Matthew One of the 12 apostles, author of the 1st gospel, and a tax-collector.

Matthias Apostle chosen by lot to replace Judas Iscariot.

Nicodemus A Pharisee who came to talk to Jesus secretly by night.

Nathanael One of the disciples of Jesus, possibly the same as Bartholomew.

Paul Apostle to the Gentiles who, before his conversion, was called Saul, and persecuted Christians; author of 13 epistles.

Peter (Simon) Apostle and leader of the early Church; denied Jesus before the crucifixion but later became 'the rock' on which Church was founded.

Philip One of the 12 apostles.

Pilate Roman procurator of Judea who allowed Jesus to be crucified.

Prodigal Son Main character of one of Jesus's parables; errant younger son who squandered his money before returning to a forgiving father.

Sadducees Jewish religious group made up of a few influential people opposed to Pharisees.

Salome (1) Wife of Zebedee, mother of James and John, present at crucifixion; (2) daughter of Herodias who danced before Herod and was rewarded with John the Baptist's head.

Saul of Tarsus See *Paul*.

Silas Paul's companion on his 2nd and 3rd missionary journeys.

Simon (1) Simon Peter (see *Peter*); (2) Simon the Canaanite, one of the 12 apostles; (3) one of Jesus's four 'brothers'; (4) Simon the Leper, in whose house Jesus was anointed; (5) Simon of Cyrene, who carried Jesus's cross; (6) Simon the Tanner, in whose house Peter had his vision.

Stephen The first Christian martyr, who was stoned to death.

Thomas One of the 12 apostles; known as 'doubting Thomas' because he at first doubted resurrection.

Timothy Paul's young helper and fellow-missionary; there are two letters to him from Paul. He was responsible for looking after the Church at Ephesus.

Titus Convert of Paul's and his travelling companion; Paul sent him one letter.

Zebedee Father of the apostles James and John.

Lucky Dip

Seeing Isn't Believing!

Learning how to see things involves far more than just learning how to use your eyes. It also involves learning how to make sense of the things the eyes and the brain tell us we are seeing. This is called *perception.*

Perception is a matter of relating what we see to the many other occasions on which we have seen the same object. We know that we are looking at a chair whether we see it from the front or the back, or from the side, or from above or below. The images of the chair that our retina absorb may well be different depending on where we stand. Nevertheless, we know that we are looking at a chair.

Similarly, people on the opposite side of the street appear to be the same size as people on our own side, although the images we receive of them are smaller. Our brain automatically organizes the images it receives in such a way that what we perceive makes sense to us.

Illusions

The brain is often deceived, however. At night, for instance, what we think is one thing often turns out to be something quite different. The images it casts on the retina are so weak that the brain misunderstands them. Sometimes, too, objects can give out conflicting images. Is the picture at the bottom of this page of a vase or of two faces?

Sometimes the brain can be deceived. Have you ever noticed how large the moon looks when it rises behind trees or houses? When it is high in the sky it looks smaller because there is nothing with which to compare it.

At first glance the picture on the right seems quite normal, because the mind is used to taking account of the size and distance of objects. A closer look reveals that the artist has tricked the mind.

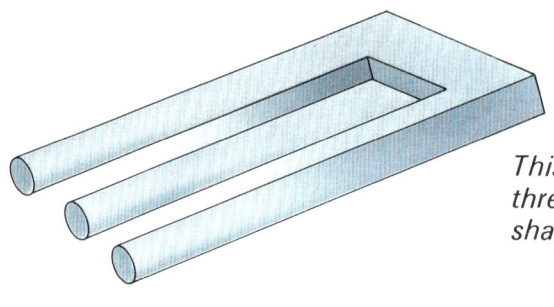

This impossible object appears to have three prongs at one end, but only a U-shape at the other.

Is this a vase or a pair of faces? The brain perceives the drawing in two ways and cannot choose between them.

Below: What size are the centre circles in these two drawings? One seems smaller than the other because of the other circles nearby, but in fact they are the same size.

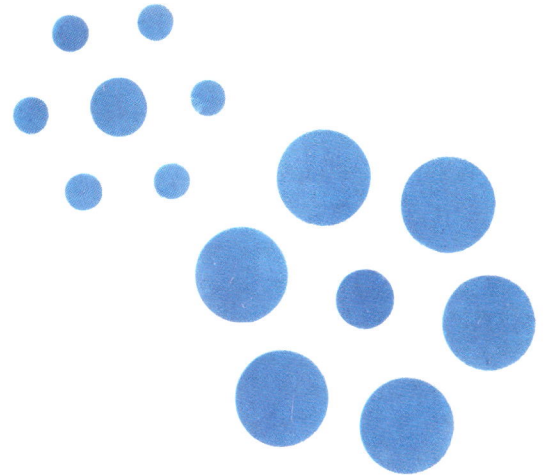

Your brain may tell you that this is a drawing of a dog. In fact it is a group of 22 blobs arranged in such a way that you perceive it as a dog.

This illusionist painting by the Dutch artist Maurits Escher defies the normal world and makes water appear to flow uphill.

How many colours appear in this drawing? Your brain may tell you there are four. In fact there are only three. The centre circles are the same colour. The different colours of the outer circles appear to change that of the inner one.

Popular Sayings

If you want a thing done well, do it yourself.

All work and no play makes Jack a dull boy.

Neither a borrower nor a lender be.

It's never too late to mend.

East, west, Home's best.

The hasty angler loses the fish.

A stitch in time saves nine.

Early to bed and early to rise makes a man healthy, wealthy and wise.

Never spend your money before you have it.

Never put off till tomorrow what you can do today.

Fire is a good servant but a bad master.

A liar should have a good memory.

Bustle is not industry, nor is impudence courage.

Knowledge makes humble.

A clear conscience fears no accusation.

Shallow brooks are noisy, deep rivers flow with silent majesty.

Knowledge talks lowly: ignorance makes proud.

Plain words make the most ornamental sentences.

Tell no home secrets out of doors.

Every day in your life is a page in your history.

Revenge is the only debt which it is wrong to pay.

Time and tide wait for no man.

Judge not, that ye be not judged.

Wilful waster makes woeful want.

Absence makes the heart grow fonder.

The bravest are the tenderest.

Brevity is the soul of wit.

Some common knots, and how they are tied. Tie your knots loosely and tighten them gently, but not completely, then wet the line and firmly pull the knot.

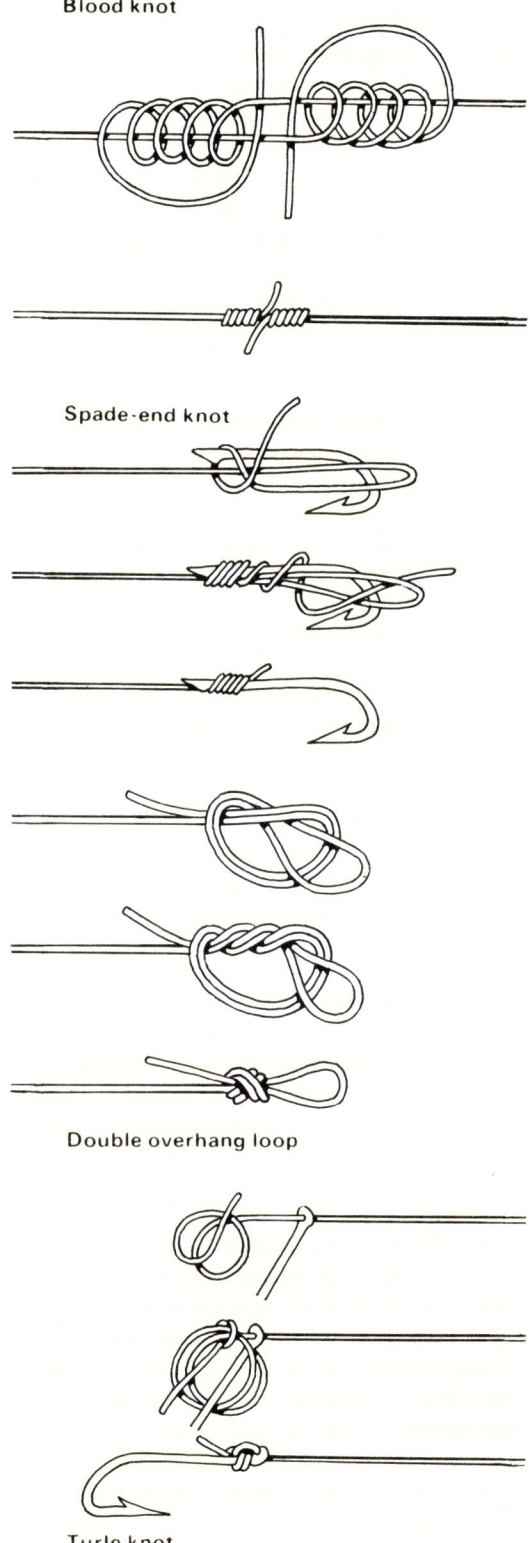

Blood knot

Spade-end knot

Double overhang loop

Turle knot

How Do You Write?

Graphology is the art of judging character from handwriting. Perhaps you have seen detective programmes on television where a graphologist is called in to give an opinion of the character of an unknown criminal simply by studying a piece of the offender's handwriting. Graphologists are able to tell the character of a person whose handwriting they have seen but whom they have never met. This is not fortune telling, but only claims to reveal personality.

Do you write using very small letters or large letters? Do you write tidily or untidily? Does the writing slope to the right, to the left, or is it bolt upright? Do you place your letters close together so that you get a maximum of words into a minimum of space, or is your handwriting scrawling or 'elongated' so that you cover many lines without saying much?

Now if your writing slopes to the *right* the graphologist will tell you that you are a determined character who likes planning ahead, even if the plans do not always work out to your liking. You feel you must sketch out tomorrow's programme on paper beforehand.

If your handwriting slopes to the *left* you are not a planner. You would rather think about what has been than what is to be. In fact, the future does not worry you at all.

The *upright* handwriters are ambitious personalities with strong will-power; and though they may not always achieve the goals they plan, they will get near to them. They are usually creative,

have their wits about them. Often they are very good judges of other people's character.

Now, do you write in an *elongated* way? That is, do you spread your words across the line, using a great deal of space without sloping to right or left? This, say our experts, reveals a person of unruffled calm who is not easily upset about anything and who is a very good friend to have in an upset of any kind.

If you always employ *close* writing – that is, condensing your words and letters – you have an artistic or literary temperament, are a quick thinker and also something of an economist. You like to day-dream, but for the most part you are intensely practical.

Let's look at the *small* letter writer. We have to be careful here because small writing is not always characteristic of the writer. People in a nervous state, who are recovering from an illness or are experiencing an acute lack of confidence in themselves, often find themselves writing in mini-style. But those who *always* write in small characters are usually the very careful types who take great pains in any task they have to perform. They are often bank clerks or schoolteachers; very precise about money and details, and therefore very careful in all they say and do. Graphologists do not say that all these people have all these attributes but it is likely that each may possess one or more of them.

The *large* letter writer is a good-humoured, generous individual with no particular 'phobias'. Such people are constantly friendly and will never betray a confidence.

The Subway on the Sidewalk

(American words and their British equivalents)

aluminum aluminium
attorney lawyer
apartment flat
automobile car
baby carriage pram
baggage luggage
bill banknote
billboard hoarding
biscuit a bread roll or scone
bit $\frac{1}{8}$ of a dollar
bug any insect
candy sweets
carousel roundabout
casket coffin
check cheque
checkers draughts
cookie sweet biscuit
clerk shop assistant
cracker biscuit
davenport couch
diaper baby's nappy
drugstore chemist's shop, also sells a variety of goods including refreshments.
doughboy infantry soldier
dove past tense of dive
elevator lift
engineer engine driver
fall autumn
fender car bumper
faucet tap
first floor ground floor
garbage can dustbin
gasoline (gas) petrol
given name christian name
grab bag lucky dip
greenbacks paper money
gridiron football field
highway main road
hog pig
homely plain, ugly
homicide murder
hood car bonnet

janitor caretaker
jumping rope skipping rope
line queue
lumber timber
lot plot of ground
major specialize in a subject
make out get along, manage
mortician undertaker
name for name after
notion department haberdashery in a department store
of before 'He left at ten minutes of six'.
pants trousers
pass up decline, refuse
peek-a-boo hide and seek
pie a tart
pocketbook handbag
purse handbag
porch verandah
railroad railway
ranch farm
realtor estate agent
rooster cockbird
round-trip ticket return ticket
sidewalk pavement
skillet frying pan
slingshot catapult
sneakers gym shoes
spool cotton reel
streetcar tram
string shoelace
subway underground railway
suspenders braces
tag day flag day
through 'Tuesday through Thursday' – from Tuesday to Thursday. Also: finished, ended
thumb tack drawing pin
tightwad miser
trash rubbish
trunk car boot
uptown residential part of a city
undershirt vest
vest waistcoat
washroom lavatory
windshield windscreen

Foreign Words in English

INDIAN WORDS

chapatti Round flat cake of whole wheat flour.

chula Small clay stove.

curry Spicy dish of eggs, meat, fish, or vegetables.

dhobi Washerman.

dhoti Simple white garment for men, wrapped round the body and between the legs.

durbar Body of officials at an Indian court.

ghee Clarified butter.

panchayat Elected council of village elders.

pilau Rice mixed with ghee and spices.

purdah Seclusion of women.

rajah King or prince.

sari Garment for women made up of a long straight piece of cloth wrapped round the body to form a dress.

Shiva, Vishnu Principal Hindu gods.

sitar Stringed instrument resembling a huge guitar.

CHINESE WORDS

Cathay Medieval European and poetic name for China.

ch'a Tea.

chopsticks Two small sticks of wood, bone, ivory, or plastic used in eating. The Pidgin English word means 'quick sticks'. The correct Chinese term is *kwaitsze* – 'the quick ones'.

chow Food.

Forbidden City Walled enclosure in Peking (1020 x 760 m) with imperial palaces, temples, apartments, and audience halls.

hua pen Scripts used by story-tellers popular in the AD 1000s.

junk Chinese sailing boat with high forecastle and poop, usually three-masted.

mah jongg table game played with small painted 'tiles', usually of ivory.

paddy or **cut** Water-covered field for growing rice.

Peking opera Form of drama, including songs and dialogue, that originated in Peking in the 1700s.

p'i p'a Ancient lute-like instrument.

sampan Shallow 'family' boat, partly covered by awnings and usually propelled by a single scull over the stern.

JAPANESE WORDS

banzai A shouted greeting '(May you live) ten thousand years'.

bonsai Miniature tree culture.

bushido warrior code of chivalry.

geisha Dancing girl.

haiku Short verse form.

hara-kari Ceremonious suicide by disembowelment.

ikebana Artistic flower-arranging.

judo A type of wrestling.

karate Unarmed self-defence, including lethal blows with hands and feet.

kamikaze 'Divine wind' refers to the typhoon that wrecked the ships of Kublai Khan in 1274 and saved Japan from conquest. The term was adopted by Japanese suicide pilots in World War II.

kimono Traditional long loose robe of cotton or silk.

mikado Foreigners' title for the Emperor.

netsuke Small ornament or figurine made of bone or wood.

Nippon Japan, literally, 'origin of the sun'.

noh Drama developed from a religious dance.

sake Rice beer.

shogun Military dictator.

LUCKY DIP

Boys' Names and Their Meaning

Aaron	Hebrew	*lofty*
Adam	Hebrew	*red skin*
Adrian	Latin	*of the Adriatic*
Alan, Allen	Celtic	*harmony*
Albert	Saxon	*nobly bright*
Alexander, Alistair	Greek	*defending men*
Andrew	Greek	*manly*
Anthony	Latin	*praiseworthy*
Barry	Gaelic	*a spear*
Benjamin	Hebrew	*son of the South*
Bernard	German	*brave as a bear*
Brian	Celtic	*strong*
Charles	German	*manly*
Christopher	Greek	*carrier of Christ*
Clifford	English	*ford by the slope*
Clive	English	*dweller by the cliff*
Conrad	German	*bold counsel*
Craig	English	*dweller by the crag*
Daniel	Hebrew	*God has judged*
David	Hebrew	*friend*
Dean	English	*dweller in the valley*
Denis, Dennis	Greek	*belonging to the god of wine*
Derek	German	*ruler of the people*
Desmond	Gaelic	*man from south Munster*
Donald	Gaelic	*world mighty*
Douglas	Gaelic	*dark blue*
Duncan	Gaelic	*brown warrior*
Edward	English	*happy guardian*
Edwin	English	*happy friend*
Eric	Norse	*ruler*
Francis, Frank	Latin	*a Frenchman*
Frederick	German	*peaceful ruler*
Geoffrey	Norman	*peace*
George	Greek	*farmer*
Gerald	Norman	*spear power*
Giles	Greek	*young goat*
Gordon	Gaelic	*great hill*
Graham	English	*Granta's homestead*
Gregory	Greek	*watchful*
Guy	Norman	*leader*
Henry	German	*home ruler*
Howard	German	*brave of heart*
Hugh	German	*heart and mind*
Ian	Gaelic form of John	
James	Latin	*a supplanter*
Jeremy	Hebrew	*exalted of the Lord*
John	Hebrew	*favoured by God*
Joseph	Hebrew	*added by God*
Julian	Latin	*soft haired*
Justin	Latin	*just*
Keith	Celtic	*wood*
Kenneth	Gaelic	*handsome*
Lance	German	*land*
Laurence	Latin	*crowned with laurels*
Leonard	German	*lion-bold*
Leslie	Gaelic	*garden of holly*
Lewis, Louis	German	*famous fighter*
Malcolm	Gaelic	*servant of St Columba*
Mark,	Latin	*a hammer*
Martin	Latin	*martial*
Matthew	Hebrew	*gift of God*
Michael	Hebrew	*who is like God?*
Neil, Neal	Gaelic	*a champion*
Nicholas	Greek	*victory of the people*
Nigel	Latin form of Neil	
Noël	French	*born on Christmas day*
Norman	German	*northman*
Oliver	French	*olive tree*
Owen	Welsh	*well-born*
Patrick	Latin	*a nobleman*
Paul	Latin	*small*
Peter	Greek	*stone*
Philip	Greek	*lover of horses*
Ralph, Randolph	Norse	*counsel wolf*
Raymond	German	*wise protection*
Reginald, Ronald	English	*powerful might*
Richard	Norman	*stern ruler*
Robert, Rupert	Norman	*bright fame*
Roderick	German	*fame rule*
Rodney	English	*Hroda's island*
Roger	Norman	*fame-spear*
Roy	Gaelic	*red*
Samuel	Hebrew	*name of God*
Sebastian	Latin	*venerable*
Simon	Hebrew	*obedient*
Stanley	English	*stone field*
Stephen	Greek	*crown*
Stuart	English	*steward*
Terence	Latin	*a Roman clan*
Theodore	Greek	*God's gift*
Thomas	Aramaic	*twin*
Timothy	Greek	*honoured*
Trevor	Welsh	*big village*
Victor	Latin	*conqueror*
Vincent	Latin	*conquering*
Walter	German	*rule folk*
William	Norman	*helmet of will*

Girls' Names and Their Meaning

Feminine forms of male names are not shown in the list unless they are not easily recognizable as such, since the feminine names have the same meaning as their male counterparts.*

Alice, Alison	German	nobility
Amanda	Latin	lovable
Angela	Greek	messenger
Ann, Anne, Hannah	Hebrew	God has favoured me
Annabelle	Latin	lovable
Audrey	English	noble
Barbara	Greek	foreign
Belinda	German	useful
Brenda	Norse	sword
Bridget	Celtic	the high one
Camilla	Latin	attendant at a sacrifice
Chloë	Greek	young green shoot
Christina, Christine	English	Christian
Claire, Clare	Latin	bright, clear
Cynthia	Greek	a goddess of the Moon
Deborah	Hebrew	a bee
Diana	Greek	goddess of the Moon
Dorothy	Greek	gift of God
Elaine, Eleanor	A form of Helen	
Elizabeth	Hebrew	oath of God
Emily	Latin	a Roman clan
Emma	German	whole, universal
Esther	Persian	star
Eve	Hebrew	lively
Evelyn	Latin	hazel
Felicity	Latin	happiness
Fiona	Gaelic	fair, white
Helen	Greek	the bright one
Hilary	Latin	cheerful
Ingrid	Norse	beautiful
Isabel	Spanish form of Elizabeth	
Jennifer	Cornish	white-cheeked
Jessica	Hebrew	God beholds
Joyce	Celtic	merry, joyful
Judith, Judy	Hebrew	a Jewess
Juliana, Gillian	Feminine of Julian	
Karen	Danish form of Katherine	
Katherine	Greek	pure
Kathleen	Irish form of Katherine	
Lucy	Latin	light
Madeleine	Hebrew	woman of Magdala
Margaret	Greek	pearl
Mary	Hebrew	wished for child
Monica	Greek	alone
Naomi	Hebrew	pleasant one
Natalie	Latin	Christmas Day
Olivia	Latin	olive
Pamela	Greek	all sweetness
Penelope	Greek	a weaver
Rachel	Hebrew	ewe
Rebecca	Hebrew	snare
Samantha	Aramaic	listener
Sarah	Hebrew	princess
Sharon	Hebrew	a plain
Sophia, Sonia	Greek	wisdom
Susan, Susannah	Hebrew	lily
Sylvia	Latin	wood
Teresa, Theresa	Greek	a reaper
Veronica	Latin	true image
Victoria	Latin	victory
Virginia	Latin	a virgin
Zoe	Greek	life

*Feminine Forms of male Names

Female	Male	Female	Male
Adrienne	Adrian	Jane	John
Alexandra	Alexander	Janet	John
Andrea	Andrew	Jean	John
Antonia	Anthony	Josephine	Joseph
Carla	Charles	Julia, Julie	Julian
Carol, Caroline	Charles	Laura	Laurence
Caroline	Charles	Lesley	Leslie
Charlene	Charles	Louisa,	Louis
Charlotte	Charles	Marcia	Mark
Danielle	Daniel	Martine	Martin
Davina	David	Maxine	Maximilian
Denise	Denis	Michaela	Michael
Edwina	Edwin	Michelle	Michael
Frances	Francis	Nicola	Nicholas
Georgina	George	Norma	Norman
Geraldine	Gerald	Patricia	Patrick
Gillian	Julian	Paula	Paul
Harriet	Henry	Pauline	Paul
Henrietta	Henry	Simone	Simon
Jacqueline	Jacques (Jacob, James)	Stephanie	Stephen
		Victoria	Victor
		Vivienne	Vivian
		Yvonne	Yves

LUCKY DIP

Greek		
Letter	Name	Transliteration
A α	alpha	a
B β	beta	b
Γ γ	gamma	g
Δ δ	delta	d
E ε	epsilon	e
Z ζ	zeta	z
H η	eta	ē
Θ θ	theta	th
I ι	iota	i
K κ	kappa	k
Λ λ	lambda	l
M μ	mu	m
N ν	nu	n
Ξ ξ	xi	x (ks)
O ο	omicron	o
Π π	pi	p
P ρ	rho	r
Σ σ,ς*	sigma	s
T τ	tau	t
Υ υ	upsilon	u, y
Φ φ	phi	ph
X χ	chi	kh, ch
Ψ ψ	psi	ps
Ω ω	omega	o

Hebrew		
Letter	Name	Transliteration
א	aleph†	ʾ
ב	beth	b
ג	gimel	g
ד	daleth	d
ה	heh	h
ו	waw	w
ז	zayin	z
ח	heth	ḥ
ט	teth	ṭ
י	yod	y
ךכ*	kaph	k, kh
ל	lamed	l
םמ*	mem	m
ןנ*	nun	n
ס	samekh	s
ע	ayin	ʿ
ףפ*	peh	p, ph
ץצ*	sadhe	ṣ
ק	qoph	q
ר	resh	r
שׁ	shin	sh
שׂ	sin	ś
ת	taw	t

Russian		
Letter		Transliteration
А	а	a
Б	б	b
В	в	v
Г	г	g
Д	д	d
Е	е	e, ye
Ж	ж	zh
З	з	z
И	и	i
Й	й	i
К	к	k
Л	л	l
М	м	m
Н	н	n
О	о	o
П	п	p
Р	р	r
С	с	s
Т	т	t
У	у	u
Ф	ф	f
Х	х	kh
Ц	ц	ts
Ч	ч	ch
Ш	ш	sh
Щ	щ	shch
	ы	i
	ь	'
Э	э	e
Ю	ю	yu
Я	я	ya

Letters and Alphabets

The alphabet which we use in Europe and many other parts of the world is called the Latin alphabet, because it is largely based on that used in ancient Rome. This book is printed in the Latin alphabet. The Romans got their letters from another people living in Italy called the Etruscans, who in turn took their letters from the Greeks. The Greeks had taken their alphabet from that used by the Phoenicians, a people who came from the area of the Middle East which is at the present day occupied by Syria and the Lebanon.

There are other alphabets used in Europe and Asia Minor, most of which came from the same source – an area somewhere in the Nile Delta, in very early times. So this means that the Latin, Hebrew and Arabic alphabets are all distantly related, although they look very different nowadays. The Greek alphabet is still used in Modern Greece and the nearby Mediterranean islands, while the Russian alphabet is somewhat similar. It does contain some extra letters which represent sounds in Russian and other Slavonic tongues which are not to be found in Greek. Christian missionaries were travelling into the various Slav countries in early times, and in the 9th century, St Cyril and another monk called St Methodius adapted the Greek letters to suit Russian and its related languages. They added one or two signs from the Coptic and Hebrew alphabets.

Somewhat distantly related to the Hebrew and Nile delta alphabets are the various writing systems used in India and countries nearby. However, India has many languages, and some need different alphabets from others, so that there is not one single alphabet which can be used for the whole area.

Chinese writing is not alphabetic, since each character represents a word or an idea. Chinese characters were originally pictures, but are now reduced to a number of careful brush strokes.

Japanese has a somewhat similar look, but in fact is quite different from Chinese. It uses a writing system made up of syllables rather than letters. You can even write English words in the Japanese syllable system, spelling them out phonetically. For instance, you would need six Japanese characters to spell AUSTRALIA – like this:

O SU TA RA RI A

If you pronounce the syllables quickly, you will hear the word 'Australia'. However, the Japanese do not distinguish between R and L, using a sound somewhere in between!

From top to bottom: letters from our alphabet, the Russian, the Japanese phonetic, the Greek and Arabic alphabets.

The Morse Code is used for sending messages by sound or by flashing lights.

A	·–	S	···	J	·———	2	··———
B	—···	T	—	K	—·—	3	···——
C	—·—·	U	··—	L	·—··	4	····—
D	—··	V	···—	M	——	5	·····
E	·	W	·——	N	—·	6	—····
F	··—·	X	—··—	O	———	7	——···
G	——·	Y	—·——	P	·——·	8	———··
H	····	Z	——··	Q	——·—	9	————·
I	··	1	·————	R	·—·	0	—————

Weights and Measures

Length
Metric units
millimetre (mm)
10 mm = 1 centimetre (cm)
100 cm = 1 metre (m)
1000 m = 1 kilometre (km)
1 micron (μ) = 10^{-6} m
1 millimicron (mμ) = 10^{-9} m
1 angstrom (Å) = 10^{-10} m

Imperial units
inch (in)
12 in = 1 yard (yd)
1760 yd = 1 mile = 5280 ft

Area
Metric units
square millimetre (mm²)
100 mm² = 1 square centimetre (cm²)
10,000 cm² = 1 square metre (m²)
100 m² = 1 are (a) = 1 square
  decametre
100 a = 1 hectare (ha) = 1 square
  hectometre
100 ha = 1 square kilometre (km²)

Imperial units
square inch (in²)
144 in² = 1 square foot (ft²)
9 ft² = 1 square yard (yd²)
4840 yd² = 1 acre
640 acres = 1 square mile (mile²)

Volume
Metric units
cubic millimetre (mm³)
1000 mm³ = 1 cubic centimetre (cm³)
1000 cm³ = 1 cubic decimetre (dm³) =
  1 litre
1000 dm³ = 1 cubic metre (m³)
1,000,000,000 m³ = 1 cubic kilometre (km³)

Imperial units
cubic inch (in³)
1728 in³ = 1 cubic foot (ft³)
27 ft³ = 1 cubic yard (yd³)
5,451,776,000 yd³ = 1 cubic mile (mile³)

Capacity
Metric units
millilitre (ml)
1000 ml = 1 litre (l)
100 l = 1 hectolitre (hl)

Imperial units
gill
4 gills = 1 pint
2 pints = 1 quart
4 quarts = 1 gallon = 277.274 in³

(dry)
2 gallons = 1 peck
4 pecks = 1 bushel
8 bushels = 1 quarter
36 bushels = 1 chaldron

(Apothecaries' fluid)
minim (min)
60 min = fluid drachm (fl dr)
8 fl dr = 1 fluid ounce (fl oz)
5 fl oz = 1 gill
20 fl oz = 1 pint

US units
1 US gallon (liquid) = 0·8327 gallon
(imp)
1 US gallon (dry) = 0·9689 gallon (imp)
1 fluid oz (US) = 1·0408 fl oz (apoth)

Weight
Metric units
milligram (mg)
1000 mg = 1 gram (g)
1000 g = 1 kilogram (kg)
100 kg = 1 quintal (q)
1000 kg = 1 metric ton, or tonne (t)

Imperial units (Avoirdupois)
grain (gr); dram (dr)
7000 gr = 1 pound (lb)
16 dr = 1 ounce (oz)
16 oz = 1 lb
14 lb = 1 stone
28 lb = 1 quarter
112 lb = 1 hundredweight (cwt)
20 cwt = 1 (long) ton = 2240 lb
2000 lb = 1 short ton (US)

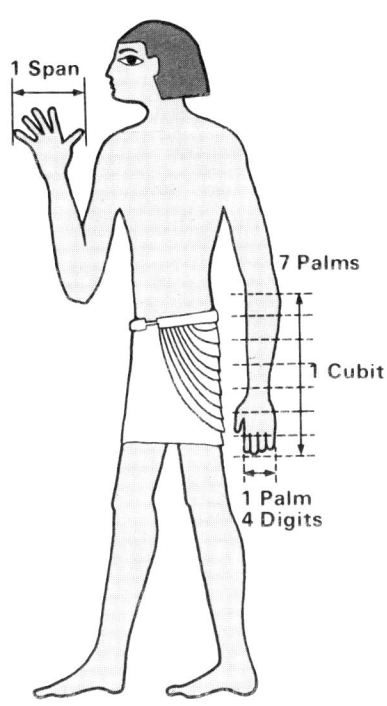

The ancient Egyptians based their measurements on the proportions of the body.

Nautical Measurement

1 fathom = 6 ft
1 nautical mile (old) = 6080 ft
1 nautical mile (international) = 1·151 statute mile (= 1852 metres)
60 nautical miles = 1 degree
3 nautical miles = 1 league (nautical)
1 knot = 1 nautical mile per hour

Conversion Factors

1 acre = 0·4047 hectares
1 bushel (imperial) = 36·369 litres
1 centimetre = 0·3937 inch
1 cubic centimetre = 0·0610 cubic inch
1 cubic decimetre = 61·024 cubic inches
1 cubic foot = 0·0283 cubic metre
1 cubic inch = 16·387 cubic centimetres
1 cubic metre = 35·3146 cubic feet = 1·3079 cubic yards
1 cubic yard = 0·7646 cubic metre
1 fluid oz (apoth) = 28·4131 millilitres
1 foot = 0·3048 metre = 30·48 centimetres

1 foot per second = 0·6818 mph = 1.097 km/h
1 gallon (imperial) = 4·5461 litres
1 gill = 0·142 litre
1 grain = 0·0648 gram
1 gram = 0·0353 ounce = 0·002205 pound = 15.43 grains = 0·0321 ounce (Troy)
1 hectare = 2·4710 acres
1 hectolitre = 2·750 bushels
1 hundredweight = 50·80 kilograms
1 inch = 2·54 centimetres
1 kilogram = 2·2046 pounds
1 kilometre = 0·6214 mile = 1093·6 yards
1 knot (international) = 0·5144 metres/sec = 1·852 km/h
1 litre = 0·220 gallon (imperial) = 0·2642 gallon (US) = 1·7598 pints (imperial) = 0·8799 quarts
1 metre = 39·3701 in = 3·2808 ft = 1·0936 yd
1 metric ton = 0·9842 long ton = 1·1023 short ton
1 mile (statute) = 1·6093 kilometres
1 mile (nautical) = 1·852 kilometres
1 millimetre = 0·03937 inch
1 ounce = 28·350 grams
1 pint (imperial) = 0·5683 litre
1 pound = 0·4536 kilogram
1 quart (imperial) = 1·1365 litres
1 square centimetre = 0·1550 square inch
1 square foot = 0·0929 square metre
1 square inch = 6·4516 square centimetres
1 square kilometre = 0·3860 square mile
1 square metre = 10·7639 square feet = 1·1960 square yards
1 square mile = 2·5900 square kilometres
1 square yard = 0·8361 square metre
1 stone = 6·350 kilograms
1 ton (long) = 1·0160 metric tons (tonnes)
1 ton (short) = 0·9072 metric tone (tonne)
1 yard = 0·9144 metre

English Homonyms

A homonym is a word which, although differently spelled, and with a different meaning, sounds like another. The following list shows typical homonyms:

adds	adze	billed	build
ail	ale	bird	burred
air	ere, e'er, heir	blew	blue
airy	aerie, eyrie	bloc	block
aisle	I'll, isle	boar	bore
all	awl	board	bored
allowed	aloud	boarder	border
altar	alter	bode	bowed
arc	ark	bold	bowled
ate	eight	bolder	boulder
auger	augur	bole	bowl
aught	ought	born	borne
auricle	oracle	bough	bow
away	aweigh	boy	buoy
aye	eye, I	braise	brays, braze
bad	bade	braid	brayed
bail	bale	brake	break
bait	bate	bray	brae
band	banned	breach	breech
banns	bans	bread	bred
bard	barred	brewed	brood
bare	bear	brews	bruise
baron	barren	bridal	bridle
based	baste	but	butt
bass	base	buy	by, bye
be	bee	byre	buyer
beach	beech	cannon	canon
bearing	baring	canvas	canvass
beat	beet	carrot	carat
been	bean	cash	cache
beer	bier	cast	caste
bell	belle	cause	caws
berry	bury	ceiling	sealing
berth	birth	cell	sell
bey	bay	cellar	seller
bight	bite	censor	censer
		cereal	serial
		chaste	chased
		cheap	cheep
		choir	quire
		choose	chews
		chronicle	chronical
		clack	claque
		clause	claws
		climb	clime
		clue	clew

coal	cole
coarse	course
coax	cokes
collar	choler
colonel	kernel
compliment	complement
coo	coup
cord	cored, chord
core	corps
correspondents	
	correspondence
council	counsel
cousin	cozen
coward	cowered
creak	creek
cruise	crews
cue	queue
currant	current
dam	damn
daze	days
dear	deer
dense	dents
dependence	dependents
desert	dessert
dew	due
die	dye
dire	dyer
discreet	discrete
dissidence	dissidents
doe	dough
done	dun
dual	duel
duct	ducked
dust	dost
earn	urn
eve	eave
faint	feint
fair	fare
faker	fakir
fate	fete
fawn	faun
fay	fey
feat	feet
feign	fain
find	fined
fir	fur

flair	flare	hoop	whoop	mantle	mantel
flea	flee	hose	hoes	mare	mayor
flew	flue, 'flu	humorous	humerus	marshal	martial
flex	flecks	idle	idol	martin	marten
flocks	phlox	in	inn	maul	mall
flour	flower	incidence	incidents	mean	mien
flow	floe	innocence	innocents	meat	meet, mete
fold	foaled	instance	instants	medal	meddle
for	fore, four	intense	intents	metal	mettle
forward	foreward	invade	inveighed	might	mite
foul	fowl	its	it's	mince	mints
frank	franc	jam	jamb	mind	mined
freeze	frees, frieze	key	quay	miner	minor
furs	furze	knave	nave	minx	minks
gamble	gambol	knew	gnu, new	mist	missed
gate	gait	knight	night	moan	mown
gauge	gage	knit	nit	moat	mote
gild	guild	knot	not	mode	mowed
gilt	guilt	know	no	mood	mooed
gored	gourd	lamb	lam	moose	mousse
gorilla	guerilla	lane	lain	morn	mourn
graze	greys	lapse	laps	mule	mewl
greater	grater	lax	lacks	muscle	mussel
grill	grille	laze	lays	muse	mews
grisly	grizzly	lea	lee	mustard	mustered
groan	grown	lead	led	naval	navel
guest	guessed	leak	leek	need	knead
guise	guys	least	leased	neigh	nay
hail	hale	leech	leach	none	nun
hair	hare	lesson	lessen	nose	knows
hall	haul	liar	lyre	oar	or, ore, o'er
heal	heel, he'll	lichen	liken	ode	owed
heard	herd	lie	lye	one	won
heart	hart	literal	littoral	our	hour
heed	he'd	load	lode, lowed	owe	oh
here	hear	loan	lone	pact	packed
hew	hue	low	lo	pail	pale
hide	hied	lumber	lumbar	pain	pane
high	hie	lute	loot	pair	pear, pare
him	hymn	lynx	links	palate	palette,
hire	higher	magnet	magnate		pallet
hoard	horde	maid	made	past	passed
hoarse	horse	mail	male	paste	paced
hold	holed	main	mane	patience	patients
holy	holey	maize	maze	pause	paws
	wholly	manner	manor	peace	piece

LUCKY DIP

peak	pique	roe	row	tact	tacked
peal	peel	roll	role	tail	tale
pearl	purl	rose	roes, rows	taught	taut
pedal	peddle	rough	ruff	tax	tacks
peer	pier	rouse	rows	tea	tee
pend	penned	rude	rood, rued	team	teem
phase	faze	rung	wrung	tear	tare
phrase	frays	rye	wry	tear	tier
pistol	pistil	sail	sale	tease	teas, tees
place	plaice	sailor	sailer	tense	tents
plain	plane	scene	seen	their	there
please	pleas	seam	seem	throne	thrown
plum	plumb	seize	seas, sees	through	threw
pole	poll	sense	cents, scents	tide	tied
pour	pore	sew	so, sow	time	thyme
praise	prays, preys	shake	sheik	to	too, two
pray	prey	shear	sheer	toad	toed, towed
presence	presents	shire	shyer	toe	tow
pride	pried	shoe	shoo	told	tolled
prince	prints	shoot	chute	tract	tracked
principal	principle	side	sighed	troop	troupe
prize	pries	sign	sine	trust	trussed
profit	prophet	signet	cygnet	turn	tern
purr	per	size	sighs	vain	vane, vein
quartz	quarts	slay	sleigh	veil	vale
rack	wrack	slight	sleight	wade	weighed
raid	rayed	slow	sloe	wane	wain
rain	reign, rein	soar	sore	waist	waste
raise	rays, raze	sold	soled	wait	weight
rancour	ranker	some	sum	war	wore
rap	wrap	son	sun	warn	worn
rapt	rapped, wrapped	soul	sole	wave	waive
read	reed	staid	stayed	way	weigh, whey
real	reel	stair	stare	we	wee
red	read	stake	steak	weak	week
reek	wreak	stationary	stationery	wear	ware, where
residence	residents	steal	steel	weave	we've
rest	wrest	step	steppe	weed	we'd
review	revue	straight	strait	weir	we're
rhyme	rime	style	stile	whole	hole
right	rite, wright, write	suede	swayed	wind	wined
rigour	rigger	surf	serf	wood	would
ring	wring	surge	serge	wretch	retch
road	rode, rowed	sweet	suite	wrote	rote
		sv⸱ ⸱	soared	yoke	yolk
		sy⸱	cymbal	you	ewe

Pronunciation of Surnames

Some British surnames are not pronounced as they are spelt. Here is a list showing some which do not follow the usual rules of spelling.

Bagehot	Bag'got
Bartelot	Bart'lett
Beauchamp	Beech'em
Beauclerc	Bo'clair
Beaulieu	Bew'ly
Belvoir	Beaver
Bethune	Beeton
Bicester	Bister
Bohun	Boon
Boleyn	Bullen
Boucher, Bourchier	Bow'cher
Bough	Boff
Chandos	Shandos
Charteris	Charters
Cheyne	Cheen, Chain Cheyney
Chisholm	Chizum
Chivas, Shives	Chives, Shee'vus
Cholmondeley	Chum'ley
Cochrane	Coch'ran*
Cockburn	Co'burn
Colquhoun	Co'hoon
Cowper	Cooper
Dalziel	Dee-ell
Donoghue	Dun-no-hew
Drogheda	Dro-heda
Dynevor	Din'never
Elgin	El'Gin**
Eyre	Air
Farquhar	Faɪ'har
Featherstonehaugh	Fan'shaw
Fiennes	Fynes

Fildes	Fyldes+
Foulis	Fowls
Gallagher	Gal'laher
Geoghegan, Gahagan	Gay'gan
Glamis	Glahms
Gough	Goff
Grieg	Greg
Grierson	Greerson
Grosvenor	Gro'venor
Hawarden	Har'den
Hepburn	Heb'burn
Home	Hume
Iveagh	Ivah
Iverach	Eeverach*
Ives	Ivs
Ker, Kerr	Kar or Ker
Kirkby	Kir'by
Maclean	Mac-lane
Macleay	Mac-lay
Macleod	Mac-loud
Macmahon	Mac-mahn
Mainwaring	Man'nering
Marjoribanks	Marshbanks
Maugham	Mawm
Maughan	Mawn

Menzies	Mengis
Methven	Meffen
Meyrick	Merrick
Pepys	Peeps
Powell	Powell or Pole
Powys, Powis	Powis or Po'is
Pugh	Pew
Reay	Ray
Rees, Rhys	Reece
Ruthven	Riven or Ruffen
St John	Sin-jun
Strachoan	Strawn ob Stra-han
Tredegar	Tread-eager
Urquhart	Ur-chart*
Wemyss	Weems
Wolseley	Wools'ly

* 'ch' is pronounced gutturally, as in Scottish 'loch'.
** Hard 'g' as in 'get'.
+ Long 'i' as in 'wild'.

Traditional Anniversary Names

Year	Name	Year	Name
1	paper	14	ivory
2	cotton	15	crystal
3	leather	20	china
4	fruit, flowers	25	silver
5	wood	30	pearl
6	iron, sugar	35	coral
7	wool, copper	40	ruby
8	bronze	45	sapphire
9	pottery	50	golden
10	tin, aluminium	55	emerald
11	steel	60	diamond
12	silk, fine linen	75	diamond
13	lace		

Pets and who kept them

Dogs are descended from wolves, jackals and coyotes. They first became tame when cubs were brought back to camp by hunters.

People in Çatal Hüyük, Anatolia, 6000 BC, kept leopards as sacred pets.

Egyptian queens used to keep pet baboons.

In Anatolia, pet dogs accompanied their dead owners into the grave, so that they could be together in the after-life.

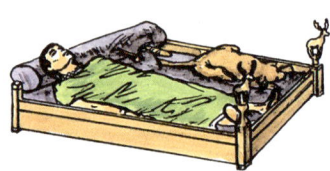

Chinese fishermen use cormorants to catch fish. They are on a lead and wear a neck ring so they cannot swallow the catch.

An unkind girl plays with her pet tortoise (left). Roman emperor Caligula used to have a lion that took part in banquets (right).

A little girl takes her pet dog for a run, 1700.

Mongooses are still kept as pets in India. They kill snakes and seem to be immune to their venom.

Below: Hawking was a popular pastime.

The Aztecs kept parrots (left) as pets. They also made good guards, warning off intruders. In 16th-century Italy (middle), bored women tried to keep themselves amused by tending exotic pets. Europeans take dogs for walks. The Muslims of the 16th century had monkeys (right).

Playing Cards

1.–2. Two trump cards from a modern Marseilles tarot pack, showing No. XIII 'Death', and No. VI 'The Lovers'. 3. A Jack of Clubs from an early French pack. 4. The Seven of Sheep from an early German animal pack. 5. A Jack of Spades from an Italian geographical pack of about 1670. 6. The Six of Swords from a modern Italian pack.

7. Trump No. XXXV from a Minchiate pack of about 1790. 8. Trump No. XVII from a German animal tarot pack from about 1800. 9. Le Jeu de Blocus pack commemorating the Napoleonic Wars. 10. Trump No. XIX from a modern Austrian tarot pack. 11. The Seven of Diamonds from a German literature pack of 1839. 12. The King of Diamonds (representing the actor Becker) from a German pack of 1840.

13. The King of Spades from an English pack of 1880. 14. The King of Clubs from an Austrian pack made for the jubilee of the Emperor, 1900. 15. The Ober of Leaves from a German 'war effort' pack of 1917. 16. A Belgian pack with deaf and dumb signs inset, made recently.

These playing-cards from different countries look unlike the familiar English pack. German cards have Acorns, Leaves, Hearts and Bells as suits, and in Italy, you will find Swords, Batons, Money and Cups. Some cards are from tarot packs. A number of games can be played with tarots, which use up to 78 different cards in one pack.

Magic

Conjuring is one of the oldest forms of entertainment. It was first mentioned in writing in the *Westcar Papyrus* over 3500 years ago. This records how the great magician Jajamanekh recovered an ornament lost in a lake by splitting the lake in two and stacking one half on top of the other. After picking up the jewel, he returned to the shore, clapped his hands and the water fell back into place!

Since then there are hundreds of records of magicians – working in the streets or at markets and fairs, or putting on shows in private houses and large theatres. Many are famous for creating specific tricks or elaborate illusions that still amaze and entertain audiences today. One of the greatest magicians of the past was the Frenchman Robert-Houdin whose 'Soirées Fantastiques' opened in Paris in 1845. He performed a wide range of magic and his presentation was completely original – he performed in ordinary evening dress rather than the long flowing robes of earlier magicians and treated magic in a scientific way. For this reason he is regarded as the 'father of modern magic'.

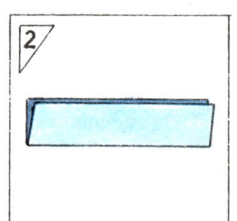
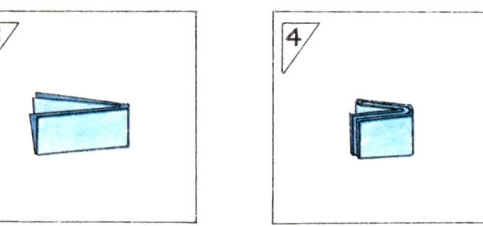
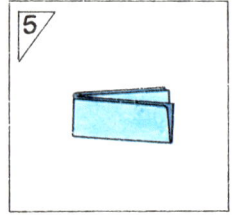
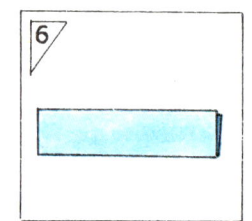

Topsy Turvy Note

Hold a bank note the right way up and facing the audience (1). The illustrations show each move from the audience's point of view. Fold the note up from the bottom to fold it in half lengthways (2). Fold it in half towards you (3).

Fold it in half again (4). Pause for a second. Hold the note steady in clear view of the audience. Look at the note as if something is puzzling you about it. Now unfold it from the front (5), (6). Continue to make your movements as slow, deliberate, and as mysterious as you can.

When, at last, the note is completely unfolded it is seen to have miraculously turned itself upside down (7). Although the slow-motion working sequence is automatic this trick is extremely effective if presented correctly.

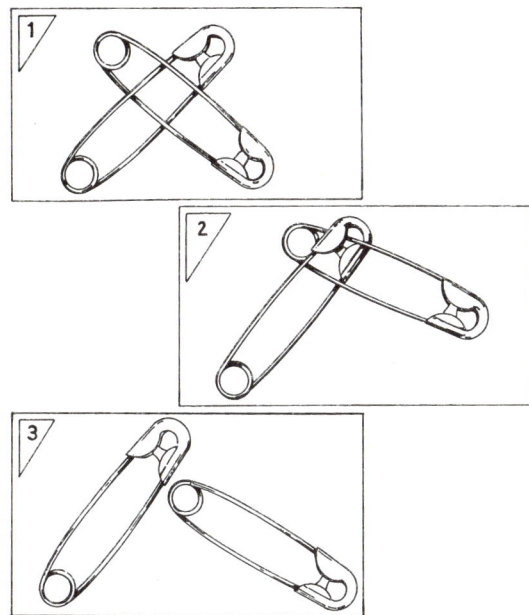

Anti-Magnetic Matches

Equipment: Two spent matches.

Place a used match on your left hand with its head overhanging your palm. Hold a used second match halfway along its length between the thumb and first finger of the right hand. The edge of the nail of the second finger of this hand is positioned against the end of the match, the same side as the first finger (1).

Bring the right hand, palm downwards, towards the left until the two match heads almost touch. Just before they make contact flick the end of the right-hand match with your finger nail. The impact will cause the head of this match to strike the other with such force that the left-hand match will leap from your hand and into the air in a spectacular way (2).

As the attention of the spectators is focused on the spectacularly dramatic movement of the match springing from your left hand no one notices the small flick made by the match in the right hand.

Piff, Paff, Pouff

Equipment: Two large safety pins.

Show your audience the two pins and then link them together (1). Hold the base of one pin in the left hand and the head of the second pin in the right hand. The uppermost bar of the second pin should be held close to the head of the first pin.

Give a secret word or blow on the pins and pull the pins apart with a definite downward movement of the right-hand pin (2).

This movement actually opens the first pin for a moment to release the second pin. But because it happens so quickly the audience is not aware that the pin has been opened and it appears that one pin has melted through the other by magic (3).

1

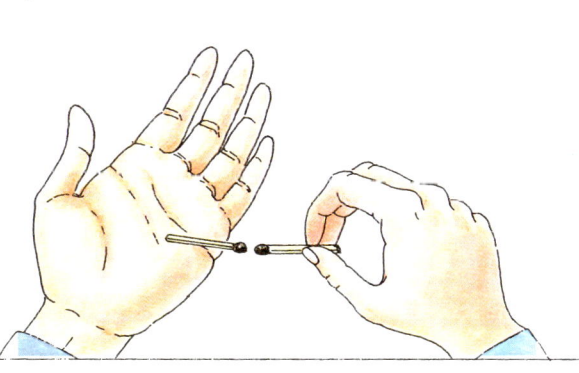

2

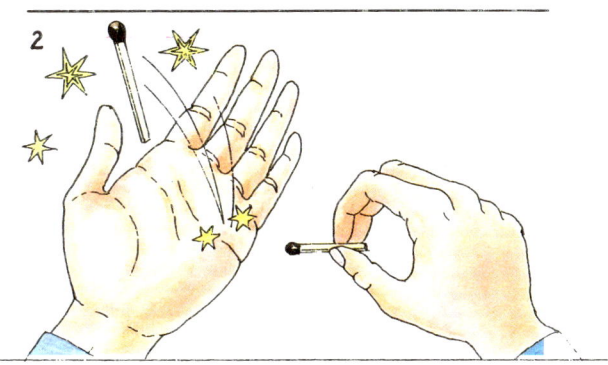

Pre-Columbian clay dog on wheels from an early Mexican culture.

Right: Greek terracotta dolls, 5th c. BC. The arms and legs are secured to the body with metal pins. The doll is probably mankind's oldest toy. The first dolls were flat pieces of wood. Today's dolls talk and walk and even wet their pants!

Bowling a hoop goes back to the earliest times. The first hoops were made from twisted reeds.

The Napoleonic Wars boosted interest in toy soldiers. This one is made of wood, 1800. Middle left: Picture blocks, 1890s. Middle right: Teddy bear 1910. Right: Toy Mercedes 28/32, 1908.

Among the simplest of toys is the cup and ball game. This one is made from turned wood 1800s.

Above: One of the earliest electric trains. A Bing steeple locomotive and carriage in gauge 3.

Right: Space invaders game, 1980s.

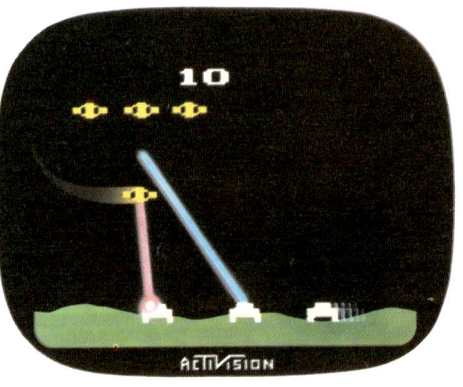

Toys

Children's toys have been used since very early times. Examples have been found in Egyptian tombs – dolls, balls, wooden animals. They were also popular in Greece and Rome. In Europe, marbles, drums and toy soldiers have been known for centuries, and a patent mechanical toy was made in England in 1672. In France and Germany, many more clever ideas were used in making toys, which are now made all over the world.

Codes and Ciphers

What most people call codes are really ciphers. Codes are usually not secret, and are simply a convenient way of sending information. A cipher is the correct name for the kinds of secret systems used by spies and secret agents.

There are two main kinds of ciphers – transposition and substitution. Most children have tried their hands at simple transposition ciphers. If you sent your friend a message such as ERUSAERT NEDDIH EHT SI EREHW it would not take him long to find out that it was simply the phrase WHERE IS THE HIDDEN TREASURE spelled backwards.

Perhaps you have tried the kind of puzzle called an acrostic. Here is an example:

        T R A D E
        H A R E M
        E X I S T
        B A T O N
        O L I V E
        O M E N S
        K N A V E
        S L A S H

It hides a simple phrase. If you read down the first column, and up the last, you will find the message THE BOOKS HE SENT ME. This is a kind of cipher, but naturally you would want to send a much longer message than that.

If that message was all jumbled up, it would be difficult to read, but it can be done so that only the sender and the person receiving it can work it out.

Here is a simple transposition cipher. Let us suppose we want to send the message: TEN MORE TRACTORS NEEDED TO WORK ON NEW FORESTRY PLANS. First, we run the whole message together, like this:

TENMORETRACTORSNEEDEDTO
WORKONNEWFORESTRYPLANS
Then, we arrange the letters in a block, like this:

        T E N M O R E T R
        A C T O R S N E E
        D E D T O W O R K
        O N N E W F O R E
        S T R Y P L A N S

We then send the message, reading the lines as they appear above, but reading *downwards*: TADOS ECENT NTDNR MOTEY OROWP RSWFL ENOOA REKES. Even this is not easy to work out, but it is better if we work with a Keyword. To fit our cipher message, we need a keyword with nine letters, all different. Let us choose PARCHMENT. We place the keyword at the top of our cipher block, like this:

        P A R C H M E N T
        T E N M O R E T R
        A C T O R S N E E
        D E D T O W O R K
        O N N E W F O R E
        S T R Y P L A N S

The next step is to place each column in alphabetical order. We write down above each letter of the keyword a figure which shows the order in which it appears in the alphabet:

        7 1 8 2 4 5 3 6 9
        P A R C H M E N T

The letters of the keyword, and also the letters appearing in each of the columns below it, should now be arranged in the correct numerical order:

        1 2 3 4 5 6 7 8 9
        A C E H M N P R T
        E M E O R T T N R
        C O N R S E A T E
        E T O O W R D D K
        N E O W F R O N E
        T Y A P L N S R S

Leaving off the keyword letters, we can now write down the message in groups as they appear in the block: EMEORTTNR CONRSEATE ETOOWRDDK NEOWFRONE TYAPLNSRS. This makes a very mysterious-looking message, but it can be deciphered by the person receiving it. He or she simply writes down the message in block form. He then places the keyword above it, but with the keyword letters in *alphabetical order*. So we write the word PARCHMENT as ACEHMNPRT. When the block has been written in, we rearrange the columns in the correct order of the word PARCHMENT, and then the message can be read off.

Memory Aids

Most people need something to jog their memory from time to time. For instance, in spelling, there is the rule I before E except after C. There are other little rhymes of this kind, and these are called mnemonics.

A useful one is 'Richard of York gave battle in vain', in which the initial letters set out the colours of the spectrum in their correct order – red, orange, yellow, green, blue, indigo and violet.

On the same principle, if you are learning to read music, you must know that 'Every Good Boy Deserves Food' or 'Eat Good Bread Dear Father' is the key to the lines on the treble clef.

Perhaps one of the best known ways of remembering one famous date is: 'in fourteen hundred and ninety-two, Columbus sailed the ocean blue.' A weather-forecasting rhyme is:

Oak before Ash,
You're in for a splash.
Ash before Oak,
You're in for a soak.

Another one is:

November leaves upon the trees
Foretell a winter when you'll freeze.

And the old favourite:

Red sky at night –
Shepherd's delight.
Red sky in the morning –
Shepherd's warning.

The seasons and the weather also have a lot of different rhymes attached to them. There is that useful verse:

Thirty days hath September,
April, June and November.
All the rest have thirty-one
Excepting February alone
Which has twenty-eight days clear,
And twenty-nine in each Leap Year.

Foreign Words and Phrases

(Abbreviations – F: French; G: German; L: Latin).

ad hoc (L) for this special object.
ad infinitum (L) for ever, to infinity.
ad libitum (ad lib.) (L) at pleasure.
ad nauseam (L) to a sickening degree.
à la carte (F) from the full menu.
à la mode (F) In the fashion.
amour-propre (F) self-respect.

à propos (F) to the point.
au courant (F) fully acquainted (with).
auf wiedersehen (G) till we meet again.
au pair (F) on mutual terms.
au revoir (F) till we meet again.
à votre santé (F) to your health!
bête noire (F) one's pet hate.
bona fide (L) in good faith, genuine.
bon voyage (F) have a good journey.
carpe diem (L) enjoy today.
carte blanche (F) full powers.
caveat emptor (L) let the buyer beware.

chacun à son goût (F)   everyone to his or her taste.

chef-d'oeuvre (F)   masterpiece.

corps de ballet (F)   team of ballet dancers.

corps diplomatique (F)   group of diplomats in a capital city.

cum grano salis (L)   with a grain of salt.

de facto (L)   in fact.

Dei gratia (L)   by the grace of God.

de luxe (F)   luxurious

dernier cri (F)   the very latest (fashion).

de trop (F)   superfluous; not wanted.

Dieu et mon droit (F)   God and my right (motto of the British Crown).

embarras de richesse (F)   having too many good things.

en famille (F)   within the family, informal.

en fête (F)   celebrating.

en passant (F)   in passing, by the way.

en rapport (F)   in sympathy.

entre nous (F)   between ourselves, confidentially.

ex cathedra (L)   from the chair of office, with authority.

ex libris (L)   from the books (of).

fait accompli (F)   an accomplished fact.

faux pas (F)   false step, mistake, blunder.

fiat lux (L)   let there be light.

honi soit qui mal y pense (F)   Shamed be he who thinks evil of it. (motto of the Order of the Garter).

hors de combat (F)   no longer able to fight, disabled.

ibidem (ibid.) (L)   in the same place

ich dien (G)   I serve, (motto of the Prince of Wales).

idée fixe (F)   obsession, fixed idea.

infra dignitatem (infra dig.) (L)   beneath one's dignity.

in loco parentis (L)   in the place of a parent.

in memoriam (L)   In memory (of).

in situ (L)   in position.

ipso facto (L)   from the facts.

mea culpa (L)   my fault.

modus operandi (L)   method of working.

nihil (L)   nothing.

noblesse oblige (F)   noble birth imposes obligations.

nom de plume (F)   pen name.

non sequitur (L)   it does not follow logically.

nota bene (N.B.) (L)   note well.

opus (L)   work (of art, music or literature).

par exemple (F)   for example.

passim (L)   everywhere, throughout.

per annum (L)   yearly.

per capita (L)   by the head.

per centum (per cent) (L)   by the hundred.

persona non grata (L)   an unacceptable person.

pièce de résistance (F)   chief dish of meal; main item.

prima donna (I)   principal female singer in an opera.

pro tempore (L)   for the time being.

quid pro quo (L)   something offered in return, an equivalent.

raison d'être (F)   reason for existence.

rendez-vous (F)   meeting place.

requiescat in pace (L)   Rest in peace.

résumé (F)   summary.

status quo (L)   the existing state of affairs.

stet (L)   let it stand (ignore correction marks).

table d'hôte (F)   a set meal at a fixed price.

tempus fugit (L)   time flies.

tête-à-tête (F)   private talk between two people.

ubique (L)   everywhere.

vade mecum (L)   a handbook of reference.

versus (L)   against.

vice versa (L)   the order being reversed.

vis-à-vis (F)   face to face.

LUCKY DIP

Abbreviations

AC Aircraftman; alternating current
ACT Australian Capital Territory
ACW Aircraftwoman
AD *anno Domini,* in the year of the Lord
ADC Aide-de-camp
ad lib. *ad libitum,* at pleasure
Adm. Admiral.
adv. adverb
advt. advertisement
AFC Air Force Cross
AFM Air Force Medal
Ala. Alabama
Alas. Alaska
Alba. Alberta
a.m. *ante meridiem,* before noon
AM amplitude modulation
Am., **Amer**. America; American
anon. anonymous
Ariz. Arizona
Ark. Arkansas
ASM air-to-surface missile
Ass., **Assoc**. Association
AWOL absent without official leave
BA *Baccalaureus Artium,* Bachelor of Arts
B and B. bed and breakfast
BAOR British Army of the Rhine
Bart. Baronet
bat, batt battalion; battery
BBC British Broadcasting Corporation
BC Before Christ; British Columbia
Beds Bedfordshire
BEM British Empire Medal
Berks Berkshire
bhp brake horsepower
bldg. building
B Lit(t) *Baccalaureus Lit(t) erarum,* Bachelor of Literature or Letters
BM Bachelor of Medicine; British Museum
B Mus Bachelor of Music
bn. battalion
BP British Pharmacopoeia; British Petroleum
Br., **Bro**. Brother
Brig. Brigadier
Brig.-Gen. Brigadier-General
Brit. Britain; Britannia; British; Briton
B Sc Bachelor of Science
BSI British Standards Institution
BST British Summer Time; British Standard Time
Bt. Baronet
Btu British Thermal Unit
Bucks Buckinghamshire
Bulg. Bulgaria; Bulgarian
C. Conservative
°C degree(s) Celsius, centigrade
C *circa*. about
ca. *circa*. about
Cal., **Calif**. California

Cam., **Camb**. Cambridge
Cambs Cambridgeshire
Cantab. *Cantabrigiensis,* of Cambridge
Capt. Captain
Cards Cardiganshire
Cath. Catholic
CB Companion of the Order of the Bath
CBE Commander of the Order of the British Empire
CBS Columbia Broadcasting System
CC County Council; Cricket Club
cc cubic centimetre(s)
CD *Corps Diplomatique.* Diplomatic Corps; Civil Defence
Cdr. Commander
CDSO Companion of the Distinguished Service Order
CENTO Central Treaty Organization
CET Central European Time
CH Companion of Honour
c.h. central heating
CI Channel Islands
CIA Central Intelligence Agency (USA)
CID Criminal Investigation Department
C.-in-C. Commander-in-Chief
cm centimetre(s)
CND Campaign for Nuclear Disarmament
CNR Canadian National Railway
CO Commanding Officer
Co. Company; County
c/o care of
c.o.d. cash (or collect) on delivery
C of E Church of England
Col. Colonel; Colorado; Colossians
col. column
coll. college; colleague; collector; colloquial
colloq. colloquial; colloquially
Coloss. Colossians
Com. Commander; Commodore; Commonwealth; Communist
Comdr Commander
Comdt Commandant
COMECON Council for Mutual Economic Aid, or Assistance (Communist Nations)
conj. conjunction; conjunctive
Conn. Connecticut
cont., **contd**. continued
co-op. co-operative
Cor. Corinthians; Coroner
Corn. Cornish; Cornwall
Corp. Corporation; Corporal
Cpl. Corporal
CPR Canadian Pacific Railway
CST Central Standard Time
Ct. Connecticut
cu., **cub**. cubic
c.v. *curriculum vitae,* course of life
CVO Commander of the (Royal) Victorian Order

c.w.o. cash with order
cwt hundredweight(s)
DA District Attorney; Diploma of Art
DBE Dame Commander of the Order of the British Empire
DC District of Columbia; direct current; District Commissioner
d.c. direct current
DCL Doctor of Civil Law
DCM Distinguished Conduct Medal
DCVO Dame Commander of the (Royal) Victorian Order
DD *Divinitatis Doctor,* Doctor of Divinity
Del. Delaware
DFC Distinguished Flying Cross
DFM Distinguished Flying Medal
DG *Dei gratia,* by the grace of God
Dip. Diploma
DIY Do-it-yourself
D Lit(t) *Doctor litterarum* or *litteraturae,* Doctor of Letters or Literature
D Mus Doctor of Music
DP Displaced Person; data processing
D Ph, or **D Phil** *Doctor Philosophiae,* Doctor of Philosophy
Dr Debtor; Doctor; Driver
D Sc. *Scientiae Doctor,* Doctor of Science
DSC Distinguished Service Cross
DSM Distinguished Service Medal
DSO Distinguished Service Order
E. and O.E. errors and omissions excepted
Ebor. *Eboracum,* York
ECG electrocardiogram (-graph)
ECSC European Coal and Steel Community
EDC European Defence Community
EEC European Economic Community
EEG electroencephalogram (-graph)
EFTA European Free Trade Association
e.g., **eg**, **ex. gr**. *exempli gratia,* for example
EPNS electroplated nickel silver
ER *Elizabetha Regina,* Queen Elizabeth
ESP extra-sensory perception
Esq., **Esqr**. Esquire
ETA (or **D**) Estimated time of arrival (or departure)
F Fahrenheit; farad; fellow
Fa. Florida
FA Football Association
FAO Food and Agriculture Organization
FBI Federal Bureau of Investigation (US)
FC Football Club
FSO Foreign and Commonwealth Office
F.D. *Fidei Defensor,* Defender of the Faith

308

ABBREVIATIONS

fig. figure; figuratively
Fla. Flor. Florida
fl. oz. fluid ounce
F.M. Field-Marshal
FM frequency modulation
F.O. Field-Officer; Flying Officer
FRCP Fellow of the Royal College
of Physicians
FRCS Fellow of the Royal College
of Surgeons
FRS Fellow of the Royal Society
Ga. Georgia
GATT General Agreement on Tariffs
and Trade
GB Great Britain
g.b.h. grievous bodily harm
GC George Cross
GHQ General Headquarters
GI (US Army) government (or
general) issue; hence, common
soldier.
Gib. Gibraltar
Gk Greek
Glam. Glamorganshire
GLC Greater London Council
Glos. Gloucestershire
GM George Medal
GMT Greenwich Mean Time
G.O.C. General Officer
Commanding
Gov. Governor; Government (also
Govt.)
GR Georgius Rex; George, King
h and c hot and cold (water laid on)
Hants Hampshire
Herts Hertfordshire
HGV Heavy goods vehicle
HM His (or Her) Majesty
HMS His (or Her) Majesty's Ship or
Service
HMSO His (or Her) Majesty's
Stationery Office
Hon. Honourable, Honorary
HRH His (or Her) Royal Highness
Hunts Huntingdonshire
Ia. Iowa
ICAO International Civil Aviation
Organization
ICBM Intercontinental ballistic
missile
ICI Imperial Chemical Industries
ICJ International Court of Justice
Id. Idaho
Ill. Illinois
ILO International Labour
Organization
IMCO Inter-Governmental Maritime
Consultative Organization
IMF International Monetary Fund
Ind. Indiana; Independent
inst. instant—the present month;
institute (also Inst.)
intro., introd. introduction
IOM Isle of Man
IOU I owe you
IOW Isle of Wight
IQ Intelligence Quotient

IRA Irish Republican Army
Irel. Ireland
ISBN International Standard Book
Number
ITU International
Telecommunications Union
JP Justice of the Peace
Jr., Jun., Junr. Junior
Kan. Kansas
KB Knight of the Bath; Knight
Bachelor; King's Bench
KBE Knight Commander of the
Order of the British Empire
KC King's Counsel
kc kilocycle(s)
KCB Knight Commander of the
Bath
KCVO Knight Commander of the
Royal Victorian Order
Ken. Kentucky
kg kilogram(s)
KG Knight of the Order of the Garter
KGB Komitet Gosudarstvennoi
Bezopasnosti (Russian Committee
of State Security)
KGCB Knight of the Grand Cross of
the Bath
kilo kilogram; kilometre
KKK Ku Klux Klan
KLM Koninkijke Luchtvaart
Maatschappij (Royal Dutch
Airlines)
km kilometre(s)
Kt Knight
kW kilowatt
Ky. Kentucky
La. Louisiana
Lab. Labour
Lancs Lancashire
Lat. Latin
lat. latitude
lb. libra, pound
lbw leg before wicket (in cricket)
lc lower-case (in printing)
Leics Leicestershire
Lieut. Lieutenant
Lincs Lincolnshire
Lit(t) D Litterarum Doctor, Doctor
of Letters
LLB Legum Baccalaureus, Bachelor
of Laws
Lt. Lieutenant
Lt.-Col. Lieutenant-Colonel
Ltd. Limited
Lt-Gen. Lieutenant-General
M. Monsieur (Fr.), Mr (pl. MM.)
M or m. mille, a thousand
m metre; mile
MA Magister Artium, Master of Arts
Maj. Major
Mass. Massachusetts
MB Medicinae Baccalaureus,
Bachelor of Medicine
MBE Member of the Order of the
British Empire
MC Member of Congress; Master of
Ceremonies; Military Cross

MCC Marylebone Cricket Club
Mc/s megacycles per second
Md. Maryland
MD Medicinae Doctor, Doctor of
Medicine
Me. Maine
memo. memorandum
Messrs Messieurs (Fr.), Sirs,
Gentleman
Mex. Mexico; Mexican
mg milligram(s)
Mgr Monseigneur; Monsignor
Mi. Mississippi
Mich. Michigan
Middx Middlesex
Minn. Minnesota
misc. miscellaneous; miscellany
Miss. Mississippi
Mlle (pl. Mlles) Mademoiselle (Fr.)
(pl. Mesdemoiselles)
MM. Messieurs (Fr.), Gentlemen or
Sirs
MM Military Medal
mm millimetre(s)
Mme (pl. Mmes) Madame (Fr.)
(pl. Mesdames)
Mo. Missouri
MO Medical Officer
Mon. Monmouthshire; Monday
Mont. Montana; Montgomeryshire
MP Member of Parliament; Military
Police
MRA Moral Rearmament
MS (MSS) manuscript
(manuscripts)
MS Master of Surgery; multiple
sclerosis
M Sc Master of Science
Mt, mt mount
Mus B (ac) Bachelor of Music
Mus D, Doc Doctor of Music
Mus M Master of Music
NASA National Aeronautics and
Space Administration (USA)
NATO North Atlantic Treaty
Organization
NB New Brunswick; North Britain;
North British
NB, nb nota bene, note well, or take
notice
N.C. North Carolina
NCO non-commissioned officer
N.D., N. Dak. North Dakota
Neb., Nebr. Nebraska
Nev. Nevada
NF, Nfd. Newfoundland
N.H. New Hampshire
NI Northern Ireland
N.J. New Jersey
N.M., N. Mex. New Mexico
Northants Northamptonshire
Northumb. Northumberland
Notts Nottinghamshire
NS New Style; Nova Scotia
NSW New South Wales
NT New Testament; Northern
Territory

LUCKY DIP

NY New York (city or state)
NYC New York City
NZ New Zealand
O. Ohio
OAS On active service; Organization of American States
OAU Organization of African Unity
OBE Officer of the Order of the British Empire
OECD Organization for Economic Co-operation and Development
OED Oxford English Dictionary
O.H.M.S. On His (or Her) Majesty's Service
Okla. Oklahoma
OM Order of Merit; Old Measurement
o.n.o. or near offer
Ont. Ontario
Or., Ore., Oreg. Oregon
OS Old Style; Ordinary Seaman; outsize
Oxon. *Oxonia,* Oxford; *Oxoniensis,* of Oxford
Pa. (or **Penn.**) Pennsylvania
P. & O. Peninsular and Oriental (Steamship Company)
PC Privy Councillor; Police Constable
Penn. Pennsylvania
Ph. D., Ph D *Philosophiae Doctor,* Doctor of Philosophy
PLA Port of London Authority
PMG Postmaster-General
P.O. post-office (also PO); Petty Officer; Pilot Officer
POW prisoner of war
PR proportional representation
PRO Public Relations Officer
pro tem. *pro tempore,* for the time being
PS *post scriptum,* written after; a postscript
PTO please turn over
QC Queen's Counsel
Q.E.D. *quod erat demonstrandum,* which was to be demonstrated
Q.M. Quartermaster
Q.M.S. Quartermaster-Sergeant
q.v. *quod vide,* which see
RA Royal Academy or Academician; Royal Artillery; Rear Admiral
RAAF Royal Australian Air Force
RAF Royal Air Force
RAN Royal Australian Navy
RC Roman Catholic; Red Cross
RCAF Royal Canadian Air Force
Rev. revise; revision; Revelation; (or **Revd.**) Reverend
RI Rhode Island
R.I.P. *requiescat in pace,* may he (or she) rest in peace
Rly, rly railway
RM Royal Marines
RMA Royal Military Academy
RN Royal Navy
RNA ribonucleic acids

RSFSR Russian Soviet Federated Socialist Republic
RSM Regimental Sergeant-Major
RSV Revised Standard Version
RSVP *répondez s'il vous plaît* (Fr.), reply if you please
Rt Hon Right Honourable
Rt Rev. Right Reverend
SA South Africa; South America; South Australia; Salvation Army
SAA South African Airways
SABENA (*Société anonyme belge d'exploitation de la navigation aérienne*) Belgian national airline
s.a.e. stamped addressed envelope
SALT Strategic Arms Limitation Talks
SAM surface-to-air missile
SAS Scandinavian Airlines System
Sask. Saskatchewan
S.C. South Carolina
sci. fi. science fiction
S.D., S. Dak. South Dakota
SDP Social Democratic Party
SEATO South-East Asia Treaty Organization
SHAPE Supreme Headquarters Allied Powers Europe
SNP Scottish National Party
SPCK Society for Promoting Christian Knowledge
SS or S.S. *Schutzstaffel* (Hitler's bodyguard)
Staffs Staffordshire
STD subscriber trunk dialling
STOL Short Take-Off and Landing
TB tuberculosis
Ten., Tenn. Tennessee
Tex. Texas
TIR *Transports Internationaux Routiers,* International Road Transport
TNT trinitrotoluene
TUC Trades Union Congress
TV television
TVA Tennessee Valley Authority
UDC Urban District Council
UDI Unilateral Declaration of Independence
UFO unidentified flying object
UHF Ultra high frequency
UK United Kingdom
UN United Nations
UNESCO United Nations Educational, Scientific and Cultural Organization
UNICEF United Nations International Children's Emergency Fund
UNO United Nations Organization
UNRRA United Nations Relief and Rehabilitation Administration
UPA Universal Postal Union
US United States; Under-secretary
USA United States of America; United States Army
USSR Union of Soviet Socialist

Republics
Ut. Utah
Va. Virginia
VAT Value-added Tax
Vat. Vatican
VC Vice-Chancellor; Vice-Consul; Victoria Cross
VE Victory in Europe
VHF very high frequency
v.i. verb intransitive
VIP Very Important Person
VR *Victoria Regina,* Queen Victoria
Vt. Vermont; verb transitive
VTO Vertical Take-off (and Landing)
WA West Africa; Western Australia
Wash. Washington
WHO World Health Organization
WI West Indies
Wilts Wiltshire
Wis. Wisconsin
WMO World Meteorological Organization
WNP Welsh Nationalist Party
WO War Office; Warrant Officer
Worcs Worcestershire
WRAC Women's Royal Army Corps
WRAF Women's Royal Air Force
WRNS Women's Royal Naval Service
W. Va. West Virginia
Wy., Wyo. Wyoming
Xm., Xmas. Christmas
YHA Youth Hostels Association
YMCA Young Men's Christian Association
Yorks Yorkshire
YWCA Young Women's Christian Association

INDEX

Page numbers in *italics* refer to pictures.

311

312

313

Kitchen-sink drama 210
Kiwis *78, 138*
Klee, Paul 190
Knieval, Evel 220
Knighthoods 88
Knot (boat speed) 244
Knots 286, *286*
Koalas *78*
Korbut, Olga 230
Korda, Sandor 214
Korea, North 58
Korea, South 58
Korean War 116
Kornberg, Arthur 166
Krak des Chevaliers 188, *188*
Krill 127
Kshatryas 276
Kush 54
Kuwait 58

L

Labours of Hercules 272
Lacrosse 230–1
Laker, James Charles 220
Lakes, world's largest 33
Languages 204–5, *204–5*;
  European 74
Laocoön 272
Laos 58
Lao Tzu 279
Lapland 74
Lapps 69
Lares 270
Larva 127
Laser 182
Latent heat 182
Latitude 38
Lauda, Niki 220
Laughton, Charles 214
Laurel, Stan 214
Laver, Rodney George 220
Lavoisier, Antoine 166
Law, Denis 220
Lawrence, D. H. 208
Lazarus 282
Leadbetter's possum 143
Lear, Edward 206
Lebanon 58
Legume 156
Lenglen, Suzanne 220
Lenin, Vladimir 108
Lens 182, *239*
Leonardo da Vinci 190
Leopards *145, 300*
Lepanto, Battle of 117
Lesotho 52
Le Repas (Gauguin) *193*
Lesseps, Ferdinand de 186
Lever 182
Leyte Gulf, Battle of 117
Liberia 52
Libya 52
Liechtenstein 70; monarch 88
Life sciences 167
Lightning 30
Light Red over Black
  (Rothko) *193*
Lillee, Dennis 220
Limericks 206
Lime tree, common *157*
Lincoln Cathedral 187
Lions 149, *300*
Liquids 166, 182
Lister, Joseph 170, 171
Liszt, Franz 201
Literature 206–8
Litmus 182

Liverworts *154*
Livingstone, David 104
Llanos 68
Lizards 127, 134, 135, *135*
Lloyd, Harold Clayton 214
Loki 270
Lombardy poplar *156*
Longden, Johnny 220
Longitude 38
Lonsdale, 5th Earl 220
Louis, Joe 220–1
Low Countries 74
Lowell, Percival 11
LSI (computer term) 240
Luke 282
Luna 272
Lunar eclipse *13, 15*
Lungs 168, *168*, 172
Lunn, Sir Arnold 221
Lusitania (liner) 247
Luther, Martin 279
Lutherans 278
Luxembourg 70; monarch 88
Lyric poem 206

M

Macão 58
McBride, Willie John 221
Macedonia 74
McEnroe, John 221
Mach number 268
Machu Picchu 68
Mackerel *132*
Madagascar 52
Madonna and Child
  (Raphael) *192*
Magellan, Ferdinand 97, 104
Magic (tricks) 302–3, *302–3*
Magnets *179*
Mahler, Gustav 201
Mahomet 275, 279
Maidenhair tree 157
Malawi 52
Malaysia 58
Maldives 58
Mali 52, 54–5
Malta 70–2
Mammals 127, 142–51, *144–51*; migration 132
Man 142, *142, 143*, 152, *152*
Mangala dam 186
Maoris 78
Mao Tse-tung 108
Map-projections 34–5, *34–5*
Maracaibo, Lake 68
Marathon, Battle of 117
Marciano, Rocky 221
Marconi, Guglielmo 238
Maria Theresa 108
Marine Iguana *134*
Mark St. 282
Mars (god) 270
Mars (planet) 17, 166
Marsupials 127, 142
Martha (New Testament) 282
Martinique 62
Marx, Karl 108
Mary Celeste 247
Masai 55
Mascots: motor cars 256–7, *256–7*
Maser 182–3
Mastodon 123
Masts 244
Mathematics 167
Matthew St. 282
Matthews, Sir Stanley 221

Matthias 282
Mauritania 52
Mauritius 52
Mausolus, tomb of *102*, 103
Mayer, Louis Burt 214
Mayotte 52
Meads, Colin Earl 221
Measures 294–5
Mechanics 167
Medals *89*
Medicine 167, 170–1
Mediterranean climate 38
Mediterranean Sea 74
Melanesia 78
Melodrama 210
Melting point 183
Memory (computer) 240–1
Memory aids 306
Mendeleyev, Dmitri 166
Mercator, Gerhardus 34
Mercury (god) 270
Mercury (planet) 17
Merganser duck 138, *138*
Mesopotamia 60
Mesosphere 31
Mesozoic Era 120, *120*
Metal 183
Metallurgy 167
Metamorphosis 127
Metazoa 127
Meteorites 19
Meteorology 30, 167
Meteors 19
Methodists 278
Mexico 62
Michelangelo Buonarroti 190
Microelectronics 241
Micronesia 78
Microprocessor 241
Midas 272
Midway, Battle of 117
Migration 132, 141
Milky Way 10, 17
Millipede *130*
Milton, John 208
Mime 210
Mimicry (in animals) 127
Minerals 40–1, *40, 41*
Minerva 270
Miriam (Old Testament) 281
Mississippi river 65
Mixture (chemical) 183
Modern Pentathlon 231
Mohammed 275, 279
Molecule 183
Molière 209
Molluscs 127
Momentum 183
Monaco 72; monarch 88
Monarch butterflies 132, 141
Monarchs 88
Monarchy 80
Monet, Claude 193
Money 84–7, *84–7*
Mongolia 58
Mongoose *300*
Monkeys 142, 143
Monocotyledons *154*
Monotremes 128, 142
Monsoon 30, 38
Montezuma cypress 157
Montgolfier brothers 243, 266
Montgomery, Bernard *116*
Montserrat 62
Moody, Helen 221
Moon, the 13, 14–15, *14, 15*, 166
Moore, Henry 195
Moore, Robert Frederick

(Bobby) 221
Moors (of North Africa) 55
Moraine 39
Moravians 278
More, Sir Thomas 108
Mormons 278
Morocco 52; monarch 88
Morphine 170
Morse code 293, *293*
Morton, William 170
Moses 281
Moss, Stirling 221
Mosses *154*
Moths *131*, 132
Motion, Newton's laws of
  183
Motor cars 252–9, *252, 254, 255, 259*
Motorcycles 259, *259*
Motorcycling sport 231
Motor Sport 231
Mountains, world's highest
  32
Mozambique 52
Mozart, Wolfgang Amadeus
  201
Muhammad 275, 279
Murray 78
Muses 272
Mushrooms 160, *160*
Music 199–203
Musical instruments 200, *201*
Musical terms 199
Music hall 210
Muslims 273, 275
Mystery play 210
Mythology 270–71

N

Naismith, Dr James A. 221
Namibia 52
Napoleon Bonaparte 108,
  108
Napoleonic Wars 115
Narcissus 272
Nasser, Gamal Abdel 108
Nastase, Ilie 221
NATO (North Atlantic Treaty
  Organization) 88
Nauru 75
Navratilova, Martina 221
Neap tides 45, *45*
Nebuchadnezzar 281
Nectar 156
Negroes 55, 65–6
Nehru, Jawahalal 108
Nelson, Horatio 108
Nematodes 128
Nepal 58–9; monarch 88
Nepia, George 221
Neptune (god) 270
Neptune (planet) 18
Nero 108–9
Nervous system 128
Netball 231
Netherlands 72; monarch 88
Netherlands Antilles 62
Neutron 183
New Cornelia Trailings dam
  186
New Guinea 78
New River Gorge 187
New Testament people 281–2
Newton, Sir Isaac 11, 166
Newts 134, *135*
New York 251
New Zealand 75